At the Feet of Abraham

At the Feet of Abraham

A Day-to-Day Dialogic Praxis
for Muslims and Christians

Levi UC Nkwocha

Foreword by Peter J. Casarella

WIPF & STOCK · Eugene, Oregon

AT THE FEET OF ABRAHAM
A Day-to-Day Dialogic Praxis for Muslims and Christians

Wipf & Stock
An Imprint of Wipf and Stock Publishers
199 W. 8th Ave., Suite 3
Eugene, OR 97401

www.wipfandstock.com

PAPERBACK ISBN: 978-1-7252-7692-5
HARDCOVER ISBN: 978-1-7252-7691-8
EBOOK ISBN: 978-1-7252-7693-2

Manufactured in the U.S.A.   11/02/20

To my inspirational dad,
Pa Alphonsus N. Nkwocha, JP (1929–2016)

Contents

Foreword

It is both a pleasure and privilege to write the foreword to *At the Feet of Abraham*. This is a significant work in systematic theology, for the book both broadens and deepens our current view of the practice of dialogue. But my immediate praise for the work's merits is also tinted by personal memories of dialogue. For example, I have a distinct recollection of the day that Dr. Levi UC Nkwocha served as a substitute in my undergraduate class at Notre Dame on "God and Dialogue." I had to give a talk at an international conference, and Nkwocha had prepared two lectures on the ethics of hospitality according to Emmanuel Levinas and Paul Ricoeur. He was very well prepared academically for the lecture, but I was much less prepared when I returned to evaluate the videotape. His lecture added a dimension I had not anticipated. Only with retrospect was I able to make sense out of my initial shortsightedness. Since his main topic was the openness to hospitality, he began the first lecture by explaining to the awe-struck nineteen-year-olds the symbolism of the kola nut ritual.

The kola nut is a special nut (with multiple lobes) of the kola tree, which is found in the rainforests of Nigeria. The lobes range from two to eight. It has ample medicinal and dynamic benefits, but Nkwocha focused on its use in a symbolized act of welcome to a known guest or stranger, mostly ritualized among the Igbos (in the southeastern region). The welcome ritual has multiple connotations. Usually, the host presents the kola nut to all present, including the stranger, then has it blessed, broken, and shared. Because of its symbolic emphasis on communitarian spirit, a kola nut without lobe is considered abnormal, and so cannot be presented to guests. While the multiple lobes are communally shared and eaten, a fruitful bond is initiated with the guest. The guest is also invited to take one kola nut home and extend the gesture of hospitality received.

No seminar on pedagogy for the twenty-first century could have imparted this lesson plan. My students retained the story until the end of the semester. The kola nut was the perfect prelude to a discussion of Levinas and Ricoeur! No assiduous study on my part could have made this lesson as memorable as Nkwocha's voice from the global South.

It is with similar delight and wonder that I offer a few prefatory remarks to this work. *At the Feet of Abraham* is unusually praiseworthy in its scope and originality. The work is remarkable for the synthesis of three elements: a phenomenological ethics and Levinasian approach to radical hospitality, the Catholic understanding of dialogue of life as a form of interreligious encounter, and the particular promises, ruptures, and exigencies of a peaceful social life in a pluralistic Nigeria today. Combining any two of these three elements would have already qualified as a tremendous achievement in many first works by young scholars.

This book excels precisely because of the equal weight placed upon each of the feet of this tripod. As such, the illuminating engagements from Levinas shine through in the sections on Catholic theology and vice versa. Problems would arise, I think, if one of these three modes of discourse were too dominant. Although the question of how to relate philosophy to theology in an intercultural context was not the direct focus of this investigation, I think that there are genuine strides made on this level as well. One might ask whether this work belongs to philosophical ethics or systematic theology, but I do not think that one must necessarily choose one or the other. In general, I was impressed by the circularity of the relationship between philosophy and theology. In this case, circularity is not an abstraction (the "vicious circle" of the philosophers) but a lived and engaged circularity. Maintaining an equilibrium between these two distinct modes of inquiry seemed prudent as well as generative of a genuinely synthetic set of new insights.

At the Feet of Abraham provides much needed clarity on the notion of the *dialogue of life* and its relationship to an ethics of hospitality. The very notion of a dialogue of life has been endorsed not only by the Catholic Church but through diverse academic studies. "Life" is not pursued *in opposition to* the other major forms of dialogue: theology, religious experience, and action. It complements these still vital tasks. Life is the field in which both human happiness and tribal violence take root. We know from too many historical examples how fraught the reality of life can be. Pope Francis, a strong proponent of the model of the dialogue of life, also writes: "Time is greater than space."[1] Dialogue accordingly cannot just focus on an agreement on ideas and plans. The end result must also include a meaningful form of existence that is sustainable over time and that offers generative life to two parties that formerly were in conflict.

The dialogue of life is hence more about people-building than the possessive occupying of territory with expensive edifices for conducting one's own business. To interrogate the conditions for dialogue beyond (but not without) doctrine, prayer, and social action sheds light on the very conditions that will lead to a sustainable peace for Africa and other regions of the world as well. The focus on African projects like the dialogical efforts of Cardinal Nzapalainga in the Central African Republic (CAR) was thus not only appropriate but necessary in this context. This moving example also underscores the element of the witnessing of faith in the hospitality model.

In general, this work represents one of the most sophisticated approaches to the ethics and theology of hospitality that I have ever read. Many sources are engaged by Nkwocha, but the position he articulates is in the end distinctively his own. He prudently restricts his borrowing from John Milbank of the terminology of "asymmetric reciprocity" since this position is still inadequately intercultural. Here he draws instead and with equal judiciousness upon Michael Purcell, Catherine Cornille, and the late Jean Vanier. The vast erudition raises other interesting questions.

The first one that came to my mind has to do with the theology of life. This is a major theme in both Levinas and in the Gospel of John. Nkwocha approaches the former in terms of an Abrahamic exodus from home and the model of Jesus as a pilgrim. He approaches the latter in terms of a detailed and convincing analysis of the Samaritan woman at the well in John 4. Although the encounter is in many ways an odd one, it is still an extension of an ethics of radical hospitality already present in the Hebrew Bible. It then becomes determinative in Nkwocha's religious ethics. Through their encounter, both Jesus and the woman retained their otherness but still experienced growth. Such asymmetrical but mutual hospitality is paradigmatic for the form of total hospitality that Nkwocha is proposing.

This work makes a unique contribution to the very notion of alterity. The assimilation of Levinasian hospitality with the ethics of hospitality defined more immanently by Jacques Derrida, especially in

---

1. Pope Francis, *Joy of the Gospel*, 222–25.

Derrida's difficult text *Adieu to Emmanuel Levinas*, does not follow the usual course that one encounters in Euroamerican discourse. Nkwocha notes that their positions cannot be assimilated to one another. Theologically both French thinkers move beyond Heidegger's critique of metaphysics, but religiously they make this move in radically different ways. They nonetheless both defend an absolute hospitality that disregards the consequences to one's own self. Richard Kearney, as Nkwocha notes, is right to denominate this form of hospitality as hyperbolic.[2] The fear of sharing a space with a total stranger can be real and terrifying. The risk of hospitality cannot be overcome by the modern Western notion of justice as fairness. Hospitality cannot be homogenized. Its universality is unmistakable but is exercised responsibly with respect to one's own location.

Instead of the Western notion of Rawlsian liberalism, we are introduced to a distinctively African and Christian way of sharing one's home. Levinas's faith in an infinite God that mirrors our own fear of and responsibility to the other is finally more persuasive than Derrida's theology of justice. For example, Nkwocha writes: "Levinas's 'self-recollection' at home, parallel to Panikkar's intra-religious dialogue, prods the host into absolute service to the other, to an extent of being a hostage."[3] One must be confident of the traditions of hospitality one has received from one's ancestors in order to take such a great risk of offering hyperbolic hospitality. The Western Christian with his colonializing tendencies is seldom able to make this leap of faith. Nkwocha consequently finds his own way home in the process of negotiating the subtle ethical and religious difference between the two French thinkers. The result of this incisive interchange is an obvious enrichment of global Catholic theology and the forging of a new path for the people of Nigeria.

A final point thus has to do with African hospitality, a polysemic term that is examined in great depth and variety, especially with regard to the *ubuntu* and the Yoruba traditions. The former undergirds the evolving human reality of "being-with-others." Our personhood develops in communion with other persons. The sharing of food, as in the New Testament, is a mere cipher for a spontaneous ethical act of welcoming the stranger. In Yorubaland, the ideas of common ancestry and respect for the elders as well as the concrete practice of housewarming can be interpreted as a way

---

2. Kearney, *Strangers*, 243.

3. Nkwocha, *At the Feet of Abraham*, citing Levinas, *Totality and Infinity*, 38.

to promote tolerance in a pluralist setting and even in areas like Northern Nigeria, where conflicts between Muslims and Christians have flared.

The convergence between the Levinasian home (as a locus for a new source of religious ethics) and the African home represents one of the great illuminations of this work as a whole. It is nonetheless the model of the pilgrim who is faithful to his religious and cultural roots rather than the territorial hoarder of a land that guides us through this thicket. The distinction between pilgrim and tourist is critical in this work and frankly in all work that broaches the tense topic of global religion. The tourist demands a fair and equitably compensated transaction. The tourist's voyage is either prepaid or based upon the calculus of a budget. The pilgrim depends upon the surprising respect of others and can respond in turn by welcoming with generosity. The budget for this act comes from beyond the meager means of the purely self-reflexive self.

In sum, *At the Feet of Abraham* is a remarkable work. Dr. Nkwocha has illuminated the Abrahamic bond that links Christians and Muslims (and not forgetting Abraham's role in establishing God's covenant with Israel). But the vision of an Abrahamic religion presented here is not the bland settlement for a lowest common denominator. The true bond, Nkwocha demonstrates, opens up an eschatological horizon in which Christians and Muslims can see one another together as God's children, a gaze that, as Br. Christian de Chergé assayed, can only be reflected in the face of the Father of Abraham. The model of pilgrimage thus points to a common practice and a common path to self-discovery.[4] The Muslim practice and the Christian practice of pilgrimage are distinct religious practices with distinct configurations of meaning that still maintain overlapping points of reference (e.g., the old city of Jerusalem). But in both cases a wanderer stands in need of an ethics of hospitality in the present and a future home in the house of the God of Abraham. This work enables us to reflect in a comparative and intercultural manner on the bridge God builds to connect the diverse pilgrims in the present with an eschatological future.

We live in a time in which the permits—legal, cultural, and spiritual—to build such bridges are needed more than ever. Since the terrorist attacks of September 11, 2001, global governments have responded with new security measures. In itself, the defense of a border against the attack made against innocents is just. But we have also witnessed the exceptional maltreatment of the stranger as a means for the enforcement of

4. On the contemporary meaning of how pilgrimage provokes self-discovery among young people today, see Jason, "Deliberate Walk."

the power of the state. The exception is now the norm. With the advent of COVID-19, new measures like the suspension of all green cards in the United States have augmented the reach and dominion of this state of exception. The insights in this work regarding hospitality are not being heeded by our leaders. Listening to the other and offering a home is now more than ever a matter that impacts global politics. Consequently, I thank God for the gift of *At the Feet of Abraham* and commend it to your reading and reflection. This is a book that speaks to some of the deepest needs that the people who share a faith in the God of Abraham are facing today.

Peter J. Casarella
Professor
The Divinity School at Duke University

Preface

THIS BOOK RESEARCH ADVANCES an Abrahamic "asymmetric-mutual substitutive" model of hospitality in order to guide interfaith relations between Muslims and Christians, particularly in the Nigerian context. Responding to Pope Francis's urgent call for a "dialogue of life" that seeks to complement other familiar forms of dialogue, such as theological discourse, religious experience, and action, this book sees holistic, everyday expressions of altruistic hospitality as key to overcoming legacies of hostility and suspicion among Christians and Muslims.

As an interdisciplinary discourse, this book systematizes Emmanuel Levinas's ethical hospitality and its African perspective into an Abrahamic interfaith dialogical pattern. Even though Levinas proposes substitutive responsibility from an ethico-philosophical view, it is the claim of this book that a healthy theology can be constructed from its principles by stimulating asymmetric-mutual substitutive responsibility among Muslims and Christians. Such transition validates a scholastic maxim: "philosophy is the handmaid of theology."

The merits of the work include its helpful survey of the four models of interfaith dialogue and its clear exposition of the dialogue of life; its constructive use of the philosophy of Levinas, particularly in supporting its vision of asymmetrical moral responsibility; and its familiarity with an extensive philosophical literature on alterity, gift-= exchange, and responsibility (Derrida, Ricoeur, Volf, and others). The book also demonstrates strong command of the relevant Christian and Muslim scriptures and Catholic teaching on interfaith relations, in addition to a wide range of background material on the African *ubuntu* spirit, visible in Nigerian sociocultural and religious interdependent relations.

Through a consistent engagement of these philosophical, ethical, and cultural dimensions, the Abrahamic theology of hospitality is ingeniously crafted to fill the age-old gap—mutual inability to deal with religious otherness. At once, the book provokes further scholarship inquiries on and around the identified concerns. Its commonness and concreteness, with the proposed respect for each other's faith commitment, further underscores its quality.

The eleven-chapters structure articulates: stating the problem, identifying previous inadequate responses, and establishing the contribution of the book. In establishing the problem that this book intends to address, the first chapter critically explores a broad review of the age-old Christian-Muslim mutual antagonistic perceptions, which have led to incessant violent attacks and deaths. Reviewing the ambivalence of both scriptures concerning other religions, this chapter argues against religious otherness as the problem, but strongly blames the problem on the mutual inability to handle faith divergences. Consequently, the internal exclusive perceptions rapidly erupted into violent space contests. The first two chapters aim to provide historical background on the origins and development of Christian/Muslim unpleasant relations.

The second chapter builds off from the inherent problem identified in the previous chapter and highlights the grave consequences of botching religious otherness. It demonstrates the dangers of supersessionist proselytization. It also argues that the major Muslim-Christian problem lies in the inability to accept each other's faith on their own terms. As a result, mutual distorted perceptions from the past to the present caused great harms to both sides. In fact, the largest human and material losses in the history of religious conflicts owe a lot to the ideology of killing and looting in the name of God.

From a global perception of the problem, chapter 3 turns more specifically to the state of these biased relations in Nigeria. It exposes an ongoing Muslim-Christian antagonism and rivalry in a contemporary society. Such religious colored unrest and supremacy tussle, in which over 187 million lives are at stake, validate the urgency of the concern of this book.

After a complete exposition of the distorted perceptions towards each religion and the prolonged consequential impacts of rivalry, wars, and inherent suspicions between Muslims and Christians, chapter 4 introduces a phase of efforts made to bridge the noticed gap. First, it appreciates available individual views in search of workable solutions, but also uncovers their limitations. This fourth chapter sketches various theories of interfaith engagement ("inclusivism," "pluralism," etc.), followed by two other chapters that present the dialogue of life as an unexplored alternative.

Similarly, chapter 5 leads a turn to dialogue, which challenges this book into searching out possible development of positive views in both Islamic and Christian traditions. The search seeks contributions that likely informed the dialogic approach, upon which the hospitality approach, as a way forward, can be constructed. Besides identifying germane pioneering intuitions viable for dialogic engagements, this chapter also explored the rich but bold extension of a hand of friendship from the Vatican to the Islamic world. Within this friendship initiative are the four forms of dialogue defined, including the unexplored dialogue of life.

As a major approach for this book research, and prior to the establishment of the hospitality model, chapter 6 provides a necessary transition or connection between practical dialogue and hospitality. The chapter accentuates the essence of space creation and sharing as basis for the possibility of dialogic hospitality.

With a well-set background on dialogue of life, chapter 7 investigates, but also appreciates, the enduring hospitality values from the philosophical and ethical perspectives, especially the Levinasian thoughts, which are relevant for the substitutive altruistic formulation. The chapter concludes with identifying the limits of ethical and philosophical views of hospitality. Chapters 7 and 8 situate hospitality as central to the dialogue of life, drawing upon the philosophy of Levinas and African notions of *ubuntu*.

From an African cultural perspective, chapter 8 proposes additional workable practice toward the coexistence of Muslims and Christians through the introduction of the *ubuntu* spirit. The African *ubuntu* metaphor emphasizes the relational responsibility that exists between persons and other persons, and with the entire community. This chapter, while appreciating *ubuntu's* inter human dependence, aligns its cultural values to the hospitality model in focus.

Chapter 9 returns to the context of Nigeria and offers the Yoruba people (of the southwestern region) as a template of Muslim-Christian dialogic hospitality. It situates the interdependent elements of African *ubuntu* in a Yoruba context, and carefully gleans out the inherent substitutive altruism that pervades the Muslim-Christian relations there. This chapter argues that if common ancestry could substantiate the Yorubaness over and above political and religious differences, then the Abrahamic ancestry claim for both Muslims and Christians could also provide healthier understanding and coexistence.

Chapter 10 introduces a theological transition that carefully articulated the Levinasian idea of substitutive hospitality as well as the African *ubuntu* spirit, but creatively remodels their principles into an Abrahamic theology of asymmetric-mutual responsibility. This tenth chapter and the last attempt to render more explicit the theological resources within Christianity and Islam that can motivate and expand the proposed model of interfaith hospitality.

Chapter 11 is critically shown as ethically and theologically substitutive via hospitality, because Abraham freely embarked on his covenantal journey in order to be available for the services of the divine Other through the human others. Understood as such, the Abrahamic substitutive theology is therefore argued as great inspiration for Muslims and Christians to live for and with each other. The book closes by evoking the scriptural scene of Abrahamic hospitality at the Oak of Mamre as a unifying image of interfaith relations going forward.

Acknowledgments

I ACKNOWLEDGE THE IMMENSE largesse of God available to me. My appreciation goes to my archbishop, Most Rev. Dr. Anthony Obinna, the Metopolitan of the Catholic Archdiocese of Owerri, Nigeria. In particular, I am indebted to the gifts of my family, friends, and mentors. I owe a lot to the University of Notre Dame, Indiana, my *alma mater*, whose prestigious home for holistic growth informed the development of this book project. I would also like to thank my academic advisor, Dr. Bradley Malkovsky, and Dr. Peter Casarella, who graciously wrote the foreword, for their collaborative guidance and interest toward my academic growth. Equal gratitude goes to my other committee members for their inspiring feedback.

Specifically, I remain grateful to my friends Scott and Kim Welch for their financial support in the accomplishment of this book project. Finally, I thank all: the faculty, the staff, and the students of my Notre Dame family, who contributed to the timely completion of this book research.

Abbreviations

AIC	African Independent Church
BICMURA	*Bulletin on Islam and Christian-Muslim Relations in Africa*
BYM	Borno Youth Movement
CAN	Christian Association of Nigeria
CAR	Central African Republic
CBCN	Catholic Bishop Conference of Nigeria
CSN	Catholic Secretariat of Nigeria
DM	*Dialogue and Mission* (full title: *The Attitude of the Church Toward Followers of Other Religions: Reflections and Orientations on Dialogue and Mission*)
DP	*Dialogue and Proclamation*
DPNC	Democratic Party of Nigeria and Cameroon
FCS	Fellowship of Christian Students
IFMC	Inter Faith Mediation Center
ITU	Igbira Tribal Union
IU	Igala Union
JNI	Jamalat-ul-Nasril Islam
LRA	Lord's Resistance Army
MDF	Midwest Democratic Front
NA	*Nostra Aetate*
NCNC	National Council of Nigeria and the Cameroon

NIREC	Nigerian Interreligious Council
NSCIA	Nigeria Supreme Council for Islamic Affairs
NYSC	National Youth Service Corps
OIC	Organization of Islamic Conference
PCID	Pontifical Council for Interreligious Dialogue

Introduction

I

As the global consciousness for a pluralistic society continues emerging, the responsibility of engaging diversities, especially the religious other, increases. Islam and Christianity, being the world's most growing and populous religions, exert great decisive impact on world peace. Unfortunately, the relationship between the two religions throughout history has been charged with rivalry, leading to mutual violence. Consequently, mutual antagonisms and suspicious isolations describe their relations. Recently than ever, scholars from both religions are striving towards establishing a healthier dialogic relationship that can sustain peaceful coexistence.

This book aims at addressing the said concern. It is the principal position of the book to argue that mutual substitutive hospitality between Muslims and Christians at the base level, especially in Nigeria, will diminish the age-old antagonism and suspicious isolation. Equally, such warm praxis will generate growth through improved openness for the respect of each other's otherness, while it deepens particular faith commitments. In essence, the book will establish that mutual substitutive hospitality, without the intent of reciprocity, provides sustainable locus for dialogue of life between these two religious rivals.

Specifically, the state of Christian-Muslim relations in Nigeria, where the populations of both groups are roughly equal, presents a microcosm of Christian-Muslim conflict in the world today. Nonetheless, Yorubaland (southwestern region) offers a superb testing ground for how interreligious hospitality and peaceful coexistence can be fostered. Yorubaland, with equal percentage of Muslims and Christians, radically disapproves the broader conclusion that an even split between the

1

predominantly Muslim North and the Christian South is the root cause for the known religious tensions and rivalry in Nigeria. Actually, the healthy coexistence in the Yoruba context, ingrained in mutual substitutive hospitality, succinctly speaks to other Muslims and Christians in the world on three counts: 1) for a deeper understanding of Abrahamic hospitality; 2) for teaching of both traditional hospitality and mutual existence; 3) for translating scriptural altruistic doctrines into effective theological praxis.

The scholarly significance of this book transits from a particular context to its universal applicability. As an interdisciplinary discourse, this book systematizes Emmanuel Levinas's ethical hospitality and its African perspective into an Abrahamic interfaith dialogic pattern. Levinasian altruism has provoked several scholarly discussions in both philosophical and ethical perceptions, but never as a tool for interfaith dialogue. Similarly, hospitality has been presented as a model for missions and for intermonastic spiritual exchanges. None, however, has considered Abrahamic hospitality as key for Muslim-Christian dialogue of life. Moreover, dialogue through hospitality, fairly present in both Muslim and Christian traditions, lacks a theological systematization of its principles for interfaith purposes. This book fills in that theological gap.

Even though Levinas proposes substitutive responsibility from an ethico-philosophical view, it is the argument of this book that a healthy theology can be constructed from its principles by stimulating asymmetric-mutual substitutive responsibility among Muslims and Christians. Such transition reassures one of the scholastic maxims that *philosophia ancillia theologia*—philosophy is the handmaid of theology.

Following Pope Francis's recent call for "dialogue of life"[1] in ecumenical and interfaith interactions, the future of this research is assured. Francis's directives for theologians to explore the dynamics of dialogue of life, beyond the theoretical discourses, will not only motivate the engagement of this work, but will also open up further scholarship inquiries on and around this topic. Above all, the creatively theological systematization of hospitality through the consistent engagement of its philosophical

1. In his keynote address, Bishop Brian Farrell, LC, secretary of the Pontifical Council for Promoting Christian Unity, stated Pope Francis's preference for the "dialogue of life," for the journey toward non-Catholics, especially the religious other, at the International Conference on "Muslin-Christian relations," organized by the World Religions, World Church area of the theology department at the University of Notre Dame, in collaboration with the Pontifical Institute for Arabic and Islamic Studies (PISAI), held in Rome, January 8–10, 2018.

and cultural dimensions within a dialogue of life strengthens the capti-
vating newness of this work.

As the major approach, dialogue of life is one of the four forms of
dialogue (others include: dialogue of action, dialogue of spiritual experience, and dialogue of theological discourse) defined by the 1984 document (*Dialogue and Mission*) of the Pontifical Council for Interreligious
Dialogue and reiterated by another in 1991 (*Dialogue and Proclamation*).
Dialogue of life represents a spontaneous, daily, practical approach of
interfaith witnessing toward the distinct but inseparable love of God and
neighbors. Obviously, it is not a replacement, but a complementary application of the ongoing theological discourses. Regrettably, dialogue of
life is the most understudied among the four forms.

The book, therefore, advocates for a turn towards millions of ordinary Christians and Muslims, who constitute the highest percentage
of endangered species (both victims and machineries) in every religious
crisis. By so doing, it will demonstrate that despite the several violent
interreligious crises between Muslims and Christians, there are still millions of adherents of these two religions who manifest practices related
to dialogue of life, daily. The research further aims at learning from their
much-understudied elements of dialogue of life, but also seeks to articulate them into a theology of hospitality, for the sustenance of peaceful
coexistence. The primary goal of the book is to harness those useful in-
gredients of dialogue of life, in view of complementing other ongoing
forms of dialogue in the academy, among spiritual experiential experts,
and among pluralistic societies facing sociopolitical and religious crises.

The radical asymmetric altruism of Emmanuel Levinas, in which
the face of the other demands a non-reciprocal sacrificial responsibility from the self, is partially adopted for the achievement of a healthy
dialogue of life between Christians and Muslims. This book appropriates
Levinas's radical substitutive responsibility toward the other, without its
asymmetric restriction. The reason being that interreligious dialogue,
in the form of a remolded theological hospitality pattern (Abrahamic
pilgrim model), has mutuality as a principal element. Moreover, mutual
hospitality is a common practice in both Islamic and Christian theological teachings. This is true because while the Qur'an (5:48) and the Bible
(Luke 6:27–28) command their respective believers to lavishly engage in
altruistic works, never do they condemn mutuality of good deeds, even
as they expect rewards from God alone.

The impact of this book, besides arousing the eagerness of interfaith theologians, will enthrall the interests of scholars in humanities, social scientists, fieldwork researchers, ardent spiritual leaders, but also committed religious adherents, whose daily life experiences are in focus. Its emphasis on the practical approach across religious borders also provides a testing ground for the ongoing dialogic discourses.

The practical richness of this book provides a resource base for an undergraduate's fundamental course in interfaith dialogue with concentration on Muslim-Christian relations. It can as well form part of a graduate course requirement for a Vatican II-based Catholicism in conversation with non-Christian faiths. In addition, this book can be recommended for a scripture course on Abrahamic faith, and a philosophical ethics class on Emmanuel Levinas. Moreover, its cultural aspect will offer significant knowledge for a course on theopolitical African studies.

Broadly speaking, the major problem of Muslim-Christian relation is typically identified as the persistent inability to manage religious otherness by harmonizing it with communion. Such a problem, therefore, calls for mutual substitutive responsibility as hyped by dialogue of life via Abrahamic hospitality. Fittingly, this book aims at addressing the identified interfaith relational gap.

Subsequently, the hospitality key demonstrates the possibility of the intended harmony between otherness and communion. Jayme Reaves's three distinctions of hospitality, namely, table fellowship, the intellectual, and the protective, underscore the fact that the need of the other, while demanding positive responses, sets the agenda. As a rule, the need of the other should be responded to, without absorbing the otherness of her personality. Such renewed ethical standard agrees with Levinasian altruism as well as the African communitarian responsibility, beautifully couched in the "*ubuntu* spirit"[2] metaphor.

With the traditional significances of hospitality properly explored, the book plunges deeper and unveils the centrality of the theological praxis of hospitality, clearly mandated in both Islamic and Christian scriptures, as inevitable eschatological conditions. These distinct but related theological mandates are articulated here as "the theology of Abrahamic substitutive hospitality."

2. The Ubuntu spirit (expressed in the Zulu adage, *Umuntu ngumuntu ngabantu*, "A person is a person with other persons") seeks unity by appreciating otherness, and therefore promotes mutual substitutive hospitality.

Substitutive responsibility expresses the mutual exchange of disparate gifts, thereby excluding indebtedness. By assuring otherness through resisting assimilation, the Abrahamic hospitality allows the gift of newness from the other to activate the process of correcting distorted perceptions. Abrahamic ethical substitution, as explored, models an equilibrium concerning the love of God and love of neighbor mandate. Therefore, his substitutive theology can inspire Muslims and Christians into coexistent living. As a preferred model, Abrahamic altruism was always done for the sake of God.[3]

Accordingly, Muslims and Christians are called to treat the other, not necessarily as bad as the other deserves, but rather as good as each adherent is, since a true theistic religion is defined by its evidential ability of achieving healthy relations between the love of God and the love of neighbor.

In order to attain its goal, this book sets out to awaken mutual hospitable awareness among Muslims and Christians through its eleven chapters. Chapter 1, "The Problem: Religious Otherness?," attempts a general review of the age-old Christian-Muslim mutual antagonistic perceptions. The evaluation extends to chapter 2, "Mismanaged Problem: Mutual Blame," which highlights the grave consequences of botching religious otherness. Chapter 3, "Contextual Rivalry: The Nigerian Experience," exposes an ongoing Muslim-Christian antagonism in a contemporary society, thereby advocating the urgency of this book. The review narrows down to chapter 4, "Inadequate Reactions to Religious Otherness," which appreciates available views on solutions, but concludes with exposing their limitations.

Then, chapter 5, "The Development of Positive Views," leads a turn which challenges this book into searching out possible dialogic contributions in both Islamic and Christian traditions, presumably preparatory for the hospitality approach, as a way forward. Prior to developing the hospitality model, chapter 6, "Dialogue of Life as Faith Witnessing," provides a necessary transition or connection between practical dialogue and hospitality. This chapter accentuates the essence of space creation and sharing as basis for the possibility of dialogic hospitality.

With the background well set, chapter 7, "The Hospitality Key," explores and appreciates the enduring hospitality values from philosophical and ethical perspectives, especially the Levinasian thoughts driving

3. Bethune, "Interreligious Dialogue," 8.

the substitutive altruistic formulation. And from a cultural perspective, chapter 8, "Hospitality and African Communality," presents additional workable practice toward the coexistence of Muslims and Christians by substantiating the substitutive altruism through the "Yoruba Example" in chapter 9.

Chapters 10, "Hospitality a Theological Dimension," introduces a theological transition that carefully articulates the Levinasian idea of substitutive hospitality as well as the African *ubuntu* spirit, and creatively remodeled their principles into an Abrahamic theology of asymmetric-mutual responsibility.

Finally, in chapter 11, "The Abrahamic Model" is critically shown as ethically and theologically substitutive via hospitality. Inductively, the Abrahamic substitutive theology is therefore presented as that priceless stimulus for Muslims and Christians to live for and with each other.

As an interfaith proposal, this book does not claim to have the last word on Muslim-Christian dialogic hospitality relation. The envisaged fruits of this book research notwithstanding, its concrete applications might remain challenging, especially due to the informality that governs dialogue of life. However, the encouragement for the pursuance of this book's thesis lies in the strength of its commonness and concreteness, without necessarily involving doctrinal polemics and proselytization for conversion, known to provoke rudeness toward otherness.

II

Understanding otherness is fundamental at this point. The existential, social, and spiritual challenge of the otherness of the human person, unlike the encounter with other realities, is as old as humanity itself. Consequently, throughout history, people have grappled with how best to appreciate otherness. In the most part, suspicion, aversion and conflict have marked religious differences. However, the awareness for improved appreciation of otherness is gradually emerging.

Even though the emergence of otherness in the academy dates back to the time of Aristotle, especially in his treatise on friendship, its wider engagement in humanities can be traced to about four decades ago,[4] with literature prominently in philosophy, psychology, anthropology, sociology, et cetera.

4. Miller, "Otherness," 587.

In German philosophy, Georg Wilhelm Friedrich Hegel (1770–831) was the first to introduce the concept of the other,[5] while Edmund Husserl (1859–1938) focused attention on moving alterity from the domain of ontology (Heidegger) to phenomenological discourses.[6] It was through the partial influence of Husserl that the scholarship of Levinas radically situated alterity into ethics. The radicality of ethical values in Levinas knows no comparison among his contemporaries and beyond, in questioning the logical claims of ontology and totality.[7] Levinasian ethical concern has ever since inspired great thoughts for otherness among some prominent twentieth-century French philosophers, like Jean Paul Satre, Jacques Derrida, and Paul Ricoeur.

In essence, the German philosopher Michael Theunissen (1932–2015) paved way for interests in Levinasian alterity. In his work *Der Andere: Studien zur Sozialontologie der Gegenwart*[8] (*The Other: Studies in the Contemporary Social Ontology of Husserl, Heidegger, Satre, and Buber*), Theunissen distinguished himself as a primal critic of modern philosophers on the other. As a university colleague with Hans-Georg Gadamer, Theunissen engaged philosophical themes like phenomenology, ancient philosophy and social philosophy, which include the works of philosophical figures like Hegel and Heidegger. Overall, Samuel Moyn affirms that Theunissen's work was famed before the interest in Levinas was really present, and so he stands as a predecessor to the appreciation of the Levinasian approach to alterity.[9]

In the words of Mitchell Miller, "Otherness is a condition or quality of being different or 'other,' particularly if the differences in question are strange, bizarre, or exotic."[10] Otherness, however, gains a clearer understanding, when studied in contrast to the notion of the self. In other words, otherness primarily connotes the undeniable reality of a certain uniqueness that defines the other person as different from oneself. And despite shared commonalities between the other and oneself, the other cannot simply be a replication of the self, because of the uniqueness that marks the other.

---

5. See Hegel, *Phenomenology of the Spirit.*

6. "Otherness," in *New Fontana Dictionary*, 620.

7. Min, *Solidarity of Others*, 7.

8. See Theunissen, *Andere.*

9. See Moyn, *Origins of the Other.*

10. Miller, "Otherness," 587.

According to Levinas, "The absolutely other is the Other."[11] Levinas emphasizes the inalienable character of not only the divine other, but primarily also the human other. The self (subject), he claims, can only access the divine through the "face" of the human other.[12] The face is key to understanding Levinasian interpersonal hospitality. The face designates that the infinite other is beyond comprehension by the self. In essence, the self cannot but remain overwhelmed by the constant epiphany of the face, which comes as a surprise.

Levinas gives reason for his radical altruism: "My ethical relation of love for the other stems from the fact that the self cannot survive by itself alone, cannot find meaning within its own being-in-the world, within the ontology of sameness."[13] As argued by Levinas, the other is so indispensable that it enjoys an absolute transcendence beyond human comprehensibility, but can only communicate part of itself to the self.

The said infinity of the other by Levinas introduces an improved paradigm of perception that could effectively correct the mutual distorted notions shared among Muslims and Christians. One way of achieving that is by posing the big question: between Muslims and Christians, who should be the other, and who should be the self? In response, this book will argue that each of these two religions has maintained flexibility of identity for being both the self and the other. In essence, mutual blame can be justifiably established between Muslims and Christians in their history of interaction. An important Vatican document concerning Christian-Muslim relations through history confirms the reality of mutual blame: "Christians may lament the loss of North Africa to the Arabs and the fall of Constantinople to the Turks, while Muslims write eloquent laments about losing Cordoba and the disappearance of Andalus, and still feel outraged by the Crusades."[14]

Using Levinas's ethical approach as a working tool, Christianity and Islam, even though being the world's two most populous monotheistic religions, are explored in this book as two different belief systems that perceive God through unique lenses. Consequently, it will be argued that the age-old use of mutual subjective lenses toward each other has caused enormous antagonism and hateful relations between the two religions,

---

11. Levinas, *Totality and Infinity,* 39.

12. Min, *Solidarity of Others,* 12.

13. Levinas, *Ethics and Infinity,* 60.

14. Michel and Fitzgerald, *Recognize the Spiritual Bonds,* 2.

not only at the global level, but also at the local levels, such as the Nigerian context. Therefore, this study aims at proposing a truer perception of the religious other. The task is to awaken a sustainable consciousness for the appreciation of otherness as defined by no other than the other.

In essence, the challenge of otherness, which has engaged humanity at various times and in various cultures, often exposes the insecurity of self-sufficient autonomy. Doctrinal absolutism has been persistent in the religious exclusivity practiced in Christendom and Islam.[15] Depending on whose lens is used, the treatment of the other, especially the religious other, has been tainted with mistrust at best and hatred at worst.

Basically, the persistent problem simply underscores humanity's inability to welcome and accept otherness in its inviolable reality. In response to this problem, Marianne Moyaert accentuates the demands of such inescapable engagement. She reminds us, "Plurality of cultures, traditions and worldviews claim that the religious other deserved our respect and had a right to our recognition and appreciation."[16]

Similarly, the hospitality key this book proposes attempts to provide a renewed lens through which the Islamic or Christian antagonized otherness unveils itself as that inviolable other. The Levinasian ethical thought offers a foundational basis, which this book intends borrowing, remodeling and constructing into a theological model for Muslim-Christian dialogue of life. As a result, introducing Levinas at this moment will be preparatory for a lucid engagement of his distinctively altruistic thinking.

III

Levinas was born in Kaunas, Lithuania, on January 12, 1906, "where he received a traditional Jewish family education."[17] As a prisoner of war in a Stalag camp in Germany (1940–945), his French citizenship saved his life during the Holocaust, while his friend Maurice Blanchot hid his wife and daughter in a French monastery.[18] Levinas lost all other relatives in his extended family. This experience of hostility and persecution deeply shaped Levinas's own philosophical thought, as reflected in his second

---

15. Michel and Fitzgerald, *Recognize the Spiritual Bonds*, 2.

16. See Marianne Moyaert, *Absorption or Hospitality*, 61.

17. Shepherd, *Gift of the Other*, 17.

18. Shepherd, *Gift of the Other*, 17.

major work, *Otherwise than Being, or Beyond Essence*,[19] which was dedicated to close relatives of the six million victims of the Holocaust.[20]

Levinas accentuated a brand of asymmetrical altruism in which otherness enjoys a unique transcendence and even infinity.[21] His primary philosophical concern was to reverse the Western enthronement of the self as the beginning of reflection on interpersonal relationality.[22] Consequently, he called for a compensatory ethical substitutive imperative, in which the self (as host) is infinitely responsible for the abused other.[23] He seeks to correct the starting point of the self with a metaphorical argument about the human face, which resists all attempts to be contained but initiates a call to the self for a one-way responsibility towards itself.[24]

Basically, it is the task of this book to judiciously adapt the Levinasian call for responsibility toward the other, without restricting the mandate to either Muslims or Christians. Rather, the responsibility weighs equally on both. By adopting and remodeling Levinasian ethical responsibility into an Abrahamic asymmetric-mutual substitutive model, it will be argued that the renewed perception of the other might clarify and correct the persistent subjective image of the other, which has so often marred the contours of interreligious dialogue. Muslim-Christian relation is a victim of such mutual distorted approaches.

Christian-Muslim theological responses to religious otherness will be assessed by the degree to which otherness is appreciated, using Levinas's substitutive ethical key. No developed dialogic language and approach were present at the outset of the Muslim-Christian encounters and even later. Therefore, both Islamic and Christian histories show an interwoven process between self-identification, boundary creation, and Othering.[25]

In rejection of the ancient Socratic "knowledge as remembering," Levinas contests that the self does not possess and cannot possess the knowledge of the other. Rather, it is the face of the other that unveils itself, though never exhaustively, to the self. Truth and knowledge rather than issue from within the self, comes from the external other. For example,

19. Levinas, *Otherwise than Being*.

20. Shepherd, *Gift of the Other*, 17.

21. Levinas, *Totality and Infinity*, 51.

22. Shepherd, *Gift of the Other*, 18.

23. Levinas, *Totality and Infinity*, 85.

24. Levinas, *Totality and Infinity*, 194–96.

25. Lamptey, *Never Wholly Other*, 18.

"teaching is not reducible to maieutics; it comes from the exterior and brings me more than I contain."[26]

Between Socrates and Levinas, Thomas G. Casey identifies a semi-permeable border through which a bit of memory is possible for the infinite. The infinite somewhat displays certain familiarity. According to Casey, this closeness manifests itself in two ways: "Firstly, by the fact that it is present in the subject before time as a claim that the Other makes upon it; it presupposes an interiority in the subject by virtue of which the subject allows itself to be invaded by the strangeness of the idea of the infinite."[27]

Casey's mediation opens up further concerns. A major concern interrogates the difficulty for the subject, known for its self-centeredness, to host the uncontainable infinite. However, standing beyond itself by being relational and humble, the self makes room for itself to recognize the infiniteness of the other. Basically, Casey affirms that, in order to create space for the infinite, "I (self) must be relational subject, capable of interaction. I must be a humble subject capable of recognizing that I am not the primary locus of reality."[28] In this regard, Casey's relational and humble dimension resonates with the preparatory disposition of the subject to interact with the other, as discussed in the intrareligious dialogue (or making of space) section.

Levinas's insistence on the submissiveness of the self in relation to the infinite suggests his Talmudic influence, by which God gratuitously reveals Godself to humanity, and not by humanity's effort. Based on such divine dimension, it could be misleading to conclude that the Levinasian infinite is one and the same with Descartes' infinite in his Third Meditation. In fact, the Levinasian God is extremely transcendent (almost to the point of atheism) except that his presence can only be possible through the face of the human other. Nevertheless, the presence of this infinite other is totally transcendent and so makes itself impossible for the self to comprehend. Contrarily, the self, on the receiving end, is humbled by the manifestation that comes from the infinite other.

The face can manifest its infinite presence in multiple forms. 1) The face does not import its meaning from the exterior. It inheres its meaning, which precedes any signification from the self. In other words, the other (face) cannot proceed from the self (a Husserlian reversion). 2)

26. Lamptey, *Never Wholly Other,* 51.

27. Casey, "Levinas' Idea," 394.

28. Casey, "Levinas' Idea," 394.

Due to the lack of exterior power and control over the face, it can be deduced from Levinasian logic that existence transcends being. 3) The face provokes newness of description. Contrary to phenomenology, in which observation produces meaning, the Levinasian face communicates its inherent meanings through interpellation. The immediate (face) cannot be perceived through vision or seeing, but through the spoken (the said). In accord, Levinas asserts, "The immediate is the interpellation, and, if we may speak thus, the imperative of language . . . The immediate is the face to face."[29] Therefore, Levinas emphasizes the importance of language as the revelation for the infinity of the other.[30]

Only the other (face) can communicate itself to the self through a discourse. Here, communication necessitates epiphany. And so, there is no disconnection between what is manifested and what manifests. This manifestation "does not consist in its being disclosed, its being exposed to the gaze that would take it as a theme for interpretation, and would command an absolute position dominating the object." In essence, what explains the face is epiphany as opposed to phenomenon. Even though epiphany as characterized by light and vision could be ambiguous, Levinas differentiates it from phenomenon. The face is not a visual expression as much as it is expressed by conversation. For this reason, Levinas says, "The face speaks, the manifestation of the face is already discourse."[31]

Unlike the emphasis on disclosure among phenomenologists, Levinas rejects disclosure because of its inappropriateness for the face. Such departure also distances Levinas from the Western philosophy, where the likes of Plato, Husserl and Heidegger conceive of truth as disclosure. To locate truth in the realm of disclosure, as Levinas argues, is to confine it within the control of the self. Rather than disclosure, which is possible for phenomena, Levinas insists that only through dialogic discourse can the face communicate some aspects of itself to the self. This implies that the self relates to the other (in its epiphany) uniquely from the manner he relates to things. Instead of the self, constituting the other (Husserl), Levinas teaches that the other expresses itself.[32] When accused by his critics of stripping the other of its ethical responsibility, while keeping the self in servitude, Levinas argues that the self can only achieve its fullest

29. Levinas, *Totality and Infinity*, 52.

30. Casey, "Levinas' Idea," 401.

31. Levinas, *Totality and Infinity*, 66, 193.

32. Levinas, *Totality and Infinity*, 399.

realization of being by relentlessly being at the service of the other.[33] The self, on its part, receives the newness of the face as a surprise that leads to growth. Therefore, in the face-to-face encounter, linguistic discourse enables the self to share in the infinitude of the other.

Obviously, Levinas absolves the other of any reciprocation, since her face always reminds the subject of his endless responsibility toward her.

The major shift of priority from the Husserlian "I" to the Levinasian "other" could provoke a suspicion of a Levinasian infiltration of theology into phenomenology. Levinas, however, objected to doing theology.[34] It is not necessarily a shift in the subject of study (phenomena), but in the approach taken (responsibility). The shift noticed is not necessarily on the what, but on the how.

Corroboratively, analyzing God's question to Cain in Genesis 4:9, "Where is your brother?," and Cain's reply, "Am I my brother's keeper?," shows a radical departure from ethical responsibility to ontological response.[35] In contrast, the methodological shift in Levinas primarily harmonizes both questions by allowing the other to set the agenda for every intersubjective relation. For Levinas, if Cain had respected the otherness of Abel, he would have realized his yawning responsibility toward him. In other words, it is a shift of center from the dominant self to the neglected other. It is like introducing a telescopic lens, which draws the distant other near, in place of the Western ontological microscopic lens, which magnifies the self.

What would possibly be the underlying motivation of the self, since it must depend on the epiphany of the other? According to Casey, Levinas in response distinguishes between human need and desire. Human need motivates but ends when the needed is provided. Such hunger is satisfied. Needs primarily belong to phenomenology. However, the ethical motivation commanded by the face is sought through desire. Infinity according to Levinas can only be accessed through desire, which transcends the theoretical and situates itself at the relational.[36] Whereas, Descartes guarantees self-consciousness as the channel into the infinite, Levinas, concretizes its primness through desire.

---

33. Levinas, *Totality and Infinity*, 197.
34. Levinas, *Totality and Infinity*, 197.
35. Levinas, *Totality and Infinity*, 42.
36. Levinas, *Totality and Infinity*, 395.

From the Latin *ligare* (to link), which is the root of "religion," a religious perspective of desire brings together two dissimilar terms: the self and the other. It purposefully seeks equality between the two. In the words of Levinas, "It (Desire) is the surplus possible in a society of equals, that of glorious humility, responsibility and sacrifice, which are the condition for equality itself."[37] Equality between self and the other sounds unusual to Levinasian prioritization of the other. It could be that by desiring the infinite, the self is redeemed from its egotism, and attains fulfillment, thereby accomplishing equality status with the other.

Levinas agrees with the assertion, "The face of the Other at each moment destroys and overflows the plastic image it leaves me, the idea existing to my own measure and to the measure of my ideatum—the adequate idea."[38] In desiring, the self is drawn toward the infinite, and often surpasses itself.[39] Helpful enough, Casey summarizes, "Desire is not striving for possession, but a striving which is possessed by that after which it yearns."[40] Desire is unquenchable as it seeks the infinite. The deeper it dives, the more profound it becomes. In other words, the face represents that inordinateness measured by desire.[41]

As noted by Andrew Shepherd, desire in both Levinas and Derrida lacks a "*telos* or eventual rest to desire."[42] This is confirmed by Levinas's assertion: "The Other is not a term: he does not stop the movement of desire. The other that Desire desires is again Desire."[43] Shepherd identifies the danger of ceaseless desire by linking it to the foundational cause of consumerism in later capitalism. With the lack of *telos* and unbridled emphasis on separateness and distance, as seen in Levinas's desire and modern consumerism, William T. Cavanaugh reverses a popular opinion that "greed is not attachment, but rather detachment."[44] That is detachment from the concerns of the other.

Shepherd, in agreement with Cavanaugh, affirms that "we perceive ourselves as detached—that is separate and distant—from what

---

37. Levinas, *Totality and Infinity*, 64.

38. Levinas, *Totality and Infinity*, 50–51.

39. Casey, "Levinas' Idea," 397.

40. Casey, "Levinas' Idea," 399.

41. Levinas, *Totality and Infinity*, 62.

42. Shepherd, *Gift of the Other*, 196.

43. Levinas, *Totality and Infinity*, 269.

44. Cavanaugh, *Being Consumed*, 157.

is Other (whether human or non-human)—that provides the basis for the acquiring of consumer items and/or relationships, their subsequent use, and then their disposal—freeing us up for acquisition of the next commodity."[45] However, if Shepherd's reading of Cavanaugh provides useful insights for the craving over material possession, why is interhuman relationship still waning by day?

Going forward, the Levinasian altruistic-responsibility shift, as just presented, offers a reliable framework in support of this book's main thesis for a healthier Muslim-Christian dialogue of life. In truth, both religious groups need telescopic lenses to harmonize their respective myopic lenses.

Nevertheless, Levinas's altruistic ethical option is as well very important in Muslim-Christian relations, because it deflects attention from the self (egocentric) and focuses on the obligation of the self to respond to the need of the other (altruistic).[46] From historic Muslim-Christian encounters (to be analyzed in chapter 1), the inability to properly appreciate and respect the other marred their age-old relations. In reaction to their unsettled problem, the Levinasian ethical template, which puts the self at the obligatory service of the other, has provided a radical turn toward that neglected "anonymous" other. Such ethical standard undergirds John F. Kennedy's famed injunction: "My fellow Americans, ask not what your country can do for you, ask what you can do for your country." Prioritizing doing good for the other among Muslims and Christians is the primary goal of this book's research.

---

45. Shepherd, *Gift of the Other*, 196–97.
46. Ferreira, "Total Altruism," 447.

1

The Problem

Religious Otherness?

THIS FIRST CHAPTER ARGUES that the mutual subjective perceptions adopted at the initial encounter between Christians and Muslims have indeed impacted their unsettled relations. The chapter purposefully accentuates subjective perception, rather than condemn either the religions or their representative actors, because it agrees with Raimon Panikkar, a mystic-pluralistic religious scholar,[1] that the cleaner our windows into reality are, the better we perceive reality.[2] This means that the more unbiased our minds are, the clearer we appreciate the significance of diversities in life, because biases, like dirt, smear our windows, forcing the other to look dirty. Moreover, this approach fits into the overall argument of this book, which claims that the existing Christian-Muslim antagonisms can be drastically diminished when the other is allowed to define its identity on her own terms.

Distorted portraiture of the other, as is argued, reflects in broad strokes what defines Christian-Muslim relations from its inception to the present time. The Muslim-Christian relational problems engaging this research fit into four broad questions that form the road maps: 1) What were the possible root causes of subjective perceptions among Muslims and Christians? 2) To what extent were their sacred texts instrumental? 3) What were the resultant effects of their antagonized perceptions at

1. See Paul F. Knitter, "The Pluralist Path: Where We've been and Where We're Going," in Harris et al., *Twenty-First Century Theologies of Religions*, 145.

2. Panikkar, *Invisible Harmony*, 171–72.

both global and local settings? 4) When, and what factors, might have engendered some improved relations, leading to dialogic option? Closely engaged attempts on these questions will not only be expository, but will also confirm the inherent danger of living with distorted imagination of the religious other.

In the meantime, however, a brief historical review of the age-old mistrust between Muslims and Christians at the universal level will first expose the possible root causes and then provide a roadmap for a better comprehension of what is particular to the Nigerian context.

The Arabian soil was host to Christianity for about two centuries before the sudden emergence of Islam. Two suppositions have been posited to account for the advent and spread of Christianity in Arabia. The first assumption is linked to the biblical Paul of Tarsus, after his retirement (Gal 1:17), while the second is traced to the "south-to-north mission" by the Syrian desert monks.[3] Despite historical uncertainty of both accounts, Christianity, no doubt, inadvertently influenced grounds for the implantation of Islam.

In the Arabian Peninsula, Christianity was not the sole religion. It rather coexisted with Judaism, Zoroastrianism, and traditional polytheism up to the early seventh century, when what became today's Islam began to emerge. Prior to the Medina experience, Muhammad had launched his prophetic mission in Mecca and also attracted some followers, about AD 618. At this earliest stage, historians suggest a tiny community of Christians, mostly artisans.[4] Before the *hijra* (flight), the few Christian presences in Mecca were the Nestorians and the Monophysites. More recently, the research of Hans Küng showed that the most popular form of Christianity to Meccans was a distinct Jewish Christian community that rejected the theological formulations of the Byzantine Church. These Jewish Christians in their doctrinal simplicity would accept the messianic mission of Jesus, but not his divinity.[5] The Medina context was no different. It was more or less a Jewish settlement, rather than Christian.

Christian missionary efforts at this period had more than the idolatrous locals as targets. They were known for promoting conversion, through polemics on other religions, while at the same time

---

3. Jomier, *How to Understand Islam*, 104.

4. Watt, *Muslim-Christian Encounters*, 7.

5. Küng et al., *Christianity and World Religions*, 100–107.

extolling their own doctrinal practices as solely authoritative. Judaism, even though treated with greater tolerance by Christians, was not entirely exempt from the latter's triumphalism.[6]

Besides these disparaged religious others, however, existed the other within Christianity. As Christianity confronted these distant religious others of the Arabian context, doctrinal disagreements weakened her strength from within. Basically, christological debates gave birth to different varieties of Christianity in pre-Islamic Arabia.

An informative example would be the dissonance between the Byzantine Eastern Church and the Western Roman Church. Following the decline of the three churches, i.e., Jerusalem, Alexandria, and Antioch, the institutionalized authorities in Christianity were reduced to the Byzantine (Constantinople) and the Roman Churches. The Byzantine and Roman Churches were torn between the political and religious struggles subsequent to aligning themselves respectively to Greek tradition and Latin tradition.[7] Besides political and social issues, the two church authorities were divided along theological lines, especially because of the christological controversies.[8]

Emperor Constantine in AD 313 influenced the tolerance of Christian worship and later, about 330, forestalled her greatness as a church in the Byzantine Empire. He is said to have convened and chaired[9] the Council of Nicea in 325, at which the consubstantiality of Christ with the Father was defined.

The three main groups of Christians that possibly encountered Islam at its nascent stage were Monophysites (the Egyptian Coptics and the Jacobites or western Syrians), the Nestorians (or eastern Syrians), and the Byzantines.[10] Each differed in their christological doctrines based on their cultural orientations. In the Egyptian Coptic Church, with the influence of the pre-Christian practice of mummification, which was a typical response to the human problem of mortality, they understood the incarnation of Christ as a one-nature liberation from mortality. Similarly, the Syrian Nestorians, whose goal was in protection of Christ's divinity, consequently emphasized his humanity. However, the Great Byzantine

---

6. Neusner, "Judaism," 31.

7. Anees, "Dialogue of History," 6–7.

8. Neusner, "Judaism," 86.

9. Neusner, "Judaism," 86.

10. Reynolds, *Emergence of Islam,* 46.

Church condemned the christological doctrines of both Monophysites and Nestorians as heretical and expelled them about AD 600. About the same year, the expelled folks were received in Iraq, where they established their main center in the Sassanian (Persian) Empire.[11]

In essence, Muhammad and his earliest companions experienced a destabilized Christianity in the Arabian context. William Montgomery Watt identifies three factors that substantiated the weakness of Christianity at this period.[12] Such internal crises heavily impacted the unity and universal character of the church. First, the Meccans considered their "trading interests" and carefully avoided unnecessary categorization into either of the two divided Christian groups, the Byzantine and Sassanian Empires. Second, the official Christology approved at Nicaea sounded abstract to the average Christians, who had no good knowledge of Greek philosophy. In defense of their positions, the Nestorians and Monophysites landed into more abstract formulations. As a result, when confronted by the pagan Meccans about their religions, most of these non-theologians (Christians) lacked the clarity of ideas for the explanation of their theology. Third, the expulsion of the Copts, Jacobites, and Nestorians by the Great Byzantine Church possibly prepared grounds for conversions to Islam.[13] Such earliest display of Christianity's inability to tolerate diversity must account for the abysmal failure of the gospel in the Arabian Peninsula today.

A divided Christianity in both doctrines and practices must have encouraged the conclusion of the earliest Muslims that the revealed Christian message suffered distortion over time, just as most Muslims continue to perceive it to date. Jacques Jomier affirms that the Muslims' accusation of Christians drifting from the original revealed message of Jesus led to the call and response of Muhammad.[14] Similarly, Watt believes such period experienced "a religious vacuum in Mecca, which Christianity could not fill."[15] According to Fatmir M. Shehu, such apparent void of a religious guide explains the prophetic call of Muhammad to Islam aimed at social and religious reformations.[16]

---

11. Watt, *Muslim-Christian Encounters*, 1.

12. Shehu, *Nostra Aetate*, 177.

13. Watt, *Muslim-Christian Encounters*, 7.

14. Jomier, *How to Understand Islam*, 103.

15. Watt, *Muslim-Christian Encounters*, 28.

16. Shehu, *Nostra Aetate*, 177.

Based on these weaknesses, the nascent Islam respected both Judaism and Christianity as "People of the Book" (or those with the revealed message), but also accuse them as those who at some point in their history altered the word of Allah. Traditional Muslims believe that Christians (as well as Jews) corrupted their scriptures[17] and in the process removed the prophecies concerning the coming of Muhammad.[18] Therefore, many traditional Muslims identify the expected *Paraclete* in the gospel as Muhammad[19] and also claim that "the rider on camel" in Isaiah 21:7 refers to him. On the contrary, biblical scholars interpret this text in parallel to King Cyrus's instrumentality to the fall of Babylon.[20]

Such speculations depict inadequate understanding of Christianity. From the same limited Islamic perspective, Judaism is considered guilty of reverting a universal call from Allah to a national election by their emphasis on the covenant,[21] while Christianity's doctrine of incarnation and atonement typically contradicts the Qur'anic teaching on the absolute transcendence of Allah.[22] Consequently, Islam from the outset imagines itself as that true religion of total submission to Allah and as that ancient Abrahamic faith (a *hanif*, or true monotheist), but whose warner (Muhammad) about the Last Day reinstated the right understanding of God.

A *hanif*, in the description of Jerusha T. Lampety, "is a person who has *din al-fitra* (natural monotheistic faith) but didn't belong to any religion."[23] In Islam, Abraham the *hanif* (neither a Jew nor a Christian) is exemplified as a true manifestation of lived monotheism.[24] His unconditional readiness to execute a rare and difficult task in obedience to God (sacrifice of Ishmael) undergirds the connection his life epitomizes in common with Islam as total submission to Allah. Based on this Abrahamic heritage, Islam in its self-identity rejects being regarded as a

---

17. Mingana, *Woodbrooke Studies*, 35, 56–58. This volume contains the two days' discussion between a Christian called Timothy, the Catholicos or head of the Nestorians in Iraq, and the caliph al-Mahdi in the year 781.

18. Mingana, *Woodbrooke Studies*, 64.

19. Mingana, *Woodbrooke Studies*, 33–35.

20. Isaiah 45:1–3.

21. McDermott, *World Religions*, 34.

22. Watt, *Muslim-Christian Encounters*, 63.

23. Lamptey, *Never Wholly Other*, 77.

24. Troll, *Dialogue and Difference*, 145.

mere new religion, when it sees itself also as a purification of that ancient monotheism for humanity that was intended by Allah.[25]

Gabriel Said Reynolds articulates this triumphalist acclaim by outlining three popular deductions from the Islamic emergence narrative: 1) Islam is the completion and corrector of Christianity; 2) Muhammad is a fulfillment of biblical prophets; and 3) the struggle between monotheism and paganism persists.[26] However, one should be aware that an Islamic universal claim was gradual. The fact that the Prophet recognized the validity of the monotheistic religions (People of the Book) and followed the Zoroastrian praxis of *Dhimmi*, which was continued by his successors during the expansion of Islam, is a critique of this claim, at its earliest time. Nonetheless, Reynolds concludes that, "from the outset Islam demonstrated a combination of religious and military supremacy."[27] Consequent upon the supremacy claim, subjective centrism underscores the Christian-Muslim relations toward each other. Accordingly, it has been noticed that "Muslims have acknowledged an Islamized Christianity and Christians have often Christianized Islam."[28]

Already, pre-Islamic Christianity understood itself as the divinely instituted consummation of the Law and the Prophets because of her christocentric advantage. Christ, as the incarnated God and the founder of Christianity, engendered in Christians an attitude of promoting their religion not only as the true religion, but also as the converging point of all other religions. In this regard, Christianity avowedly defended itself as the fulfillment of Judaism.[29]

Contrary to how Judaism defines itself, Christianity appropriated this more ancient monotheistic religion of the Mediterranean region,[30] and regarded it as preparatory ground for her later development. In other words, from a traditional Christian perspective, Judaism has meaning so long as it orients itself towards Christianity. When Pope John Paul II, for example, refers to Jews as "our older brothers,"[31] a tonal continuity and fulfillment can be inferred. By so doing, Christianity accentuates her implied

25. Troll, *Dialogue and Difference*, 52.

26. Reynolds, *Emergence of Islam*, 12.

27. Reynolds, *Emergence of Islam*, 69.

28. Orman, *Muslim View*, 69.

29. Neusner, "Judaism," 29.

30. McDermott, *World Religions*, 26.

31. McDermott, *World Religions*, 26.

continuity through the establishment of the new covenant in Christ, which is seen to be the completion of what came before.[32] This form of appropriation by Christianity infuriates adherents of Judaism and has created a continuing tension between these two monotheistic religions.

In return, Judaism ridicules the Christian claim of Jesus as Messiah.[33] For adherents of Judaism, Jesus can be seen as a historic human who might be regarded by some Jews as a prophet of sorts, but never as a God-man.[34] The expected messiahship, by Judaistic reckoning, would either be an emergence of a man (traditionalist Jews) or a messianic age (modernist Jews) in which her divine election will be established. Both opinions, however, agree that Jesus cannot be the Messiah because of his failure to achieve world peace and a universal leadership.[35] From that perspective, his proclaimed divinity constitutes a divisive obstacle for Jewish-Christian relations, because it contradicts Judaism's transcendental notion of Yahweh. From this comparative analysis, therefore, one can notice the strong self-awareness among the three religions.

In comparison to the Judeo-Christianity relation, Islam goes beyond the continuity narrative. First, it "maintains that it completes Christianity."[36] Then it also defines itself "as an end of the story: a return to the purity of the original and perennial message, rather than a process, leading to its revelation."[37] For Jacob Neuser, "Islam views Moses and Jesus (among others) as prophets, whose message is completed by the prophet Muhammad."[38]

An Islamic theologian, Tim Winter (also known as Abdul-Hakim Murad) confirms Islam's abrogation (*naskh*) of prior religions: "As in the treatment of Judaism, but more sharply, the Muslim revelation deploys arguments against a historically-evolved Christianity in order to justify the latest divine intervention (Islam)."[39] In his attempt to vindicate Islamic supersessionism, he first criticized the anti-supersession position of Paul Knitter, John Hick, and some of the Muslim pluralist

---

32. Neusner, "Judaism," 29.

33. See Neusner, *Rabbi Talks with Jesus*

34. Levenson, "Judaism Addresses Christianity," 588.

35. McDermott, *World Religions*, 36.

36. Neusner, "Judaism," 29.

37. Madigan, "Muslim-Christian Dialogue," 245.

38. Neusner, "Judaism," 29.

39. Winter, "Last Trump Card, 142.

theologians like Fazlur Rahman, Farid Esack, and Mahmoud Ayoub, for identifying supersessionism with divisiveness.[40] Then he concluded, "Supersessionism . . . has negative implications for dialogue only when read as cause for triumphalism, rather than as a spur to the contrite awareness of a heavy responsibility."[41]

Like Christianity, Islam is a complex religion, and not monolithic. The Qur'an's approach to the religious belief of others is nuanced in the sense that it displays ambivalent attitudes. As such, not all Muslims are exclusivists. Nonetheless, these mutually perceived grounds for rivalries between Christians and Muslims paved way for misconceived identities across many centuries.

The age-old antagonism and isolation between Muslims and Christians impacted their historical encounter. One of the earliest Christian engagements with Islam came from John Damascene (ca. 654–749), who, together with his father, served at the court of the Umayyad caliphs.[42] In his treatise *De Haeresibus*, he developed a chapter on "The Heresy of the Ishmaelites"[43] through his knowledge of Arabic and Greek. This textual engagement of the Qur'an from a Christian was the first attempt.[44] At this earliest time, his approach was basically apologetic rather than polemic.[45] Listing Islam among the heresies that affected Christianity,[46] Damascene acknowledged some common grounds because an outsider of the faith can hardly be a heretic. Even though his attack on major Islamic doctrines has been described as "calm and charitable in tone,"[47] it was considered preparatory for subsequent Muslim-Christian polemics.

From the ninth century, when Islamic scholars (especially the *Mu'tazila*)[48] almost rivaled their Christian counterparts in intellectual sophistication, Byzantium produced more irenic writings about Islam.

40. See Leirvik, "Towards a Relational and Humanizing Theology, 225.

41. Winter, "Last Trump Card," 152.

42. Madigan, "Muslim-Christian Dialogue," 246.

43. Earliest Christian written treatise against the Muslims, with an uncertain date between John Damascene's supposed date of birth (654) to his supposed date of death (749).

44. See Sahas, *John of Damascus on Islam*; cited in Zebiri, *Muslims and Christians*, 24.

45. Zebiri, *Muslims and Christians*, 24.

46. Madigan, "Muslim-Christian Dialogue," 247.

47. Daniel, *Islam and the West*, 15.

48. This is reckoned as the first school of scholastic theologians in Islam.

Perhaps "they were freer to express open hostility."[49] Much of such polemics derived from near ignorance about Islam, until the twelfth century, when significant academic communications cut across Arabic and
European scholars through the availability of some classic philosophical
texts in Arabic (such as Aristotle and Neoplatonists) and in Latin (like
Ibn Sina, d. AH 428/1037, and Ibn Rushd, d. AH 595/1198). This period ushered in some positive appreciation towards Islam, as European
scholarship approached the threshold of its Enlightenment. Reliable information waned the fabricated stereotyping of Islam (as external threat),
which Europe used as antithesis to its own self-image.[50]

The Renaissance period introduced individual scholars' critical perception of Islam, such as Nicholas of Cusa and John of Segovia. With the
establishments of Arab studies in the eighteenth century and Orientalist
studies in the nineteenth century, Islam in the West experienced an organized scholarship. Far from dissolving distorted conceptions, the openness to studies introduced scholars to reliable information about Islam.

From the nineteenth century, accurate information concerning
Muhammad and his prophetic mission started correcting earlier prejudices. The twentieth century, through globally increased migration and
education, offered more conciliatory opportunities between Muslims
and Christians.

A historic study on the evolution of Arabic scholarship on Christianity encountered major obstacles. Besides the inaccessibility of Muslim materials, it was almost disdainful[51] for Muslims scholars to engage
European Christendom in writing. The simple truth centers on the Ori-
entalists' misconception of Christianity as European imperialism. For
these Easterners, European secularism, which synonymously defined
Christianity, has Islam as its next positioned target. Consequently, it
was not uncommon that the term *kafirun* (infidels) was used to refer to
Christians in some languages like Persian, Turkish, and Arabic, while the
Ottoman tradition encouraged the inclusion of insults and curses to the
names of Europe.[52] Paradoxically, it was colonialism and the missionizing
impacts on Muslims that recorded greater positive influence on Muslim

49. Zebiri, *Muslims and Christians*, 29.

50. Zebiri, *Muslims and Christians*, 26.

51. Lewis, *Culture in Conflict*, 13.

52. Lewis, *The Muslim Discovery*, 172–74.

attitudes towards Christianity than ever.[53] Through these encounters both religions somewhat gained improved understanding of the other, to the extent their sacred scriptures approved.

The Role of Sacred Texts

Although Christians and Muslims pride their sacred texts as the revealed Word of God, it is imperative to recognize that, between the two faiths, the Word of God addressed to the human race is understood in significantly different ways.[54] The Christian uniqueness of Christ as the Son of God and the fulfillment of all revelation, by whose death and resurrection salvation was merited for humanity, sounds totally absurd to Muslims. It is absurd not only because of the incarnation and atonement doctrines, but also because the average Muslim reads Christianity through the unparalleled authority of the Qur'an.[55] In other words, the Qur'anic "emphasis (23 times) on Jesus as the son of Mary is a pointed denial of the Christian affirmation of him as the Son of God."[56] These divergent and convergent characteristics of Islam in relation to Christianity reveal the enormous difficulty that one confronts in perceiving one religion through the lens of the other. The difficulty, of course, breeds "confusion and irrelevant criticism."[57]

Seeing through the other's lens implies reading her sacred text accordingly. The Bible and the Qur'an vary in style, composition, and content. As sacred texts, "the Qur'an is about the same length as the New Testament," [or just over half of it][58] "but the similarity stops there."[59] Whereas biblical inspiration permits divine-human collaboration,[60] in which human agents communicated the Word in various styles and characters, in Muslim faith, the angel Gabriel (*jibrīl*) dictated the Word

53. Zebiri, *Muslims and Christians*, 28.

54. Troll, *Dialogue and Difference*, 132.

55. Zebiri, *Muslims and Christians*, 15.

56. Madigan, "Muslim-Christian Dialogue," 245.

57. Borrmans, *Guidelines for Dialogue*, 104–5.

58. Reynolds, *Emergence of Islam*, 93.

59. McDermott, *World Religions*, 107.

60. Zebiri, *Muslims and Christians*, 10.

of God to Muhammad "over the nearly twenty-three-year period of his mission from approximately 610 C.E to his death 632 C.E."[61]

According to the most widely held Islamic view, these series of revelations were only sustained orally by the earliest Muslims, until after the death of Mohammad and the subsequent death of his companions in battle. Foreseeing the danger of losing the original messages over time, one of his close associates, 'Umar b. al-Khattab, got the approval of caliph Abu Bakr for the documentation. It was through the supervision of Mohammad's secretary, Zayd b. Thabit, that the Qur'anic text was established. Qur'anic sources included all collections, "whether written on palm branches or thin stones or preserved in the hearts of men."[62] This first draft served its purpose until an edited version appeared some eighteen years later under the caliphate of Uthman b. 'Affan.[63] Despite the edited work, most Muslims accept this later version as "true to the revelation received by the prophet, and is clearly dated to his lifetime."[64]

However, sacred text critics, like John Wansbrough, argue in support of gradual collections of Qur'anic verses up till the ninth century.[65] This shows a much later dating than what is traditionally held. In contrast, another scholar, John Burton, points to an earliest composition of the Qur'an attributed to Muhammad himself.[66] Such non-consensual views among scholars on the chronology and provenance of the Qur'an amount to uncertain conclusions about its organization, leaving the option for its complexity as a better choice.[67] Reuven Firestone strongly concludes that the uncertainties and organizational redactions in the course of the Qur'anic composition "affected the nature of the Qur'an in its present form."[68]

Nonetheless, Muslims revere the Qur'an as the reported speech of Allah from the mouth of Muhammad. Representing an Islamic majority voice, Seyyed Hossein Nasr affirms, "no Muslim would accept any other view than that, the Qur'an came verbatim from heaven."[69] Nasr's affirmation is forged from two Qur'anic terms, *wahy* and *tanzil* (both translated

61. Firestone, *Jihad*, 43.

62. Firestone, *Jihad*, 43.

63. Firestone, *Jihad*, 43.

64. Firestone, *Jihad*, 43.

65. Wansbrough, *Quranic Studies*, 44–46.

66. Burton, *Collection of the Qur'an*, 239–40.

67. Firestone, *Jihad*, 44.

68. Firestone, *Jihad*, 46.

69. Nasr, "Response to Hans Küng's," 98.

as "externality of" revelation). Some Muslim scholars translate *tanzil* as "sending down" and *wahy* as the process that expresses the verbatim conveyance of Allah's word to his prophet.[70] In contrast, most Christians, in particular, the Catholic Church, recognize the few inconsistencies from human agencies in the composition and compilation of the Bible, which have been carefully explained in accord with the divine inspiration.[71]

In the strict sense, most Muslims believe that revelation through verbal dictation and to a designated messenger, i.e., the Prophet Muhammad, guarantees the ideal and error-free text.[72] They interpret the Christian teaching of a divine partnering with human beings in the creation of sacred scripture as a direct indicator of doubt and/or infiltration of errors in the original message. However, from a broader perspective, revelation as divine act contains certain nuances in both Christian and Muslim understandings.

That Islam by default has a broader appreciation of revelation than any other religion has been argued in academic circles. Muslims, according to Asghar Ali Engineer, recognize that "divine revelation is granted through all time to all nations."[73] Engineer further asserts that "a Muslim admits the truth of all prophets and revelations."[74] Again, he conclusively supported his argument by referencing a group of Islamic thinkers, who, in the spirit of dialogue, "have added prophets not mentioned in the Qur'an to the list of prophets sent by Allah. Some Sufi saints, such as Mazhar Jan-i-Janan, have accepted some highly revered Hindu religious figures, including Ram and Krishna, as prophets."[75] Such openness to religious pluralism, present even at the inception of Islam (seventh century), is uncommon among other religions. Indeed, "the Qur'an accepted the truth of other religions and sought their cooperation."[76]

By comparison, the fullness of revelation, uniquely identified by Christians in the person of Christ, is rather professed by Muslims as the Qur'an, which, in their belief, was handed over to Muhammad in its purest form. From a Catholic perspective, sacred tradition and sacred

70. Zebiri, *Muslims and Christians*, 9.

71. Zebiri, *Muslims and Christians*, 11.

72. Zebiri, *Muslims and Christians*, 11.

73. Engineer, "Da'wah or Dialogue," 28.

74. Engineer, "Da'wah or Dialogue," 28

75. Engineer, "Da'wah or Dialogue," 27.

76. Engineer, "Da'wah or Dialogue," 29.

scripture form one single source of God's revelation in Christ, which is entrusted to the church.[77] In general, the church teaches that revelation ended with the death of the last apostle.

Traditional Muslims, while recognizing the validity of the prophetic tradition in the Bible, consider it problematic to accept its textual contents as a whole. Through the doctrine of *tahrif* (scriptural alteration or falsification),[78] many Muslims read the scriptures of Jews and Christians through the Qur'anic verses. Without engaging the details of such scholarship, the doctrine of *tahrif* simply implies falsification of Jewish and Christian scriptures. In other words, these Muslims who believe in *tahrif* highlight some selective biblical verses, in particular, those that seems to suggest the coming of Mohammad and others that support the humanity of Jesus (Qur'an 9:30). Reynolds confirms that pro-*tahrif* Islamicists do not recommend the Bible for religious purposes; rather, it could be used for Islamic apologetics (*da'wa*).[79] By inference, therefore, those passages that question this Islamic perspective form the basis for the distortion argument.

Nevertheless, some common grounds between Islam and Christianity are still possible. Both Christianity and Islam believe in one God[80] (though with varied approaches), who communicates through revelation, and also in the Last Day. Each holds in esteem its own sacred texts as revealed. At once, unfortunately, each tends to highlight perceived inadequacies in the other's text, even to the extent of mistrusting its authenticity. However, we must not lose sight of Maulana Muhammad Ali's commentary on 29:46, which says, "The fundamental principle of religion is that God exists and that He reveals Himself to man, and it is common to all revealed religions."[81]

Overall, both the Bible and the Qur'an contain, at the very least, encouraging passages that can ensure fair engagement of the other. Although the Bible does not mention Muslims because none existed at the time of its composition, the love of neighbor principle (Philippians 2:3), which includes even enemies (Matthew 5:44), stands tall in this regard. Beyond this Christian dimension of the golden rule, apparently present

---

77. *Dei Verbum*, #10, in Flannery, ed., *Vatican Council II*.

78. *Tahrif* is severally used in the Qur'an, such as in 2:27; 4:46; 5:31; 5:41, etc.

79. Reynolds, "Gavin D'Costa," 293.

80. *NA*, #3, in Flannery, ed., *Vatican Council II*.

81. Ali, *Holy Qur'an*, 769.

in other religions, the Bible denotes a universalistic outlook that encourages religious pluralism. Two texts, one from the Old Testament and one from the New Testament, might suffice.

The prophecy of Malachi 1:11 reads, "For from the rising of the sun to its setting my name is great among the nations, and in every place incense is offered in my name, and pure offering, for my name is great among the nations, says the Lord of hosts." Acts 14:16–17 testifies, "In past generations he allowed all the nations to walk in their own ways; yet he did not leave himself without witness, for he did good and gave you from heaven rains and fruitful seasons, satisfying your hearts with food and gladness." Inasmuch as these universalistic texts suggest God's presence (revelation) among different peoples, they do not provide a roadmap for interreligious relations.

Antonie Wessels's review of three additional texts—Genesis 14:18–20; Matthew 15:21–28; and Acts 10:9–29; (34–36)—more or less echoes biblical grounds for interreligious encounters. Genesis 14:18–20 recounts Abraham's meeting with Melchizedek, the king of Salem. Shortly before this encounter, Abraham had been blessed by God (12:2) and was victorious over the kings of Sodom and Gomorrah (14:1–11). On his way home (Canaan), an interreligious hospitality scene, initiated by Melchizedek, was established. As a token of appreciation, Abraham gave Melchizedek his tithe from his loots, because he recognized the latter as a priest-king.

According to Wessels, Abraham's action was an overt acknowledgement of *El* (the God of Melchizedek) as identical with his own *Yahweh*,[82] who called him from Ur in Chaldea. In essence, the same priesthood and kingship of Melchizedek was linked first to the Davidic dynasty (Psalm 110:4), and later became the prototype of Christ's priesthood (Hebrews 7:17). In other words, the universality of God permits appreciation and respect for the God of the other. Therefore, *El* could be *Yahweh*, but differently perceived by the people.

The encounter between Jesus and the Canaanite woman (Matthew 15:21–28) presents the second instance of interfaith dialogue. In general, it represents a model for interfaith encounter, in which two most important principles are present. The first is the inviolable respect for otherness. Christ vividly reminded the woman of their respective cultural and religious otherness: "It is not fair to take the children's bread and throw to the dogs" (Matthew 15:25); which she was not ashamed in

---

82. Wessels, "Some Biblical," 56.

acknowledging, "Yes, Lord, even the dogs eat the crumbs that fall from their master's table" (15:27). However, she expressed commitment to her faith background, and still showed openness to the newness of Jesus' miraculous power.

The second is mutual spiritual growth. The Canaanite woman (outside of Israel) manifested an amazing faith, similar to that of the Centurion (Matthew 8:10), that surprised Jesus. Basing his argument on passages like "Jesus increased in wisdom and in stature, and in favor with God and man" (Luke 2:52), Wessels suggests that Jesus experienced surprise at an impressive faith from a religious other.[83]

Lastly, Peter's application of Christ's model of interreligious relations led to an exemplar form of conversion, which happened as fruit of the encounter, not as the goal. His acceptance of hospitality in the house of Simon the tanner (a despicable job) was preparatory to the divine approval of "unclean foods," through his vision at Joppa. That Peter, a typical Jew, offered and received hospitality from heathens shows inner transformation over religio-cultural biases. This led to his assurance to Cornelius, whom he honored his invitation "without objection" (Acts 10:29).

It is only after mutual appreciation of respective otherness that enriching fruits can emerge in interfaith encounter. Thus, Wessels concludes that through this encounter one notices that "'conversion' is not predictable but may take a shape and course different from what is expected."[84] These biblical texts, and probably more, lend grounds for Muslim-Christian dialogue of life, through establishment of its possibility, approach, and fruits.

Technically, the Qur'an identifies diversity as an act of God in the establishment of one human family. Qur'an 30:22 states, "surely in the diversity of your languages and your colors, there is a divine sign if you can only understand."[85] Drawing on this particular Qur'anic verse, Mahmoud Ayoud[86] concludes: "Diversity is not bad; it is an act of divine mercy that

---

83. Wessels, "Some Biblical," 58.

84. Wessels, "Some Biblical," 62.

85. Diversity here would include cultures as well.

86. Mahmoud Ayoub was born in 1935 in Lebanon (a mixed city of Muslims and Christians), raised a Muslim, converted to Christianity in his youth, and then returned to Islam while doing graduate studies at Harvard. He knows both religions from the inside in a very unique way. His background, especially his Shi'ite persuasion, underscores his authority with regard to Islamic religious pluralism.

we are different, that we can have a rich spirituality that takes different forms and different traditions."[87] Ayoub's disposition to pluralism will not be much a surprise, since Shi'ites disagree with the infallibility of authority attributed to the Ulamas,[88] which occludes the independent analysis of the Qur'an and Islamic law.[89] Similarly, religious pluralism in the Qur'anic context is considered as God's plan[90] with the purpose of putting humanity to a test of going astray.

The idea of a test satisfies humanity's accountability toward God, in appreciation of religious pluralism. This accords with the Qur'an: "And you will surely be called to account for all that you ever did" (16:93). Diversity being God's design from the outset necessitated the vital role of prophets as guides, coordinators, and warners, such that different peoples with divergent views would not go astray. In essence, Issa J. Boullata confirms that no peoples were meant to lack God's guidance toward the Truth.[91] Rather, Allah commands, immediately following these pluralistic verses, the fruitful way of harnessing humanity's differences: "so be you forward in good works" (2:148).

Boullata acknowledges different versions of this command and their shades of meanings, and insists they all point to "Qur'anic principle of interfaith relations, based on a harmonious religious pluralism, and urging believers of all faith to do good."[92] Even though the Qur'an does not name specific religion(s) in this regard, elsewhere it does acknowledge that the divine reward of salvation exists among some other religious groups like Jews, Christians, and Sabians (2:62), on the tripod of conditions that they believe in God, believe in the Last Day, and do righteous deeds.[93] From the foregoing, aiming at outdoing the other in good deeds[94] manifests the sustainable way of maintaining humanity's unity through the appreciation of diversities.

87. Orman, *Muslim View*, 15.

88. *Ulamas* are Islamic scholars whose consensus on moral right and wrong are faith based.

89. McDermott, *World Religions*, 113.

90. The importance of pluralism is emphasized in four different suras: 5:48; 11:118; 16:93; 42:8.

91. Boullata, "Fastabiqul-Khairat," 44.

92. Boullata, "Fastabiqul-Khairat," 44

93. Boullata, "Fastabiqul-Khairat," 45.

94. This mandate is present in both the Qur'an and the Bible. Its theological implications will be a major concern in chapters 10 and 11.

The Qur'anic command, *fa-stabiqu'l-khayrat*, compete in good deeds (with its other nuanced English translations), emphasizes the priority of practicing good deeds toward others. Two questions are paramount from this command, according to Mun'im Sirry: Who are the addressees? And what does the command demand from them? Some prominent Muslim scholars' responses to these questions attest to its interfaith support.

Al-Tabari (d. AD 923), one of the earliest Islamic commentators, in his famous magnum opus, *Tafsir*, reviews (Qur'an 2:148 and 5:48). Analyzing two interpretations of *li-kull-in* (unto each), one referring to the community of Muhammad (Muslims) and the other suggesting people of different religious communities, al-Tabari settles with the second consideration.[95] His interpretation guarantees certain openness to Christian-Muslim relations, since Allah gave each people a law and a prophet. Another Muslim exegete, al-Baydawi (d. AD 1286), following the steps of al-Tabari, confirms its universal addressees, but also "amplifies the meaning of the command in these words: 'hasten to them (good deeds) in order to seize the opportunity and achieve the merit of precedence and priority.'"[96]

Two modern Islamic exegetes also lent their voices to the two verses on good deeds. Rashid Rida, in his *Tafsir al-Manar*, provides elaborate answers to who and what the texts meant:

> It is incumbent on all of you to hasten to good deeds and to hurry to them because they are specifically the intended purpose of all laws and ways of religion. Why then, O people, do you look at the difference and dissimilarity [among religious communities] without seeing the wisdom of difference and the intention of religion and law? Is this not abandoning guidance and following the ways of passion? . . . And so, you should consider [different] laws to be a cause for competition in good deeds, and not a cause for enmity by rivalry in deeds of bigotry.[97]

Rida's argument in favor of all peoples emphasizes the fact that since Muslims already have responded to the same divine call, *fa-stabiqu 'l-khayrat*, in Qur'an 2:148 refers to any religious community, not specifically to Islam.

---

95. Boullata, "Fastabiqul-Khairat," 46–47.

96. Boullata, "Fastabiqul-Khairat," 48.

97. Boullata, "Fastabiqul-Khairat," 49.

In contrast, Sayyid Qutb insists that the Qur'anic command addresses the specificity and distinctiveness of the Muslim community, which imply all peoples embracing Islam and its sharia for the assurance of justice, peace, and salvation.[98] His position opposes interfaith relations, based on the condition that the supremacy of Islam and that of its sharia are recognized.[99] Despite Qutb's insistence on Islamic supremacy, his earlier exegeses were closer to the inclusive voice of the verses by many Qur'anic commentators. Moreover, since Qur'an 2:256 forbids coercion in religious matters, it greatly supports the command on good deeds in paving way for Muslim-Christian interfaith relations.

Similarly, Ayoub is definitive in his reminder to adherents of both Islam and Christianity regarding the one human family under God: "Theological doctrines may divide us, but faith unites us."[100] Faith serves as a common ground for both Muslims and Christians: "The truth is that Christianity and Islam constitute one complex faith, one starting with person, another with the Word. Their separateness does not denote two areas of conflicting truths, but a dialogical necessity."[101] Again, Ayoub's analysis is strongly representative of pluralists' voices in scholarship.

In corroboration, various verses of the Qur'an depict language of respect for People of the Book, i.e., Jews, Christians, Sabians, and sometimes Zoroastrians. Human diversity reminds us that we ought not be the same, even while humbly appreciating our similarities as one human genus, because the reason for our differences is also fundamental to our being. Diversity originates from the will of God. Actually, diversity is meant not to constitute division, but rather to encourage healthy competition in doing good works (Qur'an 5:48). Therefore, the crux of diversity is primarily positive. "Doing good for the other" will be fully developed into a workable theology in chapter 10.

Meanwhile, between Jews and Christians, the Qur'an shows a bit of a favor for the latter. In fact, that "Christians are the nearest people in amity to the Muslims" is a popular Quranic command.[102] When threatened by his Qurashite kinsmen,[103] Muhammad ordered some of his men to seek

98. Boullata, "Fastabiqul-Khairat," 50.

99. Boullata, "Fastabiqul-Khairat," 50

100. McDermott, *World Religions*, 113.

101. Askari, "Dialogical Relationship," 485.

102. Orman, *Muslim View*, 313. Mun'im Sirry is also an important Muslim scholar in this regard.

103. Qurashites constitute the most famous tribe in Mohammad's Mecca, and the

refuge at the hands of a Christian king, Negus in Abyssinia, Ethiopia.[104] Sending them to Medina (a Jewish settlement) was an option that did not happen. This could suggest trust, especially when dear lives were at stake. Shehu actually confirms that Muhammad took the Christian option based on the moral and charitable confidence they earned.[105] In other words, asking for and providing hospitality at this earliest Muslim-Christian encounter points to historical grounds for the thesis of this research.

More so, that Christianity (as previously explained) expresses itself as the fulfillment of Judaism could be another reason. For the sake of precision, Islamic scholars have argued, "the Christianity that the Qur'an extols is not the official Christianity of Rome and Byzantium with its elaborate theology, but the popular piety of desert monks who carried on the work of healing and purification that Christ began during his earthly sojourn."[106] Nonetheless, Engineer asserts that the sura (5:82) that extols the monks "speaks of people not faiths."[107] He further clarified that the reference to "Jews as violent" was not based on faith, but on the supremacy struggle over Medina.[108]

At best, the Qur'an reveals an obvious ambivalence toward People of the Book (*Ahl al-Kitab*), especially Christians. All depends on which circumstances are addressed. From the outset, Islam enjoyed amity with Christianity and Judaism. This need not evoke much surprise, because as an ancient religion in a new garb,[109] Islam had to demonstrate its validity by appealing to the sacred texts of existing religious authorities, while emphasizing its uniqueness. At once, the Qur'an does not lack strong and hateful languages toward People of the Book; partly because Islam thought that People of the Book antagonize each other,[110] and partly because antagonizing the previous religions largely assures Islam's necessity.

---

guardians of the Kaaba.

104. See McAuliffe, *Quranic Christians*, 204–39 (especially ch. 7).

105. Shehu, *Nostra Aetate*, 178.

106. Ayoub, "Christian-Muslim Dialogue," 313.

107. Engineer, "Daw'ah or Dialogue," 27.

108. Engineer, "Daw'ah or Dialogue," 27. Medina was formerly a Jewish settlement until the *hijra* (AD 622), which they tried defending (violently) against the new Islamic power threat. Such power tussle was not seen among Christians because they were not in Medina. The closest encounter that Muhammad had was with priests and monks who lacked interest in territorial control.

109. Ammah, "Muslim-Christian," 141.

110. See Qur'an 2:113.

In the foregoing, the Qur'anic ambivalence towards People of the Book will be eked out.

At the earliest stage of distinguishing its identity, Islam "borrowed" but "remolded" certain Arabian cultural elements as well as ideas from People of the Book.[111] Even though some Christian Islamicists like Reynolds see close parallels between the Bible and the Qur'an,[112] Ayoub considers the terms "borrowing and remolding" more fitting for the Islamic tradition than for the Qur'an, because traditional Muslims believe the words of the Qur'an were dictated to Muhammad.

In terms of historicity, it was Christianity, as a self-proclaimed fulfillment of Judaism, that offered Islam a platform for the confirmation of its needed authenticity. The Qur'an vividly testifies to this initial rapport by affirming more than once the authority of some Christian witnesses (16:43 called them "people of remembrance"). To be precise, Muhammad was instructed to verify his prophetic experiences in these words: "If you are in doubt concerning what We sent down to you, ask those who read the scripture before you" (10:94).

Two accounts are available to the Islamic tradition, in which the Prophet is said to have sought and received approval. The first was from a Christian servant, Waraqah b. Nawfal,[113] the cousin of his wife Khadijah.[114] The second was from a Syrian monk called Bahirah, who confirmed Muhammad as the expected eschatological Prophet,[115] through recognition of the prophetic seal between his shoulders.[116] These oral accounts depict the cultural reminiscent of Muhammad's context, in which special men could predictably link the future by confirming the present. In addition to Christian witness, the Qur'an also references the authority of the Christian scriptures on the same matter. Qur'an 61:6 asserts that Jesus predicted another messenger who would succeed him with the name Ahmad, understood as Muhammad. Most Islamic scholars interpret such Quranic reference to the Bible as not only a proof of confirmation on the newer religion but also a claim of supremacy of Islam.

---

111. Orman, *Muslim View*, 10.

112. Reynolds, *Emergence of Islam*, 122.

113. Guillaume, *Life of Muhammad*, 107.

114. Orman, *Muslim View*, 1.

115. Orman, *Muslim View*, 79–81.

116. Orman, *Muslim View*, 80.

In acknowledgment of this Christian authority, the Qur'an confirms the divine origins of pre-Qur'anic scriptures. It states: "He [God] sent down the book to you [Muhammad] with the truth, confirming [the scriptures] that were before it, and He sent down the Torah and the Gospel aforetime, a guidance for humankind . . ." (3:3–4). A closer examination of this passage reveals that the claim simultaneously assures Qur'anic authenticity and supremacy. Its supremacy lies in the Islamic claim that it came later, not to contradict the previous scriptures, but rather to confirm and correct the Torah and the Bible and every other sacred text that God revealed before it.[117] The two major authoritative sources (Christians and the Bible) for the authentication of Muhammad's message and prophetic ministry might have paved the way for the enjoyed amity between both religions at the dawn of Islam.

Islamic tradition also records cordiality by Muhammad himself. The Prophet is said to have allowed a delegation of a Christian community from the valley of Najran in South Arabia to stay with him at the time of noon prayers and pray in his mosque.[118] Muhammad's respect for his Christian guests exceeded the loud protestations of his companions.[119]

Much of the perceived appreciative attitude toward Christianity in earliest Islam could also be considered by virtue of the fittingness of the latter within the Qur'anic four basic requirements of a true religion. The four principles include: ownership of a revealed scripture (or sacred law), being monotheistic, profession of faith in God and the Last Day, and the fostering of righteous living.[120] Based on these four principles, Islam demonstrates certain openness to pluralism and diversity[121] within monotheistic religions, whereby any true religion can be both particularistic and universal.[122]

Grounds for religious plurality have often been traced in the Qur'an as divinely instituted. 49:13 speaks about diversity in an even clearer tone: "O mankind! We created you from a single (pair) of a male and a female, and made you into nations and tribes, that ye may know each other not

117. Rahman, *Major Themes*, 162–70.

118. Shehu, *Nostra Aetate*, 181.

119. Ayoub, *Qur'an and Its Interpreters*, 2:188–91. The Qur'an makes no direct reference to such a delegation, but exegetical tradition has generally linked 3:61 to the Christians of Najran.

120. Orman, *Muslim View*, 2.

121. Orman, *Muslim View*, 3.

122. Orman, *Muslim View*, 2.

that ye may despise (each other)." This sura does not only infer diversity as a divine intent, but also disapproves of triumphalism, since despising the other is forbidden, and Allah is the common goal. Furthermore, the four Qur'anic principles (mentioned above) also support the oneness of God, in whom the truth of the faith of Muslims, Jews, Christians, and Sabaeans (see 2:62; 5:69) rest.

However, the few inconsistencies present in Qur'anic verses with regard to Christians are quite revealing. As previously noted, the Qur'an that recognizes unity with Christians regarding the oneness of God also rejects the latter's Trinitarian and christological doctrines. In a related sense, its approval of Christians as one's safest neighbors contrasts with its command for war against People of the Book, who reject faith in God and the Last Day, until they remit the *jizyah*, or poll tax (Qur'an 9:29). Sura 5, in particular, speaks in overtly exclusivist language: "Oh ye who believe! Take not the Jews and the Christians for your friends and pro-tectors!" (5:51). Sura 5 has sparked various reactions among Islamicists scholars, giving rise to different interpretations ranging from exclusivism to pluralist interpretations.[123]

Despite the ambivalence of the Qur'an toward Christians,[124] it still invites People of the Book to a friendly dialogue (3:64). The Qur'an un-equivocally attests to the unity of faith professed by both Christians and Muslims. It asserts, "we accept faith in that which was sent down to us and that which was sent down to you. Our God and your God is One, and to Him we are Submitters" (29:46). The unity of faith expressed in this Qur'anic language emphasizes more the concrete responsive submission to God than it does doctrinal theories. From the Islamic perspective, it could be adduced that it is not religion per se, but rather true conformity to God's will, that saves. Hence, it concludes that:

> It is not in accordance with your [Muslims] wishes, nor the wishes of the people of the Book; rather, whoever does evil, s/he will be recompensed for it, nor will s/he find any friend or helper against God. And, anyone who performs righteous deeds—male or female- and is a person of faith, those will enter the garden [of paradise] and they will not be wronged in the least.[125]

---

123. Sirry, "Compete," 424.

124. Orman, *Muslim View*, 314.

125. Qur'an 4:123–24.

One way of appreciating the language of the Qur'an is by recognizing that the Qur'an doubles as "a book of moral and pious precepts and also as the primary source of the sacred law of God, toward the establishment of the (Umma) Islamic state."[126] Similar to the Bible, the Qur'an speaks a language that attracts careful interpretations. As in Christianity, the universal claim in Islam can be explained either exclusively or inclusively. Islamic pluralists like Farid Esack, Mahmoud Ayoub, Mahmut Aydin Abdulaziz, Sachedina,[127] and Ashar Ali Engineer manifest significant openness toward other religions, but the Muslim majority disagrees with their scholarly exegesis of Qur'anic injunctions in regard to pluralism. Most anti-Islamic pluralists emphasize their standpoint through the abrogation argument, by which the latest religion (Islam) supplants the former.

Medieval scholars like Muhammad Husein al-Dahabi, al-Qurtubī, and Ibn Kathir[128] had thoughts deeply influenced by abrogation theory. Abrogation theory implies the finality[129] of Mohammad's prophetic mission. Being the Seal of the Prophets, according to Perry Schmit-Leukel, means that Muhammad is the corrector and confirmation of previous authentic revelations, and more so that he was the last of the prophets.[130] Contrasting conclusions such as abrogation of previous prophetic messages and the openness to revelations in other Abrahamic faith communities reflect the side of the interpreter. Sirry, a contemporary Islamic scholar, confirms that Muqatil ibn Sulaymān, though an earliest exegete, provided a more systemic account of how pluralism could be understood among the Abrahamic religions.[131] Muqatil explains:

> The sharī'a of the people of the Torah on [the punishment for] unlawful killing is retribution (qisas) with no blood money (diya), and stoning for a married man and woman who commit adultery. The sharī'a of the people of the Gospel on [the punishment for] unlawful killing is forgiveness, no qisas for them nor blood money, and their sharī'a on adultery is whipping (jald) without stoning. The sharī'a of the people of Muhammad, peace be upon him, on [the punishment for] unlawful

126. Orman, *Muslim View*, 314.

127. Esack, *Qur'an, Liberation*, 173–75.

128. al-Dahabi, "Israelitic Narratives," 659.

129. Shehu, *Nostra Aetate*, 57.

130. See Perry Schmit-Leukel, "Pluralistic Approaches in Some Major Non-Christian Religions," in Harris et al., *Twenty-First Century Theologies of Religions*, 165.

131. Sirry, "Compete," 426.

killing is *qisas*, blood money, and forgiveness, and their sharī'a
on adultery is whipping for unmarried and stoning for mar-
ried [men and women].[132]

Muqatil argues how the same God established different sharia for
different people. Such divine pluralistic plan, in his argument, prohibits
one particular people from judging others with their own sharia. Modern scholarship seems not to follow the pluralism paradigm defined by
Muqatil. While some past and present commentators like M. Plessner,
and Muhammad b. 'Abd al-Rahmān al-Maghrāwī[133] vehemently condemned his analysis, a few others like Imam al-Shāfi'ī extoled his scholarly input as a landmark for any serious Quranic studies.[134]

A more recent pluralistic clarification by Schmidt-Leukel contains
a distinction between "islam" (with lower case 'i') as a religious attitude
meaning submission to God, and "Islam" as designating the "socio-cultural phenomenon of the religion Islam."[135] Muslim pluralists, he stresses,
counter the traditionalist thinking on some referenced suras (3:19, 85)
in which Islam/islam are mentioned as a condition for salvation. They
argue that, rather than the Islamic institution per se, the verses refer to
personal submissive attitude to Allah, open to all humanity. They further
identify divine promise in the traditionalists' legal directives as the correct interpretation of 2:62, "those who believe and those who follow the
Jewish and the Christian and the Sabeans—any who believe in Allah and
the Last Day, and work righteousness, shall have their reward with the
Lord: on them shall be no fear, nor shall they grieve." 2:62, in the Muslim
pluralists' conclusion, cannot be read as abrogation verse because of the
irrevocability of divine promises, and the repetition of the same verse
toward the last suras of the Medina period.[136]

Still, against the Islamic traditional exclusivist claim, Farid Esack
interprets Muhammad's mission as a serious reminder to Jews and Christians of that ancient Abrahamic faith, and the submissiveness it requires,
which can either be accomplished in the various religious communities

132. See Muqātil ibn Sulaymān (1979), 482; cited in Sirry, "Compete," 426.

133. See Plessner, "Mukatil b. Sulaiman."

134. Sirry, "Compete," 427.

135. See Perry Schmit-Leukel, "Pluralistic Approaches in Some Major Non-Christian Religions," in Harris et al., *Twenty-First Century Theologies of Religions*, 165.

136. See Perry Schmit-Leukel, "Pluralistic Approaches in Some Major Non-Christian Religions," in Harris et al., *Twenty-First Century Theologies of Religions*, 166.

or within Islam.[137] Invariably, both traditionalists' view and pluralists' understanding undergird their arguments from the words of the Qur'an, proving its ambivalent character.

The prejudice of Western Christianity started with the emergence of Islam. Christianity typically considered the Arabian Peninsula prior to Islamic conquest of seventh century as a *haeresium ferax* (breeding region of heresies).[138] It was the tremendous rise of Islam, according to Reuven Firestone, that orchestrated unimaginable threat for several millennia. For Firestone, successes in both religious and sociopolitical spheres such as these: "From the conquest of Spain in the early eight century to the siege of Vienna by Ottoman Turks in 1683, Islam represented a threat to the very physical existence of Christendom,"[139] blacklisted Islam. Such earliest negative stereotyping of Islam "as cruel evil, and uncivilized"[140] started from the heydays of Islam, but has endured to date.

History shows in later Muslim-Christian encounters that their common triumphalist and proselytizing tendencies stimulated greater mutual antagonisms and hate. According to John Esposito, historical encounters between Muslims and Christians have "often found the two communities in competition, and locked at times in deadly combat, for power, land, and souls."[141] Whereas Muslims have vigorously challenged basic Christian doctrines and have generally condemned Christians as polytheists, the latter have voraciously labeled Islam as a movement of the biblically foretold Antichrist, and Muslims as barbaric people without any moral or spiritual values.[142] Such distorted perceptions engendered the mutual inflictions of memorial wounds.

137. Esack, *Qur'an, Liberation,* 172–72.

138. Denny, *Introduction to Islam,* 59.

139. Firestone, *Jihad,* 13.

140. Firestone, *Jihad,* 13.

141. Esposito, *Islamic Threat,* 46.

142. Orman, *Muslim View,* 315.

2

Mismanaged Problem

Mutual Blame

THIS RESEARCH PERFECTLY AGREES with Ayoub that the major Muslim-Christian problem lies in the inability to accept each other's faith on their own terms.[1] Alternatively, each partner needs to clean the stain of suspicion and biases off her lens, or better still, learn to see the other through their own lens. Mutual distorted perceptions from the past to the present have caused great harm to both sides. The largest human and material losses in the history of religious conflicts owe a lot to the ideology of killing and looting in the name of God.

The most remarkable religious mayhem recorded in history happened "in the name of God," be it Islamic jihad or Christian crusade. Even though debates are unsettled as to what justifies such militancy within these peace-inclined religions, this research considers it relevant to critically explore in the next section these two major displays of violence, in order to highlight steps to be avoided so as to assure mutual respect and appreciation of the religious other. Muslim jihad, which, even though ongoing, is as old as Islam, will be the first to be explored.

The concept of holy war is not uncommon among world civilizations, particularly within the popular monotheistic religions that witnessed the emergence of Islam. There can be no doubt concerning some religious influences from Christianity and Judaism on the nascent Islam,[2] however,

---

1. Orman, *Muslim View*, 318.

2. Firestone, *Jihad*, 19.

41

in terms of religious war, it is strongly contested that the existing parallels are basically phenomenological, but not biblical influences.[3]

Jihad in General

Jihad means more than a religious battle. The practice of jihad among Muslims is highly undisputed. There abounds classical and modern litera- ture in support of its practices. However, its centrality in Islamic practices has attracted several complex developmental interpretations throughout Islamic history. David Cook, an Islamicist, confirms an evolution of meaning of jihad: "From the initially straightforward conquest of Mecca by the prophet Muhammad, to the multifaceted Islamic conquests of the following century, to the defensive jihads against the Crusaders and the Mongols, to the revivalists and defensive jihads of the nineteenth century, there are considerable twists."[4] According to Cook, great concern con- fronts scholars as they struggle to ascertain if the word "jihad has lost all coherence" due to various usages within the fourteen centuries of Islamic existence. For example, most Muslims are perturbed in explaining how the globalist radical jihads replicate or relate to the classical concept of the term. Until these polarized notions of jihad are resolved, the majority of non-Muslims still perceive radical Islam as legitimate Islamic practice, thereby awaiting its declaration to be apostasy. When viewed through the lens of non-Muslims, the only perceived difference is that radical Islamists disregard a legitimate Islamic authority such as a caliph or an imam for the declaration of jihad.[5] Fortunately, jihad implies deeper understanding in unpacking its complexities.

One direction of understanding jihad is reading through its de- velopmental analyses in three historic periods as charted by Firestone: 1) jihad in the nascent Islam, 2) jihad in the Qur'an and its foundation, and 3) jihad in oral tradition. In summary, jihad for the earliest Muslims was perceived through its connotation as miraculous events[6] (due to the numerous conquests achieved by fewer hands) that confirmed the divine

---

3. Firestone, *Jihad*, 19.

4. Cook, *Understanding Jihad*, 163.

5. See ur-Rehmaan, *Jihaad: Fardh ayn or fardh kifaayah*, which is a summary of Nasir al-Din al-Albani's discussions with radical Muslims, Fatawa al-Shaykh al-Albani, 294–310.

6. Cook, *Understanding Jihad*, 30.

legitimacy of Islam. Muslim scholars feel nostalgic drawing profusely from this cradle period of their faith, which has sustained "the crucial importance of jihad in Islamic history."[7] Cook seems to reject any strict differentiation between "greater" and "lesser" jihad. He argues: "The spiritual, internal jihad is the derivative form, and not the contrary."[8] He further substantiates his point by alluding to the absence of "greater jihad" in the earliest hadith books, compared to the abundance of literature for the "lesser jihad." Besides few examples on the praxis of "Greater jihad," which includes Ayatullah al-Khumayni's contemporary book, and Eric Geoffroy's *Jihad et Contemplation*,[9] Cook concludes that the apocalyptic fervor that in particular targeted the conquest of the Byzantines (besieged in 676–80 and 715–17), and other Roman Empire provinces played a major role for walking along Allah's path. This dream lives on in the apocalyptic literature, but also impacted the Islamic spread.

Cook captures vividly the complementarity that existed between Islamic messianic and missionizing goals: "Although Islam was not spread by the sword, as is commonly imagined, conquest and jihad created the preconditions for conversion, and conversion or proclamation was one of the goals of the jihad."[10]

Like some other major themes, jihad in the Qur'an and its foundation abound in ambivalent language. As previously discussed, the Qur'anic tone consistently shifts back and forth from non-violent approaches, through to strict conditional terms, to strong war advocacies. Looking at jihad in oral tradition, Cook believes that the earliest conquest stories of Mohammad and his followers, which were aggressive and expansive, extremely shaped the abundance of militant understandings in the hadith literature today. Subsequently, this hadith collection was codified and legalized. It is not the point that the importance of Islamic jihad connotes aggressiveness. Rather, the point is that most Muslims scholars feel nostalgic concerning these classic narratives.

Another major question that has engaged Islamic minds is whether jihad is offensive or defensive. To the popular Western thinking that Islam is a religion of the sword, many Muslim scholars reacted variously as apologists, revivalists, or some with polemics. The works of apologists

7. Cook, *Understanding Jihad*, 30.

8. Cook, *Understanding Jihad*, 46.

9. Though a thoughtful study on greater jihad, but it was written in European language for non-Muslims.

10. Cook, *Understanding Jihad*, 25.

range from "the writings of Maulawi Cheragh 'Ali in India and Rashid Rida in Egypt to Ayatullah Ahmad Jannati's *Defence and Jihad in the Qur'an* and S. K. Malik's *The Qur'anic Concept of War*."[11] Islamic revivalist works, such as John Laffin's alarmist *Holy War: Islam Fights* and the Hindu revivalist Suhas Majumdar's *Jihad: The Islamic Doctrine of Permanent War*, embraced a more radical approach than the apologists by legitimizing jihad as a divine command.[12] Whereas the apologists presented jihad as defensive, the revivalists preferred its offensive dimension, or both at least, grounding their arguments on divine approval. With their limited notions, Firestone criticizes these approaches, whether as apologists, revivalists, or polemics, for emphasizing one aspect of jihad at the expense of the complex whole.[13]

As a way forward, Firestone agrees that the process of organizational redaction contributed to the disorderliness of some Qur'anic verses, especially on jihad. He therefore suggests four categories for Qur'anic verses on fighting: "1) Verses expressing non-militant means of propagating or defending the faith; 2) Verses expressing restrictions on fighting; 3) Verses expressing conflict between God's command and the reaction of Mohammad's followers; 4) Verses strongly advocating war for God's religion."[14]

Non-violent verses will include four Meccan verses referring to idolaters before the *hijra* (Qur'an 6:106; 15:94; 16:125; 50:39) and four Medina verses referring to People of the Book (2:109; 5:13; 29:46; 42:15). The restrictive verses refer to restrictions for the sacred month (2:194), on defense (22:39–40), and on divine command (2:216). Though "not exhaustive," Firestone's categorization firmly supports our thesis that jihad is more than aggressive fighting in Islam.

Jihad, an Arabic verbal noun, derives from the (Arabic) root *j.h.d* (*jahada*), which classically refers to "exerting one's utmost power, efforts, endeavors, or ability in contending with an object of disapprobation."[15] Different kinds of jihad include: "Jihad of the heart" (aimed at internal struggle against vices), "Jihad of the tongue" (verbal witnessing to truth and justice), and "Jihad of the sword" (actively defending Islam and

---

11. Firestone, *Jihad*, 4.

12. Firestone, *Jihad*, 4.

13. Firestone, *Jihad*, 4.

14. Firestone, *Jihad*, 69.

15. Lane, *Arabic-English Lexicon*, 473.

propagating the faith).[16] Similar to Firestone's categorization, it can be deduced from this classification that there are other notions of jihad that are achieved without warfare.

The Prophet Mohammad, as attributed in his Sunna (a body of Islamic customs and practices derived from Muhammad's words and deeds), approves all three kinds of jihad as true marks of a believer.[17] In addition, the saying "The best jihad is [speaking] a word of justice to a tyrannical ruler"[18] is also credited to him. However, among Westerners, "jihad of the sword" was popularized by Rudolf Peters[19] as a word that "has a basic connotation of endeavor towards a praiseworthy aim."[20] Such narrow understanding of jihad has gained much acceptance in the Western world, especially after the 9/11 tragedies in the US.[21] Despite its popularity, Peters's idea of jihad barely uncovers its full meaning.

Jihad in its full Arabic expression reads, "*jihad fi sabil Allah*" (jihad in the path of God).[22] Broadly speaking, jihad expresses firm resistance to any form of obstacle in doing Allah's will or walking along Allah's path. In other words, jihad can be launched against both spiritual and human inhibitors or obstacles. Muslim thinkers, especially Sufi mystics, distinguish between interior struggles against the self, known as the "greater jihad" (*al-jihad al-akbar*), and "lesser jihad" (*al-jihad al-asghar*), denoting warring in the path of God.[23]

Even though the legitimate call for jihad by Muslim religious authority as contained in Islamic law literature reflects the legality of just war theory in Christianity, it will amount to gross injustice to demean jihad as mere holy war. Firestone further affirms that "even 'jihad of the sword' is not quite equivalent to the common Western understanding of holy war."[24] To throw more light on the misconstrued term jihad, Firestone recalls the distinction between two Qur'anic terms: *harb* (war), referring to all warring not legitimized by Muslim authority, and *quital* (fighting),

---

16. Firestone, *Jihad*, 17.

17. Firestone, *Jihad*, 17.

18. Firestone, *Jihad*, 17.

19. Rudolph Peters is a Dutch-born renowned Islamic scholar of law.

20. Peters, *Jihad in Classical*, 1.

21. Nsofor, "Muslim-Christian Relations," 79.

22. Firestone, *Jihad*, 17.

23. Watt, "Islamic Conceptions," 155.

24. Firestone, *Jihad*, 18.

which is synonymous with jihad because of its primary purpose of warring in the path of God.[25]

Nevertheless, in the latter half of the eighth century, when the need for conquests drastically dropped, other kinds of jihads took the center stage. The post-conquest period (later eighth century) ushered in a shift of emphasis on Islamic jihad through martyrdom.

The concept of martyr (*shahid*) in Islam is quite different from its Judeo-Christian teaching. According to Cook, martyrdom in Islam has a much more active sense. The prospective martyr is called to seek out situations in which martyrdom can be achieved.[26] Besides dying in battle, the Islamic *Kitab al-jihad* tradition includes seven other forms, like death by stomach complaint, by drowning, of a plague, of pleurisy, in a structural collapse, in a fire, or at childbirth (woman).[27] Nonetheless, dying in battle is motivated through the hopeful rewards of gaining the earthly forbidden, the women of paradise, fame, and honor (since martyrdom is ranked the highest of the one hundred ranks in paradise). This *primus inter pares* status empowers the martyr to play the role of an intercessor on behalf of his relative and friends (seventy or more in number) on the Judgment Day.[28] Above all, attention will be given to the lesser jihad because of its misconceived notions and its impact on Christian-Muslim relations.

Lesser Jihad

Islam as a way of life permeates the cultural, the sociopolitical, and the religious aspects from its earliest stage through its historical developments. Its establishment integrally involved these three aspects of life; hence, conflicts and tensions with established authorities were inevitable. For example, in Mecca, Muhammad and his followers met great opposition and persecution from his idolatrous Quraysh people, which led to his flight to safety (*hijra*) in July 622[29] to Yathrib (later renamed Medina). The Meccan rejection and death attempt on Muhammad by his fellow Qurayshites created an unfriendly relationship between him and his people, until their eventual subjugation.

25. Firestone, *Jihad*, 18.

26. Cook, *Understanding Jihad*, 26.

27. See Ibn al-Mubarak, *Jihad*, 63–68.

28. Cook, *Understanding Jihad*, 27–29.

29. *Hijra* marks the start of the Islamic calendar.

Muhammad's period of sojourn in Medina had its own peculiar story. While he was in exile in Medina, conquering Mecca never ceased being a central goal for Muhammad and his companions. Consequently, it took several strategies to gain possession of Mecca, which is the traditional geographic center of Islam. Raids and ambush, common forms of conquest in the Bedouin culture, were employed for the destabilization of the Meccans' economy and military might, even before a revelation on jihad was given.

In the second *Anno Hijra*, AH 2 (AD 624), an arrow shot by Abdul ibn Jahsh (Muhammad's commander), killed Amr ibn al-Hadrami, a Qurayshite, in the month of *Rajab*, and his caravan was looted. C. F. Nsofor explains the importance of this event in the history of Islam based on two counts. First, the death of Hadrami is alleged as the first Islamic shedding of blood. Second, the month it occurred in was regarded as holy, and thus provoked condemnation from both Jews and Qurayshites, in accord with the Arabian custom.[30] As popularly held among Muslims, Muhammad almost regretted this initial raid, and refused accepting his portion of the loot, before Allah spoke to him. In the midst of the confusion, Allah sent his words (Qur'an 2:216–18) approving this first lesser jihad and later reinforced it with subsequent encouragements:

> Fighting is prescribed for you, though it is hateful to you. You may happen to hate a thing though it is good for you, and you may happen to love a thing though it is bad for you. God knows and you do not know. They ask about the sacred month—(about) fighting during it. Say: 'fighting during it is serious (matter); but keeping (people) from the way of God—and disbelief in Him—and the sacred Mosque, and expelling its people from it, (are even) more serious in the sight of God'. Persecution is more serious than killing. They will not stop fighting you until they turn you back from your religion, if they can. Whoever of you turns away from his religion and dies while he is a disbeliever, those—their deeds have come to nothing in this world and the Hereafter. Those are the compassions of the Fire. Surely those who believe, and those who have emigrated and struggled in the way of God, those—they hope for the mercy of God. God is forgiving, compassionate.[31]

30. Nsofor, *Muslim-Christian Relations*, 83.
31. Quotation taken from Droge, *Qur'an*.

Nsofor argues against any perception of a lesser jihad as mere war of self-defense, based on the noted approval by Allah and the Islamic commitment to submission to his will.[32] In contrast to Nsofor's evaluation, Reynolds affirms: "Muslim apologists, in particular, the writings of Muhammad Abdel Haleem and the record of Ibn Ishaq, agree that Muhammad fought in self-defense."[33] And as a proof of Allah's support, Muhammad's victories should be attributed to Allah's intervention (miracles), rather than to his own chivalry and valor.[34]

From a hermeneutic perspective, there is a huge gulf of difference between the Christian and Muslim understanding of lesser jihad. For Muslims, to engage in this form of jihad means an extension of submission to Allah, which is the goal of every serious Muslim. In lesser jihad, what Christians emphasize as killings Muslims see as a legitimate Islamic approach to confronting obstacles of faith. Muhammad H. Haykal's explanation affirms the noticed implication of divine approval on jihad. He notes:

> Jihad or war for the sake of God is clearly defined in the verses, which we have mentioned and which were revealed in connection with the expedition of Abdull ibn Jahsh. Its definite meaning is to fight those who sway the Muslims away from his religion and prevent him from walking in the path of God. This fight is waged solely for the freedom to call men unto God and unto his religion. To use a modern expression consonant with the usage of the present age, we may say that war in Islam is permitted . . . nay, it is rather a duty . . . when undertaken in defense of freedom of thought and opinion.[35]

Haykal explains lesser jihad in connection with the greater jihad. He views lesser jihad from a theological perspective in defense of faith.

In regard to Haykal's analysis, one wonders to what extent divine mandates could be rationalized. Obeying divine orders borders on faith understanding and expression. Faith as a universal religious attitude cuts across religions. Faith expresses an indeterminate conscious relationship with the divine.

Wilfred Cantwell Smith (1964–1973), a Canadian-born comparative religionist, distinguished between faith and belief. His conviction about the convergence of world religions undergirds his affirmation on

32. Nsofor, "Muslim-Christian Relations," 88.

33. Reynolds, *Emergence of Islam*, 32.

34. Reynolds, *Emergence of Islam*, 32.

35. Haykal, *Life of Muhammad*, 211.

the legitimacy and necessity of faith in contrast to the temporality and relativity of belief. He calls for a distinction between the faith of a particular people and the pattern through which it is expressed.[36] The modern view on belief, according to Smith, differs from knowledge and therefore suggests uncertainty and open neutrality as to what is believed.[37] In other words, universalistic faith is distinguished from the relativity in belief systems that differ from one religious community to another.[38] Such an important distinction between faith and belief systems challenges researchers to further evaluate what properly constitutes obstacles to faith and what defines the scope of one's religious freedom in relation to the dignity of the religious other. In accord, Smith envisions a theology that can articulate the faith of world religions, taking into account the pluralistic world character, without diluting either Christian faith or Muslim faith or Hindu faith.[39]

Nonetheless, the words of Bishop Léon-Etienne Duval of Constantine, Algeria warn Muslims and Christians against blind obedience: "The virtue of obedience needed to be rooted in faith and required the use of intelligence and discernment. Committing evil by blind obedience would be inexcusable."[40] Blind obedience has no place among liberal Islamic thinkers, who define the relationship between rights to freedom and religious duties differently. According to them, "revealed norms can be put into practice only by way of personal, free commitment, and not by way of external compulsion. This is so because carrying out revealed norms in their view should be a moral act and so necessarily also a free act."[41]

Concerning human free will, should the religious other be labeled an obstacle to faith, and by what standard, and by whose faith? Attempts to address these questions show, on the one hand, that there is room for hermeneutic understanding of Qur'anic literalness in Islam, especially when issues bordering on the beliefs of the other are at stake. On the other hand, both Christianity and Islam need some internal evaluations of faith commitment as moderated by openness to the faith values of the other.

---

36. Wainwright, "Wilfred Cantwell Smith," 353.

37. Smith, *Faith and Belief,* 35.

38. Panikkar, *Intra-Religious Dialogue,* 41–59.

39. Smith, *Toward a World Theology,* 125.

40. Maskulak, "Mission and Dialogue," 433.

41. Wielandt, "Menschenwürde und Freiheit," 199.

In retrospective accord, Muhammad's earliest position against the Byzantine Christians would have more sociopolitical reasons than religious. The conversion of Emperor Constantine in the fourth century contributed to the transformation of the church from the persecuted minority to a distinguished Christendom deeply tied to the sociopolitical power of the empire. Such intimacy with the empire strengthened some internal disaccord. Confirming the Christian disunity, Kate Zebiri wrote: "The Muslim conquerors encountered a divided Christendom, and some Christians, particularly the Copts in Egypt, had reason to prefer their new masters to their Byzantine oppressors."[42] This unholy marriage of the religious and the state empires, otherwise called caesaropapism, and the complexity of Muhammad's Islam (in which the religious, the cultural, and the political finely interplay) makes it difficult to arrive at a clear picture of what truly defined Muslim-Christian relation at that earliest stage.

Christian Troll draws attention to the ambivalent character of the Qur'an toward violent attacks on Christians. He notes that besides its commendation for People of the Book, Christians in particular, Qur'an 9:29 states that "the Muslims are called upon to fight not only against the pagans but also against the 'people of the Book,' until they accept the subordinate but protected position as *dhimmis* appropriate to them within the framework of Islamic rule."[43] Religiously induced violent attacks have received sharp criticisms among scholars, especially since such mayhem widens the gulf between Muslims and Christians. Ayoub, with his pluralistic predispositions, vehemently condemns brutality in defense of God:

> The religious idolatry in the name of God and the faith has been the cause of untold suffering, misery and bloodshed. Whether it is the martyrs' movement in Spain, the Inquisition, or the Crusades, the result has been the same: lives were lost and noble principles violated to no purpose. The Crusades ended leaving scars that have yet to be healed. The Muslims were expelled from Spain and Islam was washed away with blood . . . Muslims have equally been guilty of this religious idolatry in the name of God and Islam. They too contributed to the collapse of the Hispano-Arabic experiment. Had they sought to realize the moral imperatives of the Qur'an instead of reducing them to lifeless and often

42. Zebiri, *Muslims and Christians*, 23.

43. Troll, *Dialogue and Difference*, 150.

bigoted laws, the history of Muslim-Christian relations would have been more humane, and no doubt, more promising.[44]

To further ridicule religious killings, Ayoub reminds us that "what Muslims won through conquest and war was lost. But what was achieved through "wisdom and fair exhortation" (via pious traders and Sufis), continues to grow and to prosper."[45] Whether the brutal Crusades and the terrifying stakes of the Inquisition or the ferocious Islamic jihads, the blame should be shared, because both religious traditions essentially claim being the supreme custodians of peace and love. While still unresolved as to which of the religious traditions should take the bigger blame for the several violent Muslim-Christian historical encounters, the mid-twelfth-century Aleppan chronicler al-'Azimi recorded: "The people of the Syrian ports prevented Frankish and Byzantine pilgrims from crossing to Jerusalem. Those of them who survived spread the news about that to their country. So they prepared themselves for military invasion."[46] Al-'Azimi might account for the immediate cause of the Muslim-Christian "holy wars," but there were some remote causes.

From a Christian perspective, Islam was quick in assuming the status of a proximate other (a rival), mainly through conquests. In history, both religions manifested "mutual exclusive claims to universality and finality."[47] Even their common monotheistic ancestry in Abraham is fraught with discord and envy. Islam threads safely in acknowledging the prophetic traditions in Christianity as recorded in the Qur'an, but Christianity cannot accept any element of continuity towards Islam without "undermining the finality and the ultimacy of the revelation in Christ."[48] Islam, for many Christians, is therefore that close rival that challenges centuries-old supremacy held by Christianity. William Muir[49] articulates the pre-twentieth-century Christian description of Islam as "the only disguised and formidable antagonist of Christianity."[50] Such

---

44. Orman, *Muslim View*, 30.

45. Orman, *Muslim View*, 30.

46. al-Azimi, "La Chronique Abregee," 369.

47. Zebiri, *Muslims and Christians*, 5.

48. Zebiri, *Muslims and Christians*, 5.

49. He was a nineteenth-century colonial administrator and supporter of missions.

50. See William Muir, cited in Hourani, *Islam in European Thought*, 19.

tensed rivalry resulted into strained relations or antagonized isolation[51] on the one hand, and crises and wars on the other.

The first major war between Islam and Christian forces happened at the Battle of Tours in AD 732. Although Islam suffered internal civil strife between the Shi'ite and the Sunni factions shortly after the death of Mohammad, still they united and organized a formidable force that conquered Africa and Southern Europe before 732.[52]

Within the first century of Islam, there were not only tremendous conquests recorded in its favor, but also monumental assaults for its acclaimed supremacy over Judaism and Christianity. As the Dome of the Rock in Jerusalem was intentionally erected on the Jewish Temple Mount in 691 for the purposes of dominance,[53] so did the Great Mosque of Damascus (AD 715), which replaced the Cathedral of St. John, account for the Islamic superiority over an alleged corrupt Christianity.[54]

The Dome of the Rock and the Great Mosque are for the Muslims the third and fourth holiest places in Islam, after Mecca and Medina. The Dome of the Rock symbolizes the Abrahamic heritage of Muslims in the city of Jerusalem. Jerusalem, captured by the Muslims in 638 from the Greek Christians of Byzantium, was a precious target, not only because Muslims perceive it as part of Islam's Abrahamic heritage, but also as the location of Muhammad's Night Journey (believed as the eschatological locus).[55] However, Bukhari's hadith version of the Night Journey omits Jerusalem and locates it in Mecca.[56] But because these two Islamic sacred spaces are monumental encroachments on the religious other, the provocation was fiercely confronted in the Christendom world.

The account below describes the defeat of Abd-er Rahman, leader of the Spanish Islamic army, by Charles Martel (688–741), leader of the Spanish Christian military, in October 732 outside of Tours. According to the chronicler, the basilica of St. Martin of Tours was a monumental target of the Muslims. This "most accurate account of the battle"[57] of Tours states:

51. Zebiri, *Christians and Muslims*, 7.

52. Caner and Caner, *Christian Jihad*, 69.

53. Caner and Caner, *Christian Jihad*, 70.

54. Braswell, *Islam*, 26.

55. Asbridge, *Crusades*, 19.

56. al-Bukhari, *Sahih al-Bukhari*, 345.

57. Asbridge, *Crusades*, 19.

[Abd-er Rahman] destroyed palaces, burned churches, and imagined he could pillage the basilica of St. Martin of Tours. It is then that he found himself face to face with the lord of Austrasia, Charles, a mighty warrior from his youth, and trained in all the occasions of arms. For almost seven days the two armies watched one another, awaiting anxiously the moment for joining the struggle. Finally they made ready for combat. And in the shock of the battle the men of the North seemed like a sea that cannot be moved. Firmly they stood, one close to another, forming as it were a bulwark of ice; and with great blows of their swords they hewed down the Arabs. Drawn up in a band around their chief, the people of the Austrasians carried all before them. Their tireless hands drove their swords down to the breast [of the foe].[58]

After this initial victory by the Spanish Christians, Christendom in 1099 recorded another triumph in a fiercer battle in contention for the control of Jerusalem.

The Crusades

In response to the urgent call from Alexis, the eastern emperor, who was under assault by the Muslims, Pope Urban II launched the First Crusade in 1095 at the Council of Clermont with these words:

You, brothers and fellow bishops; you, fellow priests and sharers with us in Christ, make this same announcement through churches committed to you, and with your whole soul vigorously preach the journey to Jerusalem. When they have confessed the disgrace of their sins, do you, secure in Christ, grant them speedy pardon. Moreover, you who are to go shall have us praying for you; we shall have you fighting for God's people. It is our duty to pray, yours to fight the Amalakites. With Moses, we shall extend unwearied hands in prayer to Heaven, while you go forth and brandish the sword, like dauntless warriors, against Amalek.[59]

Enthused by the unanimous support from the clergy at Clermont, Urban II addressed the Christian military force and sanctified the war ahead: "Let this then be your war-cry in combats, because this word is

58. See Isidore of Beja's Chronicle, in Davis, *Readings in Ancient History*, 362–64.

59. Krey, *First Crusade*, 103. The language about the Amalakites is from the Hebrew Scriptures (1 Sam 15: 2–3), where God commanded Saul to destroy everything alive in Amalek because they waylaid the Israelites on their way home from Egypt.

given to you by God. When an armed attack is made upon the enemy, let this one cry be raised by all soldiers of God: It is the will of God! It is the will of God!"[60]

Pope Urban II has received serious criticism not as much for approving a war as for the motivations that undergirded the process of reclaiming the Holy Land from Muslims. His approach was accused of falling short of the distinction Augustine of Hippo proffered between aggressive and defensive war.[61] The three prerequisites of a just war formulated later by Augustine were: "1) proclamation by a 'legitimate authority,' such as a king or a bishop; 2) a 'just cause' defense against enemy attack or recovery of lost property; 3) and prosecution with 'right intention,' that is, with the least possible violence."[62] Unfortunately, the third was fundamentally violated. Even though the three prerequisites would together guarantee a just war, still "they fell far short of advocating the sanctification of war."[63] In support, a school of thought believe that a just war with rules of engagement would not have resulted into a sea of blood caused by a conquest mandate, "Christian Jihad."[64] Shehu characterizes the Crusades with "rivers of blood" in contradistinction to the jihads that respected the vulnerable lives of elderly people, women, and children.[65]

With the emblem of the cross on the battle armor, and an irrevocable pledge for conquest (retraction was threatened with banishment) from Pope Urban II, the Christian army was sufficiently empowered. Ergun Mehmet Caner and Emir Fethi Caner express the clear implication of such a militant strategy: "Without the emblem of the cross, there would be no salvation."[66] Invariably, the motivation for this earliest Crusade could parallel Islamic jihad, since in both instances killings were done in the name of God.

Urban II, the Vicar of Christ, and Mohammad, the Prophet of Allah, motivated their armies with unwavering belief in eternal rewards for victims of holy wars. For Urban II, "All who die by the way, whether by land or sea, or in battle against the pagans, shall have immediate remission

---

60. Munro, *Urban and the Crusaders*, 6–7.

61. Augustine, *Contra Faustum*, 442.

62. Asbridge, *Crusades*, 15.

63. Asbridge, *Crusades*, 15.

64. Caner and Caner, *Christian Jihad*, 91.

65. Shehu, *Nostra Aetate*, 58.

66. Caner and Caner, *Christian Jihad*, 92.

of sins. This I grant them through the power of God with which I am invested."[67] Similarly, the hadith of al-Bukhari instructs:

> The prophet (peace be upon him) said: The person who participates (in Holy battle) in Allah's cause and nothing compels him to do so except his belief in Allah and His Apostle, will be recompensed by Allah either with a reward, or booty (if he survives) or will be admitted to paradise (if he is killed in the battle as a martyr) . . . Our Prophet (peace be upon him) has informed us that our Lord says: Whoever among us is killed (i.e. martyred), will go to Paradise to lead such a luxurious life as he has never seen.[68]

Although the hadith does not speak the same language of remission of sins, which is offensive in Islam, still the promise of eternal rewards in the exhortations fired the zeal and determination for self-sacrifice and bloodshed. In essence, such Islamic standard also paralleled the violent agenda of eleventh-century Christendom.

Even though the victory of the first crusaders cannot be attributed to a foreknowledge of the internal feud between the *Abbasids* (Sunni faction) and *Fatimids* (Shi'ite faction) in the eleventh-century Mediterranean world, the rift, as argued, "prevented the Muslim rulers of Egypt and Iraq from offering any form of coordinated or concerted resistance to Christian invasion."[69] More so, "the timing of the First Crusade was remarkably propitious."[70] However, the noticed "unbridled carnage"[71] was a huge mutual loss, because apart from the First Crusade (1095–1099), the Muslims were victorious in the subsequent attempts for control over the Holy Land, which ended in 1291. It is confirmed that even though "the dream of Christian victory lived on, the Muslim world prevailed, securing lasting possession of Jerusalem and the Near East."[72]

Military activity might have sneaked into the papacy in the late eleventh century, but the intention predates the pontificate of Urban II. If Urban II shoulders the responsibility of causing the First Crusade in 1095, his predecessor, Pope Gregory VI, would be regarded as the first

67. Thatcher and McNeal, *Source Book*, 513–17.

68. al-Bukhari, *Hadith of al-Bukhari*.

69. Asbridge, *Crusades*, 21.

70. Berkley, *Formation of Islam*, 100.

71. Berkley, *Formation of Islam*, 100.

72. Asbridge, *Crusades*, 2.

real desirer of a crusade.[73] His great military desire in 1074 was aimed toward the eastern Mediterranean in defense of the Byzantine Church, although his failure in attracting significant recruitment should be noted.

Given the rivalry of supremacy claims between Muslims and Christians in terms of religious finality and the Last Day,[74] it is still remarkable how both soiled their hands in blood as *de iure divino* (by the will of God). Thomas Asbridge concurs by raising some puzzling questions: "How did two of the world's great religions come to advocate violence in the name of God, convince followers that fighting for their faith would open the gates to Heaven or Paradise? And why did endless thousands of Christians and Muslims answer the call to crusade and jihad, knowing full well that they might face intense suffering and even death?"[75] These questions are considered very important, since they expose these historic excesses, which this research seeks to prevent. Fundamentally, this research identifies the problem of killing in the name of God as a misconstrued dualism between love of God and love of neighbor. Therefore, its primal goal seeks to establish the love of God made manifest in the love of neighbor.

At the universal level, the violent, hateful attacks were unarguably mutual.[76] Even if the Christian Crusades were motivated by self-defense and control,[77] the bigger question is: How does the Bible view violence and retaliation? Moreover, if most Muslims defend lesser jihad as an act of obedience to Qur'anic injunction,[78] can Christians substantively make similar claims? Besides the Hebrew Bible, where God sanctioned genocide,[79] lack of such a mandate in the New Testament texts, from the Muslims' perception, strengthens grounds for their belief that Christians indeed drifted away from their revealed message and embraced violence.[80] However, as shown above, global violent attacks championed by both religious traditions inflicted wounds still to be completely healed. To what extent, therefore, would the mutual blame at the global scene reflect Muslim-Christian relations in the Nigerian context?

73. Asbridge, *Crusades*, 16.

74. Ammah, *Christian-Muslim Relations*, 142.

75. Caner and Caner, *Christian Jihad*, 3–4.

76. Shehu, *Nostra Aetate*, 57.

77. Shehu, *Nostra Aetate*, 59.

78. Shehu, *Nostra Aetate*, 58.

79. See 1 Samuel 15.

80. One of Nsofor's learned Islamic interviewees confirms this; see Nsofor, "Muslim-Christian Relations," 100–101.

3

Contextual Rivalry

The Nigerian Experience

THIS CHAPTER SEEKS TO address the following pertinent questions, and perhaps more: 1) Who or what receives supreme allegiance in Nigeria—country, tribe, or religion? 2) Who owns and controls Nigeria through conquest and occupation rhetoric as well as religious and political maneuvering? 3) How does resource control and political activism lead to boundary switching: Muslim versus Christian, North versus South, military versus civilian? 4) How manipulative is the population figure of Nigeria? 5) What leads to confrontations and violence? 6) What are the roles of the government (state and federal) in violence? And who defines violence and by what standard? The underlying aim of reviewing these questions is to demonstrate the huge impact of religion in the sociopolitical terrain of Nigeria.

The choice of Nigeria is based on a twofold relevance: 1) As the most populous nation in Africa, it plays host to a rare even split of Muslims and Christians. 2) The religious tolerance in its southwestern region (Yorubaland) can be instructive as a working template for a dialogue of life even outside the Nigerian context.

In contrast to the Muslim-Christian mutual violence on the global level, the Nigerian context shows uneven generation of crises. The predominately Northern Hausa-Fulani Muslims have mostly been labeled the aggressors by Christian voices.[1] In defense, the Muslim voices

---

1. Adogame, "Politicization of Religion," 130.

adjudge Christian activities as conversion oriented (especially through Western education) and therefore, provocative. In fact, the complexity of Muslim-Christian unhealthy coexistence centers on the "very high proselytizing propensity"[2] that typifies both religions. Their mutual proselytizing tendency deeply impacts not only their religious and cultural but also their sociopolitical relationships. From their first interactions in the late nineteenth century, to date, their relationship could best be described as neighbors insulated from each other. J. M. Gaudeul articulates the huge ignorance of each to the other. For a Muslim, "Islam is the religion of Africa, whereas Christianity is a 'foreign religion'. For his part, the Christian asserts that Christianity is the religion of progress, while Islam entails stagnation."[3] A concise historical background of the Northern Islamic hegemony and the Southern Christian strategies will hopefully expose the alluded intricacy that marks the context of study.

The nation-state of Nigeria experienced a reverse of Christianity's precedence over Islam in Arabia. From the Berbers and Arabs, Islam first arrived in the Kanem-Bornu kingdom (Kanuri people of modern northeastern Nigeria) about the early eleventh century[4] through commerce and mission.[5] Islam quickly took root in this kingdom and spread throughout the entire Northern region, including also some parts of the South. At that time, Islam had only the traditional religions to contend with, because Christianity first touched the soil of (southern) Nigeria much later, in the fifteenth century, at Warri and Benin kingdoms, and only penetrated into the Northern part in the late nineteenth century.

Unlike Christianity, whose first converts in the South were mainly the ordinary people, from its inception, the Northern Islam targeted political leaders and elites. Part of the reason for the failure of the Portuguese mission at Warri was its entanglement with palace royalties and their corrupt business practices with the foreigners. On the contrary, while it took a long time for the masses to become Muslims,[6] "Islam was at first adopted among the Hausa as a class religion, chiefly by the ruling group.[7] Such elites assimilated Islamic principles into the administration

2. Nwaiwu, "Inter-Religious Dialogue," 100.

3. Gaudeul, "Christianity, Islam, and Nation-Building," 5.

4. Iwuchukwu, *Muslim-Christian Dialogue*, 2.

5. Iwuchukwu, *Muslim-Christian Dialogue*, 1.

6. Ifemesia, "States of the Central Sudan," 94.

7. Ifemesia, "States of the Central Sudan," 94.

and juridical activities of their communities.[8] C. C. Ifemesia confirms: "The political, legal, judicial and other institutions of the country are on the Muslim pattern. Social life is to a great extent ruled by Muslim norms, and Islam provides the framework for intellectual development."[9] This enduring factor undergirds the sociopolitical and religious mix currently visible among the Nigerian Muslims.

Nigerian Muslims through the *umma* concept understand themselves as a religious community that has all it takes to be a nation-state. The brotherhood cohesion seems stronger with other Muslims outside Nigeria than with non-Muslim fellow citizens.[10] Islam is not just a religion, but indeed a way of life, a state. The convolution of such mentality occasionally conflicts with the recognition of Nigeria as a secular state. For the traditional Muslim and as taught by Islamic jurists, the world is divided into two states or houses: *Dar al-Islam* (the House of Islam), with a provision for *Ahl al-Dhimma* (people under conditioned Islamic protection), and *Dar al-Harb* (the House of War).[11] This two-world dualism provides the legitimate prism through which these Muslims perceive reality, including the sociopolitical dimension. Unlike Christianity, Islam is oriented toward the realization of *Dar al-Islam* even when a nation-state like Nigeria is equally shared by non-Muslims. In this regard, secularism is perceived as dangerous and threatening to the Islamic faith. Muslims therefore aim at instituting particular sociopolitical systems, which embody sharia law. A later section in this chapter provides details on sharia in Nigeria. Meanwhile, scholars have noticed certain peculiarities of Nigerian Islam, which underscores its complexity.

Nigerian Islam is too complex to be homogeneous. William F. S. Miles, the Northeastern University professor with research interest in West Africa, has identified the heterogeneous identity of Nigerian Islam. Miles argues that "Islam in northern Nigeria is itself multiple and multi-stranded: it comprises contrasting organizational and theological tendencies, and thus must pluralize the very paradigm of pluralism for the present-day northern Nigeria."[12] The jihad of Usman dan Fodio provides,

8. Iwuchukwu, *Muslim-Christian Dialogue*, 1.

9. Ifemesia, "States of the Central Sudan," 93.

10. Nwaiwu, *Inter-Religious Dialogue*, 101.

11. Kenny, "Sharia in Nigeria," 10. Also see Qur'an 3:102–4.

12. Miles, "Religious Pluralism," 109.

according to scholars, one of the most reliable prism for understanding Northern (Nigerian) Islam.

The jihad of Usman dan Fodio (1804–1808) established the Sokoto-Fulani caliphate (the largest political unit in the nineteenth century, West Africa).[13] Through the serial conquests and dethronement of the indigenous Hausa majority leaderships, dan Fodio also posed a serious threat to the Kanuri people of Kanem-Bornu kingdom before the intervention of the British colonists in 1903.[14] The Sokoto caliphate as noted by Murray Last was first a religious and cultural entity.[15] John N. Paden confirms the prior establishment of its religious integration before the achievement of its sociopolitical dimension.[16] However, after the jihadic conquests, the Fulani-Muslim leadership, with the aim of retaining control, adopted a policy of *taqiyya* toward the British, which, in the description of Miles, means "a strategic combination of outward submission to superior force with continued inner fealty to Islam."[17]

Dan Fodio's unrivaled victories throughout western Sudan[18] have been challenged as the exception to the rule of Islamic expansion in Africa,[19] due to its sanitization motive. However, Fodio's conquests have been contested as being more a religious reformation (because of the already existing Islam in the North) than jihad per se. A popular contemporary Christian convert from Islam, Lamin Sanneh, attests: "In most places . . . Muslims embraced local versions of pluralism and tolerance rather than committing themselves and others to inflexible compliance with religious code."[20]

To date, the legacy of dan Fodio elevated his Fulani minority ethnic group[21] to the religiopolitical rulers of the entire Hausa majority, including the rival Kanuri kingdom. The Kanem-Bornu kingdom consisted of extended Bornu territories and the vassal states with their puppet chiefs.[22] The great old empire of Kanem-Bornu suffered defeat first in

13. Iwuchukwu, *Muslim-Christian Dialogue*, 9.

14. Miles, "Religious Pluralism," 210.

15. Last, *Sokoto lip*.

16. Paden, *Religion and Political Culture*, 391.

17. Miles, "Religious Pluralism," 211.

18. Iwuchukwu, *Muslim-Christian Dialogue*, 8.

19. Iwuchukwu, *Muslim-Christian Dialogue*, 9.

20. Sanneh, *Piety and Power*, 2.

21. Morel, *Nigeria*, 99.

22. Hodgkin, *Nigeria Perspectives*, 92.

1893 by the fierce force of Rabeh from eastern Sudan. Later in 1900, the French colonists conquered the Rabeh, leading to the partitioning of the old kingdom into four bordering countries: Chad, Cameroun, Niger, and Nigeria.[23] Before the British halted the Islamic expansion of the Sokoto caliphate toward the Nigerian part of the Kanem-Bornu kingdom, her courageous king and committed Islamic cleric, Shehu Mohammad El-Kanemi, had resisted the jihadists (Sokoto caliphate) in 1811.[24] Islam was not mandatory for the people of the Kanem-Bornu empire.[25] However, "all Kanuri people were, of course, expected to be Muslims."[26]

The Kanem-Bornu and Sokoto caliphates' divide, which preceded the advent of Christianity, together with other contrasting organizational and theological tendencies, offer grounds for writers to acknowledge the Muslim-North heterogeneity.[27] Nigeria Northern Islam exhibits intra shades of Muslims. Miles categorizes these shades of Muslims into Sunnis, Sufis, and Mahdis.[28] He prefers not to identify the Kanem-Bornu caliphate as a true representation of Shi'ites. Nigeria Sufism criticized by the Islamic purists for their veneration of saints[29] generated two very important brotherhoods: the Qadiriyya and the Tijaniyya. As early as the seventeenth century, the Qadriyya brotherhood, which traces its root to Baghdad, consisted of conservative elites with defined political ambition in the preindependence era. In reaction to their perceived marginalization, the Tijaniyya brotherhood rose about the twentieth century, gaining massive support among the ordinary people.[30] Their differences extend to worship.

At prayer, while the Qadaris keep their arms parallel to their sides, the Tijanis cross their arms across their chest (*kabalu*). The *kabalu* is considered heretical by the Qadaris.[31] As such, these brotherhoods perceive each other as rival groups in both religious and political terrains.

23. Iwuchukwu, *Muslim-Christian Dialogue*, 4.

24. Iwuchukwu, *Muslim-Christian Dialogue*, 2.

25. Iwuchukwu, *Muslim-Christian Dialogue*, 4.

26. Ifemesia, "Bornu Under the Shehus," 92.

27. Miles, "Religious Pluralism," 209.

28. Miles, "Religious Pluralism," 213.

29. See Muhammad S. Umar, "Changing Islamic Identity," cited in Miles, *Religious Pluralism*, 214.

30. See Muhammad S. Umar, "Changing Islamic Identity," cited in Miles, *Religious Pluralism*, 214.

31. Clarke and Linden, *Islam in Modern Nigeria*, 45.

About the mid twentieth century, a radical Sunni group labeled the Sufi brotherhoods as a colonialist corrupted version of Muslims. Abubakar Gummi, the grand *kadi* of the north, became the most prominent Sunni reformer, and was against Sufi practices, especially through his translation of the Qur'an into Hausa vernacular. His militant approach, enforced by the Yan Izala group and the Muslim Students Society, had a retrieval of the "common northern Nigeria legacy of Uthman dan Fodio's jihad."[32] The Mahdiyya, on its part, shares similarities with a late-nineteenth-century Sudanese movement. Several violent crises that erupted in Northern Nigeria were ascribed to its militant activities.

In general, the Fulani-led Sokoto caliphate constitutes the Sunni Muslim majority, while the Kanem-Bornu version of Islam is predominantly the Shi'ite minority. Ifemesia articulates the relationship between the two factions of Nigerian Islam: "There was little love between the houses of Dan Fodio and Al-kanemi throughout most of the nineteenth century and beyond."[33] Regardless of their internal differences, the British in 1903 merged the two caliphates and formed the Northern Protectorate.[34] In today's Nigeria, the two exist as the northeastern (Kanem-Bornu caliphate) and northwestern regions (Sokoto caliphate), but still without any noticed improvement in their relationship as affirmed by Ifemesia.

Even though a greater percentage of Nigerian Muslims are Sunnis, the population of the Shi'ite minority exceeds the totality of Muslims in some other African nations. A 2009 Pew Research Center report numbered about 5 percent of Nigerians as Shi'ites.[35] With the estimated population of 185 million Nigerians, as of 2015,[36] Shi'ites (5 percent) get close to about 9.3 million people. This statistic amazes when compared to Senegal, a predominantly Islamic state, with a total population of a little more than 12 million people,[37] and to Ghanaian Muslims, estimated at 15 percent of her 25.37 million people.

Even at the global level, the Pew Research Center survey of 2011 shows that Shi'ites form the majority of Muslims in Iraq—as many as

---

32. Clarke and Linden, *Islam in Modern Nigeria*, 215.

33. Hodgkin, *Nigeria Perspectives*, 289.

34. Iwuchukwu, *Muslim-Christian Dialogue*, 4.

35. Pew Research Center, "Mapping the Global Muslim Population."

36. World Bank population figure. http://www.dataworldbank.org/country/nigeria.

37. Dowd, *Christianity, Islam*, 105.

19.8 million, accounting for 51 percent, out of a population of 30.7 million.[38] In comparison, therefore, Nigerian Shi'ites, estimated at 9.3 million, come very close to half of the Iraqi Shi'ites (the home of Shi'ites). So, whether as Sunnis or as Shi'ites or both, Nigerian Muslims (estimated at 52 percent) are enough to populate four independent nations in Africa.

The importance of establishing intra-Muslim heterogeneity in Nigeria explains some major doctrinal impact in one region that lacks in another. The creation and supremacy of the Sokoto caliphate in the northwest, as explained earlier, deserves a recall. In the northeast, the ancient Kanem-Bornu empire, which was not overrun by the dan Fodio jihad, exists as a rival caliphate known as the Bornu caliphate. If there exists a homogenous Northern Nigerian Islam, why is the notorious Islamic terrorist group Boko Haram operating only in the northeast (the Sambisa Forest in Bornu state) and not in the northwest (Sokoto caliphate)? The internal divide also plays out on why the recent Shi'ite religious procession (Ashura festival) [39] was violently suppressed by the military in the city of Kano (Nigeria), and their leader, Ibraheem Zakzaky, jailed under (Sunni) Muslim leadership in Nigeria; whereas several massacres across the nation by the Sunni Muslim-Fulani herdsmen are still to receive official condemnation or military intervention. Answers to these questions are pointers to the reality of heterogeneity and divisiveness among Nigerian Muslims.

Another peculiar factor of Nigerian Islam centers on the barring of Christianity by the British administrator Frederick Lugard from having any encounter with the Muslim North,[40] until the Toronto Industrial Mission at Pategi in 1899.[41] The simple reason hinges on the bilateral gains associated with the "indirect rule" between the British and the Muslim North. Since the existing Islamic structure in the North supported the strategy of indirect rule, the British, in appreciation, protected the Islamic territory. In sustenance of the British Lugard's bilateral agreement, subsequent colonial administrators upheld the Christian missionizing ban.

Nevertheless, within the first half of the twentieth century, Christians, through interdenominational missions from America and Europe, recorded an initial success among the Northern minority groups (areas barely hit by the jihadists), collectively known as the "Middle Belt." In the

38. Pew Research Center, "Sunni and Shia Muslims."

39. On November 14, 2015.

40. Miles, "Religious Pluralism," 211.

41. Iwuchukwu, *Muslim-Christian Dialogue*, 24.

1930s, many Southern Christians were able to penetrate the core Muslim North, through government jobs and search for business ventures. After a decade effort, the Christian population in the North showed a slow but steady increase.[42]

The Nigerian brand of "Africanization of Islam, prior to the jihad"[43] because of its tolerance for certain African Traditional Religion's (hereafter ATR) ritual practices claims itself as part of a much local tradition intolerant to Christianity. In other words, Northern Muslims perceive the Southern Christians as traitors who embraced Europeanized religion and culture, because Islam associates Christians as part of Western imperialists.

Paradoxically, the colonial rule, with its defined economic interests, did not only sustain the existing Islamic framework, it invigorated it. The obvious British political and economic predilection towards the Islamic North also created deep suspicion among the Southerners. A major factor of suspicion includes the Muslim Hausa-Fulani acclaimed proprietorship of the British-amalgamated Nigeria. Lugard's address at the inception of the British indirect rule implies such supremacy clause:

> The Fulani in old times under Dan Fodio conquered this country. They took the right to rule over, to levy taxes, to depose kings and to create kings . . . All these things . . . do now pass to the British . . . [But] all men are free to worship God as they please. Mosques and prayer places will be treated with respect by us . . . You need have no fear regarding British rule, it is our wish to learn your customs and fashion.[44]

Lugard's assertion demonstrates recognition of the existing Sokoto caliphate, but it also confers "a stamp of legitimacy on Muslim leadership and Islamic governance and culture."[45]

The British, for easier taxation, had a special interest in the Muslim North, because Northern Nigeria provided a local administrative model that favored British indirect rule.[46] Despite the agitation of non-Muslim minority groups in the North, the colonists preserved the influence of the Sokoto caliphate through indirect rule, a system that imposed on non-Islamic people Muslim rulers who owed allegiance to the jihadists.

---

42. Ojo, "Pentecostal Movements," 177.

43. Iwuchukwu, *Muslim-Christian Dialogue*, 7.

44. Ifemesia, "Bornu Under the Shehus," 284–93.

45. Miles, "Religious Pluralism," 212.

46. Miles, "Religious Pluralism," 211.

Indirect rule consolidated the religious authority of the emirs and broadened Islamic control. Ever since, the Muslim-Christian coexistence in Nigeria has been marked with mutual mistrust. Eventually, the sustenance of such a tilted framework was challenged, leading to pockets of agitation among minority groups in the twentieth century.

The Northern Fulani-Islam was initially planned to be a nation-state until the colonists surprisingly realized the overt inability of the North toward sustaining their commerce treaty due to very insufficient natural resources. Nigeria was not a consolidated colony when Lugard in his first administration made a treaty with the major Islamic emirates of Sokoto in 1903.[47] By the early nineteenth century, commerce was the primary interest of Britain, through the Royal Niger Company, until its collapse in 1900, and then colonization as a royal enterprise proceeded systematically.[48] Commerce allowed a bilateral bargain that was lost during the colonial era. This initial interest is confirmed by the fact that the northern Fulani-Sokoto caliphate, to which other emirates owed fealty, was Lugard's test and prize.[49]

It was not until his second commission (back to Nigeria from Hong Kong) as the governor of Southern and Northern protectorates (1912–1913) that Lugard effected the amalgamation of Northern and Southern regions in 1914, in order to salvage the former.[50] This "amalgamation ghost" still haunts its product, Nigeria. Even though the amalgamation was signed into law for a hundred years (1914–2014), the long struggle for self-actualization by the Biafrans (South Eastern region), which culminated in the 1967–1970 civil war, is still ongoing. Lugard's amalgamation created a persistent gulf of an even split along religious, ethnic, and political lines. The inherent danger of such an even divide has perpetuated rivalry and internal insecurity to date.

Invariably, minor provocations intensified into several violent crises. Within the several decades of Muslim-Christian coexistence, the Northern region of Nigeria has experienced many religious/political conflicts. The 1980s Islamic vandalism of churches and mosques in Kaduna resulted in four hundred deaths. Simultaneously, Muslim students'

---

47. Hiskett, *Development of Islam*.
48. Miles, "Religious Pluralism," 209.
49. Miles, "Religious Pluralism," 210.
50. Iwuchukwu, *Muslim-Christian Dialogue*, 28.

violent demonstration (1982) at Sabon Gari, Kano, claimed many lives.[51] These violent attacks were not only between Muslims and Christians, but also between the different cleavages within Islam.

The Maitatsine riots in 1980 and 1984 against corruption and corrupt Muslim leaders in Nigeria and the world at large claimed over five thousand people, including Alhaji Muhammadu Marwa (Maitatsine) himself.[52] Tensions between the two major brotherhood factions, *Tijaniyya* and *Qadriyya*, resulted in tolls of deaths from the 1950s up to the mid 1960s.[53] There were also the *Yan Izala* movement and Sufi brotherhood clashes, *Boko Haram*, and *Sara Suka*, which respectively disrupted Islamic cohesion in the early 1990s and most recently.[54]

Christian authors usually present Christians as major victims of several interreligious crises in Nigerian history. In contrast, Islamic writers often defend Muslim attacks for the most part as a reaction to hateful Christian provocations as well as the Westernized structures believed to be aimed at Islamic suppression. Samuel Huntington captures such sentiments vividly:

> The underlying problem for the west is not Islamic fundamentalism. It is Islam, a different civilisation whose people are convinced of the superiority of their culture . . . The problem for Islam is not the CIA or the U.S Department of Defense. It is the West, a different civilisation whose people are convinced of the universality of their culture . . . These are the basic ingredients that fuel conflict between Islam and the West.[55]

In agreement with Huntington's perceived Islamic-Western rivalry, Ayoub identifies three Western systematic approaches toward Islam—colonialism, evangelization, and orientalism[56]—in destabilizing an Islamic opposition. However, today statistics show that there are more Muslims living in the Western Hemisphere than in some of the Islamic countries.

Similarly, Matthew Hassan Kukah, a Nigerian Catholic bishop and scholar, situates the Nigerian Muslim-Christian feud on a tripod with a troubling structure: colonization, Shehu Usman dan Fodio's jihad, and

51. Bongo, *Christianity in Danger*, 3–4.

52. Miles, "Religious Pluralisms," 219.

53. Miles, "Religious Pluralisms," 219.

54. Kukah and McGarvey, "Christian Muslim Dialogue," 17–18.

55. Huntington, *Clash of Civilizations*, 217–18.

56. Orman, *Muslim View*, 43.

the Christian mission approach.[57] Ojo agrees with Kukah on the negative impacts of this tripartite legacy that has shaped the Nigerian geopolitics and religions.[58] Concerning colonialism, Lugard considered British colonialism in Africa not for philanthropic reason, but purely on economic advantages.[59] Shortly before the 1914 amalgamation, Lugard adamantly disregarded the warning voices of Charles Temple (the lieutenant-governor of the North) and E. D. Morel (the editor of the *African Mail*) against merging both protectorates for reasons of incompatibility. Rather than one country for the Northern and Southern polarized geographic areas, the two prophetic voices proposed "four or seven countries, provinces or even confederated units."[60] They were prophetic because today, more than ever, their proposals are the options being hotly debated in the National Assembly and across the country—a typical evidence that the amalgamation is a failed British project.

Asonzeh Ukah, another Nigerian scholar, agrees with Kukah on the negative impact of the Muslim-Christian even split in Nigeria. He blames the colonial policies that prevented early Christian evangelization in the North and the predominance of Islam in that region through Dan Fodio's jihad, but seems to sympathize with the helpless experiences of the Christian missionaries.[61] Afe Adogame, also a Nigerian scholar of religion, notes how the consequences of British power stratification in favor of the North intensified the mistrust and hatred toward the South, who through the missionaries embraced Western education. At the center of Nigeria Muslim-Christian problematic relation, Adogame rightly links the perceived inequality between the North and the South to the current religious coloration of politics in Nigeria. He describes such manipulative practices among key religious and political elites as "religionization of politics and politicization of religion."[62] Within the entire discourse, ethnicity subtly plays an undercurrent role in the even divide between the predominantly Muslim North and the predominantly Christian South in Nigeria. It as well questions the erroneous homogeneity of Northern Muslims.

---

57. Kukah and McGarvey, "Christian Muslim Dialogue," 14–18.

58. Ojo, "Pentecostal Movements," 176.

59. Boer, *Missionary Messengers*, 60.

60. Gailey, *Lugard*, 48–50.

61. Ukah, "Born-Again Muslims," 45–47.

62. Adogame, "Politicization of Religion," 125.

With a broad-strokes portrait of the religious and sociopolitical situation in Nigeria, the tension created by the resultant even split between the Muslim North and the Christian South is evidenced. Nigerian Christian-Muslim tension constitutes an obvious interreligious challenge.[63] And as such her millions of citizens respond to it differently. The informal daily attempts to navigate the murky waters of such tension among the ordinary religious adherents will be evaluated in the later chapters, as important grounds for the goal of this research, which aims at mitigating such persistent mistrust.

A major cause of the existing animosity between Nigerian Muslims and Christians has been identified as the obvious inability of the government to manage the evenly split structure of postcolonial Nigeria. Nigeria's (even) divide has been compared to the Sudan (a nation whose north is Muslim but whose south is non-Muslim), whereby the demarcation line follows a "northern Muslim vs. southern Christian" dichotomy.[64]

Some other factors shaped the divide even in the postcolonial period. Culturally and politically, Nigerians are yet to perceive themselves as one people. Ethnic interests overrule national cohesion. Ojo captures the negativity of ethnic priority even from the time there came a hint of autonomy from colonial imperialism. He noted that "During the decades preceding independence, gaps between the North and the South, and between Christianity and Islam, widened as the political parties assumed an ethnic and regional complexion, while the religious divide still existed in the background."[65] In corroboration with Ojo, the first republic following the 1960 independence never had a unifying ideology of a political party with a national character. Rather, with a fair exemption of National Council of Nigeria and the Cameroons/National Convention of Nigerian Citizens (NCNC), the then political parties—Action Group (AG), Borno Youth Movement (BYM), Democratic Party of Nigeria and Cameroon (DPNC), Dynamic Party (DP), Igala Union (IU), Igbira Tribal Union (ITU), Midwest Democratic Front (MDF)—had something in common. They all reflected ethnic blocks, which has not ceased paralyzing sociopolitical, economic, and religious developments.

Although current political parties can be said to reflect national characters, in reality, ethnicity and religious sentimentalism still breed

63. Adogame, "Politicization of Religion," 128–29.

64. Miles, "Religious Pluralism," 210.

65. Ojo, "Pentecostal Movements," 178.

division from the high to the low places. The failed leadership roles in Nigeria, especially the dominant northern military regimes (first junta 1966–79, second junta 1983–99), created a dysfunctional political system that shuns equity and development.[66] Even though citizens of a multi-ethnic nation, Nigerians from the South have experienced a continuation of dan Fodio's feudalistic leadership in many sectors, most obviously in education and job opportunities, through the "quota system."

The quota system, a preindependence (1960) introduction for the benefit of the northern, less privileged Western education areas, has proven a manipulative device against the federal character enshrined in the 1979 constitution, in order to perpetuate the Hausa-Fulani supremacy. As a sociopolitical concept, the quota system in Nigeria compromises national standards in favor of the Fulani oligarchy. In other words, the quota system is a "tilted table" on which merit is daily sacrificed for ethnic mediocrity. Such a sad situation disregards the most qualified and fills national opportunities with the least qualified based on tribal sentimentalism.

This unjust selective tool has penetrated almost all the ambience of the nation, especially the economic sector. As an oil-endowed nation, it is disheartening to note that 83 percent of the oil blocks in Nigeria are controlled by individual elites from Northern Nigeria, even though these oil wells are located in the South. Nevertheless, Northern scholars like Kukah decry the incredible poverty level in the North. These elements of incendiaries point to a clear portraiture of a failed political leadership in Nigeria. As such, the dysfunctional political state of Nigeria has engendered competitive interests among Muslims and Christians for natural resources.[67]

Sharia and the Contest for Political Space since the 1980s

Ab initio, sharia law, was not a major concern for non-Muslims in Nigeria. Rather, the enforcement targeted lax Muslims. Joseph Kenny notices that for over seven centuries of Islam in Northern Nigeria, the Hausa kings perceived themselves as custodians of both Islamic and non-Islamic cultures and traditions.[68] Under their leadership, the Islamic law was toned with the traditional practices of pre-Islamic Hausa land. H.

---

66. Adogame, "Politicization of Religion," 125.

67. Adogame, "Politicization of Religion," 130.

68. Kenny, "Islam and Christianity," 339.

Fisher described these Islamic rulers as "mixers."[69] As already discussed, dan Fodio carried out a cleansing war against this syncretic institution in Hausa and toppled it. Dan Fodio's reform was "aimed at the formation of Islamic state based on sharia."[70] His primary targets were lax Muslims,[71] but later extended to traditionalists.

Despite the initial status of sharia in Nigeria, it has overtime undergone substantial transformations through both constitutional and non-constitutional means. Most Christians strongly believe the ongoing Muslim attempts to impose sharia law on Christians is the long-term goal. Such red alert has generated greater resistance from Christians. In other words, sharia has graduated from a religious concern into becoming a political tool.

The exclusivity of the sharia law is a basic problem in religiously pluralistic African nations. Rather than achieving peace (al-Islam), it distorts it. Ahmad Khurshid, in the Pregny-Chambesy, Geneva conference, confirms the exclusive impact of sharia law: "When a religious system is concerned not merely to provide for the spiritual reform and uplift of the individual but to go on to create the framework of the state as is Islam, freedom can only have meaning within the framework and not outside it." For the sake of peace in nations with Muslims as minorities, sharia law is seriously restricted to within the Muslim context. But in accord with Khurshid, the implementation of sharia law in polarized nations has failed peace in a Muslim-dominated nation like Sudan (currently in civil war),[72] whereas its heated controversy in Nigeria has remained provocative.[73] Twelve out of the thirty-six states in Nigeria were declared sharia states. Rather than abide by the ordinances of the constitution of the country, residence of these twelve states are constrained to living under Muslim laws irrespective of their religious faith. Paradoxically, in politics, Islam puts no boundaries in participation, at least, as moderate as most church leaders would advocate.

Similarly, in the Graeco-Roman world and technically across the rest of Europe and America, Christianity displayed obvious exclusive control towards non-Christian cultures. Rather than impose the

---

69. Fisher, "Conversion Reconsidered," 73.

70. Kenny, "Islam and Christianity," 339.

71. Last, "Some Economic Aspects," 237.

72. al-Abidin, "Introduction," 1–12.

73. Kenny, "Sharia in Nigeria," 1–21.

Christian corpus of laws on their host communities,[74] the infiltration of doctrine and practices were achieved through education, health care services, commerce, and power. While doing so, Christians believe that through the implantation of newness of spirit, rather than legislation, non-Christians would also achieve the collective pursuit of human virtues, like truth, freedom, justice, human dignity, love, and rectitude.

In essence, J. W. Evans and L. N. Ward argue that Christianity approves of a pluralistic notion of state, where peoples of different philosophical and religious backgrounds collaborate, "provided they similarly assent to the charter and basic tenets of a society of free man."[75] So, the collaboration inspired by Christian tolerance in the modern world constitutes a superfluous rapprochement with secularism, when viewed from a predominant Islamic perspective. Most Muslims reject secularism because it has irreligious and atheistic overtones.

The expressed tension between the different forms of proselytization in the Islamic movement towards the *umma* and in Christianity's missionizing fervor might not be overtly perceptible in either Uganda (Christian predominance) or Senegal (Muslim predominance). However, its presence in a religiously even-split nation like Nigeria can be telling. The tension between Muslims and Christians in Nigeria is characterized by mutual suspicion, confrontation, and manipulation of statistics[76] as a struggle to show supremacy.

Championed by the Neo-Pentecostals and their counterparts, the radical Islamic front, these two highly intolerant (semi-independent) religious groups in Nigeria have remained in continuous competition for sacred spaces from the 1970s until now. Mistrust and hatred have colored their mutual perceptions towards each other. The bone of contention goes beyond search for souls to include winning "attention for dominance and for access to the resources of the state (land, patronage, economic advantage, etc.)."[77]

74. "Christian Concept," 5.

75. Evans and Ward, *Social and Political*, 169.

76. Census manipulations can be noticed in the restrictions surrounding its accuracy. Ever since the 1963 census that put Muslims at 45 percent of the population, the Northern Fulani hegemony have resisted the inclusion of nativity and religion in subsequent head counts of Nigerian citizens, thereby making it impossible to either confirm the said claim or debunk it.

77. Ojo, "Pentecostal Movements," 175.

The tussle, however, has experienced some developmental shifts within this period. At first, the impenetrable Northern Islamic territory started experiencing from the 1940s a gradual but steadily infiltration of Christians. Proselytization was an undercurrent goal of such brave steps. The first three decades witnessed the efforts of foreign evangelicals from North America and Europe. However, the pre- and post-independence periods heralded indigenous control of not only political but also religious affairs. The African Indigenous Church (hereafter AIC) emerged as a concrete expression of the rejection of the missionaries' flat condemnation of African values and traits as idolatry. Although manifested in distinct strands, the AIC's common goal sought ways of incarnating the gospel in African categories.

Unlike the AIC, the new-wave charismatic experience distances itself from African Traditional Religion and claims an international identity. In January 1970, university students in Ibadan (Southern Nigeria) were the first caught by the charismatic spirit spreading across the globe from Asuza Street, Los Angeles. Drawn together by a revivalist fervor, these students through evangelistic activities spread to other campuses. Matthew Ojo notices that by 1973 campuses in the North, like Ahmadu Bello University, Zaria, and the University of Jos,[78] started feeling the presence of these charismatic groups under the name Fellowship of Christian Students (FCS).[79]

Among the three phases of efforts by the Southern charismatic groups in evangelizing the Muslims, the earliest was the college graduate evangelical students deployed by the government to the north as National Youth Service Corps (hereafter NYSC) members.[80] The efforts of these evangelical students laid the foundation for renewal through undercurrent approaches in the institutions where they were deployed.

78. University of Jos operated at that time as a campus of University of Ibadan. It became an autonomous university in 1975.

79. Ojo, "Pentecostal Movements," 179.

80. National Youth Service Corps is a post–Nigeria civil war unifying initiative of General Yakubu Gowon as part of the reintegration policy of his administration. Founded in 1973, it is a one-year patriotic service program with the primary objective of enabling college graduates the opportunity for deeper integration of cultures, and promotion of unity among the diverse ethnic groups in Nigeria. As a result, graduating students are deployed in states other than their native states with a long-term plan of getting them assimilated into those states of residence through job opportunities and intertribal marriages. However, corrupt governance and godfatherism have obstructed the desired fruits of this program.

With quasi-immunity as government special personnel, some of them dared into remote Muslims areas like Sokoto. Their activities were virtually unnoticed since they founded no defined denominations. Some who got jobs stayed back and continued subtle evangelization as leaders of charismatic groups. Ojo believes that the cumulative efforts of these evangelical NYSC students raised the Pentecostal status in the North from "obscurity into prominence."[81]

The second category of Christians that entered the North in the 1970s and 1980s facilitated Pentecostal growth in the North. These were a different generation of evangelicals with less education than the NYSC members. Whether as government employees or as private businessmen and women, these Pentecostals were instrumental to the establishment of Pentecostal churches in the cities in and around the universities. The goal was evangelizing Muslims and Pentecostalizing Christians.

Despite an earliest establishment of a Pentecostal church in Jos by Thompson Nwosu with the name Redeemed Peoples' Mission Incorporated in 1975, Kaduna as the hub and gateway into other Northern states was a target for these Southern evangelists. That goal was soon accomplished.

In 1980, the Kaduna Pentecostal Youth Fellowship was established, which bonded most Pentecostal groups and stimulated their resolute determinations. The Living Faith Church (Winners' Chapel), founded in 1985, recorded outstanding growth after a successful crusade in the city of Kaduna.[82] Similarly, other Pentecostal churches, like Deeper Life, started emerging. By the mid 1980s, several Pentecostal organizations spread across the Northern region, though heavily populated by Southern Igbos and some Yorubas, but not without the Northern indigenous presence. Their Christian good works and neighborliness gradually impacted their new societies due to years of interactions that enabled significant understanding of the language, culture, and religion of their Muslim hosts.

The peak of Christian success came about when some Northern charismatic natives took leadership roles as Pentecostal pastors. Ojo articulates a plethora of Northern indigenous pioneers that founded Pentecostal churches. He accounts:

> In Kaduna, the first of such Northern indigenes to shoot into the limelight was Samuel Kujiyat, a veterinary doctor, who left the ECWA church to establish Rhema Living Word Church in 1984.

81. Ojo, "Pentecostal Movements," 179.
82. Ojo, "Pentecostal Movements," 180.

The church has a substantial number of Northerners among its members. Another prominent leader was Simon Kwasau, a polytechnic graduate, who established the Love Divine Ministry in 1986. In the same city, there was also Peter Ohidah, another college graduate, who established the Healing the Nations Bible Church. In Zaria, Professor Ishaya Audu, Nigeria's Foreign Minister (1979–1983), after retiring from public service, established the Faith and Charity Ministries. Likewise, John Akpam, a medical doctor, established the Christian Teaching Centre, and its Chapel of Revival. Maiwaizi Dandaura, a health technologist, and Steve Onoja, a medical doctor, were two other Northern indigenes that have shot into the limelight in Jos as leaders of charismatic organizations. Their organizations, Prevailing Faith Ministries and Faith Deliverance Ministries, were established in 1980 and 1986, respectively.[83]

This monumental Christian success recorded by Ojo in Muslim territory was more a political breakthrough than religious. By becoming founders of churches, these northern pastors began assuring the stability of Christian presence in the North, thereby weakening the tensed dichotomy between the Muslim North and the Christian South.

In contrast, the Christian-Muslim relation in the southwestern region (Yorubaland) reflected neither exactly the Northern picture nor a scenario entirely different from it. In its uniqueness (to be explored in chapter 9), Yorubaland has not been a haven of peace for Muslims and Christians. The major difference in approach could be that interreligious agitations were technically nipped in the bud.

Two factors are said to be contributory. First, scholars have attested to the Yoruba common ancestry as a prioritized indomitable bond rather than the religious or the national tie. Joseph Kenny confirms the identity consciousness of a common root ancestry (Oduduwa's sons and daughters) as the reason that makes all Yoruba people perceive themselves first as Yoruba, second as Muslims or Christians (or traditionalists), and lastly as Nigerians.[84] Like the Northern-Fulani Uthman dan Fodio's hegemony, the Oduduwa dynasty might be the strength of the Yoruba people, but invariably a serious weakness to the sociopolitical nationalistic goal of Nigeria. Kenny further justified the Yoruba bonding by drawing attention

83. Ojo, "Pentecostal Movements," 180–82.

84. Kenny, "Spread of Islam in Nigeria," 5–6.

to their religious pluralism. As he observed, one "can find both Muslims and Christians in some involvement in the traditional religion."[85]

Despite the ideology of a blood bond among Yoruba people, an influx of religious fundamentalism can be inevitable. The several times that adherents of African Traditional Religion and Islam in Yorubaland met Christian missionaries were mostly friendly encounters.[86] On few occasions, however, "intolerance or outright hostile attitude was expressed by the Muslim community towards the Christian missionaries."[87] Such negative attitudes occurred in Muslim dominated areas. A case in point is the mid-nineteenth-century Muslim resistance against the Christian evangelization and settlement rights in Iseyin, granted by King Aseyi at his court in 1851. T. G. O. Gbadamosi affirms:

> The Aseyin, like most Yoruba Obas, maintained the policy of open-mindedness and apparent support to all religions. When approached by Townsend in 1856, he had little hesitation in granting permission to the solicitous missionary to build a mission station; but when the Rev. G. F. Buhler, on the strength of this permission, came along in April to establish there, he met in spite of the welcome of the king, stiff opposition from Muslims whom he described as 'very angry' when they heard of his arrival. Indeed before his arrival, they had endeavored to prevent the Christian from settling down at Iseyin . . . [88]

According to Francis Adedigba's research findings, Christian missionaries experienced similar unfriendly attitudes from some Muslims in communities where Islam has firmly rooted itself, such as in Iwo and Epe. More so, Anna Hinderer[89] described a false alert used by Muslim teachers against Christian missionaries with a purported claim that Europeans transmit a deadly poison to Africans.[90] Such prejudices yielded some initial results, which couldn't be sustained as reality unfolded.

More recently, a more organized Muslim opposition group surfaced under the name *Tabliq* in Yorubaland. This radical Islamic group lives a life of material renouncement, and they wear knee-length shorts. They usually travel on foot. The goal of this sect was best known to their

85. Kenny, "Spread of Islam in Nigeria," 6–7.

86. Adedigba, "Roles of Jesus," 133.

87. Adedigba, "Roles of Jesus," 133.

88. Gbadamosi, *Growth of Islam*, 125.

89. Wife of the Rev. David Hinderer, CMS missionary in Western Africa.

90. Hone and Hone, *Seventeen Years*, 171–72.

members only. However, their presence at Ogbomosho in 2001 taking photographs of churches alerted the king, who chased them out from his town for fear of possible attack on churches.

Yorubaland is the hub of most famous global charismatic churches in Nigeria. It could be that Europe and American members who either reside in or fly into the country for worship were the targets. Precisely in February 2013, the directorate for State Security Service (DSS) in Nigeria claimed to have arrested Abdullahi Mustapha Berende and his two associates for terrorist charges. These purported terrorists have allegiance with Iran, and were trained to spy and attack mostly Americans and Isrealis wherever they worship in Yorubaland.[91] Fortunately, negative religious machinations by some radical Muslims against Christians in Yorubaland have not been successful.

The closest known incident toward interreligious crisis was a case of public denouncement of Islamic faith at Osun state in Yorubaland. Abiodun Alao narrates an incident of an Islamic convert to Christianity who publicly compared the Qur'an and the Bible at an open-air city crusade. He recounts:

> In Iwo, Osun state, in October 2007, during a Christian crusade, a former Muslim who had become Christian told the audience: "if you want to know about God, go to the Qur'an, but if you really want to know God, go to the Bible." Muslims found this unacceptable, as they argued that the statement presupposes that Qur'an only talked about God without really revealing God. Issues like this have been known to result in violence.[92]

Adedigba agrees that such statements should be labeled provocative and avoided. Even if the radical groups decide to read it mildly in order to prevent violence, enough damage could be impacted on Muslim-Christian relation, which might eventually result to similar continuous rivalry in the Northern region.

The Yoruba context, as explained, enjoys a more ancestral bond, which moderates interreligious coexistence, contrasted with the heterogeneity of the Northern region. Unlike the religious pluralism seen in Yorubaland, the Northern Muslim hegemony still preaches religious exclusivity within its domain, thereby tacitly restricting Christian activities. In reaction, the Christians have unceasingly been forging strategic

---

91. Eboh, "Nigeria (DSS) Arrests Iran-Linked Cell."

92. Abiodun Alao, "Islamic Radicalization," 35; cited in Adedigba, "Role of Jesus."

means of occupying substantial space in the North. Besides the initial efforts of NYSC members, evangelical government workers, and some indigenous Pentecostal pastors in the Northern evangelization project, few pioneer Pentecostal pastors from the South later took the bull by the horn to establish branches in the Muslim North.

In collaboration with some prominent Southern charismatic leaders such as A. A. Idahosa, more Pentecostal pastors were sponsored and commissioned to the Islamic North, in resistance to the suspected Muslim agenda of Islamizing Christians. The coalition of Northern and Southern charismatic leaders under the Christian Association of Nigeria (CAN) produced a formidable voice for Christians against the presumed Muslim supremacy.[93] Muslims perceived such moves for space from the Christians as provocative. Mutual suspicion of the other, indeed, triggered unprecedented violence.

From the 1960 independence to date, no decade witnessed greater religiously instigated crisis in Nigeria than the 1980s. First, the violent demonstration of Muslim students in Kano, which provoked sympathizers in some other Northern universities, extended to major cities. The agitation was for implementation of sharia laws in lieu of secular constitutions for both Muslims and Christians. In the end, Christian lives and properties were victimized. The collective pains of losses united Christians more in the resolve for self-defense. To crown it all, the military dictatorship of General Ibrahim Babangida's secret registration of Nigeria in 1986 as a member of Organization of Islamic Conference (OIC) sparked off conclusion on the suspected Islamization agenda.

The consequential controversy created by the OIC membership outrageously lingered. In the midst of the controversy, Muslim-Christian relations deteriorated. Christians under the Christian Association of Nigeria umbrella adopted the cliché that "the best defense is a well-articulated and executed attack." As a surprise package, the hate speeches of Abubakar Gummi and the violent activities of his Zumarat followers were hit by Christian violent retaliation. Violence, even though unacceptable in Christian teaching, succeeded in pushing back Muslim assaults, when they realized the collective strength of Christians. For radical Christians, these Islamic attacks and agenda against Christians have confirmed reasons for their continued demonization of Islam.

93. Adogame, "Politicization of Religion," 131.

The violent approach, however, came with obvious lessons. Ojo notices that between the 1980s and 1990s the demonization of Islamic fundamentalism championed by some Christian fundamental revivalists, in particular, Neo-Pentecostals and evangelicals, was dropped and they embraced a subtle strategy aimed at winning the contest. Through a bifurcated counterattack, they aimed at undermining the prolonged Islamic supremacy tendencies in Nigerian politics. First, active partisan politicking under the consolidated aegis of Christian Association of Nigeria was intended to capture the political leadership control in Nigeria. Political activism initiated by mostly Southern Pentecostals living in the North later gained the support of Northern indigenous Christians. Thus pulpits, conferences, and crusades became grounds for political campaigns. The second strategy centered on lobbying Muslim elites with political ambitions in embracing prosperity theology. Prosperity theology, a.k.a., "sowing seeds" for richer blessings, was inspired by the philosophy: the more you give God (in the church), the more blessings you attract. Actually, this second strategy fuels the first. In other words, the millions of naira tacitly reclaimed from Muslims politicians are used for sponsoring Christian political candidates.

Additional tension was sustained between the policy of centralization of power advocated by Muslim fundamentalists and the decentralization ideology advanced by the Pentecostals. The latter resonates with the Holy Spirit's empowerment of individual freedom and charisma. In this regard, while the Islamic fundamentalists target the sanitization of anomalies in modern societies, Pentecostals aim at correcting individual missteps. However, as this research develops, the unsettled religious otherness among Nigerian Muslims and Christians will be kept in focus, while immediate attention will be given to the exploration of some insufficient positive reactions toward (interreligious) the management of otherness.

4

Inadequate Reactions
to Religious Otherness

FROM THE MUSLIM-CHRISTIAN HISTORICAL encounters previously analyzed, the inability to properly appreciate and respect the other marred
their age-old relations.

Describing the status quo, Francis Peters, while through an Islamic
lens, describe Christianity as "the-Other-who-can-never-be-wholly-
other,"[1] and names this continuity-discontinuity dynamic "problematic continuity."[2] In other words, the religious other has been a serious
threat to each religion. Such a challenging process exemplifies Muslims
and Christians in a continuous and contextual assemblage and reassem-
blage.[3] Consequently, the other is often silenced or objectivized in order
to illuminate and reassure the faith of the self.[4] Theologians, therefore,
have responded by providing certain relational approaches. The exploration of these approaches will determine whether or not there is need to
search further for a healthier Muslim-Christian relation.

Generally speaking, although significant achievements have been
made within Christianity, especially in the area of interreligious dialogue,
still more efforts are needed in regard to Christian-Muslim relations. In
Christianity, the most famous attempts toward assessing religious otherness constitute the threefold categorization by Race (1983), namely:

1. Lamptey, *Never Wholly Other*, 47.

2. Peters, "Alius or Alter," 169–70.

3. Peters, "Alius or Alter," 174.

4. Aydin, "Religious Pluralism," 335.

exclusivism, inclusivism, and pluralism. Alan Race was the first person to make the tripartite distinction of exclusivism, inclusivism, and pluralism. This distinction has often been challenged in recent decades, but has been fairly recently defended by Perry Schmidt-Leukel.[5] Race's threefold distinction reflects a "dialectical process," starting with the "least open," the "half-open," and finally the "dialogical virtue of openness."[6]

Exclusivism

In the Catholic Church, for example, exclusivism reflects the longstanding predominant approach to otherness, in which the "*extra ecclesiam nulla salus*" of Cyprian (d. AD 258),[7] shaped a significant part of pre-Vatican II theology of the other. The Fourth Lateran Council (AD 1215) approved this exclusivist formula, verbatim.[8] During this period, the notion of truth was absolute, static, and monologic,[9] and basically entrusted to the church. Like a barricaded city, the envisaged salvation is open only to whoever stays inside, but not to those outside the "imaginary" wall. In fact, the Council of Florence (AD 1442) confirmed that pagans, Jews, heretics, and schismatics have by choice condemned themselves to hellfire.[10]

To be more precise, the Roman Catholic Church was projected as the one center that awaited the return of entire humanity. Among Christians, the "return" theory of the Council of Florence (1438–1445) was a second attempt on reunion, after the first attempt at the Council of Lyons (1274). The Great Schism between East and West in 1054 necessitated both. Not much changed about four centuries later. Pope Pius XI, through his encyclical of 1928, *Mortalium Animos*, forbade all ecumenical invitations from the World Council of Churches,[11] based on the "return" theory

5. See Perry Schmidt-Leukel, "Pluralist Approaches in Some Major Non-Christian Religions," in Harris et al., *Twenty-First Century Theologies*, 159–87.

6. See Marianne Moyaert, "Christianity as the Measure of Religion? Materializing the Theology of Religions," in Harris et al., *Twenty First Century Theologies*, 242.

7. Cyprian of Carthage, *Ep. 73*, 21. This exclusivist formula was repeated in the Pronouncement of Pope Boniface VIII (1235–1303); in the papal bull *Unam Sanctam* (1302); also in the Athanasian Creed.

8. Adam, *Spirit of Catholicism*, 161–62.

9. Swidler, "Age of Global Dialogue," 275–76.

10. Adam, *Spirit of Catholicism*, 162.

11. Swidler, "Age of Global Dialogue," 282–83.

that persisted in the Vatican for ages.[12] Such a persistent idea of one true church shaped the missionary impulse in the history of the church, especially in Africa, till about the mid twentieth century. The weight of these ecclesial signatures intensified existing negative perceptions toward the church, especially from the Muslims.

Even though the earliest period of Christianity and the Middle Ages experienced some shades of inclusivism, such differing voice was scarcely heard. It was the voice of the teaching authority of the church that was mostly heard. Muslim scholars frown at Cyprian's famous exclusivist quote from *On the Unity of the Church*: "He can no longer have God for his Father, who has not the church for his mother."[13] While some in defense interpret later Muslims' hateful attitudes toward Christians as possible responses to the noticed Christian exclusivism, a few among them have traced exclusive language also to Muhammad. It is alleged that Muhammad said, "whoever died in the faith of Jesus, and died in Islam before he heard of me, his lot shall be good. But whoever hears of me today and yet does not assent to me, he shall surely perish."[14]

The earliest mutual exclusivist thrust between Islam and Christianity can be accurately described as the manifestation of the "age of invincible ignorance,"[15] up till the mid fifteenth century, when interfaith scholarship based on respect and openness started emerging.[16] However, from such exclusive perception, the dignity of the other was totally violated and her mysterious personhood reduced to a mere object.[17]

An exclusivist thrust gained weight in the mid twentieth century, especially among the Islamic academy, in rejection of what was considered Western control. Ideologies that presented Islam as the last authentic religious opportunity for the salvation of mankind defined the impulse of these later evolving spirits.[18] Sayyid Qutb, the Egyptian

12. Other Vatican documents that encouraged solipsism in the Catholic Church include: *Monitum* (1948), *Instructio* (1949), and one in 1954 barring of Catholics from participation in the Second World Council of Churches at Evanston.

13. Cyprian of Carthage, *Ep. 74*, 7; see Cross and Livingstone, *Oxford Dictionary of the Christian Church*.

14. Ayoub, *Qur'an and Its Interpreters*, 1:112.

15. Age of invincible ignorance describes a long period of unsubstantiated conclusions between Muslims and Christians.

16. D'Costa, *Vatican II*, 161–64.

17. Panikkar, *Christophany*, 171.

18. For a survey of these movements, see Hourani, *Arab Thought*.

scholar and distinguished adherent of the Society of Muslim Brothers, builds his argument on the universalist-finalist theory of Islam. His approach toward Christianity was reductionistic because he considered Christianity as a transitory religion whose limited goal was only for the revival of Judaic legalism and *"preparatio evangelica"* for Islam.[19] In this sense, Christianity, the religious other, is overtly demeaned. In essence, through exclusivism, the centeredness of the self is virtually threatened by the reality of the other.

Overall, exclusivists' lens had exacerbated the initial antagonisms between Muslims and Christians, which resulted in mutual hatred and killings, as epitomized in the several crusades and the numerous jihads. As deduced, it might be argued that the mutual supersessionist exclusivism has often been instigated by political rather than purely religious considerations.[20] On account of this causal distinction, a shift in perspective gradually emerged that challenged exclusivism. Broadly speaking, adherents of a different assessment of the other, called inclusivism, were mostly drawn from the circle of critics of exclusivism.

Inclusivism

Inclusivists often see themselves as diametrically opposed to exclusivist approaches to other religions. Inclusivism attempts a balance between openness and commitment to religious identity.[21] Simply put, inclusivists believe unity assures a soteriological openness to all humanity. Christian inclusivists seek to resolve the universality of God's salvific will with the uniqueness and mediating function of Christ and the church. Within the same spectrum, religious otherness can be tolerated, so long as the salvific uniqueness of Christ is unthreatened.[22] To a large extent, inclusivism shares this one-centeredness with exclusivism, but goes beyond the latter in accepting that elements of the truth can exist outside of the church.[23] Nevertheless, some brand of exclusivists would concede to the existence of traces of truth elsewhere, but find them

19. See Sayyid Qutb, *Al-Adala al-ijtima'iyyah*, 6–12; cited in Ayoub, *Qur'an and Its Interpreters*, 1:112–13.

20. Orman, *Muslim View*, 45.

21. Moyaert, *Fragile Identities*, 81.

22. Kaplan, *Different Paths*, 1–2.

23. Shehu, *Nostra Aetate*, 9.

insignificant for salvation. Traces of pre-Vatican II inclusivism can be found among the distinct mission approaches of the Jesuit Roberto de Nobili's inculturation rite.

De Nobili (1577–1656), for the Indian Christians, adopted the rites of controversy initiated by Matteo Ricci (1552–1610), which the latter first experimented with in China. Although the debates on the rites of controversy could not get Vatican approval for over two hundred years, still the possibility of salvation from de Nobili's perspective could be inferred by his non-insistence on conversion for Hindus.[24] However, scholars noticed that de Nobili had strongly desired conversion to Catholicism and indeed recorded much success, especially with the Brahmins. Nevertheless, a more precise account of appreciating local values happened earlier through the defense of the Dominican Bartholomé de Las Casas for the Indian natives.[25] Las Casas's argument centers on human dignity and freedom of worship, which suggests a foundational anticipation for religious freedom witnessed at the Second Vatican Council.[26]

Despite the implied respect for the religious other, inclusivists in some sense promote one-centeredness. In their improved recognition of the religious other, the consciousness of the supremacy of their own religion remains intact. Specifically, the validity of the other only derives from their own theological starting point. This approach suggests assimilation. The case of Ruth, the Moabite, who became Jesus' ancestor,[27] though she converted by choice,[28] shows how Judaism and Christianity assimilated many foreign religious and cultural elements. If exclusivism prevents openness to otherness, in inclusivism the problem of otherness shifts from exclusion to assimilation. The high risk includes the inability to accept "non-integrateable differences."[29] A one-centeredness approach toward the other oppresses and even diminishes him or her.

Inclusivism would be no less guilty than the Husserlian ego or the Homeric Odysseus's homeward voyage.[30] Both analyses demonstrate a round trip that begins from the self and terminates in the self. In such

24. Müller et al., *Dictionary of Mission*, 398–99.

25. Gutierrez, *Las Casas*, 62.

26. *Dignitatis Humanae*, in Flannery, ed., *Vatican Council II*.

27. Matthew 1:5.

28. Ruth replied to Naomi (her widowed and childless mother-in-law): "Your people shall be my people and your God shall be my God" (Ruth 1:16).

29. Moyaert, *Fragile Identities*, 82.

30. Homer, *Odyssey* 14.56–58.

circular movements the inviolable other is occluded. Said differently, the openness advocated by inclusivism gradually wanes into tacit exclusive conclusions. Therefore, an inclusive approach to interreligious dialogue between Muslims and Christians cannot exceed an impasse in which Muslims might be Christianized or Christians Islamized.

How inclusive was the Second Vatican Council (Vatican II)? The Second Vatican Council, initiated on October 11, 1962 by Pope John XXIII and concluded on December 8, 1965 by Pope Paul VI, has remained a watershed[31] in the mission and general engagement of the Catholic Church towards larger society. Great theologians like Agustin Bea (1881–1968), Karl Rahner (1904–1984), George Anawati (1905–1994), Franz Konig (1905–2004), Hans Küng (1928 to date), Robert Caspar, etc. were behind the success of Vatican II. While Caspar describes the Vatican II newness as "a revolution"[32] and Anawati calls it "a radical novelty,"[33] Gavin D'Costa wonders whether the newness "was the shift in pastoral attitude or a shift of doctrine"[34] and prefers holding a continuity position.

As students of Massignon and members of the drafting committee at Vatican II, Caspar and Anawati almost reflected the thoughts of their master, whose influence by the Muslim mystic al-Hallaj[35] led to his affirmation of close parallels between the latter's death and the atoning crucifixion of Christ.[36] However, both D'Costa and Christian Troll showed that Massignon's liberal teaching (that Islam has a legitimate heredity from Abraham through Ishmael) was seriously contested at the Council.[37]

Massignon's emphasis on Islam in contradistinction to Vatican II's stress on Muslims generated three opinions among scholars. While the first group argues that Islam was not mentioned in the documents (*Lumen Gentium* and *Nostra Aetate*), and the second denies the endorsement of Islam as a religion because it houses true and false doctrines, the third

---

31. Knitter, *No Other Name?*, 123–24.

32. Caspar, "Islam According to Vatican II," 2. Gavin D'Costa notes that Louis Massignon first used the same term, "revolution," in its Copernican sense, as a new attitude for Christians toward Islamic doctrines.

33. Anawati, "Assessment," 52.

34. D'Costa, *Vatican II*, 161.

35. See Massignon, *Passion of al-Hallaj*.

36. D'Costa, *Vatican II*, 166.

37. Troll, "Changing Catholic Views," 28.

camp (Caspar and Anawati) thinks that the word "submission" used in the document implies Islam.[38]

Similarly, Muslim thinkers received Vatican II's newness in *Nostra Aetate* (hereafter *NA*) with mixed expressions. The unprecedented turn and acknowledged "respect" for the faith of Muslims were obviously appreciated by interreligious Muslim scholars as great invitation for dialogue. However, some, like Murad Wilfried Hofman, Seyyed Hossein Nasr, Mahmoud M. Ayoub and Iran Abdul Hameed Fattah, couldn't hide their reservations on the insufficiency of *NA*.

Generally, the common and major lack was the omission of Islam, the Qur'an, and the chosen prophet, Muhammad.[39] In reaction, whereas Nasr describes the lack in *NA* as a case of isolation,[40] Mahmut Ayudin interprets it as a recognition of Muslims only as individuals without a defined religion,[41] and Ayoub terms it an "absolute minimum"[42] towards Islam, Fattah thinks it failed to achieve the goal of Muslim-Christian dialogue.[43] In summary, Hofman encourages Christians to shun exclusivism, not only formally (as in *NA*), but also in mind.[44] However, such minimalist contribution in *NA* might also suggest that it only provided a dialogic framework that challenges Islamic and Christian theologians for its greater enrichment.

In essence, the demand from the Catholic patriarchs and Eastern bishops for deepening of the church's relationship, not only to Jews, but also to Muslims, gave birth to two touchstone documents of the Second Vatican Council concerning other religions. In the first document, *Lumen Gentium*, no. 16c, Islam is prioritized among the other known religions that recognize the creator, God, because of her expressed profession in the common faith with Abraham, which also is shared by Christians. Troll notices in Islam not only a semblance but also a deeper faith relationship with the Abrahamic profession, operating at a personal level.[45]

---

38. D'Costa, *Vatican II*, 167.

39. Shehu, *Nostra Aetate*, 222.

40. Nasr, "Response to Hans Küng's," 98–99.

41. Aydin, "Towards a Theological Dialogue," 2.

42. Ayoub, "Roots of Muslim-Christian Conflict," 42.

43. Shehu, *Nostra Aetate*, 224.

44. Hofman, *Al-Islam Kabadil*, 61–62.

45. Troll, *Dialogue and Difference*, 153.

The Council carefully accentuated two theological shared beliefs in the one God of Muslims and Christians. One pertains to God's personal attribute as a merciful creator, and the other refers to his action as eschatological judge. Even though the merciful God teaching of the Muslims questions the Christian belief in the propitiatory role of Christ, both religions at least accept worshipping a God who does not relent in forgiving human frailty. In essence, both religions agree that the gravity of one's sins is nothing in comparison to the immensity of God's mercy.

However, the Christian understanding of mercy in relation to justice weighs far greater than the Muslim understanding of God's stand on human judgment. Whereas Islam emphasizes personal righteousness, Christianity balances human efforts with the merits of Christ's atonement.

The second text, *NA*, contains a rather detailed appreciation of Islam in the section 3. After a general instruction on non-Christian religions, *NA* not only emphasizes openness to what is good and true in Islam but also urges honest effort toward the realization of mutual understanding. Section 3 of *NA* therefore asserts:

> Upon the Muslims, too, the Church looks with esteem. They adore one God, living and enduring, merciful and all-powerful, Maker of heaven and earth and speaker to men. They strive to submit wholeheartedly even to His inscrutable decrees, just as did Abraham, with whom the Islamic faith is pleased to associate itself. Though they do not acknowledge Jesus as God, they revere him as prophet. They also honor Mary, his virgin mother; at times they call on her, too, with devotion. In addition, they await the day of judgment when God will give each man his due after raising him up. Consequently, they prize the moral life, and give worship to God especially through prayer, almsgiving, and fasting.[46]

When viewed from the context of the history of the Catholic Church, the inclusive language of *NA* on the relationship of the Church with non-Christian religions signals an important breakthrough. Although the intention of the Synod of Bishops was to develop a document on ecumenism and to correct Catholicism's existing troubled relation with Judaism, *NA* emerged as a fruit of a long debate, reflecting sensitivity to "the signs of the times."[47]

---

46. *NA*, #3, in Flannery, ed., *Vatican Council II*.

47. *Gaudium et Spes*, #4, in Flannery, ed., *Vatican Council II*.

The signs of the times, as envisioned by John XXIII, invited the church, among other things, to mediate and address diversities in a pluralistic world. *Nostra Aetate's* exhortation, on the one hand, calls for respect for the truth and genuine holiness in other religions (*NA*, 2), and on the other hand, insists on an unwavering proclamation of Christ, the way, the truth, and the life, in whom all people find their fulfillment (*NA*, 2). This christocentric demand of *NA* has not only created an unresolved tension and dilemma but also engages its pluralistic beauty. It could be said that *NA* sets the agenda for interreligious dialogue without a corresponding road map. This is because Vatican II was more pastoral than systematic in its articulations.

Nostra Aetate concludes its section on Islam with the following words: "Over the centuries many quarrels and dissensions have arisen between Christians and Muslims. This sacred council pleads with all to forget the past and urges that a sincere effort be made to achieve mutual understanding; for the benefit of all, let them together preserve and promote peace, liberty, social justice, moral values."[48]

Two great points are very clearly stated in the structure and language of this section 3 of NA. First, the beginning paragraph is exhortative, thereby appealing to convergences between Christianity and Islam, but not without drawing lines of differences. Second, the concluding paragraph emphasizes dialogic potentials and needs, despite a shared inglorious past; and it marks a new beginning, initiating a practical step in confirming the *Credo in Unum Deum*.[49] The wisdom of the Council reflects her great care in teasing out the commonalities but also paying attention to the inherent differences in both the meaning and understanding of God's names and attributes.[50] It is equally revealing that the eleventh-century Pope Gregory VII (1073–1085), in his letter (cited in the footnote to the council text) to the emir of Mauritania, addressed him as "his brother in Abraham" and as a believer in the one God, the creator.[51]

Nonetheless, Anawati comments on Vatican II's silence concerning three Islamic features: an ancestral link to Abraham and his son, Ishmael; the person of Muhammad; and the prophetic character of Muhammad.

48. *NA*, #3, in Flannery, ed., *Vatican Council II*.
49. Troll, *Dialogue and Difference*, 154.
50. Troll, *Dialogue and Difference*, 154.
51. Troll, *Dialogue and Difference*, 154.

In these very words he notes, "it can be said that the Council's declaration gives an account in the shortest possible form, of the Moslem theodicy, but not of the essence of the Moslem faith, which includes among its most important elements belief in the prophetic mission of Muhammad."[52] Also, three of the five pillars of Islam were named (prayer, almsgiving, and fasting)[53] but the Islamic faith in the *shahada* and pilgrimage were overlooked; and Troll thinks it was deliberate.[54]

Above all, in *NA*, the tension between the two foci of inclusivism, i.e., the divine universal will to save and the salvific uniqueness of Christ, though dominant in both Vatican and post-Vatican II periods, still awaits a definitive resolution. Hence, "Christian theologians of religions are trapped at the crossroads of affirming the universality of God and Christ as the unique locus of salvation."[55]

Consequently, the obvious reality of otherness, which remained unresolved by both the exclusivist and inclusivist approaches, as well as by Vatican II's innovative intervention, might have prompted the emergence of the third category, pluralism. It has been argued that Vatican II laid a foundation for a pluralistic theology of religions,[56] even though the Council of Bishops, according to Karl Rahner (1979), did not intend to do so. In other words, as explained by Paul Knitter, Vatican II's *aggiornamento* successfully transcended the Catholic Church's traditional exclusivism, but it could not navigate beyond the inclusivist's confines. Therefore, Vatican II in its watershed shift barely transcended liberal inclusivism.[57] Vatican II did not develop any theology of religions but instead left it for her theologians: "The Church therefore urges her sons to engage with prudence and charity into the dialogue and collaboration with members of other religions."[58]

In that regard, Moyaert warns against the inclusive danger of absorbing other religions into Christianity. She rather envisions "theologians who take seriously the messy complexities of trans-religious and cross-cultural transformations, who are unafraid to cross borders and

---

52. Anawati, "Excursus on Islam," 153.

53. *NA*, #3, in Flannery, ed., *Vatican Council II*.

54. Troll, *Dialogue and Difference*, 156.

55. Kärkkäinen, *Introduction*, 20.

56. See Paul F. Knitter, "The Pluralistic Path: Where We've been and Where We're Going" in Harris et al., *Twenty-First Century Theologies of Religions*, 143.

57. Hick, *Disputed Questions*, 82.

58. *NA*, #2, in Flannery, ed., *Vatican Council II*.

refrain from the tendency towards apriori systematization."[59] Can pluralists satisfy the challenges of Moyaert?

Pluralism

The proponents of pluralism were more of twentieth-century thinkers who claimed their position addresses the limitations of exclusivism and inclusivism. Pluralists advocate a major shift from self-centeredness to reality-centeredness, if salvation is open to all humanity. While trying to sustain universal salvation, the pluralist alternative presupposes the soteriological sameness of all the religions.[60] In other words, all religions offer distinct paths to "Salvation / Liberation / Enlightenment."[61] However, as the name "pluralism" suggests, its advocates teach equal validity of religions from several perspectives. One of the pioneer pluralists contends that pluralism

> marks a break with exclusivist and inclusivist outlook because it does not interpret religious plurality from the perspective of Christian absolutism. It allows for the distinctiveness of the Christian voice, but it neither elevates Christian faith into a position of superiority, finality, unsurpassability, or exclusivity, nor renders other faith-traditions as lesser versions of what has emerged through the greater tradition.[62]

From this perspective, it is unclear how realizable pluralists' claims could be.

Nonetheless, pluralistic theology emerged as a fruit of authentic dialogue of religions. The growth of such fruit was enabled by the World Council of Churches and followed the exemplary steps of Vatican II. In the 1970s, its calls for interreligious dialogue increased under the leadership of Stanley Jedidiah Samartha.[63]

---

59. See Marianne Moyaert, "Christianity as the Measure of Religions? Materializing the Theologies of Religions," in Harris et al., *Twenty-First Century Theologies of Religions*, 249.

60. Moyaert, *Fragile Identities*, 82.

61. Shehu, *Nostra Aetate*, #9.

62. Race, *Interfaith Encounter*, 3.

63. Stanley Jedidiah Samartha was born in Karkala, Karnataka, India on October 7, 1920. As a theologian he promoted interreligious dialogue through the World Council of Churches and once served as the director. He died on July 22, 2001.

John Hick, with his Copernican revolution work, *God and the Universe of Faiths*,[64] is regarded as the father of a pluralistic theology of religions.[65] His radical shift urges Christianity to move from a "christocentric" to a "theocentric" approach toward other religions, especially since Vatican II had moved from "ecclesiocentrism" to "christocentrism."[66]

Not only Hick, but Raimon Pannikar also "laid the first foundations of a pluralistic theology of religions."[67] Panikkar was a multiple religious belonger through dialogic practices, studies, and personal spirituality, long before the term became current.[68] His major argument in the book *The Intra-Religious Dialogue* insists that interreligious dialogue must presuppose intrareligious dialogue, in which the discovery of otherness and the newness of one's own religious tradition and identity are required.[69] The intra-engagement demands taking the other seriously as one who also has truth to be shared. Panikkar was profoundly a mystic, who saw no contradiction between one's faith and having great respect for religious otherness.[70] In chapter 6 of this book, Panikkarian intrareligious intuition will be preparatory in response to the spontaneity involved in being responsible for the other.

The Panikkarian pluralistic approach simultaneously supports faith commitment and openness to newness. While preserving the otherness among religions, Panikkar also posits a connecting bridge among them, by which mutual challenge and growth is possible in genuine dialogue.[71] In agreement, the Vatican's document *Dialogue and Proclamation* (hereafter *DP*), approves the dual ways of understanding the role of Christianity and of Christ in relation to other religions[72] by citing *NA*: "Let Christians, while witnessing to their own faith and way of life, acknowledge, preserve and encourage the spiritual and moral goods found among non-Christians, as well as their social and cultural values."[73]

---

64. See Hick, *God and the Universe*.

65. Knitter, "Pluralist Path," 144.

66. Knitter, "Pluralist Path," 145.

67. Knitter, "Pluralist Path," 145.

68. Drew, "Christian and Hindu," 247–72.

69. Knitter, "Pluralist Path," 145.

70. Knitter, "Pluralist Path," 145.

71. Panikkar, "Jordan, the Tiber," 110.

72. PCID, *DP*, #17.

73. *NA*, #2, in Flannery, ed., *Vatican Council II*.

Nonetheless, it has been argued that pluralism also leads to impe-rialism/exclusivism.[74] D'Costa, an arch critic of pluralism, coordinated an assemblage of international scholars who responded to Hick's *Myth of Christian Uniqueness* with their critical publication, *The Myth of a Pluralistic Theology of Religions*. Their major argument intended to prove that pluralists were guilty of what they intended to salvage with their theocentric shift. That all religions point in the same direction suggests that pluralism also suffocates the otherness of both theistic and non-theistic religions.[75]

It was a common view in the Christian theological circle that "Plu-ralism betrays Christian identity, because to question the salvific role of Christ is to rob Christianity of its identity."[76] Both the magisterium and many other Catholic theologians objected to the validity of the campaign set in place by Hick and his colleagues of a theistic and non-theistic un-derstanding of "the absolute." In their strong warning, theologians like Hans Küng, Monika Hellwig, Gregory Baum, and Karl Josef Kuschel, though from diverse perspectives, agree that "the pluralists' decentraliza-tion of Christ would wreak havoc among the faithful, or that it would dull liberation theology's prophetic call for justice."[77]

Paul Knitter thinks otherwise. With the observable evolutionary trend in a theology of religions from ecclesiocentrism to christocentrism, and to the theocentrism of pluralists, Knitter proposes a further move to soteriocentrism. It is soteriocentrism, he argues, that assures the collec-tive well-being in a multireligious collaboration, and therefore occupies the first act of ethical praxis. Muslim-Christian soteriological goals en-courage ethical responsibility and can be competitive (Qur'an 5:48). Fol-lowing upon soteriocentrism would be theology and dialogue, because in every multireligious context, "Dialogue would come after dia-praxis. Then, theological reflection would follow ethical collaboration."[78]

Knitter notices five outstanding models within the past two decades that have contested the Christian pluralist approach to other religions. They include particularism, deep pluralism, comparative theology,

74. Knitter, "Pluralist Path," 147.
75. Moyaert, *Fragile Identities*, 86.
76. Knitter, "Pluralist Path," 147.
77. Knitter, "Pluralist Path," 148.
78. Knitter, "Pluralist Path," 149.

feminism, and the Vatican.[79] Particularism, according to Knitter, emphasizes the dominance of incommensurability.[80] Even though Knitter lists
George Lindbeck as the initiator of particularism,[81] this research rather
recognizes his position as a cultural-linguistic approach. Supporters of
particularism insist that absolute commonalities among religions guarantee the imposition of one religion over the others.[82]

The critique of the particularists, according to Knitter, has alarmed
the pluralists about their own inclusive stand on a slippery slope of imperialism. The way out, he suggests, would entail pluralists seeking both
a defined harmony between their desired commonalities and some proportional differences among religions.[83] Nevertheless, the particularists
still have to contend with some other theologians of religion, such as
Hans Küng and Catherine Cornille, who strongly argue that a necessary
interconnectivity among religions, despite their diverse nature, leads to
world peace.[84]

In fact, the brand of pluralism that would survive these major criticisms is that whose goal is not "*Ex pluribus, unum* (from many, to one)
but *Ex pluribus unitas* (from many, to unity)."[85] While oneness dissolves
differences, unity retains differences, even though scholars like Milbank[86] see unity as reduction of plurality.[87] Likely, Knitter meant a kind
of unity that respects differences, which can be seen in a true solidarity
of individuals.

Ever since, Knitter has proposed a solidarity model as a bridge for
interreligious connectivity. Knitter's call for a mutuality model aims at a
retreat from supremacy truth claims, so that "many true religions [are]
called to dialogue."[88] In his view, the solidarity paradigm offers a reliable basis for interreligious relations. Thus he concludes, "solidarity with
the suffering ones of this earth, and with the suffering earth itself, can
provide the starting point and the [next] stage for a new praxis-initiated

79. Knitter, "Pluralist Path," 150–51.

80. Knitter, "Pluralist Path," 150.

81. Knitter, "Pluralist Path," 150.

82. D'Costa, *Meeting of Religions*, 30–39.

83. Knitter, "Pluralist Path," 152.

84. Cornille, *Im-Possibility*, 95–135.

85. Knitter, "Pluralist Path," 154.

86. See Milbank et al., *Radical Orthodoxy*; also, D'Costa, *Meeting of Religions*.

87. Moyaert, "Christianity as the Measure," 244.

88. Knitter, *Introducing Theologies*, 109–10.

interreligious dialogue. I can hope for this," writes Knitter, "because I see it already happening."[89]

Knitter resonates with Levinas to a large extent concerning his emphasis on ethical responsibility across religions. If the cliché "action speaks louder than words" still bears some ethical relevance among Muslims and Christians, the main argument of this research for interreligious competition on altruism will go a long way in wiping clean the smudged lenses of both traditions as they appreciate the reality of the other.

Like particularists, another group of critics, the deep pluralists, led by S. Mark Heim, argue that religious cultural specificity continues into the *eschaton*. Heim's notion of heaven can be understood not as a level plain, but as a sort of Alps, from which each religion can look at the other.[90] In other words, there can be Ultimate Realities,[91] which for John Cobb are marked by three possible characteristics: the theistic, the acosmic, and the cosmic.[92]

Among the four critical groups of pluralism mentioned, the comparative theologians have recorded the greatest reproaches against the pluralists. Following the lead of Francis X. Clooney and James Fredericks, pluralist theologians are presented as mere theorists with impracticable ideas or "armchair anthropologists that make sweeping claims about cultures and traditions they have not experienced."[93] In reply, Knitter contests that one cannot be a theologian of religion without equally being a comparative theologian.[94] He also believes that Perry Schmidt Leukel, Judith Berling, Diana Eck, and the late Raimon Panikkar are pluralist theologians who are already engaged in comparative theology.

Nevertheless, comparative theologians led by Fredericks have called for a momentary "moratorium" of the theology of religions (though not its quest) for two reasons: 1) Theologians of religions presuppose a substantial knowledge of other religions that they do not really possess and therefore draw hasty conclusions leading to sameness of purpose. 2.) The

89. Knitter, *One Earth, Many Religions*, 73–80.

90. Knitter, "Pluralist Path," 150.

91. Knitter, "Pluralist Path," 150.

92. Griffin, "Religious Pluralism, 3–38.

93. Clooney, *Comparative Theology*, 150.

94. Knitter, "Pluralist Path," 154.

lack of openness for Christians to learn from other believers.[95] Narrowing his objections toward theologians of religions, Fredericks affirms:

> Exclusivist theologians, like Karl Barth, see non-Christians religions as entirely different and of no consequence for Christian believers. Inclusivist theologians like Karl Rahner and pluralist theologies can have the unintended effect of rendering the differences that distinguish other religions from Christianity less interesting to Christians.[96]

Fredericks advocates for comparative analysis of faiths across religions for a deeper mutual enrichment of particular religions. However loud his call sounds, it does not seem to differ completely from the call by some theologians of religions on religious commitment and openness already discussed. Fredericks has also, in the meantime, strongly advocated for cultivating interreligious friendship as the key to a proper understanding of other religions.[97] In any case, interreligious friendship must presuppose interreligious hospitality.

Last but not least is the Vatican. In the recent past, the Vatican has constituted the fiercest critic of pluralism. As the head of the Congregation for the Doctrine of the Faith, Joseph Cardinal Ratzinger drew attention to the inherent danger of relativism and indifferentism in pluralism. In addition to explicitly naming John Hick and Paul Knitter as dangerous propagators of pluralism, Ratzinger's publication of *Dominus Iesus* (hereafter *DI*) in 2000 further challenged pluralistic theology.

Generally speaking, *DI* was seen to be unfair even by moderate inclusivists such as Walter Kasper and therefore has authority only among conservative Catholics like Gavin D'Costa. Ratzinger's radical stand in *DI* has been seen by some of its critics as having shifted the evolutionary trend of the Catholic Church decades backward, prior to Vatican II and John Paul II's *Redemptoris Missio*. Unlike *DI*, *Redemptoris Missio* spells out in greater detail the complementarity between dialogue and its relationship to proclamation, by urging the striving for openness and faith commitment.[98] The firm revival of christocentric exclusivism in *DI* shook the progressive

---

95. Fredericks, *Faith Among Faiths*, 166.

96. Fredericks, *Faith Among Faiths*, 167.

97. James Fredericks coedited a book titled *Interreligious Friendship after Nostra Aetate* on this argument with Tracy Tiemeier, his colleague at Loyola Marymount University in Los Angeles.

98. John Paul II, *Redemptoris Missio*, ##55–57.

course in interreligious dialogue, and even called for the review of some of the works of "Roger Haight, S.J, Jacques Dupuis, S.J., Jon Sobrino, S.J., Peter Phan, Tissa Balassuriya, and Sister Elizabeth Johnson."[99]

Alternatively, Knitter proposes the "distinctness" rather than the "uniqueness" of Jesus, and at once "maintains an openness to the uniqueness of other religious figures and traditions."[100] Recalling Krister Stendahl's question as to whether "I can sing my song to Jesus fully and with abandon, without feeling it necessary to belittle the faith of others,"[101] Knitter proposes a dialogic Christology, based on a kenotic and prophetic Christology.[102] In consonance with John Cobb, Knitter sees Christ as "the Way, which is open to Other Ways."[103] Knitter's portrayal of Christ as the Way among other ways questions the uniqueness of Christ's divine sonship, which is the basis for Christian theology.

In the end, the pluralists' perspective fails to acknowledge the otherness of other religious confessions. Rather, in all their efforts to promote otherness, the other is either excluded from or absorbed into one's own confessional perspective. Consequently, Moyaert insists that the confessional perspective must be transcended.[104]

Islamic Perspective

An Islamic perspective offers a rather appealing Christology to Christians. Olaf Schumann[105] objects to Christians' claim of supremacy through divine sonship, and proposes "a servant Christology that is sensitive to Muslim sensibilities and still true to basic Christian teachings."[106] Schumann argues that a servanthood perspective on Christ is a genuine form of Islam. He asserts: "Only on the cross, through the final submission

---

99. Knitter, "Pluralist Path," 152.

100. Knitter, "Pluralist Path," 155.

101. Stendahl, *Meanings*, 133.

102. Knitter, "Doing Theology Interreligiously."

103. Knitter, *Introducing Theologies of Religions*, 119–23, 156.

104. Moyaert, *Fragile Identities*, 92–98.

105. Schumann, *Der Christus der Muslime*.

106. Oddbjørn Leirvik, "Towards a Relational and Humanizing Theology: A Christian-Muslim Dialogue," in Harris, et al., *Twenty-First Century Theologies of Religions*, 231.

of will and its ambition 'to be like God' may the always present temptation of '*shirk*' be defeated."[107]

Although Schumann does not escape the snares of Arianism and Sa-
bellianism (ancient heresies that questioned Christ's divinity), a focus on
the servanthood of Christ can pave the way for a better Muslim-Christian
understanding in two ways: 1) it avoids the traditional Muslim-Christian
impasse over Christ's divinity, and 2) it approves the cross of Christ for
Muslims as noble/fervent obedience to God. Moreover, servanthood
Christology undergirds the substitutive responsibility being advanced
in this research. Overall, Schumann's notion of servanthood makes an
important connection between Islam and Christianity that Cornille and
Küng defended. Such connections between religions prepare the grounds
for an interreligious dialogue at the base level, with a hospitality key.

For the engagement of religious otherness among Islamic scholars,
Jerusha Tanner Lamptey identifies three categories of scholars. Like the
Christian pluralists and particularists, each group emphasizes either a
sameness argument, otherness argument, or a defense of their harmony.

For an Islamic theological trend of religious sameness, the work of
Ashgar Ali Engineer, an Indian Islamic activist (d. 2013), published in
Paul Knitter's edited volume *The Myth of Religious Superiority: A Multifaith Exploration* was a good attempt at exploring Islamic attitudes
toward religious pluralism. He built his argument on the Qur'anic assertion about the divine will by stressing that God could have created a
single, homogeneous people if he was against diversity. Thus he argues
that the Qur'an "not only accepts the legitimacy of the religious pluralism, but considers it as central to its system of beliefs."[108] However, he
regrets that despite the Quranic openness to otherness, religious diversity
often leads to conflicts because of the supersessionist drive of one religion
over others. Diversity, he concludes, counts as a divine gift that should
be appropriated for the sustenance of "peace and harmony among all
the communities."[109] As a support for Engineer, Qur'an 2:177 recalls that
ethical grounds, rather than doctrinal beliefs, define a fervent Muslim
submitter. Overall, Engineer's trend of argument reveals a greater sympathy for religious sameness, despite his acknowledgement of otherness.

---

107. Schumann, *Der Christus der Muslime*, 178.

108. Lamptey, *Never Wholly Other*, 51.

109. Lamptey, *Never Wholly Other*, 51.

While the Christian perspective often enough seems to situate the raison d'être of diversity in the plurality of humanity, the Islamic lens locates it in the divine intent. Juxtaposing the theistic pluralism of Hick (a Christian) and Rumi (a Muslim), both agree on a God who is greater than all religions, and one that constitutes their omega point. But in contrast to Hick, who thinks that human sociocultural projections account for religious pluralism, Rumi sees it rather as a divinely intended result of divine self-disclosure (*wujud*)[110] in the world. If Allah intends pluralism in the world, as Rumi contends, a great caution is needed before any conclusion that Muslims' dream of *umma* opposes diversity. In this regard, a major concern would be exactly how to understand diversity through an Islamic lense.

Seyyed Hossein Nasr, an Iranian philosopher and a principal representative of a harmonized sameness-and-otherness model, argues that "the fact that these elements within a particular religious universe might differ or even contradict elements belonging to another universe does not prove their falsity or destroy their absoluteness within the universe to which they belong."[111] He explains that the wholeness of homogenous traditional religions was disrupted by modern civilization, and that the remedy will entail a reaffirmation of the transcendental unity that respects obvious particularities.[112] While he blames modern approaches to diversity for their pitfalls, which include historicism, phenomenology, lowest common denominator, ecumenism, and relativism, he at one and the same time extols perennial philosophy and Sufism as the only keys to a simultaneous appreciation of otherness and sameness. His use of Sufi mysticism enables him to harmonize unity and diversity without any contradictions.

Among the representatives of a prioritization-of-otherness model, Tim Winter of Cambridge University is noteworthy. Drawing from classical Sunni speculative theology (*kalam*), Winter criticizes pluralism on the grounds that its principle violates the logic of non-contradiction. He critically rejects any platform that claims to harmonize religious monotheism and dualism. He rather insists that pluralism "requires simultaneous affirmation of contradictory elements, beliefs or doctrines."[113] In essence, he reiterates that religious pluralists deny Islam of its internal

110. Reynolds, *Muslim Theologian*, xlviii, liii, 85.

111. Nasr, "Religion and Religions," 75.

112. Lamptey, *Never Wholly Other*, 60.

113. Winter, "Last Trump Card," 135–36.

homogeneity that legitimately marks its supersessionism over previous monotheistic religions. In contrast to the interpretations of continuity that pluralists give to Qur'an 5:48, Winter takes exception by providing two different reasons why Allah gave Muhammad such a command. His reasons emphasize the validation of Islam and its role as corrector of religions. First, Muhammad's prophetic mission was to be confirmed by the existing Judeo-Christian prophetic traditions. Second, it was to establish Islam as a guardian (*muhaymin*) over surviving adherents of previous existing faith religions.[114]

The goal of all these trends can be identified within religious self-identification, through a process of trivializing the faith and values of the other religions. According to Daniel Boyarin, such resentment expresses nothing less than "a depiction of religions as separate, hermetically sealed compartments."[115]

Moving forward, Boyarin distinguishes between the distant other and the remote other. Unlike the distant other, the proximate other is that religious other whose existence intimidates the religious self, and whose presence cannot be ignored. The proximate other has a faith similar to that of the self, except that each pattern of expressions differs. While the distant other, as the insignificant voiceless or faceless other, could easily be silenced or ignored, the proximate other presents a formidable challenge to the religious self. Islam and Christianity in today's pluralistic world affirm such proximate relationship. Like Boyarin, Jonathan Z. Smith concludes that "the other, the different, is not wholly distinct or discreetly bounded. Difference—at least meaningful and meaning-making difference—is always relational, dynamic and provocative."[116] Despite the consideration of Islam and Christianity as proximate others, none of the observed Islamic trends nor Christian theology of religions has successfully provided a vivid account of the proximate other.

In his attempts at making space for the proximate other, Isma'il Raji al-Faruqui[117] logically connects two Islamic ontological concerns: the *tawhid* (oneness of God) and the *fitra* (human nature). God's oneness,

---

114. Winter, "Last Trump Card," 139.

115. Boyarin, *Border Lines*, 14.

116. Jonathan Z. Smith, cited in Lamptey, *Never Wholly Other*, 73.

117. Isma'il al-Faruqi was born in Palestine in 1921 and was an American/Egyptian-trained scholar of Islam and comparative religion. Before his death in 1986, he founded many Islamic studies programs, such as the Islamic Studies Group of the American Academy of Religion and the International Institute of Islamic Thought.

according to al-Faruqui, does not destroy human nature; rather, both exist cordially in ideally harmonious relationship. In a related manner, he argues that since all religions in some way deal with the *din al-fitra* (natural religion), none should be a gauge for the others; instead, all are accountable only to God. A *hanif*, he reiterates, is a person who has *din al-fitra* but doesn't belong to any religion.[118] In other words, no peoples on earth have been deprived of the revelation of God.

The Qur'an also teaches that the human *nafs* (the primordial soul created by God) possesses inner awareness of the *taqwa* (piety).[119] Like Christianity, Islam does not doubt the importance of human nature. Rather, the differentiating line between good and bad people lies with human acts. Goodness in people radiates one's religious identity. In essence, it is the individual's conformity to the will and purpose of God that guarantees her religious identity. However, universal human freedom, which is part of the divine endowment toward the realization of creation's goal, accounts for the differentiated attitudes toward the *taqwa* (piety). The use of freedom can be for humanity's oneness or a rejection of it. Technically, freedom guarantees humanity's ability of making choice.[120] Invariably, diversity "creates a unique characteristic in the Qur'anic discourse: from the most basic level, the Qur'an affirms all peoples, though it never affirms all actions."[121] Both sameness and difference can be deduced from this divine intention in creation. The coexistence of these opposites can be traced from the creation of *zawj* (the woman-spouse) from *nafs* (the primordial soul created by God),[122] which later resulted in cultural, religious, and color diversities within the one human genus.

Jerusha Lamptey reiterates Asma Barlas's distinction between hierarchical difference and lateral difference in society. Lateral difference distinguishes (gender) groups without attaching an evaluative measure to that. It reflects a divine purpose through which the importance of each group is guaranteed. In contrast, hierarchical difference follows the course of evaluation with respect to the *taqwa* (piety). The assessment virtually happens at the individual level. The Qur'an, according to Lamptey, offers two major supports for lateral difference. The two purposes of

118. Lamptey, *Never Wholly Other*, 77.

119. Winter, "Last Trump Card," 152–53.

120. al-Faruqi, *Islam and Other Faiths*, 133.

121. Lamptey, *Never Wholly Other*, 243.

122. See Qur'an 4:1.

lateral difference pertain to God and humanity respectively. In 30:20–22 lateral difference is designated as an *aya* (sign) of God, through which awe and reflection are provoked with regard to God. And in 49:13 lateral difference accounts for humanity's ability to live in appreciation of diversity. Lateral difference, Lamptey concludes, does not prioritize the self over the other, or vice versa; rather, both stand equally before God.[123] "Qur'anic *ayat*, which affirms the divinely intended status of lateral religious particularities (rites, laws, ways), describe the appropriate response to those particularities as racing or vying (*istabiqu*) with one another in pursuit of what is good (khayrat)."[124] True manifestation of *taqwa* is concretely shown in the daily pursuit for *khayrat*.[125]

Khayrat includes belief, prayer, almsgiving, social interactions, and the prioritization of a vertical relationship with God over horizontal human relationships.[126] The said bifurcation (between vertical and horizontal) constitutes a disturbing phenomenon because it severs humanity's responsibility toward God (theology) from its implied responsibility toward fellow humans (ethics). Rather than tend toward the identified dualism, this research advocates for a fair harmonization between otherness and sameness.

This section focused on highlighting the inadequacies in major Muslim and Christian suggested approaches toward the religious other. Moving further, therefore, the research searches further for glimpses of improved relationship between Muslims and Christians.

---

123. Lamptey, *Never Wholly Other*, 244.

124. Qur'an 2:148.

125. Qur'an 23:57–61.

126. Lamptey, *Never Wholly Other*, 251.

5

The Development of Positive Views

IN CHAPTER 1, SUFFICIENT exposition was presented in identifying the mutual antagonistic perceptions that have infested Muslim-Christian relations over time.[1] Still noted were significant moments that suggest the possibility of positive interactions.[2] Often, exacerbated relational breakdowns easily eclipse such glimpses of hope. Through an enriching document on Muslim-Christian historical relations, the Vatican reiterates the innumerable instances of dialogue of life between Muslim and Christian neighbors, unaccounted for in historical texts due to the tendentious thrust "to the dramatic, to indignities or injustices inflicted and endured, to violence and suffering."[3]

In corroboration, the World Council of Churches in an official document cautions against misplaced historical memories, in which "conflicts overshadow peaceful experiences and accusations drown the voices of understanding."[4] In light of such concerns, chapter 4 also established various theoretical responses by philosophers and religious scholars in search of a healthier dialogic relationship between the two religions.

Even though studies show significant progress within both religions, this should not mislead to unwarranted assumptions that Muslim-Christian interfaith discourse has achieved its goal of harmony and

1. Shehu, *Nostra Aetate*, 56.

2. Kimball, *Striving Together*, 37.

3. Michel and Fitzgerald, *Recognize the Spiritual Bonds*, 3.

4. World Council of Churches, Office on Interreligious Relations, "Striving Together in Dialogue," 481.

peace. In fact, scholars like Gabriel Reynolds have confirmed the great insufficiency of what the Church has said about Islam, and how that has impacted serious challenges for Catholic theologians.[5] In other words, Christian-Muslim dialogic embrace is still emerging.

This chapter primarily aims at establishing renewed awareness of altruistic responsibility among Muslims and Christians, through which the other can be appreciated as much as she freely communicates herself. It seeks to create a possible transition from the Muslim-Christian inimical past, through traces of openness for dialogic embrace, toward a renewed neighborliness.

Structurally, four questions are pertinent: 1) What are the contributory factors for the emerging turn to dialogue between Muslims and Christians? 2) Among the four types of dialogue, how is dialogue of life a path-paver across the Muslim-Christian borderline? 3) What is the relationship between dialogue of life and hospitality, or how possible is dialogue without hospitality? 4) What shades of hope does dialogue of life via hospitality offer towards the dissolution of Muslim-Christian antagonism and isolation? These questions and similar concerns constitute the framework of in this chapter.

Improved Muslim-Christian Relations

The thousandth strike that cracked a rock only evidences the invisible impact of the previous 999 strikes. It is really difficult to name one exclusive historic event that engendered a radical Muslim-Christian relational change on a broad scale. From innumerable jihads (as early as the seventh century) and crusades (from the eleventh century) to more complex forms like contemporary terrorism and media attacks, religion has not escaped the center of blame. Consequently, Muslims and Christians are gradually taking a dialogic turn toward each other in search of a healthier correlation.

So far, this research has explored both Islamic and Christian subjective lenses through their historical encounters. It has also examined recent examples of renewed openness toward the otherness of the other and highlighted their limitations. It is pertinent in this section to engage what factors might have informed the noted sudden change of attitude in both Islam and Catholicism toward the other.

5. Reynolds, "Gavin D'Costa," 291.

With the recent identification of Islam with acts of terrorism, both Muslims and some Christian Islamicists tend to distance themselves from the initial jihadist apologetics, and rather emphasize the importance of the greater jihad—the jihad of words and the pen. This turn toward greater jihad prioritizes the inner struggle over jihad of the sword. Theoretically, the current tendency among Muslim scholars reveals a profound deemphasis on lesser jihad, which has been argued as a misinterpretation of the Arabic meaning. Maulana Muhammad Ali's exegesis of 29:68 and 25:52 upholds a missionary approach through the propagation of the Qur'an only, for the establishment of Islam.[6]

Similarly, Dr. Rowan Williams, former archbishop of Canterbury, identifies a converging point between Christians and Muslims. In his opening speech at the second Building Bridges Seminar (April 7, 2003) at Doha, Qatar, Williams elucidates Muslim-Christian otherness in terms of a potential reasonable convergence.

> Christians are Christians and Muslims are Muslims because they care about the truth, and because they believe that truth alone gives life. About the nature of that absolute and life-giving truth, Christians and Muslims are not fully in agreement. Yet they are able to find words in which to explain and explore that disagreement because they also share histories and practices that make parts of their systems of belief mutually recognizable—a story reaching to God's creation of the world and God's call to Abraham; a practice of reading and absorbing scriptures and of shaping a life in response to the Word God speaks to creation . . . Listening to God and listening to one another as nations, cultures and faiths have not always had the priority they so desperately need.[7]

In corroboration with Williams, and despite the noted doctrinal and structural differences, a meeting point is still possible between the Islamic strict simple form of monotheism and the Christian Trinitarian monotheism. In support, Christian Troll explains: "While doctrinal differences certainly bear significantly on the nature of Christian-Muslim *convivencia* (coexistence), conversely, the varying ways in which the communities coexist also have a palpable influence on how each community lives out its faith and formulates its theology."[8] Troll's assertion

---

6. Ali, *Manual of Hadith*, 252.

7. Ipgrave, *Scriptures in Dialogue*, xi–xii.

8. Troll, *Dialogue and Difference*, 148.

speaks to dialogue of life as a functional option for Muslim-Christian non-doctrinal interactions.

Recently, there has been in the Islamic academy a more profound positive turn to the reality of otherness, especially the religious other, through a dialogic approach such as *Meta-Religions: Toward a Critical World Theology* (1986) by Isma 'il Raji al-Faruqi.[9] In addition to the Holocaust, which informs the works of Levinas and Buber, a more recent growing engagement with the other, some scholars argue, has been signs of reactions to the 9/11 terrorist attacks on the USA. The significances include the resulting huge losses experienced on both sides, beginning with the 9/11 attacks itself and then with their violent aftermath in Middle Eastern conflicts.[10]

In essence, the basic problem simply underscores humanity's inability to welcome and accept otherness in its inviolable reality. In response to this problem, Moyeart accentuates the need for such inescapable engagement. Her words remind us that "[p]lurality of cultures, traditions and worldviews claim that the religious other deserved our respect and had a right to our recognition and appreciation."[11]

Background to Muslim-Christian Dialogue

Traces of openness to dialogue are possible through Islamic and Christian lenses. The earliest advocacy for interreligious openness by a Catholic scholar of Islamic mysticism, Louis Massignon (1883–1962), with the great influence of Charles de Foucauld (1858–1916), his spiritual mentor, is quite remarkable. After Massignon's return to the practice of the Catholic faith in 1908, and while working in Iraq, he sought to develop a positive Christian theology of Islam with special focus on the Abrahamic figure. Against the consensus of Western Christian historians, Massignon

---

9. Isma 'il Raji al-Faruqi (1921–1986) is acknowledged as an authority on Islam and comparative studies. He is also recognized as the first Muslim thinker who promoted the necessity for Muslims to transcend from apologetic and polemic mindsets to openness for mutual respect and learning with Christians, especially in *Meta-Religions: Toward a Critical World Theology* (1986). More recent dialogic works include: Nasr, *Islamic-Christian Dialogue* (1998); Kearney and Hosting, eds., *Stranger Between Religions* (2011); Moyaert, *Fragile Identities* (2011); and Harris et al., eds., *Twenty-First Century Theologies of Religions* (2017).

10. Swidler, "History of Interreligious Dialogue," 3.

11. Moyaert, "Absorption or Hospitality," 61.

affirmed that Muhammad was indeed a descendent of Abraham through Ishmael.[12] He also claimed that despite some developmental oversteps following Muhammad's death by later Muslims, it was the Islamic mystics, through their Abrahamic spirituality, who could purify Islam from its excesses and bring it to the full truth.[13] Massignon identified the figure of Abraham as a converging rather than a diverging point for Muslims and Christians.

Massignon's spiritually was transformed when he rediscovered the root of his faith life in substitutionary discipleship as found in the life of the Sunni mystic al-Hallaj.[14] His renewed Christian faith convinced him that to be Christlike or Christian we must substitute our own lives for the salvation of others as Jesus did. His hospitality experience in a Muslim home in Baghdad marked his spiritual Copernican revolution. The experience, he writes, "overturned one by one all of my acquired reflexes, all my habitual cautions, and my sense of place in the society."[15] Massignon had a spiritual partner, Mary Kahil, a Melkite Christian, who shared a similar substitutionary vision, and on February 9, 1934 both took a vow in Damietta (Egypt) before the altar of St. Francis of Assisi. Massignon substantiated his vow with Mary through the "*Badaliya*" initiative (a prayer "home" for Christians and Muslims, established in 1934 in Cairo).[16]

The *Badaliya* was designed in terms of its appropriate recognition and impact on both Muslims and Christians. *Badaliya* is an Arabic word for substitution, which Massignon applies to the substitutive demand of Christian discipleship for the salvation of others, without aiming at conversion.[17] This renewed spirituality of Massignon and Kahil received Vatican approval in 1947. The spiritual movement also attracted impressive membership, including Cardinal Giovanni Battista Montini (later Pope Paul VI)[18] and some monks. In the resolution of members (Christian and Muslims) to pray for one another, living the gospel message of love was always an undercurrent.[19] Founded on the early Christians' spirit of

---

12. Massignon, *Testimonies and Reflections*, 3–20.

13. Madigan, "Muslim-Christian Dialogue," 250.

14. D'Costa, *Vatican II*, 166. See Massignon, *Passion of al-Hallaj*.

15. Massignon, "Visitation de l'Etranger," 282.

16. D'Costa, *Vatican II*, 166.

17. Baldick, "Massignon," 36.

18. D'Costa, *Vatican II*, 166.

19. Buck, *Model of Hope*, 2.

martyrdom and the medieval mystics' desire of suffering for others, Massignon reveals the motif of *Badaliya*: "The essence of the *Badaliya* is to lift the screen by our presence, delivering us from this kind of scandalous rivalry . . . it is necessary to maintain the presence of Jesus living in us."[20]

The screen the *Badaliya* intends lifting echoes the distorted lenses this research exposes as major Muslim-Christian obstacles. It is argued that "the greatest obstacle comes from ourselves. It is we who need to be purified, our thoughts, our visions."[21] With a proper diagnosis of the problem between Muslims and Christians, Massignon contends that "voluntary substitution abolishes an eye for an eye."[22] In other words, Massignon's *Badaliya* resonates with Levinasian substitutive responsibility for the other. It is uncertain whether Levinas knew Massignon or not, but it is rather certain, according to Derrida, that the former did not reference the latter.[23] Substitutive altruism can be explained in terms of making oneself available as an instrument for the welfare of others. The welfare of others reconnects to God's will for them. Therefore, doing ethical substitutive services for others ensures obeying God's will.

Besides Islam's position of being a major and global community, religion in general reaffirmed itself after being impacted negatively by the impulses of the Enlightenment. Presently, religion is reasserting itself,[24] not only in destructive ways (through terrorism and conflicts), but also in constructive ways, through various peace movements and reconciliation movements, seen in postapartheid South Africa, campaigned for by Martin Luther King, and especially through interreligious dialogue.[25] In corroboration, Swidler confirms this new flourishing element noticed among religions. He makes the bold claim: "Flowing out from its dim beginning in the Enlightenment, interreligious dialogue is permeating all fabric of human structures of the globe, establishing global dialogical civilization."[26]

---

20. Massignon and Kahil, *L'Hospitalite Sacre*, 208.

21. Buck, *Model of Hope*, 3.

22. Buck, *Model of Hope*, 3.

23. Derrida, *Acts of Religion*, 367.

24. Micklethwait and Wooldrige, *God Is Back*.

25. Swidler, "History," 17.

26. Swidler, "History," 17–18.

Bases Leading to Dialogic Turn

This section seeks out pro-dialogic contributions in the history of Muslim-Christian relation. The search is open and will include possible elements or traces that suggest a transitional shift from the initial antagonistic lenses toward a dialogic embrace. However, due to the negative impacts of centuries-old isolation and biases between these two world religions, there will be huge disappointments if there are expectations for robust and smooth dialogic interactions. Nevertheless, attempts will be made (where possible) to include contributions from individuals as well as institutions on both religious sides. Above all, the Vatican's four forms of dialogue will be specifically sought for in this regard.

Toward the end of this dialogic section, dialogue of life will be distinguished by establishing its relevance and purpose as the focus of this research. As the research advances, it will develop this basic form of dialogue into a theology of life that intends complementing the ongoing dialogic efforts in interfaith conversations. The choice of dialogue of life does not imply any priority or exclusivity. Rather, drawn by the need for complementarity among the four forms of dialogue, this research seeks to bring the dialogue of life onto the table of interfaith dialogic discourses, as a non-doctrinal approach.

At some point in history, despite the age-old reality of mutual antagonism and isolation between Muslims and Christians, mass migration, modern technology and Western intellectual culture narrowed the geographical and relational divide. Hardly is there an Occidental world without a Muslim presence or an Oriental world devoid of a Christian presence.[27] Most of all, Western education and culture have permeated these pluralistic societies, an acknowledgment of unity in diversity.[28] Muslim and Christian scholars are putting more efforts into unlearning and sharing each other's religious traditions from less apologetic perspectives, through a more dialogic approach.

In view of the emerging dialogic option, George Anawati categorizes Muslim-Christian relation into three periods. The first period, from Islamic inception to the twelfth century, which he calls the "age of ignorance," explains the moment of Western blindness to Islam.[29] According to Anawati, the distorted perceptions at this period could be reviewed

27. Shehu, *Nostra Aetate*, xi.
28. Watt, *Muslim-Christian Encounters*, 130.
29. Anawati, "Assessment," 52.

as being controlled by "invincible ignorance." The second period, from
the twelfth century to the fall of Constantinople in 1453, was marked by
antagonistic relation between religions and scholarship development.[30]
This period witnessed Peter the Venerable's supervision on the translation of the Qur'an into Latin, which encouraged the earliest major study
of Islam.[31] Using this translation in his later writings, Peter argued that
Islam rose as a Christian heresy that required refutation.[32] Although Islamic literature of the thirteenth century facilitated the introduction of
Aristotle to the European university curriculum,[33] and simultaneously
impacted Aquinas's synthesis,[34] still, some other historic events gradually impacted Muslim-Christian relation negatively. These include: "the
Mongol conquest of Baghdad (1258), the Fall of Acre in Palestine to the
Muslims (1291), the Crusades (eleventh to thirteenth century), and the
final fall of Constantinople in 1453 to the Ottomans."[35] In retrospect,
Peter's apologetic contributions echoed the eighth-century John Damascene's scholarship on the Arabic Qur'an and theology.

For Anawati, the official Christian perception of Islam at this second
period reflected a mixture of rivalry and serious threats, virtually targeted
on both the existence and teachings of Christianity.[36] D'Costa traces the
difference between the distorted perception of Islam at this period and its
Vatican II revision to what he terms as "invincible ignorance."[37] For him,
"invincible ignorance" implies that Muslims are heretics of Christianity
unknowingly, which suggests the pastoral attitudinal shift at Vatican II.

The third period, through Nicholas of Cusa's irenic *De Pace Fidei*
(On the Peace of Faith, 1453) and his later tougher *Cribratio Alcorani* (A
Scrutiny of the Qur'an, 1460) ushered the base argument for the possibility
of Muslim-Christian peaceful coexistence. Scholars like Anawati studied
Cusanus, while Massignon developed Cusanus's arguments by claiming
that Islam can trace legitimate ancestry to Abraham through Ishmael.[38]

30. D'Costa, *Vatican II*, 161.

31. D'Costa, *Vatican II*, 161

32. Constable, *Letters of Peter*, letter 3.

33. Menocal, *Arabic Role*, 1–7.

34. D'Costa, *Vatican II*, 162.

35. D'Costa, *Vatican II*, 162

36. Anawati, "Assessment," 53.

37. D'Costa, *Vatican II*, 163.

38. Massignon, *Testimonies and Reflections*, 3–20.

Anawati strongly contests that the new vision of Islam at Vatican II, precisely *NA*, was anticipated by Massignon's later experiences and scholarship. Even though the claim on Massignon as precursor to Vatican II's shift from negative theology has attracted several studies, D'Costa considers it as an overstatement.[39] His reasons include the downplaying of other sources like the work of Miguel Asin Palacios (d. 1944)[40] and the fact that Vatican II did not endorse Massignon's Islamic position, which would have introduced a third covenant through Ishmael after the Old Covenant with Israel and the final New Testament in Christ.[41]

D'Costa, moreover, regretted that the roles of the Eastern fathers at Vatican II were not fully represented in Anawati's presentation. D'Costa recalls the significance of the minority status of these fathers in regard to their exemplary resilience geared towards peaceful coexistence in a dominate Islamic structure.[42] Some writers who agree that the literature from such Christian minority cannot but carefully avoid apologetic language somewhat support D'Costa's argument.[43]

Anawati's systematic periodization, though instructive, does not exhaustively account for Muslim-Christian dialogic embrace in history. His periodization seems not to account for the positive interactions among Jews, Christians, and Muslims in Iberia, particularly from 711 to 1492, prior to the expulsion of Muslims and Jews from unified Spain under Isabela and Ferdinand. Again, Muslim-Christian relations in the kingdom of Abyssinia beginning from the start of Islam questions the claim made by Anawati as universal, unless it could be limited to Western societies. Therefore, this research searches beyond his periodization.

Some bold steps from Muslim scholars were taken with at least two earliest contributions. As early as the mid nineteenth century, Sir Sayyid Ahmad Khan (1817–1898) began a commentary on the Bible, but was unable to go beyond "the first eleven chapters of Genesis and the first five chapters of Matthew."[44] Similarly, a twentieth-century Egyptian writer, M. Kamel Hussein (1901–1977), in his novel *Qarya Zalima* (City of God), avoided talking about the crucifixion of Jesus, but instead engaged

39. D'Costa, *Vatican II*, 165.

40. Palacios, *On Muslim Influences.*

41. D'Costa, *Vatican II*, 165.

42. D'Costa, *Vatican II*, 162.

43. Griffith, *Arabic Christianity*, 99–142. See Caspar, *Historical Introduction*, 24–32.

44. Troll, "Christian-Muslim Relations," 126.

the events before and after it. By this tact, he evaded asserting or denying Christ's immolation on the cross, considered absurd in Islamic tradition. However, his other works suggest that he disagrees with the doctrine of biblical corruption, and so is open to interfaith dialogue.[45]

Still on the Muslim side, interfaith support received some of its greatest contributions from the blind Lebanese Muslim Mahmoud Ayoub (b. 1935).[46] As noted earlier in chapter 1,[47] his academic background and Shi'ite persuasion influenced his pluralistic tendency. The titles of his two works, *Redemptive Suffering in Islam* and *Toward an Islamic Christology* (1975),[48] demonstrate the depth of Ayoub's commitment to Christian-Muslim relations. In particular, he exposed the rich images of Christ in (Shi'ite) Islamic piety by drawing on the Muslim spiritual tradition.

Even though Ayoub's understanding of Christ is distinct from standard Christian Christology, he acknowledges Christ as the Word of God and God's "spirit," which, he reminds his readers, are Qur'anic terms.[49] Further, he concludes that the Qur'an does not dismiss the death of Christ. Rather, Christ's death was a judgment not against a particular people, but against all of humanity. Ayoub concludes that humanity in its foolishness thought it could destroy the divine Word, Jesus Christ, the Messenger of God.[50]

Similarly, Prince Ghazi bin Muhammad of Jordan initiated the 2007 document *A Common Word between Us and You*,[51] which was an Islamic response to Pope Benedict's 2006 Regensburg Address. The document remains a monumental invitation for dialogue to Christians. This official dialogic document "has become the world's leading interfaith dialogue initiative between Christians and Muslims specifically, and has achieved historically unprecedented global acceptance and 'traction' as an interfaith theological document."[52]

---

45. Watt, *Muslim-Christian Encounters*, 126.

46. Watt, *Muslim-Christian Encounters*, 127. For some of Ayoub's works on the subject, see: *Redemptive Suffering in Islam* and *The Qur'an and Its Interpreters*. Also, his two-volume publications: Dirasat fi al-'Alaqat al-Masihiyyah al-Islamiyyah in *Arabic Studies in Christian-Muslim Relations* (2000), and *Islam: Faith and History* (2004).

47. See footnote 131.

48. Watt, *Muslim-Christian Encounters*, 127.

49. Ayoub, "Towards an Islamic Christology," 163. See Qur'an 4:171; 3:39, 45.

50. Ayoub, "Towards an Islamic Christology," 116.

51. See, https://www.acommonword.com.

52. *Common Word*, v.

Despite the initial Muslim shock and unhappy reception of Pope Benedict XVI's Regensburg Address (September 12, 2006), *A Common Word*, which was signed by 138 Muslim scholars and religious leaders, is still in effect. Many more Muslim scholars and leaders have signed the document since then. Some scholars attribute this increased Muslim interest in dialogue to Benedict XVI's speech in Turkey two months later on November 28, which reinstated a common Abrahamic faith origin between Christians and Muslims. Indeed, the Turkey speech was a soothing balm on the outcry of Muslims following Pope Benedict's earlier Regensburg non-inclusive remarks. In addition, King Abdullah of Saudi Arabia became a principal promoter of dialogue. After his meeting at the Vatican with Pope Benedict XVI in November 2007, he launched a world conference on dialogue with all the religions of the world in Spain.[53]

From the Christian perspective, it is important to recall the prompt and classic response of Pope Paul VI to the then ongoing conversations at Vatican II (1962–65), which later promoted openness for recognizing the truth and holiness in non-Christian religions. His contribution was two-fold. In 1964, the very first year of his pontificate, he wrote the encyclical *Ecclesiam Suam*[54] and also established the Secretariat for Non-Christians, which was eventually changed by Pope John Paul II to the Pontifical Council for Interreligious Dialogue (hereafter PCID) on June 28, 1988. *Ecclesiam Suam* was significant because of the central place it gave to the word "dialogue."[55] The word "dialogue" was used 68 times in the document. In addition, Pope Paul VI created the Commission for the Religious Relations with Muslims[56] to facilitate healthier encounters. As noted by the Vatican, "Pope Paul VI is remembered for his contacts with Muslims not only at a personal level, but also in the diplomatic domain."[57]

In the spirit of Paul VI, PCID at inception was duly assigned triple goals. First was the task of promoting and critically unlearning the biases toward non-Christian religions. Second, the council was to promote the riches of dialogue within the Christian faith community, especially in

---

53. The Land of the Golden Age of Inter-Religious Dialogue (Convivencia), July 16–18, 2008.

54. *Ecclesiam Suam* marks a quick intervention between the second and third sessions of Vatican II, with an aim of supporting a new perspective in the Church for a dialogical engagement of the modern world, especially non-Christian religions.

55. Paul VI, *Ecclesiam Suam*, ##81–82.

56. Michel and Fitzgerald, *Recognize the Spiritual*, 48.

57. Michel, and Fitzgerald, *Recognize the Spiritual*, 10.

interacting with other faith adherents. Lastly, the council had to initiate dialogic interactions with non-Christians.[58] These three tasks were gradually and objectively engaged under the following leaderships: Cardinal Paolo Marella (1965–1973), with emphasis on the first goal; Cardinal Sergio Pignedoli ((1973–1980) engaged the third task through several interpersonal encounters; Archbishop Jean Jadot (1980–984) emphasized the second task, with a predilection for Muslims; Cardinal Francis Arinze (1984–2007) through theological engagements prioritized Christian-Muslim relations at the local and universal levels.[59] Finally, Cardinal Jean-Louis Tauran (2007 to 2018) strengthened and developed the interfaith foundations laid by his predecessors. With his recent assumption of office, Cardinal Miguel Angel Ayuso Guixot (2019 to date) is sustaining the ongoing openness to non-Christians.

More than two decades after its establishment, the PCID followed up its initial document, *Dialogue and Mission* (hereafter *DM*) in 1984, and released another document, *Dialogue and Proclamation* (hereafter *DP*), in 1991. This later document reiterates four different forms of interreligious dialogue, first mentioned in the 1984 document of the PCID.[60] *DM* clearly affirms the distinction as well as the connection among the four forms of dialogue.[61] In its revised version, *DP* confirms the four forms of dialogue, without giving priority to any of them.[62] Rather, *DP* highlights their close affinity. The four forms include: "1) The dialogue of life, where people strive to live in an open and neighborly spirit; sharing their joys and sorrows, their human problems and preoccupations. 2) The dialogue of action, in which Christians and others collaborate for the integral development and liberation of people. 3) The dialogue of theological exchange, where specialists seek to deepen their understanding of their respective religious heritages and to appreciate each other's spiritual values. 4) The dialogue of religious experience, where persons, rooted in their own religious traditions, share their spiritual riches, for instance, with regard to prayer and contemplation, faith and ways of searching for God or the absolute."[63]

---

58. Michel, and Fitzgerald, *Recognize the Spiritual*, 48–49.

59. Michel, and Fitzgerald, *Recognize the Spiritual*, 49–51.

60. PCID, *DM*, ##28–35.

61. PCID, *DM*, #28.

62. *NA*, #42, in Flannery, ed., *Vatican Council II*.

63. PCID, *DM*, ##28–35. See PCID, *DP*, #42.

Despite the PCID's instructions mentioned above, rarely have the four forms of dialogue been treated holistically. One particular form of dialogue, the dialogue of life, has suffered significant neglect in the academy. But as this research seeks to demonstrate, the dialogue of life could be that missing arm that would strengthen ongoing Muslim-Christian relations. Its untapped resources from the day-to-day experiences of ordinary religious adherents have value to contribute toward the current dialogic discourses in the three other forms.

Above all, *DP* at once strongly accentuates the indispensability of dialogue as a complement to proclamation (of the uniqueness and salvific centrality of Christ) in evangelization, but also exhorts the practice of a peaceable mutual critique between Christianity and other religions.[64] Many theologians have too often overlooked this "mutual critique." It is not just mutual attentive listening, but rather a readiness to be corrected by the other.

Nonetheless, the two related mandates, proclamation and dialogue, have created more unresolved tension than intended, leading to the need for very careful but flexible approaches toward people of other religions. However, even though dialogue should not be understood as synonymous with proclamation (which promotes the gospel), this does not mean that it pitches the former against the latter. Rather, dialogue remains open to the possibility of proclamation.[65] The gospel of Christ calls forth a change in the human heart, and a transformation of all who hear the proclamation.

Beyond common expectation, the Congregation for the Doctrine of the Faith's September 5, 2000 controversial document, *Dominus Iesus* (hereafter *DI*), signed by Cardinal Joseph Ratzinger, expresses conversion as the proper goal of interreligious dialogue. The declaration states:

> Equality, which is a presupposition of inter-religious dialogue, refers to the equal personal dignity of the parties in dialogue, not to doctrinal content, nor even less to the position of Jesus Christ—who is God himself made man—in relation to the founders of the other religions. Indeed, the Church, guided by charity and respect for freedom (cf. Second Vatican Council, Declaration *Dignitatis humanae*, 1) must be primarily committed to proclaiming to all people the truth definitively revealed by the Lord, and to announcing the necessity of conversion to Jesus

64. PCID, *DM*, #2.
65. PCID, *DP*, #77.

Christ and of adherence to the Church through Baptism and the other sacraments, in order to participate fully in communion with God, the Father, Son and Holy Spirit.[66]

In his critical assessment of *DI*, Gregory Baum, a contemporary Catholic theologian, notices the suspicious language of the document: "Interreligious dialogue fostered a relativistic attitude and undermined the Church's evangelizing mission. Religious pluralism exists only in fact, for in principle there is only one religion, Roman Catholicism."[67] This quote is a summary of section 4 by Baum, who strongly disagrees with it. However, Panikkar's teaching that genuine dialogue not only listens and observes, but it also speaks, corrects, and is corrected, and as well aims at mutual understanding,[68] contrasts the referenced sections (4 and 22) of *DI*.

A further review of *Dominus Iesus* shows two discordant positions in reaction to the unresolved question concerning conversion. Whereas some Catholics, in consonance with *DI*, insist that conversion is the ultimate end of interreligious dialogue, opposing opinions have sought support in *NA*'s appeal "to acknowledge, preserve and promote the spiritual and moral goods found among them (other religions) as well as the values of their society and culture."[69] The goal of dialogue of life resonates with this spirit of *NA*. Baum noted that these latter theologians maintain that the purpose of interreligious dialogue is to widen the truths and values shared by the religious traditions and thus enable them to work together to serve the common good of humanity.[70]

This newness of *NA*, according to Jacques Dupuis, encourages Catholics to engage other religions in fruitful dialogues.[71] Such dialogic tone is stated in the document: "Prudently and lovingly through dialogue and collaboration with the followers of other religions, and in witness of Christian faith and life acknowledge . . . the values in their society and culture."[72] Faith commitment and appreciation of what the other holds sacred summarize this section of *NA*. Therefore, in addition to being

---

66. Ratzinger, *Dominus Iesus*, #22.

67. Baum, "Interreligious Dialogue," 10.

68. Panikkar, *Intra-Religious Dialogue*, 82.

69. *NA*, #2, in Flannery, ed., *Vatican Council II*.

70. Baum, "Interreligious Dialogue," 9.

71. Dupuis, "Inter-Religious Dialogue," 240.

72. *NA*, #2, in Flannery, ed., *Vatican Council II*.

steadfast to one's faith, the religion and culture of the other have to be learned dialogically.[73] However, D'Costa in his theology of doctrinal continuity rejects Gerard O'Collins's insistence that *NA* reversed the strict exclusivist position of the church at the Council of Florence (1439–1441).[74] D'Costa, rather, explains that at Vatican II, "invincible ignorance"[75] about Christ was considered an excuse for Jews and Muslims.[76]

Nonetheless, Pope John Paul II already acknowledged the openness found in *NA*, as evidenced in one of his earlier arguments in *Redemptoris Missio* (1990). He affirms that the redemptive mission of the church is dual: the proclamation of the gospel and the engagement in interreligious dialogue.[77] He further showed that interreligious dialogue aims at the promotion of mutual understanding and social reconciliation, knowing that we live in a diversified world marked by conflicts, inequalities, and ideological contradictions.

The movement for genuine interpersonal dialogue between religious others had a late start, and it is still undergoing developments. Textual engagements, no doubt, happened as early as the eight century, with the personal efforts of John Damascene, as well as Nicolas Cusanus in the Middle Ages. Besides the contribution of John Damascene, who died before 754, the two-day dialogue between the Abbassid caliph al-Mahid and the Nestorian patriarch Timothy I (in Baghdad) in 782 was outstanding, considering its earliest timing and politeness of language. The general motivation behind both interfaith dialoguers seems to reflect the Anselmian classic theological mission of *fides querens intellectum* (faith seeking understanding). As truth seekers, al-Mahid and Timothy I eulogized each other's religious virtues, while defending their distinct faith commitments.

Concerning doctrinal issues, whereas al-Mahid desired establishing the authenticity of the prophetic mission of Mohammad and Islam in the Torah and the *Injil* (gospel), Timothy was curious that such "prophetic" claim raises huge contradiction to the Christian faith. But on moral

73. Dhavamony, "Evangelization and Dialogue," 271–72.

74. D'Costa, *Vatican II*, 154.

75. For James L. Fredericks, "Invincible ignorance" is a medieval theological principle that has come in for considerable development in the last 150 years. "Inculpably ignorant" or "ignorant through no fault of their own" might be a better translation from the original Latin. See Fredericks, Review of Gavin D'Costa, 4.

76. D'Costa, *Vatican II*, 155.

77. John Paul II, *Redemptoris Missio*, #56.

issues, the language was more amicable, as confirmed in Timothy's assertion: "As all the prophets turned men away from wickedness and sins, and
led them to integrity and virtue, so Mohammed turned the children of
his people away from wickedness and led them to integrity and virtue."[78]

Timothy I's amicable language for Islam was echoed in the letter of
Pope Gregory VII to Sultan al-Nasir of Bejaya, Algeria in 1076. At the request of al-Nasir for a presiding bishop from among the local priests, Pope
Gregory VII in a friendly letter appreciates the charitable concern of the
Muslim ruler, which he believes draws from the immense love for all exemplified in the one God that Muslims and Christians worship.[79] Similar
interfaith dialogic encounters include the peace meeting between Francis
of Assisi and Sultan al-Malik al-Kamil in 1219, at the heart of the Fifth
Crusade in Egypt. Convinced that each knew and loved God, al-Kamil
sealed their interfaith friendship[80] by giving Francis an ivory trumpet,
which is preserved in the crypt of the Basilica of St. Francis in Assisi.

Nonetheless, record has it that only on May 30, 1254, at
Karakorum,[81] did the first world interreligious conversation in modern
history take place between representatives of the East and West. The
thirteenth-century great leader of the Mongols, Genghis Khan, staged
this religious dialogue, which lasted for a whole day. There were four
conversation groups: the Latins (the Catholic Christians), the Nestorian
Christians, the Buddhists, and the Muslims. The theme of this religious
conversation focused on God's being.[82]

The next was in 1893, when the city of Chicago played host to the
World Parliament of Religions. Participants were said to have expressed
themselves in a free and open manner, thus reflecting what qualifies as dialogue in some quarters.[83] However, it was difficult to ascertain whether
conversion was totally abrogated during the parliamentary gathering. In
its strictest sense, the template of dialogue at that earliest stage of development was technically characterized more by "monologic" interactions

---

78. Browne, "Patriarch Timothy," 43. See Dr. Mingana's English translation of the
Arabic version, in Mingana, Woodbrooke Studies, 15.

79. Michel and Fitzgerald, Recognize the Spiritual, 4.

80. Michel and Fitzgerald, Recognize the Spiritual, 4.

81. Karakorum was the Mongol empire capital (unification of groups of nomadic
peoples around Central Asia in the Mongol homeland) under the leadership of Emperor Khan about 1206.

82. Shehu, Nostra Aetate, 172–200.

83. Hedges, Controversies, 59.

than by genuine interreligious dialogue as is known and practiced today. "Ecumenism," because of scarce interfaith representation, better qualifies what happened at the Chicago summit.

Another official dialogue occurred in April 1978 at the University of al-Azhar in Cairo, between Vatican representatives and Islamic scholars. Two years earlier, in February 1976, William Montgomery Watt, as observer, witnessed Colonel Qadhafi's Seminar of Islamo-Christian Dialogue at Tripoli. According to him, this convention involved fifteen Muslims and (Vatican) Christians before five hundred observers. Watt, however, noted: "Informal meetings . . . have probably achieved more than these official occasions."[84] The relevance of informal interactions between Muslim and Christians resonates with the spontaneity of the dialogue of life being advanced in this research. Their study and documentations will definitely augment the official meetings.

Meanwhile, theologically and spiritually enriching proceedings from Muslim-Christian dialogic seminars have been annually published since 1975 by *Pontificio Istituto di Studi Islamici Arabia* in Rome.[85] In addition to the elimination of any polemical and apologetic language in this publication, it is interesting to read from some of the Muslim contributors, who are very critical of radical Islamists.[86]

Apart from these epochal religious convocations, nothing similar was heard among the leaders of Christianity until about the close of the twentieth century, when a more refined form of dialogue emerged in the Christian world. Christian openness to other religions was prompted by the ecumenical spirit of the World Council of Churches (WCC)[87] on the Protestant and Orthodox side and by Vatican II on the Catholic side.[88]

In the local context, similar dialogic efforts are noticed. In response to some of the identified religious and political crises in Nigeria, collaborative leadership efforts among Muslims and Christians in establishing peaceful coexistence through dialogue have been commendable. With the establishment of Catholic Bishops Conference of Nigeria (CBCN) and its administrative arm, the Catholic Secretariat of Nigeria (CSN), in 1956, the Department of Mission of the CSN has not rested in engaging

84. Watt, *Muslim-Christian Encounters*, 130.

85. Watt, *Muslim-Christian Encounters*, 126.

86. Watt, *Muslim-Christian Encounters*, 126

87. The World Council of Churches was inaugurated in 1948.

88. Hedges, *Controversies*, 59.

its ecumenical and interfaith objectives. Twenty years later (1976), the Christian Association of Nigeria (CAN) was founded as a uniting body for all Christians. Both CSN and CAN are promoters of dialogic approaches with Muslims. The dialogic efforts of Christians were formally augmented in 1973, with the inauguration of the Nigerian Supreme Council for Islamic Affairs (NSCIA), which aims at consolidating all Muslims politically and religiously. NSCIA has the *Jamalat-ul-Nasril Islam* (JNI) and the Council of the Ulema as its arms for education, mission, and advisory roles.[89]

Several meetings and seminars have been organized between CAN and NSCIA for the fostering of dialogic purposes. Such meetings include Abuja (2002) for Jos crisis, Kano and Kaduna (2005) on sharia debate, and in Kano (2010) a gathering of Muslim-Christian youths and religious for deliberations on peaceful coexistence.[90]

The Nigerian Interreligious Council (NIREC), created in September 1999, stands as a vivid fruit of Muslim-Christian joint efforts in promoting dialogue and mutual understanding. Together with NIREC, another Christian-Muslim interfaith coalition called InterFaith Mediation Centre (IFMC), founded by pastor James Wuye and Imam Muhammad Ashafa in Kaduna, is known for organizing workshops, lectures, seminars, meetings, and trainings.[91] They as well coordinate effective ways and means toward the fostering of interreligious dialogue.[92] Through these various forms of openness to the religious other, interreligious discussions have gradually developed toward assuming a truly interreligious dialogue. However, in order not to be too presumptuous, there is need to briefly distinguish between dialogue and dialectics.

Scholars like Raimon Panikkar have expressed serious thoughtfulness about the need for clarity between dialogue and dialectics. Dialectics can easily be misconceived as dialogue because both involve two or more different voices in a particular conversation. The end or goal, Panikkar instructs, distinguishes one from the other.[93] Whereas dialectics engages ideas in a winner-loser debate, dialogue per se involves growth of the

89. Ayegboyin, "Religious Association," 103–6.

90. Salihu, *Interreligious Dialogue*, 2005.

91. Ashafa and Wuye, *Pastor and the Imam*.

92. Okpanachi, "Building Peace."

93. Panikkar, *Intra-Religious Dialogue*, 23–40. See Panikkar, *Myth, Faith and Hermeneutics*, 232–56.

whole human person, including her emotions and biases.[94] And because human persons, and not just theories and ideas, are involved in inter-religious dialogue, Panikkar insists that mutual growth must characterize every dialogic interaction.[95] The possibility of growth, however, lies in the ability of those in dialogue to appreciate otherness and learn from it, through the use of appropriate lenses in perceiving the other. A genuine dialogue therefore "demands a radical openness, thinking through our tradition in recognition of its permeable barriers in relation to the religious other."[96] Every genuine dialogue aims at unlearning or learning something different from the other, as well as getting to know the other[97] as belonging to one whole human family.[98] Muslims and Christians might not yet be there; still, the option of adopting an effective approach can be a bold step in the right direction.

Interreligious activity in this regard is still in development, working out more profound methodological approaches. With the noted clarification between dialectics and dialogue, the four forms of dialogue enumerated by the PCID will be explored in details. The PCID invites and exhorts Christians to implement renewed active participation and collaboration between religions.

The Vatican Intervention

The four forms of dialogue proposed by the PCID more than two decades ago seem not to have been thoroughly implemented. One major reason for such lack of progress can be deduced from the obvious neglect of instruction in the document on the interdependence of the various forms of dialogue. *DP*, while asserting non-priority among the four forms of dialogue in *DM*,[99] highlights the universality of the call for dialogue, and reiterates the interconnectivity of the four forms.[100] The model of the polyhedron as a way of thinking about unity inspired by Peter Casarella's

94. Panikkar, *Intra-Religious Dialogue*, 30.

95. Panikkar, *Intra-Religious Dialogue*, 91.

96. Hedges, *Controversies*, 88.

97. Shehu, *Nostra Aetate*, 172–200.

98. Sintang, "Dialogue of Life," 69.

99. PCID, *DM*, #17.

100. PCID, *DP*, #43.

presentation at the Rome conference[101] suggests a possibility of Pope Francis's emphasis on a theology of the people reclaiming the importance of witnessing, but also involving a new configuration of the relationship between these four forms of dialogue. Today's interreligious dialogue is still to accomplish the urgent call for attention to particularity as well as interconnectivity of the four dialogic forms.

In the course of this research, it was discovered that while different degrees of attention have been given to these forms of dialogue, the one that has suffered a considerable neglect is dialogue of life. In general, as will be shown, there are available examples of three forms of dialogue between Christians and non-Christian religions. However, between Muslims and Christians only a tangential touch can be noticed.

Dialogue of Theological Discourse

The dialogue of theological discourse, as evidenced in chapter 4 (through theories of exclusivism, inclusivism, pluralism, as well as particularism), even though the most difficult form,[102] has received the greatest scholarship attention. Its difficulty lies in the perceived fear of compromising faith while engaging on doctrinal differences. The fact remains that Islam and Christianity use the same terms, like "prophesy" and "revelation," differently, but despite their conflicting understandings and relative expressions, the underlying reality in focus seems non-contradictory.[103] Nonetheless, the PCID in collaboration with an organ of Muslim leaders and scholars have organized seminars on major themes: Holiness in Islam and Christianity (Rome, 1985), Rights of the Child in a World of War (Amman, 1990), Mission and Da'wah (Rome, 1990), Women in Society (Rome, 1992), and Religion and Nationalism (Amman, 1994).[104] Similarly, the World Council of Churches greatly distinguished itself in promoting Muslim-Christian dialogic relationship. Such meetings include

101. Prof. Peter Casarella spoke on "Wholes and Parts: Ecumenism and Interreligious Encounters in the Pope Francis's Teologia del Pueblo." In his presentation, Prof. Casarella analyzed the unique ecumenical and interreligious insights of Pope Francis, which are shaped around the principle that one can work towards unity by celebrating difference. He noted that Pope Francis envisions dialogue as a "polyhedron" and not simply as a set of concentric circles by which certain groups are privileged.

102. Michel and Fitzgerald, *Recognize the Spiritual*, 69.

103. Michel and Fitzgerald, *Recognize the Spiritual*, 69.

104. Michel and Fitzgerald, *Recognize the Spiritual*, 71–76.

those held in: "Ajaltoun (1970) and Broumana (1972) in Lebanon; Accra (1974); Hong Kong (1975); Chambesy (1976), Beirut (1980); Colombo (1982); Benin (1986); Indonesia (1986), Switzerland (1992 & 1993)."[105]

As also demonstrated in chapter 4, despite the huge progress achieved, none of these theoretical approaches, due to doctrinal impasse, suffices for a healthy Muslim-Christian relation. Therefore, such doctrinal conversations are progressively ongoing. In furtherance to the successes achieved through the dialogue of theoretical discourse, this section seeks to engage a dialogue of religious experience and a dialogue of action, in view of demonstrating the complementary relevance of dialogue of life for Muslim-Christian relation. In essence, dialogue of life is being developed as a way-paver for fuller complementarity among the four dialogic forms.

Dialogue of Religious Experience

The dialogue of religious experience, practiced by monastics, has gradually gained acceptability. Rather than Muslim-Christian spiritual exchange, its focus has been between Catholic monastics and Buddhist or Hindu monastics. Up until the first half of the twentieth century, Pierre-Francois de Bethune notices that monastic authorities frowned at the idea of conceiving of similarities between Catholic and Buddhists spiritualties. Such expression, he regretted, was regarded as "apostasy," whereas blindness to its reality was considered "a monastic virtue."[106] However, the zeal for practicing the gospel inspired the lead role initiated by profound monastic spirituality in the Catholic tradition. De Bethune confirms that it was a rediscovery of the centrality of hospitality in the Bible,[107] which was grossly neglected in the church,[108] that set the basis for new visions and approaches in interspiritual exchanges.[109]

The proposal for better ways to coordinate the establishment of newer monasticism in Africa and Asia at the Benedictine abbey in 1959, by abbots Cornelius Tholens and Theodore Ghesquiere, was well received. This desire to establish monasticism in "mission lands," first conceived

---

105. Michel and Fitzgerald, *Recognize the Spiritual*, 78–79.

106. See Bethune, "Monastic Interreligious Dialogue," 35.

107. Bethune, "Interreligious Dialogue," 8.

108. Bethune, "Interreligious Dialogue," 1.

109. Bethune, "Monastic Interreligious Dialogue," 34.

among Benedictine monks, yielded fruit in 1961 when the Secretariat to Aid the Implementation of Monasticism (AIM) was founded among Benedictine and Cistercian monks. The purpose was to search for values in non-Christian monastic traditions that might enrich the spiritual life of Christians. Africa and Asia lands were the primary targets.

With the empowerment of *NA* in 1965, the openness to learn from Hindu and Buddhist monks and nuns was strengthened. The first Pan-Asiatic Intermonastic Congress took place in Bangkok in 1968, with impressive Buddhist monks in attendance. Two factors were noticed: 1) from a positive perspective, there was recognition of the Christian minority status in Asia, which necessitates dialogue; and 2) the accidental death of Father Thomas Merton drew more attention to his personal efforts toward balancing faith commitment and openness to other faiths. The Second pan-Asiatic Congress, held in Bangalore in 1973, deliberated on the theme "the experience of God in different religions."[110] Selected religious personalities, like "Hugo Enomiya-Lasselle, S.J, Vincent Shigeto Oshida, O.P, Edmond Verdiere, M. E. P, and Raimon Panikkar,"[111] were challenged to engage the theme from different perspectives. However, at his parting speech, Abbot Primate Rembert Weakland[112] regretted the lower attendance of monks at this congress.

In 1974, Cardinal Sergio Pignedoli, second president of the Secretariat for Non-Christians (later renamed PCID), commissioned abbot Primate Weakland to organize an intermonastic dialogue. Pignedoli noted that "monks represent a point of contact and mutual comprehension between Christians and Non-Christians."[113] With permission from Vatican, Pignedoli extended intermonastic consciousness to the West.

When the monastic dialogic attention focused on Europe and America, two important meetings were held in 1977,[114] which brought together monks and nuns eager to embrace intermonastic dialogue with other religious spiritualties. As a follow-up, two commissions were set up in 1978: 1) the North America Board for East-West Dialogue (NA-BEWD), and 2) the commission for Dialogue Interreligiuex Monastique

110. Bethune, "Monastic Interreligious Dialogue," 35.

111. Bethune, "Monastic Interreligious Dialogue," 35–36.

112. Weakland was an ardent proponent of monastic renewal, together with Abbot Cornelius Tholens and Father Jean Leclercq.

113. Pignedoli, "Lettre a l'Abbe Primat," 7.

114. At Petersham, Massachusetts, and Loppem, Belgium.

(DIM) for Europe.[115] Initially, the monastic pioneers relied on their faith commitment and awaited Vatican's approval. Eventually, the sincerity of their search for the truth among non-Christian spiritualties later impacted those at the seat of governance in the Vatican. In 1984, the PCID confirmed intermonastic dialogue in her publication *DM*. A section of *DM* states:

> At a deeper level, persons rooted in their own religious tradition can share their experiences of prayer, contemplation, faith and duty, as well as their expressions and ways of searching for the Absolute. This type of dialogue can be a mutual enrichment and fruitful cooperation for promoting and preserving the highest values and spiritual ideals of man.[116]

Prior to the developmental consciousness of intermonastic relations, Charles de Foucauld (1859–1916) was considered the precursor of Christian-Muslim intermonastic dialogue. About the same time (the early twentieth century), B. Upadhyay was pioneering Catholic monastic approaches to Hinduism in India. De Foucauld was born and raised a Catholic in Strasbourg. He lost his Christian faith in adolescence, having lived a pleasure-driven life. Even, as a French military officer serving in Morocco, his carnal life continued.

Surprisingly, the quietude of the North African desert captivated his inner life. His resignation from the army engendered a rediscovery of his Catholic faith through the outstanding hospitality he experienced living among the Tuaregs of Algeria. With the spiritual direction of Abbe Huvelin back in France, he returned to belief in God (as a monk) upon witnessing the vibrant faith and prayer praxis of Muslims in North Africa.[117] De Foucauld desired witnessing to the "hidden life of Jesus" among the Muslims of Tuaregs through committed practices of prayer, hospitality, and friendship.[118] On January 23, 1897, de Foucauld left the Trappist monastery in Morocco and joined the Poor Clares as their servant in Nazareth (1897–1900). Afterwards, he went to live in Beni Abbes (1901–1904), where he enjoyed the hospitality of the native Muslims. When he was seriously ill, his Muslim hosts nursed him back to health. The transformative attitude of de Foucauld toward the Muslims in North

---

115. Bethune, "Monastic Interreligious Dialogue," 36.

116. PCID, *DM* 138.

117. Zoe, "Muslim's View," 297.

118. Michel, and Fitzgerald, *Recognize the Spiritual*, 5.

Africa was informed by the hospitality he enjoyed. Through the living examples of his Muslim hosts, he learned to respect the profound value of their religion, and to appreciate its providential role in God's plan.

Previously, while appreciating the religiosity of the Muslims, de Foucauld thought that their salvation was still to be effected through the salvific mission of the church. However, having been nursed back to health by the poor and devout Muslims who fed him goat milk and cared for him, he came to realize that it was better not to evangelize the Muslims. In his words, "To preach Jesus to the Tuaregs is not, I believe, something that Jesus wishes, neither from me nor from anybody. It would be the way of retarding, not advancing, their conversion. The need is to get to know them, with great prudence and gentleness."[119] Consequently, he was further attracted by the desert lives of the Tuaregs in Algeria, from 1904 to 1916, with the intention of practicing the gospel[120] through the simple expression of hospitality.[121]

According to de Foucauld, a true Christian disciple must radiate Jesus.[122] His life based on "universal brotherhood" endeared him to many, especially the Amenukal Moussa ag Amastane, the head of the Tuareges. When de Foucauld was assassinated in Tuaregs in 1916 by a bandit at the age of fifty-eight,[123] the Amenukal wrote these words to his sister: "Charles the marabout [Islamic term for holy man] has died not only for you, he has died for us too. May God have mercy on him, and may we meet him in Paradise." De Foucauld's life and death impacted several people, both Muslims and Christians. Hersov Zoe, an Arabic translator, remarked: "Charles de Foucauld's valiant attempt to 'cry the Gospel' with his life left a profound mark on Christian spirituality."[124] As a precursor of practical interreligious dialogue, de Foucauld dedicated his entire life to dilating the difficult boundary of the church with the North African Muslims.[125] Indeed, de Foucauld's lived example sheds light to modern Christians' attitude toward Islam and Muslims.

---

119. O'Mahony and Bowe, *Catholics in Interreligious*, 47–70.

120. Patey, "Sanctity and Mission," 365.

121. Bethune, "Monastic Interreligious Dialogue," 37.

122. Foucauld, *Letters from the Desert*, 178.

123. Patey, "Sanctity and Mission," 366.

124. Zoe, "Muslim's View," 300.

125. Patey, "Sanctity and Mission," 365.

By the middle of the twentieth century, de Foucald's interest in living the gospel through simple hospitality with the Muslims, rather than through theoretical engagement, impacted hundreds of Christians. Praxis characterizes the early Catholic pioneers of interreligious dialogue with several daring approaches, especially in the pre- and post-Vatican II eras. Prominent among them are Western Catholics such as: Louis Massignon (1883–1962), Thomas Merton, OCSO (1915–1968), Henri Le Saux, OSB (Swami, Abhishiktananda) (1910–973), Bede Griffiths, OSB (1906–1993), Christian de Cherge, OSCO (1937–1996), Dr. Raimon Panikkar (1918–2010), and Aloysuis Pieris, SJ (1934–). Some of the most popular non-Christians involved in dialogue with Christians include Swami Vivekananda Bengali (1863–1902), D. T. Suzuki (1870–966), the Dalai Lama (1935–), Thich Nhat Hanh (1926–), and the Tea Master Nojiri Michiko.[126]

Much later, following the inaugural meeting of NABEWD in January 1978, the publishing of the *West-East Inter-Monastic Bulletin* began, with Pascaline Coff, OSB, as its first editor. And in January 2011 the Commission for Dialogue Interreligiuex Monastique launched *Dilatato Corde*, its online, multilingual journal, which provides personal testimonies and reflections on monastic interreligious dialogue, scholarly articles, and other helpful materials.

The attendance of Muslims in addition to Hindus and Buddhists at the third Pan-Asiatic Congress, held in Kandy, Sri Lanka in 1980, recorded another milestone achievement of intermonastic dialogue.[127] For the first time, Muslims were in attendance. Immediately after the congress, a meeting of Asian-born participants including Hindus, Buddhists, Muslims, and Christians was held. This was intended towards enriching dialogue with Asian cultural and religious values.[128] Intermonastic spiritual exchange will be futile if each religious group does not experience the reason(s) for the monastic convictions of the religious other. Mutual hospitality greatly provides that opportunity. The speech of John Paul II when visited by forty Japanese monks and their European Christian hosts at Rome,[129] after their third spiritual exchange in 1987, appreciated the hospitality fruits at this level of dialogic engagement. The pope said:

126. Bethune, "Monastic Interreligious Dialogue," 37.

127. Bethune, "Monastic Interreligious Dialogue," 38.

128. Bethune, "Monastic Interreligious Dialogue," 38

129. Both monks gathered for a symposium at Sant Anselmo, the center of Benedictine monasticism.

Your specific contribution to these initiatives consist not only in maintaining an explicit dialogue, but also in promoting a deep spiritual encounter, for your life is above all one devoted to silence, prayer and witness of community life. There is much you can do through hospitality. In opening your houses and your hearts as you have done these days, you follow well the tradition of your spiritual father, Saint Benedict. To your brother monks coming from across the world and from a very different religious tradition, you apply the beautiful chapter of the Rule concerning reception of guests. In doing so you offer a setting wherein a meeting of mind and heart can take place, a meeting characterized by shared sense of brotherhood in the one human family that opens the way of ever deeper spiritual dialogue.[130]

John Paul II's support for intermonastic interactions resonates with his inspiration for convoking a multireligious prayer[131] in 1986 at Assisi. According to D'Costa, hot theological debates in the church followed what happened at Assisi in the bid to ascertain whether it was a multireligious or an interreligious prayer, and the sustainability of either of them.[132] The question is, at Assisi: "did people come to pray together" (interreligious dialogue prayer) or did "they come together to pray"[133] (multireligious prayer)? The difference centers on the presence or absence of "co-intentionality" at prayer.[134] However, an outright response is: can't it be both?

However, de Bethune, as a consultant to the Secretariat for Non-Christians (renamed PCID), recounts a post-(Assisi) prayer remark from a Zoroastrian delegate, Homi Dhalla: "I will no longer be able to pray as I used to; from now on, I will always pray in communion with all who pray."[135] This testimony at the end of the Assisi peace prayer expresses the profound growth that accompanies genuine interreligious dialogue at any level.

---

130. PCID, "Discourse of the Pope," 5–6.

131. See D'Costa, "Interreligious Prayer between Roman Catholic Christians and Muslims," in Moyaert and Geldhof, *Ritual Participation*, 97. See John Paul II, Christmas address to the Roman Curia."

132. See Gavin D'Costa, "Interreligious Prayer between Roman Catholic Christians and Muslims," in Moyaert and Geldhof, *Ritual Participation*, 97–99.

133. Catholic Bishops' Conference, *Meeting God*, 59.

134. See D'Costa, "Interreligious Prayer between Roman Catholic Christians and Muslims," in Moyaert and Geldhof, *Ritual Participation*, 96.

135. Bethune, "Monastic Interreligious Dialogue," 39.

Nevertheless, in 1989 the Congregation for the Doctrine of the Faith (hereafter CDF) published "A Letter to the Bishops of the Catholic Church on some Aspects of Christian Meditation,"[136] drawing their attention to the possible dangers involved in Eastern forms of meditation. Authorized by the PCID (which was not consulted by the CDF) to respond to the letter, de Bethune pointed out a caveat: "any attempt to deal with matters pertaining to another religion that is not carried out in a spirit of dialogue ends up by doing more harm than good."[137] In light of his response, Arinze, the PCID's fourth president, mandated the secretariat of Aid the Implementation of Monasticism to further deliberate on the issue of meditation. The outcome of the brainstorming from monks and nuns, themed "Contemplation and Interreligious Dialogue: References and Perspectives Drawn from Experiences of Monastics," with its central recommendation for prudence and boldness, was approved and published by the PCID.

In accord with de Bethune's defense, Abbot Christian de Chergé (1937–1996)[138] was invited in 1995 to Spain by the secretariat of Aid the Implementation of Monasticism. There de Chergé introduced his practice of communion in prayer. The steps include: 1) In silence, the monks sat in a circle, with Christians and Muslims intermixed. 2) The *Dhikr* (the repetition of Muslim names for God) was done in common; however, the spontaneous invocation on God's names drew on both Islam and Christianity. 3) Six months afterwards, they reconvened and shared the fruits of their meditation and prayer, but also listened to sacred texts and exhortations. The shared prayers constitute a reminder that Muslims and Christians are believers in God. Nonetheless, Thomas Merton's correspondence with Abdul Aziz in Merton's (posthumous) *The Hidden Ground of Love* is often seen to be groundbreaking with regard to a Muslim-Christian sharing of experience and the practice of prayer.

Hitherto, Catholic intermonastic dialogue was limited to Asian Hinduism and Buddhism, until the testimony of de Chergé involved

136. Congregation for the Doctrine of Faith, "Letter to the Bishops."

137. Bethune, "Monastic Interreligious Dialogue," 40.

138. Christian de Chergé (1937–1996) was a French abbot to six other Cistercian monks at the Abbey of Our Lady of Atlas in Tibhirine, Algeria, whose hospitality (food, medical care, interfaith prayers) to the predominant Muslims and few Christian locals was remarkable. Their services to these locals attracted suspicion from the dictatorial leadership. In that crisis-ridden Algeria, through Chergé's conviction, the monks rejected the offer to flee for their own lives. Rather, they stayed with the vulnerable locals and died as martyrs in the hands of Islamists.

Muslims as part of the circle that prays.[139] De Bethune recounts the cyclic prayer setting of Catholic, Hindu, and Buddhist monastics, metaphorically articulated as a well in the desert with several paths converging at its profound depth and infinite broadness. His analysis of the well identifies its significant features of maintaining unity but also allowing the freedom for separateness.[140] In other words, interreligious dialogue does not aim at diffusing difference or even hybridization; rather, it seeks a "fruitful juxtaposition."[141]

With the discussed background commitment among the pioneer monks, and later hierarchical support, intermonastic dialogic exchange progressively became a movement.[142] Monks of different religious persuasions developed the contemporary interfaith encounter, weathering through the risk of sharing (internal and external) sacred places.[143] Catholic monastics in East and West as well as Asian and non-Asian Buddhist monastics have opened avenues for sharing grounds and religious experiences. Through hospitality and contemplative silence, both kinds of monastics have enriched their particular religious experiences, and have subsequently created enough room to accommodate the otherness of the other.

Men and women of silence ably commune across religious borders. A few days before his untimely death, Merton's talk about (intermonastic) communion in Calcutta summarized intermonastic praxis. He said, "The deepest level of communication is not communication, but communion. It is wordless. It is beyond words, and it is beyond speeches, and it is beyond concepts. Not that we discover a new unity. My brothers, we are already one. But we imagine that we are not. And what we have to recover is our original unity. What we have to be is what we are."[144] In accord, John Paul II beautifully extols this special form of dialogue, saying, "The important contribution of inter-monastic dialogue is channeled . . . to the service of all humanity and to the only God."[145] Consequently, the participants at this level of dialogue never saw any incompatibility

---

139. Bethune, "Monastic Interreligious Dialogue," 41.

140. Bethune, « Interreligious Dialogue, » 18.

141. Bethune, « Interreligious Dialogue, » 19.

142. Bethune, "Interreligious Dialogue," 41.

143. Standaert, *Sharing Sacred Space*, viii.

144. Merton, *Asian Journal*, 308.

145 Quoted in *Bulletin of the Secretariat for Non-Christian Religious* 19.2 (1984), 124.

between their monastic vocation and the vocation of true interreligious dialogue.[146] Thus, de Bethune concludes, "In dialogue, the treasure that we have to share is not a wealth that is given once and for all; it is a questioning, a poverty shared."[147]

Similarly, the Chinese saying "if you want to polish a piece of jade to make it even more beautiful, do so with another piece of jade coming from another mountain" underscores the fact that one's faith commitment can be enriched when juxtaposed with that of the other. The richness, however, might greatly be determined by the disposition of the person who encounters religious otherness.[148] In other words, what might be lacking in the Muslim-Christian antagonizing relation is not necessarily additional doctrines. Rather, it might be a shift of religious attitude in respect to that which the other essentially values.

The noted breakthrough in intermonastic spiritual exchanges notwithstanding, de Bethune reminds us that the dialogue of religious experience is ordinarily a path passable for a handful of experts.[149] What then accounts for the rest of religious people—the billions of Muslims and Christians? Despite the few significant attempts referenced—de Chergé led monks at Tibhirine, Merton's correspondence with Abdul Aziz, Massignon's *Badalyia* in Cairo, and John Paul II's initiated multireligious prayer at Assisi—Muslim-Christian dialogue, in particular, is still to witness profound dialogic activity. Nonetheless, this research argues that ordinary Muslims and Christians have a dialogic responsibility, especially in the praxis of dialogue of life.

Dialogue of Action

In the meantime, dialogue of action, as distinguished by the PCID, has fairly demonstrated in concrete terms the possibility of Muslim-Christian collaboration. Even though dialogue of action shares a thin boundary with dialogue of life, for which reason they are easily interchanged, this essay intends to maintain the distinction that *DP* draws between them, in order to appreciate their complementarity. Distinction and

---

146. Bethune, "Monks in Dialogue," 129.
147. Bethune, "Monks in Dialogue," 136.
148. Sintang, "Dialogue of Life," 86.
149. Bethune, "Interreligious Dialogue," 18.

complementarity reflect a coexistence of otherness and communion at the center of the argument of this research.

Dialogue of action primarily expresses the responsive collaborations among multireligious people living together when challenged by common goals for the sustenance and restoration of peace and harmony.[150] It might be affirmed that dialogue of action is often engendered by imminent life threats caused by sociopolitical and religiously incited crises and struggles. In other words, while dialogue of action can be described as that rapid interreligious collaborative response to critical moments,[151] dialogue of life happens within normal everyday living conditions. Again, dialogue of action most often centers on charismatic religious leaders, who act as the greatest risk-bearers in such critical moments, whereas ordinary religious people play the central role in dialogue of life.

The ongoing crises in the Central African Republic (hereafter CAR) provide a clearer picture of how dialogue of action has happened between Muslims and Christians through the instrumentality of charismatic religious leaders. Although there are individuals whose ingenious interventions united people of different faiths in pursuance of peace, CAR is chosen because of its defined collaborative activities between two different religious authorities.

The article in the New York Times "Archbishop and Imam Are United Across Battle Lines in Central African Republic" made headline news on December 23, 2013. At the center of the story, reported by Carlotta Gall, was a Catholic archbishop, Dieudonné Nzapalainga,[152] from Bangui, who opened the doors of his church to hundreds of fleeing Christians threatened by Islamic militia. In addition to the Christian refugees, he accommodated the most senior Muslim cleric, Imam Oumar Kobin Layama, whose life was also threatened by Christians seeking vengeance.

The same story was captured in the headline of BBC News Africa "CAR's Archbishop and Imam in Peace Drive."[153] Tim Whewell of the BBC joined them on one of their trips to promote peace. Ever since the Imam has sought protection at the house of the archbishop, the two

150. PCID, DM 31.

151. Michel, and Fiztgerald, Recognize the Spiritual, 68.

152. Archbishop D. Nzapalainga was among the seventeen new cardinals named by Pope Francis on Sunday, October 9, 2016. The reason for his selection, even though unsaid, is doubtfully unconnected to his active involvement in dialogue of action in CAR.

153. "CAR's Archbishop and Imam in Peace Drive."

religious leaders have travelled together, even to some Western cities, creating awareness of the ongoing mutual political pogrom between the *Seleka* movement (Islamic) and the Militia (mostly Christians in defense of the besieged locals) that the world seems to ignore.

The situation could be described as a balance of fear. Members of each religious tradition felt threatened by the other. Recounting the vulnerability of both the Muslim and Christian populace, Archbishop Nzapalainga described the situation as follows: "The people are between the hammer and anvil." For months afterward, according to Gall, the two religious leaders, along with the leading Protestant cleric, Franco Mbaye Bondoi, engaged in a dialogue of action, travelling across Congo and disseminating the reconciliatory message "We are brothers."

Crux, a Vatican newspaper, under the theme "Now a cardinal, this African prelate was already a 'saint,'" articulates the outstanding humanitarian efforts of these clerics: "Nzapalainga has become one of the 'three saints of Bangui,' together with Rev. Nicolas Guerekoyame-Gbangou, president of the country's Evangelical Alliance, and Imam Oumar Kobine Layama, president of the Islamic Council."[154] These three spiritual founders of Peace Platform, aimed at restoring unity and peace among Muslims and Christians, received the 2015 Sergio Vieira de Mello Prize (named after the UN diplomat killed alongside colleagues in a 2003 bombing in Bagdad).[155]

From an *Index Mundi* source, religions in CAR show a population of 50 percent Christian, 15 percent Muslim, and 35 percent indigenous belief, who had lived as neighbors until politicians injected divisive rhetoric among the youths.[156] And having identified a conflict of political interests and power at the root of the killings, Christian and Muslim leaders rejected the religious coloring of the crises and took repeated turns across the villages of the country in search of reconciliation. That the crises persisted and even escalated proved that their many travels could only yield modest results. But as a result of their efforts, in Bangassou, the archbishop's hometown east of the capital, Muslims and Christians still live together in peaceful coexistence. Nevertheless, the weight of unsatisfactory results seen in each of the three dialogic approaches demonstrates the inadequacy in methodology, such as the concentration of activities

154. San-Martín, "Now a Cardinal."

155. Allen, "France Eschews."

156. Minority Rights Group International, *World Directory—Central African Republic*, at https://www.refworld.org/docid/4954ce4723.html.

among the religious leaders, but without a solid connection to the majority (adherents) at the base level.

Overall, and as PCID predicted, the goal of dialogue will be far-fetched unless the four forms collaborate. The document clearly provided a blueprint laying out the interconnectivity of the four dialogic forms: "Contacts in daily life and common commitment to action will normally open the door for cooperation in promoting human and spiritual values; they may also eventually lead to the dialogue of religious experience in response to the great questions which the circumstances of life do not fail to arouse in the minds of people."[157] "Exchanges at the level of religious experience can give more life to theological discussions."[158] This research totally agrees with the PCID instruction on interconnectivity among the four forms of dialogue. Therefore, in exploring the channel of dialogue of life, it therefore seeks to enrich existing dialogic fruits.

Dialogue of Life

In corroboration with the success achieved in dialogue of action and the ongoing dialogue of theological discourse, as well as the huge progress recorded among interfaith monastics in establishing genuine neighborly relationship, the present study therefore proposes an inclusive turn for holistic interactions with the religious other. It is an attempt to study, but also to challenge, the practical lives of all believers, especially common people. The shift aims at awakening the hospitality responsibility known to the Islamic and Christian traditions, but fairly practiced in the people's daily responses to religious otherness. In this way, the thesis of this research seeks to engage and articulate a kind of practical theology of religious adherents, based on their lived experience and praxis.

The choice of the dialogue of life through hospitality in this research strongly supports the vital recommendations of the PCID. The longstanding oversight or omission of the dialogue of life is evidenced in the lack of literature about it. Bringing the dialogue of life into the larger conversation therefore satisfies the need for interconnectivity among the four dialogic forms. It as well guarantees the basic complementarity of professional dialogic contributions to the everyday dialogue among ordinary religious people.

157. PCID, *DP*, #43. See *NA*, #2, in Flannery, ed., *Vatican Council II*.
158. PCID, *DP*, #43.

In essence, the Vatican document *DM* affirms that, "dialogue (of life) is a manner of acting, an attitude and a spirit which guides one's conduct. It implies concern, respect, and hospitality towards the other. It leaves room for the other person's identity, his modes of expression, and his values."[159] By extension, the dialogue of life "is a dialogical relation to promote amicable relation with people from different religions. It begins when one encounters, lives and interacts with the others and participates in daily life activities together."[160]

The *New World Encyclopedia*[161] recognizes dialogue of life as the third trend of interreligious dialogue for the new millennium.[162] An example of the first trend, known as "institutionalization of interreligious dialogue," is the Inter Faith Network of major world religions, which was established in United Kingdom in 1987. The best example of the second trend, called "the academic institutions," was that founded at Harvard University in 1991,[163] with an aim of monitoring demographic exigencies of religious pluralism. Diana Eck, in her six types of dialogue—parliamentary, institutional, theological, spiritual, inner dialogue—also includes "dialogue in a community" or dialogue of life.[164] While acknowledging these two other sources that recognize the dialogue of life, the focus of this research will be on the PCID categorization, as mentioned earlier. Most importantly, all three sources acknowledge the distinctiveness of dialogue of life.

The dialogue of life focuses on the informal practices of ordinary people across religious differences. Pope John Paul II articulates its baseline relevance when he teaches that "the dialogue between ordinary believers, harmonious and constructive sharing in the situations of daily contacts is truly a basic form of dialogue, and the one which lays the foundation for more specialized encounters."[165] The goal of this study seeks to implement John Paul II's dialogic vision.

In confirmation of such vision, Francis Cardinal Arinze of Nigeria, the fourth president of the PCID, explained that dialogue of life happens

---

159. PCID, *DM*, #29.

160. Sintang, "Dialogue of Life," 69.

161. http://www.newworldencyclopedia.org/entry/Inter-religious_Dialogue.

162. Sintang, "Dialogue of Life," 71.

163. http://www.newworldencyclopedia.org/entry/Inter-religious_Dialogue.

164. Eck, "What Do We Mean?" 5–11.

165. John Paul II, "Address to Participants," #1.

among ordinary people who see themselves first as good neighbors before they consider their religious differences. As he argues, even though such people do not discuss religious doctrines, they allow the many ways they apply religion in their own lives to speak to the religious other(s).[166] Leading by example, John Paul II, during his long pontificate (1978–2005), displayed the ability to cement interreligious relationships with gestures and personal contacts, without restricting himself to a discussion of doctrines,[167] thereby confirming that the dialogue of life intrinsically "implies concern, respect and hospitality toward one another."[168]

Within scholarly circles, authorities like Leonard Swidler strongly assert that dialogue of life at its most basic level sustains friendship, especially during crisis at the official or political level.[169] Confirming the importance of the dialogue of life, Hasan Askari, an Indian-British Shi'ite Muslim, sees no meaning in human existence, except as inter-existence, in which "Each man becomes a neighbor."[170]

Mahmoud Ayoub explains similar interfaith collaboration as "the dialogue of concerned neighbors with their adjacent churches, and mosques, who work together . . . on issues of social justice, pollution problems, and teenage children in mixed public schools with their problems of sex and drugs and a host of other issues."[171] Even though Ayoub identifies four types of dialogue—dialogue of life, dialogue of beliefs (theological doctrines and philosophical ideas), dialogue of witnessing to one's faith, and dialogue of faith[172]—he barely distinguishes dialogue of life from dialogue of action, as seen in Arinze's classification. In other words, dialogue of life and dialogue of action for Arinze function together as one (dialogue of life) in Ayoub. However, both scholars agree on the fundamental essence of a dialogue of life, especially as it happens most frequently between the greatest numbers of religious adherents. Above all, the enormous human and material resources put at risk on this base level in every single event of religious crisis between Muslims and Christians validate a clarion call for a dialogue of life. The problem, as argued

166. Sintang, "Dialogue of Life," 71.

167. Swidler, "History," 18.

168. Sintang, "Dialogue of Life," 71.

169. Madigan, "Christian-Muslim Dialogue," 252.

170. Askari, "Dialogical Relationship," 481.

171. Orman, *Muslim View*, 68.

172. Orman, *Muslim View*, 67–68.

in this study, centers on using distorted lenses when perceiving the other. Mutual biases as evidenced throughout historical Muslim-Christian interactions have yielded terrible results.

Ayoub identifies the consequences in using such distorted lenses: "The main obstacle to true Christian-Muslim dialogue on both sides is, I believe, their unwillingness to truly admit that God's love and providence extend equally to all human beings, regardless of religious identity."[173] His standpoint both demonstrates an articulation of (one's) faith and recognition of the value of the other. Elsewhere, Ayoub cautions that both religious traditions "should not remake the other in their own image, as a precondition for acceptance. Rather they should listen and learn before they venture into the sacred precincts of each other's faith."[174]

For a sustainable interreligious praxis between Islam and Christianity, especially at the ordinary level, the dialogue of life is strongly argued as a viable starting point. Retrieving and encouraging the tradition of hospitality among adherents of religion through the dialogue of life can be preparatory for the intended transformation. Accordingly, Muslims and Christians might perhaps achieve interfaith transformation by incorporating the latent dialogue of life into ongoing theological discourses.

In Africa, Ghanaian Muslims and Christians, according to Mustpha Abdul-Hamid, have embraced the dialogue of life as a better option for undergirding peace and harmony. Abdul-Hamid unmistakably praises the outcome of neighborly interactivities between Muslims and Christians in his context of study. In comparison, he claims that the dialogue of theological discourse among Ghanaians has yielded insufficient fruits.[175] Abdul-Hamid therefore likens interfaith conferences to what Ali Mazrui calls "a dialogue of the deaf."[176]

Obviously, Abdul-Hamid's conclusion differs from the thesis of this research. Unlike his exclusive option for dialogue of life, this research argues for interconnectivity across the four forms of dialogue, as instructed by the PCID.[177] Such inherent openness acknowledges that people who engage in dialogue of life may find particular concerns that lead them

173. Orman, *Muslim View*, 69.

174. Orman, *Muslim View*, 67.

175. Abdul-Hamid, "Christian-Muslim," 25.

176. Abdul-Hamid, "Christian-Muslim," 23.

177. PCID, *DP*, #43.

into dialogue of action or even dialogue of theological exchange to better understand the religious belief of the other.

Furthermore, Standaert Benoit makes a caveat that: "Any encounter with the great religions of the world is bound to fail if its starting point is dogma as formulated and transmitted in a given culture, or if it is based on some historical expressions, which are also culturally conditioned."[178] Benoit's assertion, rather than disparage any aspect of dialogue, endorses their connectivity, but also suggest that dialoguers should begin from sharing common grounds, and then move toward engaging obvious doctrinal differences.

In this regard, interreligious hospitality known and encouraged among Muslims and Christians could be a start point, but not an end point. Such ethical practice can ensure that trust and neighborliness happens in the local contexts where religious peoples interact daily. This practical but preparatory ground for overall dialogue defines what dialogue of life stands for. In support, Abdul-Hamid, says: "The theory of the dialogue of life states that life itself offers opportunities for people of different faiths, ethnicities and backgrounds to interact as they go about their daily activities."[179] At the end, the everydayness of interactions among religious people aid in building up trust and offers better appreciation of each other. In confirmation, Abdul-Hamid concludes that interreligious "interaction builds camaraderie and understanding. It is this understanding on a personal everyday level that will ensure the peace between people of different faiths rather than yearly conferences."[180]

The dialogue of life, though spontaneous, is identifiable. For example, every day millions of Nigerian Muslims and Christians interact either as neighbors, commuters, office staffs, and worshippers or at schools, markets, and hospitals. Such interreligious socialization happens more in urban cities than in the rural areas, where the ethnic divide keeps majority of people within their own native homes.

Home in traditional Africa is generally linked to a people's ancestral origin. Despite the multireligious and multicultural sense in contemporary Africa, the traditional mentality has not entirely ceased impacting sociopolitical arrangements. In contrasts to the Western perception, the ancestral bond of unity has been impacting homogeneity, even in regard

178. Benoit, *Sharing Sacred Space*, xiii

179. Abdul-Hamid, "Christian-Muslim," 25.

180. Abdul-Hamid, "Christian-Muslim," 26.

to religious affiliation. As a result, religious diversities are uncommon in rural settings, except through the settlement of strangers who come with alternate religions. Because rural dwelling often lacks basic infrastructures for job and business opportunities that should attract the settlement of strangers and their foreign religions, homogeneity often characterizes its population. However, the Yoruba context in Nigeria will be explored in chapter 9 as an exception. Its unique context might also lend strong basis to establish the Abrahamic pilgrim metaphor, which is aimed at interrogating the ancestral ethnic home imagination.

Whether at the rural or urban setting, some degree of mutual cordiality does exist between Muslim-Christian religious peoples and their host cultures in Africa. The dualism of secular and sacred domains is difficult to comprehend for traditional Africans on account of their notorious religiosity,[181] which entails that "all things would have fallen to pieces if God did not exist."[182] Indeed, African Traditional Religion can best be described as life. This is because it perceives the entirety of life as religious.

As host, African Traditional Religion's inclusive character has variously been interpreted among scholars. On the one hand, some anthropologists, like Robin Horton (1975), with his intellectualistic theory of "explain, predict and control," interprets African religion's adaptability as an internal weakness when confronted by a macrocosmic religion.[183] On the other hand, some Africanists, like Andrew Walls, Ogbu Kalu, Kwame Bediako, and Lamin Sanneh, have demonstrated African Traditional Religion's internal strength and resilience toward Islam and Christianity.[184] Although this acknowledgement appears new, its reality has been deeply buried in the mental construct of Africans. To date, at the crossroads of life-threatening instances, African Traditional Religion beliefs resurface as the preferential option because of its holistic flexible approach.[185]

The inclusive characteristic of African Traditional Religion was very visible during the advent of the two major world religions, Islam and Christianity, in Africa. Even though scholars rarely talk about it, African Traditional Religion, no doubt played the good host to both foreign religions. Scholars like Albert J. Raboteau and Melville Herskovits have

181. Mbiti, *African Religions*, 1.

182. Idowu, *African Traditional Religions*, 104.

183. Meyer, "Christianity in Africa, 458.

184. Sanneh, *West African Christianity*, 213.

185. Bureau, "Sorcellerie et Prophetisme."

argued in defense of the African Traditional Religion's adaptive character. Herskovits insists that: "Adaptability, based upon respect for spiritual power wherever it originated, accounted for the openness of African religions to syncretism with other religious traditions and for the continuity of a distinctively African religious consciousness."[186] The African continent welcomed Islam and Christianity in such a manner that both foreign religions flourished together on competitive basis. However, the African traits penetrated and shaped each of them differently. In West Africa, about the eighteenth century, it was confirmed that: "Elements of Islam were often mixed with or adapted to forms of traditional African belief."[187] Similarly, the developmental stages of Christianity in Africa show a clearer picture of a struggle toward African Christianity.

Looking broadly at the relevance, the dialogue of life at the ordinary level is not only open to all; it also assures a recognition of the otherness of the other, in such a manner that differential energies can be utilized in achieving mutual hospitality. The Vatican document *DM* approved universality and altruistic responsibility as features of a dialogue of life when it instructs:

> Every follower of Christ, by reason of his human and Christian vocation, is called to live dialogue in his daily life, whether he finds himself in a majority situation or in that of a minority. He ought to bring the spirit of the Gospel into any environment in which he lives and works, that of family, social, educational, artistic, economic, or political life.[188]

Arinze, the fourth president for the PCID, clarified that this baseline dialogue does not necessarily involve any doctrinal discourse. Rather, it offers equal opportunities for religious people to exemplify the basic doctrines of love of God and neighbor.[189] Above all, a Vatican document on Muslim-Christian dialogue clearly states: "The main form of dialogue, the basis for all others and that to which other dialogue activities should be oriented, is what many, including Pope John Paul II, have called 'the dialogue of life.'"[190] Also in *Redemptoris Missio*, Pope John Paul II categorically

---

186. Herskovits, *Myth*.

187. Raboteau, *Slave Religion*, 5.

188. PCID, *DM*, #30.

189. The speech conveyed by Cardinal Arinze at the ASEAN conference on Christian- Muslim relation in Pattaya, Thailand in 1996; see Pratt, "Vatican," 258.

190. Michel, and Fitzgerald, *Recognize the Spiritual*, 68.

explains dialogue of life as that special form of dialogue by which "believers in different religions bear witness before each other in daily life to their own human and spiritual values, and help each other to live according to those values in order to build a more just and fraternal society."[191]

Another relevance of the dialogue of life centers on its emphasis on daily practical demonstrations of one's faith and belief systems, on the one hand, and on the other hand, it creates a humble openness to appreciating the values of the other by learning from the other. Competing with one another in good works harmonizes with the altruistic hospitality model of Levinas. In this Muslim-Christian context of study, followers of both religions can be that vulnerable other, depending on the religious affiliation of the altruist. Moreover, when these prospective altruists assume the utmost responsibility for the other, a healthy competition is established. If the other, according to Levinas, constantly reminds the self of the responsibility owed her, the egocentrism that had marked previous Muslim-Christian relations can be contrasted with a religious desire for interreligious hospitality. This approach can necessitate a focal shift by toning down exclusive claims having to do with doctrinal superiority, through interreligious altruistic works, thereby concretizing the love of God and love of humanity.

The interfaith leadership example of a Jordanian-born Archbishop Ghaleb Moussa Abdalla Bader, of Algiers, testifies to the efficacy of a dialogue of life between Muslims and Christians. As an expert in relations with Islam, he served as an adviser to the PCID from 1996 to 2001.[192] Drawing on his rich Muslim-Christian collaborative experiences,[193] Bader confirms: "Daily dialogue (of life) helps to dispel prejudices and false conceptions and leads to mutual trust and knowledge."[194] What Bader affirms in Algeria is very relevant and could apply in the Nigerian context (with its own particularities), via hospitality, as the need to genuinely engage the religious other increases. The next chapter offers an opportunity for testing the veracity of Bader's thesis. It will explore the necessary intersection between missionizing and dialogue of life. Rather than wrongly perceived as an obstacle, dialogue of life is presented as a faith-witnessing mandate.

191. John Paul II, *Redemptoris Missio*, #57.

192. *Documentation Information Catholiques Internationales*, 2012.

193. Refers to his encounters in a religiously volatile (French) Algeria.

194. Maskulak, "Mission," 436.

6

Dialogue of Life as Faith Witnessing

DIALOGUE AND MISSION CONSTITUTE vital approaches toward the goal of interreligious engagements. Mission in this regard could be synonymous with proclamation or evangelization, which gets moderated by dialogue. Such collaborative roles received strong mandate in the Vatican document *DP* and Pope John Paul II's *Redemptoris Missio*. Ever since, however, the two arms have been ongoing with recorded successes, depending on the compatibility of the basic religious orientations of the dialoguers.

In context, Islam and Christianity are two highly proselytizing religions, whose recent turn toward interfaith dialogue is still evolving, and so evokes cautionary steps. Enthused by their respective proselytizing spirits, the issue of conversion between Muslims and Christians cannot be taken for granted. No matter how subtle it could be suppressed, conversion would seem impossible to be entirely eliminated in Christian-Muslim missionizing. Each religion prides itself on what it has and rejects whatever contradicts it. The religious other, rather than being spoon-fed, enjoys the dialogic meal best when the delicacy of each religious tradition is communally shared. Asymmetric-mutual substitutive hospitality, as would be argued, offers that option.

A cursory hindsight on these two religious giants, evidenced in the first three chapters, reveals mutual mistrust and antagonism. Mutual mistrust operates as a result of blindness due to ignorance of each other's religion.[1] More so, putting into consideration the grave danger of slipping off the attained dialogic height, this research advocates for a

---

1. Adedegba, *Role of Jesus*, 137.

particular mission approach that would assure healthy relation. It is a practical witnessing better described as a *"preparatio evangelica."* Pope Paul VI admonishes that "Modern man listens more willingly to witnesses than teachers, and if he does listen to teachers, it is because they are witnesses."[2]

Hospitality as a form of witnessing accompanies evangelization by paving the way and sustaining what is shared. It is a practical gospel, and basically dialogic. This mission model aims at restructuring the existing antagonistic platform by establishing mutual trust and respect between Muslims and Christians.

Dialogic hospitality supports and paves way for evangelization as evidenced in the biblical paradigm. On this standpoint, Jean Marc Ela questions mission without witnessing among African Christians thus: "how can we escape from 'theo-logy' that forces our faith and the church to play conservative roles, wherein preachers, catechists, spiritual advisers and pastors impose on God a repressive function incompatible with Jesus' evangelical plan?"[3] Ela's concern on modern African mission includes the neglect of the christological hospitable approaches.

Christ's evangelical mandate in Luke 9:1–6 includes hospitality, where he says, "take nothing for your journey, no staff, nor bag, nor money—not even an extra tunic" (9:3). Andrew E. Arterbury interprets Christ's choice terms such as "enter, welcome, stay" as clear indicators for the "the custom of hospitality."[4] This passage can be understood in a guest-host dynamic.

The authority and power Christ gave his twelve apostles over sickness, demons, and for the proclamation of the kingdom constitute one part of the mission. As guests, the apostles' authority was purposeful for rendering spiritual and material services to their arbitrary hosts, perhaps as gifts. In return, the other part of the mission also mandated the apostles to travel light and be solely dependent on the hospitality of their hosts.[5] In essence, this mission mandate not only demands offering hospitality but also requires asking for and accepting hospitality.

2. See Paul VI, "Address to the Members of the Consilium de Laicis (2 October 1974)," in Paul VI, *Evangelii Nuntiandi,* #41.

3. Ela, *Repenser la théologie africaine,* 33.

4. Arterbury, *Entertaining Angels,* 140.

5. Siddiqui, *Hospitality and Islam,* 47.

Asking humbles. Although "everything" according to St. Francis of Assisi, "is provided by Divine Providence,"[6] they are to be asked for from their earthly stewards. R. Alan Culpepper interprets this verse on traveling light (Luke 9:3–5) as an indication of the apostles' "complete dependence on God's provision for their needs."[7] Nonetheless, God is known to act through human instruments. Summarily, Mikeal C. Parsons confirms, "Luke understands that God will provide through the hospitality of those to whom the apostles proclaim the kingdom of God."[8] Therefore, Christ instructed a mission that incorporates hospitality, in which both guests and hosts would first establish a cordial relationship.

Logically, the apostles were to hold back proclamation unless they were first welcomed—"any house they do not welcome you, dust off your feet as a testimony against such people" (Luke 9:6). Bartolomé de las Casas affirms in these words: "Christ gave his apostles permission and power to preach the gospel to those willing to hear it, and that only! Not power to punish the unwilling by force, pressure, or harshness. He granted no power to apostle or preacher of the faith to force the unwilling to listen, no power to punish even those who drove the apostles out of town."[9] In accord, this research therefore is only calling attention to that biblical mission approach that has a collaborative mandate between proclamation and hospitality, through the witnessing of faith among Christians and Muslims.

The first missionary report of the apostles was not pleasing to the master, Jesus. The content of their missionary account was partial. It exposed their lone source of joy, which drew from the fact that "even the devil submits to us" (Luke 10:17). If the authority to heal and to cast out demons was imparted to them before sending them out, should they, rather than God, be praised for being only instruments of God's power?

Jesus did not waste time in giving them an idiomatic correction. He said, "rejoice however that your names are written in heaven" (Luke 10:20). And how would their names be written in heaven, if not through hospitality? Recall that in Matthew 25 Jesus established hospitality as an eschatological gauge for heaven—I was hungry, thirsty, homeless, naked,

---

6. Moorman, *Richest of Poor Men*, 90.

7. Culpepper, "Luke," 194.

8. Parsons, *Luke*, 146.

9. Las Casas, *Only Way*, 77.

sick and you came to my rescue—because whenever and wherever hospitality is shown to the other, that other represents Jesus.

The apostles' insufficient report omitted the hospitality dimension of their mission. They might have considered their received hospitality as their right; after all, they came as teachers of the kingdom. As a result, "a laborer deserves his wages." However, their inattention or neglect of hospitality in their success story caused Jesus to reiterate the importance of hospitality for Christian evangelization.

Shortly after, an opportunity emerged. Jesus' apostles might have felt that the crowd aborted Jesus' invitation for them to rest in a lonely place by arriving at the place (via road) before them, while they traveled through the sea. Ministering to the crowd till evening, Jesus offered the apostles another opportunity to practice and learn hospitality when he said, "give them something to eat" (Luke 9:13). This would have been a way of appreciating the hospitality they received from the people. On the contrary, their expression showed inhospitality.

Why not? Why should they be friendly to this inconsiderate crowd, who ruined their time of intimacy with the master? Nonetheless, their excuses to evade hospitality were countered by Jesus. And from their insignificant food reserve, Jesus taught them that the joy of hospitality does not lie in the plenty, but rather in the satisfaction that comes from sharing.[10] The Markan episode (7:14–23) in which Jesus heals Peter's mother-in-law of fever and immediately she reciprocated his kindness with hospitality also forestalls the inseparability of Christian mission and dialogue of life.

Evangelization and dialogue of life via hospitality facilitate mission to fruition. They do not conflict. Rather, they are complementary. Drawing on the teaching of PCID that dialogic practices can happen without explicit engagement of doctrinal discourses, this research therefore seeks to explore a theology of witnessing to one's faith as part of mission. This aspect of mission emphasizes good works towards the religious other as means of evangelization. For Gustavo Gutierrez, it is "Christians' orthopraxis, as we now express it, (which) gives substance to the orthodoxy of their proclamation and wins that proclamation a hearing."[11] In other words, Gutierrez insists on Christ's mission model by drawing attention to the inseparability between verbal and concrete witnessing of the

10. Shepherd, *Gift*, 242–43.

11. Gutierrez, *Las Casas*, 161.

gospel.[12] In accord, Las Casas concludes, "Christ taught, Christ set the way, the form for preaching the gospel: deeds first, words later."[13] Since both religious traditions own similar mandates for altruistic deeds, witnessing through hospitality being developed can achieve two things.

First, it can pave the initial way for the establishment of trust while creating the openness for mutual growth in appreciation of each other. Second, it might discourage conversion as part of dialogue, but cannot oppose or deny it. Mission, in this regard, should not be a process of lobbying or baiting the other for conversion. Rather, a genuine conversion should happen in the heart, when the "aha moment" is attained through practical witnessing. True conversion, as it is, must not necessarily be the immediate goal of dialogue. Rather, it belongs to its lasting fruit. Only after the aha moment can switching of religions be ripe. From such perceptivity, dialogue of life via hospitality offers the opportunity for establishing witnessing of the faith as an urgent mission for Muslims and Christians.

For the fact that dialogue often involves verbal exchanges, which might lack existential engagement, de Bethune succinctly concludes, "dialogue (theological discourse) is necessary but not sufficient for mutual understanding between religions."[14] Here, de Bethune refers to the theoretical aspect of dialogue in order to highlight the complementary importance of its concrete dimension. He stresses that hospitality must transcend communication and be headed toward communion:

> Hospitality involves permitting another to enter one's house, or oneself entering the house of another. Communication is then made through gestures that are less explicit than words but also less ambiguous. To give lodging to a stranger, to offer him food and drink—these are gestures, which speak plainly of one's respect for him. Hospitality, then, belongs to the domain of ethos; it is an existential experience, which goes beyond logos.[15]

De Bethune was able to prove that the intermonastic dialogue between Christian and Buddhist monastics happens in silence but still exemplifies dialogue. Intermonastic spiritual exchange is basically dialogue in its concretized form. Similarly, dialogue of life belongs to this practical category and hospitality is its language of communication.

12. Gutierrez, *Las Casas,* 160.
13. Las Casas, *Only Way,* 90.
14. Bethune, "Interreligious Dialogue," 1.
15. Bethune, "Interreligious Dialogue," 6.

In accord, de Bethune's assertion traces a complementary relationship between dialogue and hospitality when he argues that the latter offers a model for much deeper understanding of the other, in regards to concrete demand on trust, welcome, and actual experiences of the otherness of the other.[16] In other words, what dialogue or hospitality could not achieve independently is possible in their collaboration because "dialogue and hospitality are mutually dependent."[17]

Islam and Christianity highly promote hospitality, even though they do so from different perspectives. But since the spontaneity inherently involved in the dialogue of life can be conventionally contaminated[18] with cultural biases and pride, hospitality is the key that provides a level ground for healthy competition. The ordinariness of the dialogue of life through a known hospitality tool undergirds the aim of sustaining unity amidst otherness, because hospitality is first and foremost an ethical practice that involves the inviolable respect of the other. Respecting otherness enriches mutual edification.

In agreement with the instructions of de Bethune, this research continues arguing that Muslim-Christian dialogue of life via hospitality is required for peaceful and mutual enriching coexistence, especially in Nigeria. Invariably, interfaith dialogue is incomplete without hospitality because the latter "is a step that is taken in order to humanize the meeting between strangers."[19] Moreover, Massignon discovered hospitality as a path to the truth when he taught:

> Truth is a purely spiritual and dispassionate relation between understandings of two partners such that the stranger becomes the host . . . Only so far as one grants hospitality to another (rather than colonizing him), and only so far as one shares with the other the same work, the same bread, can one become aware of a unifying truth. Truth can only be found through the practice of hospitality.[20]

Furthermore, the dialogue of life "implies concern, respect and hospitality towards one another. It leaves room for the other person's identity,

---

16. Bethune, "Interreligious Dialogue," 1.

17. Bethune, "Interreligious Dialogue," 7.

18. Sintang, "Dialogue of Life," 72.

19. Bethune, "Interreligious Dialogue," 3.

20. Massignon, *Opera Minora*, 608–9.

modes of expression and values."[21] In essence, *DM* unequivocally agrees that the dialogue of life provides the locus for hospitality. According to Antonie Wessels, "Interreligious contact involves interaction between addressees and addressers, a communication dialectic whereby the partners involved both give and receive."[22]

Although, according to Cardinal Arinze, doctrinal deliberations are discouraged at the level of dialogue of life, still, religious adherents are required to demonstrate their faith by a mutual exchange of good works.[23] Two major benefits are noticed in a genuine dialogue of life: 1) There is mutual prophetic witnessing toward each other. 2) Each person involved in the dialogue enriches her faith commitment. Suraya Sintang offers support in these words: "Not only does this approach [dialogue of life] foster mutual witness, it also causes one to come to a deeper understanding of his or her own faith and religious identity."[24]

Another significance of the dialogue of life revolves around spontaneous and fresh responses. The spontaneity that marks the dialogue of life articulates daily experiences where people freely express themselves, share their joys and sorrows, and together engage their challenges. From this perspective, the other, rather than the self, sets the agenda for the dialogue, to which the latter spontaneously responds. In the same vein, Oliver Davies asserts, "the self is mediated in and through the other."[25] The dialogue of life spontaneously happens in religiously pluralistic contexts, with openness and sensitivity toward the concerns of the other, such as during the celebration of festivals as well as in interactions at workplaces and markets. Within the scope of such intersubjectivity, hospitable neighborliness gradually develops into friendship, which diminishes the distorted perception of mutual mistrust and suspicion.

Moreover, Muslims and Christians have the practice of altruism enshrined in their sacred texts. Jesus' Sermon on the Mount, which includes the injunction "Love your enemies, do good to those who hate you, bless those who curse you, pray for those who mistreat you" (Luke 6:27–28), culminates in the "fruit criterion" as gauge for genuine Christian discipleship. Precisely, Luke 6:43–44 states, "No good tree bears bad fruit, nor

21. PCID, *DM*, #29.

22. Wessels, "Some Biblical Considerations," 62.

23. The speech conveyed by Arinze at the ASEAN conference on Christian- Muslim relation in Pattaya, Thailand in 1996; in Ugwoji, "Inter Religious Relations," 39.

24 Sintang, "Dialogue of Life," 72.

25. Davies, *Theology of Compassion*, 19.

does a bad tree bear good fruit. Each tree is recognized with its own fruit. People do not pick figs from thorn-bushes, or grapes from briers." The fruit metaphor somewhat agrees with the Qur'anic summon for "striving for good deeds" (5:48). In essence, Watt argues, "one can say that a religion produces good fruit when it enables the majority of members to lead meaningful lives in a harmonious community, despite the existence of pain and suffering."[26] Watt's conclusion firmly supports the argument of this research that hospitable deeds, and not rhetorical claims only, should demonstrate what is the authentic strength/center of each religion. Watt goes further to assert a pluralistic understanding of "fruit," such that each religion would appreciate the good fruits in others, since they indicate God's active presence.[27]

Muslims and Christians are called to be hospitable to others, even to the extent of self-sacrifice. Substitutive hospitality will be developed in chapter 10. Meanwhile, Levinas's teaching on radical responsibility provides the functional tool that can awaken a dying altruistic consciousness among religious adherents. Since both Muslims and Christians need this radical awakening in order to fruitfully engage in a dialogue of life, there is need for mutuality of purpose, so long as reciprocity is neither intended nor restricted. If, ultimately, reciprocity happens, that makes no significant difference. De Bethune reminds us that even if guests might visit with gifts, receiving gifts is not the aim of hospitality.[28] Hospitality, he explains, entails a *philia*, a friendship that does not carry with it an intention to be repaid for one's generosity with some sort of secondary benefit.[29] Nevertheless, giving and receiving complete a genuine hospitality.

Against payback, the reason for the choice of Levinas, instead of Martin Buber, is also worth discussing. No doubt, Buber's famous "I-Thou" relationship makes a good dialogic discourse,[30] but the contextual Muslim-Christian relation requires a greater radical impulse, only found in Levinas's infinite responsibility.[31] Buber teaches that only in reciprocity can relationship be justly established. His intersubjective

26. Watt, *Muslim-Christian Encounter*, 138–40.

27. Watt, *Muslim-Christian Encounter*, 138–40.

28. Bethune, "Interreligious Dialogue," 1.

29. Bethune, "Interreligious Dialogue," 1.

30. Silberstein, "Buber, Martin."

31. Levinas, *Totality and Infinity*, 675–76.

argument assures a kind of radical reciprocity[32] that resists self-sacrifice.[33] In essence, Buber eliminates grounds for sacrificial hospitality,
which is fundamental for the main thesis of this research. Between Muslims and Christians, Buberian consciousness for self-gain or self-protection lacks a wedge and can rapidly cause more harm than good.

Nonetheless, Buber's idea of neighbor love[34] implies distancing.
The entire argument in the trilogy of Buber (*I and Thou*, *Between Man
and Man*, and *Knowledge of Man*) can be summarized as follows: the
other is not the self and the self is not the other. Therefore, Buber introduces the notion of distancing to preserve the otherness of the other.
In fact, Levinas's critique of him is for what Buber refers to as an "I-It"
relationship, which he acknowledges as legitimate for erotic love and
love of food and so on. He reserves "I-Thou" as the ultimate relationship
for interpersonal interactions.

To love the other "as myself" or "as yourself" is contextually problematic. Scholars like Soren Kierkegaard and Paul Ricoeur agree that
"love as yourself" asserts the legitimacy of self-love but puts legitimate
limits on sacrificial love.[35] In "as yourself" formula, it is still the self that
sets the agenda, but Buber's dialogic openness to the other moderately
liberate itself from the control of the self.[36] From a radical perspective,
Levinas rejects any form of self-control over the other. Levinas prefers
the use of "responsibility to the other" in lieu of the compromised words
"love" and "neighbor," which obstruct difference.[37] He equates the biblical command on love of neighbor with "the responsibility to the other."[38]

In addition, it is not clear why Levinas points to another weakness
in Buber's argument:

> The I-Thou formalism does not determine any concrete struc-
> ture. The I-Thou is an event (*Geschehen*), a shock, a compre-
> hension, but does not enable us to account for a life other than

32. Levinas, *Totality and Infinity*, 68.

33. Buber, *I and Thou*, 33.

34. Kaufmann, "Buber's Religious Significance," 668.

35. Kierkegaard, *Works of Love*, 266. See Ricoeur, *Oneself as Another*, 192. See
Ferreira, *Love's Grateful Striving*, 31–36; 129–36.

36. Buber, *Pointing the Way*, 238.

37. Levinas, *Ethics and Infinity*, 52.

38. Levinas, *Otherwise than Being* (1981), 47.

friendship: economy, the search for happiness, the representa-
tional relation with things.[39]

Probably, Buberian friendship as remarked by Levinas neglects other aspects of life, such as radical altruistic practice. In reality, friendship
would be a secondary phase compared to the fundamentals of interfaith
hospitality between Muslims and Christians, especially at its initial stage
of assuming a responsible turn toward each other. If hospitality is the
means to achieving interfaith healthy neighborliness, friendship might
be considered as one of its fruits.

The Greek root *philadelphia* (connoting love among relatives) fits
Buberian friendship, while *philoxenia* (implying love for strangers)
agrees more with Levinasian altruism. At the earliest stage of establishing healthy coexistence, Muslims and Christians need not be friends as
much as (good) neighbors. Should Buber's preaching on reciprocity be
applied to Christians and Muslims, it would breed payback, leading to
unimaginable indebtedness.

Similarly, Arthur Sutherland notices that reciprocity above responsibility obstructs the practice of genuine hospitality. Among contemporary Americans, Sutherland argues, "the reason we do not consider
hospitality is that we think too little of responsibility and too much of
reciprocity."[40] In other words, "Hospitality is quickly diluted by concerns
for parity and reciprocity."[41] However, between reciprocity and mutuality, intentionality marks the difference. De Bethune confirms in these
words: "Hospitality also entails a *philia*, a friendship that does not carry
with it an intention to be repaid for one's generosity with some sort of
secondary benefit. True, it sometimes is accompanied by an exchange of
gifts, but this is foreign to its fundamental nature."[42] Accordingly, mutual
disparate good deeds or "asymmetric mutuality," always without payback
anticipation, can mediate between the extremity of rejecting it (Levinas's
asymmetry) and demanding it (Buber's strict reciprocity).

The essence of mutuality is to inculcate doing good to the religious
other without an expectation of reciprocity, because Allah rewards
good deeds. Doing good to the other for the sake of God might provide
a smooth passage of interaction between Muslims and Christians. A

39. Levinas, *Totality and Infinity*, 68.

40. Sutherland, *I Was a Stranger*, xiv.

41. Sutherland, *I Was a Stranger,* xv.

42. Bethune, "Interreligious Dialogue," 14.

known proverb in Islam confirms that "the hospitable one is the beloved of God" (*al-karim habib ullah*). Moreover, hospitality, in rhetoric and in practice, is "conspicuously oriented towards issues of mutual respect."[43] Insistence on reciprocity can destroy hospitality, as Derrida has argued. Hospitality does not necessarily need reciprocity in order to be complete. It is complete (with or) without reciprocation. In other words, hospitality is completed when what is given is received.

As previously explained, asymmetric mutuality provides a level and viable ground for Muslim-Christian coexistence, because each has been both aggressor and victim, and can only achieve conciliation through collaborative efforts in good deeds. One reason for this mutual approach stems from the fact that when people conscientiously engage in outdoing the other in hospitality, as a sole responsibility because of the inviolable dignity of the other and her infinite value, the shared age-old biases can be greatly diminished.

Invariably, Levinasian altruism, which requires from Christians and Muslims the bold thrust of hospitable responsibility toward the other, would become a true test of proving the genuineness of the theology of God's love and of neighbor. Good deeds toward the other, without the intent of reciprocation, reflect a perfect means of living out one's own religious commitment as a hospitality people.

Likewise, through the face-to-face encounter of Levinas, a face of a Muslim will spontaneously provoke a Christian to sincere responsibility for the former, and the converse, since "the nakedness of the face is destituteness."[44] Levinas stresses a preconceptual encounter, which not only allows the other to (verbally) communicate himself, but also guarantees genuine altruistic acts. The responsibility for the other will then assure his transformation from a threatening suspect, or apparent enemy, to that true inviolable personality. At this transformed stage, religion might cease to divide. Rather, it would embrace its abandoned ethical responsiveness towards the other.

Competing in good works is not only familiar to Muslim and Christian traditions; it also makes possible the dialogue of life. Pratt confirms that the first priority between Muslims and Christians is the dialogue of life, through which each adherent testifies to her faith and the ideals of

43. Shryock, "Thinking About Hospitality," 406.
44. Levinas, *Totality and Infinity*, 75.

her personal God.[45] In support, Hensman notices that although people of different religions have always lived together, still, the recent globalizing pluralistic society has been identified as a huge challenge for peace and harmony.[46]

In this chapter of practical witnessing to faith, this research has demonstrated the required collaboration between the dialogue of life and hospitality in regard to Muslim-Christian renewed relation. It has as well shown the relevance of asymmetric mutuality in substitutive altruistic deeds between these two religions. Subsequent to the established relevance of faith witnessing, the question of how one can be disposed or prompted into appropriate spontaneous altruistic acts needs to be addressed.

Making Space for the Religious Other

That the dialogue of life provides the locus for interreligious hospitality needs further reiteration. The characteristic elements that motivate the dialogue of life as described include: interpersonal involvement, spontaneity, belief commitment, and responsibility toward the other. But because of the tension between informality and readiness for service (as genuine hospitality demands), which are also required for the dialogue of life, scholars have argued for "space-making" across interfaith relationships. In the exploration of space-making, further dynamics bordering the fine lines between dialogue of life and hospitality, especially within the Muslim-Christian contexts, will be highlighted, using the host-guest paradigm. Prior to demonstrating host-guest mutual enrichment, better expressed as hospitality, grounds for altruistic readiness will be established.

Raimon Panikkar's turn to the subject aligns with the Levinasian call to the self for absolute responsibility toward the other. The duty Levinas stipulates for the self corresponds to the vision Panikkar offers with regard to a possible methodology. Levinas might not have explicitly advocated a particular and necessary internal disposition before meeting the other, but his approval of spontaneity presupposes an implied readiness. This characterizes spontaneity as a human act, performed in freedom. The end point of such an internal disposition, however, ensures space-making.

45. Pratt, "Vatican in Dialogue," 245–62.
46. Hensman, "Beyond Talk," 323–37.

Making space for the other to belong happens both internally and externally. If internal space-making is the disposition, space-sharing or hospitality is the act. Internal space-making has Panikkar as its prominent initiator. Panikkar dedicated a whole book, *The Intra-Religious Dialogue*, to the insufficiency of *interreligious* dialogue and advocated for *intrareligious* dialogue to complement it.

The intrareligious dialogue of Panikkar concentrates on the internal activity of the person, which substantially engages the integral self. For Panikkar, intrareligious dialogue "is the internal dialogue triggered by the thou who is not in-different to the I."[47] The movement inherently involved can be dangerously slippery. Intra-activity might either lead, in a positive sense, to purifying individualistic solitude, or it might give rise to a destructive individualistic isolation.[48] It is a personal question concerning the meaning of reality.[49] Consequently, intrareligious dialogue must maintain a priority over and above interreligious dialogue, where it rightfully belongs.

Intrareligious dialogue, in Panikkarian explanation, is an internal dialogue in which "one struggles with the angel, the *daimon*, and oneself."[50] But since not every interior activity qualifies for intrareligious dialogue, Panikkar draws a major distinction from what such dialogue is not. It is, he insists:

> Neither monologue, soliloquy, meditation on the partner's belief or religions, nor scientific research into a different worldview out of curiosity, or with a sympathetic mind. Instead, this kind of dialogue entails a profound engagement in search of salvation, and we accept being taught by others, not only by our own clan. We thus transcend the more or less unconscious attitude of private property in the religious realm.[51]

Intrareligious dialogue, as Panikkar explains, helps us to learn and discover the other. Panikkar affirms, "I am not the other, nor is the other I, but we are together because we are all sharers of the world, as the *Rig Veda* (I, 164,37) says." Although intrareligious and interreligious dialogue are complementary, the former should lead the way. Both Levinas and

47. Panikkar, *Intra-Religious Dialogue*, xvi.

48. Panikkar, *Intra-Religious Dialogue*, xvi.

49. Panikkar, *Intra-Religious Dialogue*, xvi.

50. Panikkar, *Intra-Religious Dialogue*, xvii.

51. Panikkar, *Intra-Religious Dialogue*, xvii.

Panikkar do not differ on this priority. Panikkar goes on to demonstrate his full support of this in the following remarks.

> If interreligious dialogue is to be real dialogue, an intra-religious dialogue must accompany it; that is it must begin with my questioning myself and the relativity of my beliefs (which does not mean their relativism), accepting the challenge of a change, a conversion, and the risk of upsetting my traditional patterns . . . one simply cannot enter the arena of genuine religious dialogue without such a self-critical attitude.[52]

The very necessity of such self-critique is brilliantly couched in Saint Augustine's great quote, *"Quaestio mihi factus sum"*[53] (I have made a question of myself). Through self-interrogation, the dialogue partner can be better perceived as a principal subject that demands space for establishing his or her own identity and gifts. Simply put by Levinas, "The presence of the Other is equivalent to this calling into question of my joyous possession of the world."[54] In other words, the other commands a departure from my comfort zone, in response to the need of the other.

In his attempt to emphasize the openness required for the other, Panikkar makes a sharp distinction between dialectical dialogue and dialogic dialogue. While "the dialectical dialogue is a dialogue about objects, dialogical dialogue is a dialogue among subjects, aiming at being a dialogue about subjects."[55] Dialogue between subjects resonates with Levinas's insistence on intersubjective encounter. In agreement with the dialogue of life, the concern is on persons rather than on doctrinal ideas:

> The dialogical dialogue is not so much about opinions . . . as about those who have such opinions, and eventually not about you, but about me to you. To dialogue about opinions, doctrines, views, the dialectical dialogue is indispensable. In the dialogical dialogue the partner is not an object or a subject merely putting forth some objective thoughts to be discussed, but a you, a real you and not an it. I must deal with you and not merely with your thought, and of course, vice versa. You, yourself are a source of understanding.[56]

52. Panikkar, *Intra-Religious Dialogue*, 74.

53. Augustine, *Confessions*, 10.33, 50.

54. Levinas, *Totality and Infinity*, 75–76.

55. Panikkar, *Intra-Religious Dialogue*, 29.

56. Panikkar, *Intra-Religious Dialogue*, 30.

The distinction Panikkar advances here stems from the often-misguided assumption in the academy that interreligious dialogue basically addresses religions and their belief systems, rather than the lived experiences between religious people. However, interreligious dialogue, as exemplified in the dialogue of life, enriches its goal when religious adherents deeply involve themselves in the transformation process of becoming living testimonies of what they believe.

According to the initiator, the slipperiness of intrareligious dialogue points to a twofold temptation. In both temptations, the one-centeredness subdues the beauty of otherness. First, for the powerful, "it is to build a tower of babel for the sake of unity—be it called one God, religion, or culture, or one world government, democracy, or market."[57] Second, for the powerless, "the temptation is to construct for oneself an isolated shell instead of a home open to community."[58] In both extreme situations, Panikkar regrets that the humanness is lost.[59] How then can this Panikkarian-envisioned danger be averted? Paying a humble attention to the inner self might constitute a good start, but is definitely not an end.

Silence constitutes a vital key to the success of intrareligious dialogue. It also exposes its greatest difficulty because modern society has a tendentious aversion to silence. Silence at this point needs a redefinition. Unlike in its most common forms of "silence of indifference" as well as "silence of skepticism," "there is also a silence that does not deny the word, but is aware that the silence is prior to the word and that the word simply words the silence that makes the word possible."[60] This latter kind of silence prevents passivity. It is active because it generates and shapes verbal reflection. This form of reflective silence enables the self to examine itself, discover its unnecessary obstacles, such as biases, and then strive to empty them for the sake of the other. Invariably, any space creation occurring only on the outside (without a prior internal space), in the form of hospitality, becomes more oppressing than revealing.[61] Without internal space, the other is perceived as an object of appropriation.

Panikkar totally agrees with Catherine Cornille that it is imperative not only to know one's own tradition but also to maintain a fair grasp of

---

57. Panikkar, *Intra-Religious Dialogue*, xvi.

58. Panikkar, *Intra-Religious Dialogue*, xvi.

59. Panikkar, *Intra-Religious Dialogue*, xvi.

60. Panikkar, *Intra-Religious Dialogue* , 22.

61. Nouwen, *Reaching Out*, 52.

that of the other.[62] First, he contends that very often we only discover the profound meaning of our own world after we have tasted something exotically different. Speaking from a personal experience, Panikkar affirms that "one discovers home, sweet home" when one returns from elsewhere.[63] Panikkar in his second point argues that to think of ourselves, even collectively, as self-sufficient implies a certain condemnation of others.[64] His fear comes true and can be more visible when individual religious people fail to make internal space for others to reveal themselves. Space-making cannot be a question of either external or internal preparations, but must include both.

With availability and listening, the monks create space internally and externally to accommodate the other within their own space. Availability and listening offer the other the room to feel at home and unveil her gifts and identity. Such interpersonal interactions, according to Gabriel Marcel, begin with individual availability or *disponibilité*. Marcel's paradigm confirms the necessity of space-making as a predialogic moment for a fruitful encounter with the other. In his definition of availability, space-making is highly emphasized and contrasted with an enclosed individual, who lacks spaces for the other. Availability, for Marcel, is

> to transform circumstances into opportunities, we might even say favours, thus participating in the shaping of our own destiny and marking it with our seal . . . The being who is ready for anything is the opposite of him who is occupied and cluttered up with himself. He reaches out, on the contrary, beyond his narrow self, prepared to concentrate his being to a cause which is greater than he is, but which at the same time he makes his own.[65]

Availability as defined by Marcel and practiced by the monks inherently sustains hospitality, simply understood as living for the other, without altering the otherness intrinsic to either the self or the other. To alter otherness means nothing less than to destroy being, because *ousia* (substance) and otherness ontologically constitute being.[66]

Closely related to availability is the act of listening. Humanity is guilty of neglecting listening in great measure. The struggle to be heard

---

62. Cornille, *Im-Possibility*, 84.

63. Panikkar, *Intra-Religious Dialogue*, xviii.

64. Panikkar, *Intra-Religious Dialogue*, xviii.

65. Marcel, *Homo Viator*, 23–25.

66. Zizioulas, *Communion and Otherness*, 5.

virtually overturns the arena of mutual interaction to unhealthy competition. Rivalry can be symptomatic of lack of space for the other because a winner-loser dialectic destroys conducive space for mutual relationality. By contrast, a disposition for listening, which involves "standing under the discourses of others and rhetorically listening to them,"[67] also creates space for the exchange of individual gifts.

Monks are known to be good hosts, as shown in dialogue on spiritual experiences, because they know how to listen to their guests. In monastic hospitality, fear of the other is transformed into love for them. Learning from the monks, the initial lure to aversion or suspicion between Muslims and Christians can be tempered through the making of space, which disposes one to recognize the inherent worth of the other.[68] Nevertheless, the making of space has its own challenges.

Challenges of Making Space

Henri Nouwen names two major challenges to interior space-making as "concentration" and "decongestion."[69] The human mind is overwhelmingly occupied. The restless monkey is the traditional Hindu symbol of the mind until a one-centered control is achieved through meditation. At this transformed moment, the symbol of the controlled mind is a non-flickering flame in a windless room.[70] The metaphor of this flame articulates the basic challenges of internal space-making.

There is an underlying approach that can especially facilitate the dialogue of life through hospitality. That approach is humility. Panikkar argues that "humility is not primarily a moral virtue but an ontological one; it is the awareness of the place of my ego, the truthfulness of accepting my real situation, namely, that I am a situated being, a vision's angle on the real, an existence."[71] Cornille affirms this predialogic desire because it "increases one's understanding of the other, of oneself, or of the truth. And thus presupposes humble awareness of the limitation of one's own understanding and growth."[72] For Cornille, humility may be

---

67. Ratcliffe "Rhetorical Listening," 207.

68. Jacobs, "Audacity of Hospitality," 567.

69. Nouwen, Reaching Out, 51.

70. See Schweig, Bhagavad Gītā, 6:19.

71. Panikar, Intra-Religious Dialogue, 37.

72. Cornille, Im-Possibility, 9.

understood "to denote a genuine acknowledgement of the limitation and imperfection of one's insights and accomplishments, as indeed of all human realization and self-expression."[73]

Humility exhibits two tasks for the dialogic person. First, it anticipates the perceived differences of the other. Second, it acknowledges one's finitude or limitations with regard to the whole of reality. Only through humility can most religious adherents realize that "because the intellectual content of religious belief is expressed in iconic terms, there can be no intellectual criterion of the truth of beliefs, and that doctrines which seem to be contradictory may not in fact be contradictory but perhaps complementary."[74] Armed with these two key dispositions, the creation of space between Muslims and Christians would be greatly enhanced, because it not only accommodates all that the other signifies, but also creates more room for self-growth, through healthy experience of that other.

In Cornille's submission, interreligious dialogue requires in each dialogic partner a dynamism of humility, towards both the other religion and towards one's own religious tradition.[75] Summing up his own thoughts, Pannikar concluded that no one has 360 degrees of knowledge, partly because humanity is limited in perceiving reality, and partly because of the inescapable contradictions involved in perception itself.[76] He therefore insists that only in the complementarity of individual perceptions can reality be fully understood.

The paradox of doctrinal humility calls for a self-criticism of one's doctrinal beliefs. Tolerance is insufficient for hospitality because one needs not understand, let alone respect, what one is willing to tolerate. Cornille expatiates: "While tolerance often includes an attitude of indifference or even disregard for the distinctive beliefs and practices of the other, genuine humility is accompanied by an attitude of interest in the other and by a self-critical awareness of the possibility of distortions in one's own understanding of the other."[77] Only on this basic point of self-critique can we strongly say that Panikkar echoes Augustine's *Questio mihi factus est*. Nonetheless, humility is incomplete without hospitality.

---

73. Cornille, *Im-Possibility*, 9. This radical understanding is implied in the original Latin root of "humility," which is *humus*, meaning "earth" or "ground," from which the sense of lowly or humble derives.

74. Watt, *Christian-Muslim Encounters*, 138.

75. Cornille, *Im-Possibility*, 9–10.

76. Panikkar, *Cosmotheandric Experience*, 13.

77. Cornille, *Im-Possibility*, 25.

Having exposed the need for space-making, the argument will be incomplete without addressing the actual sharing of space (hospitality).

Space Sharing with the Religious Other

The main thesis of the previous section emphasized the essence of space creation for the other to belong. The detailed exploration centered on the need for internal and external space creation through an analysis of Panikkar's intrareligious dialogue. It also identified basic steps along the course of self-critique in view of allowing the other to unveil her identity and otherness.

This current section aims at considering space, not necessarily from the internal subjective standpoint, but rather as interpersonal boundary flexibility. For hospitality to happen, space must not only exist; it must be shared.[78] And "to practice hospitality is to welcome others into what will become a shared space with the presence of another."[79]

The genuine expression of space-sharing with the other is through hospitality. Our world stands in need of interreligious hospitality that consists in transporting oneself into the sphere of meaning of a foreign tradition and in welcoming the other's narrative tradition.[80] This type of hospitality, in Paul Ricoeur's understanding, presumes an attitude of hermeneutical openness by which "believers give up part of their control and mastery to become a guest in a strange narrative tradition."[81] Moyaert's reading of Ricoeur on hospitality strongly affirms its proper understanding in this essay. For Moyaert: "The other who asks to be understood and comprehended challenges the interpreter to listen and to make room in his own identity for the strange."[82] Precisely, altruistic imagination allows the subject to see matters differently."[83] In essence, genuine hospitality consists of the ability to balance the tension between faith commitment and openness to the truth of the other.

In the first-century Mediterranean world, hospitality was generally a public duty, in which the honor of the host community was at stake,

---

78. Sutherland, *I Was a Stranger*, x.

79. Reaves, *Safeguarding the Stranger*, 39.

80. Ricoeur, *Reflections on the Just*, 30.

81. Ricoeur, *Critique and Conviction*, 191.

82. Moyaert, *Fragile Identities*, 266.

83. Ricoeur, *Reflections on the Just*, 268.

and reciprocity was more communal than individual. At that time, it connoted a sacred duty, but also an ethical process of transforming an alien into a guest, including all the risk involved. John Navone notes the three stages of transformation involved in the exercise of such hospitality: "Evaluation and testing; the incorporation of the guest under the patronage of the host (involving culture-specific obligations upon both host and guest); and the departure of the stranger-transformed into either friend or enemy."[84]

There is no consensual definition of hospitality from available literature. However, authors seem to agree on altruism as the undercurrent phenomenon, while proffering a variety of ways and means that articulate such a responsible act. Common key terms for addressing hospitality inexhaustively include "stranger," "other," and "welcome."[85] Each term has unsettled notions in regard to hospitality. For example, the stranger could be a friend or an enemy or even both. These multiple approaches to hospitality, on the one hand, suggest its obvious importance, and on the other hand, expose its degree of complexity.

Analyzing the philosophical thoughts of Ricoeur, Moyaert reiterates that hospitality is "a model for integrating identity and otherness," which simultaneously sustains the human family by "showing concern for a concrete other because she or he is human."[86] From her perspective, hospitality contradicts the ideology of sectarianism or tribalism,[87] and most importantly does not intend to alter the otherness of the other. Rather, the peculiarity of the other inspires the self in unlearning her. Unlearning entails correction of biases against the other. Through a conscious commitment toward the well-being of the other, hospitality unlocks existing religious tradition by introducing a newness of approach, which assumes "responsibility in imagination and sympathy, for the story of the other."[88]

Ricoeur tries convincing his readers into believing that such deep commitment toward the other can be possible through linguistic hospitality. Linguistic hospitality, as an act, requires "inhabiting the (world) of the Other paralleled by the act of receiving the word of the other into

---

84. Navone, "Divine and Human Hospitality," 333

85. Reaves, *Safeguarding the Stranger*, 37.

86. Moyaert, *Absorption or Hospitality*, 83.

87. Moyaert, *Absorption or Hospitality*, 83

88. Ricoeur, "Reflection on a New Ethos," 7.

one's own home, one's own dwelling."[89] Muslim-Christian dialogue of life, as explored in this research, entails encouraging theoretical aspects according to Ricoeur, but with more emphasis on practical hospitality. Both suggest a complexity that is not a contradiction. The noticed complexity embedded in hospitality has prompted scholars like Jayme Reaves to opt for the meaning rather than the definition of hospitality.[90] While hospitality, as shown, eludes stating in precise terms, its paradoxical characterizations would rather be expressed accordingly.

89. Ricoeur, *On Translation*, 10.
90. Reaves, *Safeguarding the Stranger*, 37.

7

The Hospitality Key

WHY HOSPITALITY, AND WHY are charity and compassion necessary but insufficient?

Charity and compassion, as great ethical virtues, share altruistic tendencies with hospitality, but they technically do not guarantee the inviolability of otherness. Basically, charity and compassion presuppose empathetic responses toward the other, which usually emanate from the judgment of the self. This is a major concern because hospitality's rule of thumb requires the other to always define herself.

Islamic thought makes no serious distinction between charity and hospitality. In both aspects, the poor and the needy are the predictable beneficiaries. However, Michael Bonner explains away such conclusion due to insufficient written materials in seventh-century Arabia to ascertain who the poor and their benefactors were in the sacred book.[1]

Based on the Bedouin culture of hospitality, early Islam ennobled *karam* (generosity) as part of hospitality, by ranking the latter together with chivalry and honor. Snjezana Akpinar, emphasizing the humanizing element of hospitable acts in the pre-Islamic period, asserts that "hospitality was considered as an act of unconditional surrender for the other."[2]

Again, charity and compassion seek to alter the vulnerable condition of the other, thereby touching on the sacredness of otherness. Oliver Davies, in his book *A Theology of Compassion*, affirms: "Compassion is the recognition of the otherness of the other, as an otherness, which stands

---

1. Bonner, "Poverty and Economics, 391–92.
2. Akpinar, "Hospitality and Islam," 23.

beyond our own world, beyond our own constructions of otherness. But it is also the discovery of our own nature, as a horizon of subjectivity, which is fundamentally ordered to the world of another's experience."[3] Invariably, hospitality demands a profundity of responsibility towards every other (irrespective of any status), and so "should not be confused with the contemporary understanding of charity and entertainment."[4]

Truly, intentionality is the basic determinant of altruistic acts,[5] and must not be overlooked. However, intentions could be virtuous but no less absorptive. For example, many European missionaries' charitable projects, like hospitals and schools, were inseparable from conversion to Christianity.[6] The undercurrent of intent of most charitable and compassionate acts replicates an ennobling sameness as dictated by the self. De Bethune affirms and identifies the reason for the neglect of hospitality by missionaries as one-centered imaginative assimilation.[7]

Appropriation of the other most likely happens while executing charity and compassion, because their practices usually maintain unequal relations, and could as well lead to the sort of indebtedness that Derrida's hospitality warns against. In the act of either charity or compassion, the position of the vulnerable recipient is typically static, which denies the mutuality that defines hospitality within a bidirectional host-guest paradigm. In contrast, hospitality is open to all, both the poor and the rich. Often, the poor, like the widow of Zarephath, practice hospitality.[8] Therefore, the practice of hospitality is endemic to life for genuine persons in relationship.

Meaning of Hospitality

The meaning of hospitality can be enriched with a developmental exploration of its etymological terms, either from the Greek *philoxenia* or the Latin *hospitium*. Christine D. Pohl identifies a basal commonality between love and hospitality. According to Pohl, the Greek *philoxenia* "combines the general word for love or the affection for the people who

3. Davies, A *Theology of Compassion*, 17.

4. Siddiqui, *Hospitality and Islam*, 29.

5. Davies, *Theology of Compassion*, 18.

6. Bethune, "Interreligious Dialogue," 16.

7. Bethune, "Interreligious Dialogue," 16.

8. 1 Kings 17.

are connected by kinship or faith (*phileo*), and the word for stranger (*xenos*)."[9] With the centralization of love as an integral component of hospitality, Pohl presents the latter as an inevitable element in religious practices. In other words, love exchanged between the host and the guest strongly undergirds one of the most famous practices of hospitality.[10] Pohl's approach is a bit quick in presuming a robust host-guest relationship, which doesn't represent the inherent paradoxical significances of hospitality. Therefore, tracing further the etymology of hospitality might be very insightful.

Reaves notices the unavailability of literature on the linguistic roots of hospitality, except the detailed works of Emile Benveniste, a French linguist, which has been popularized in the English world by Tracy Mc-Nulty, a literature scholar.[11] Benveniste traces hospitality to a two-(root) word coinage: *hostis*, inferring stranger/enemy/guest, and pot (*potentator*), inferring master. The closest inference from these root words suggests the Latin *hospes* (host), from which modern usage evolves.[12]

Reaves thinks that modern scholars do not go beyond the Latin *hospes*, and she therefore attempts to demonstrate what could be missing when the two root words are ignored. Reviewing the argument of Reaves on McNulty's input, it can be deduced that every subject is originally a master unto himself (*ipse*), who exercises his authority from a locus called home, which constitutes his identity as host. As McNulty puts it, the "master is eminently himself [and] offers hospitality from the place where he is 'at home."[13] So the protection and identity that derive from the subject's home can be shared or extended to a *hostis* (a homeless foreigner) through hospitality or denied through hostility. Incidentally, *hostis* is not only the root word for "hostility" and "hospitality"; it also implies guest and enemy. The tension, therefore, between hospitable and inhospitable practices contributes to the complexity of hospitality, in as much as each highlights the meaning of the other.

Reaves reads extra meaning into *hostis* and contends that reciprocity is necessarily implied. From her perspective, it cannot be hospitality when the guest is only passively involved. Levinasian asymmetric hospitality,

---

9. Pohl, *Making Room*, 31.

10. Jacobs, "Audacity of Hospitality," 568.

11. Reaves, *Safeguarding the Stranger*, 41.

12. Benveniste, "L'Hospitalite."

13. McNulty, *Hostess*, x.

partly adopted, counters Reaves's reciprocal dimension. Meanwhile, asymmetric arguments from Levinas and the reciprocity that Reaves identifies will be harmonized with an asymmetric mutuality thesis of this research in chapter 9.

Reaves's thesis echoes the position of McNulty in her description, "*hostis* is he who compensates a gift with a counter-gift."[14] The reciprocity that is in contestation resonates with the French root *hote*, which connotes both the giver (*donne*) and the receiver (*recoit*). Reciprocity as described by Reaves supports the tension that defines the host-guest relationship.

Host-Guest Dynamics

Though totally indefinite, the other could still be understood through the paradigmatic prism of guest and host. Could the host also be the guest? Yes, on two accounts: 1) When a host leaves her home, she eventually becomes a guest, which converges with cultural and biblical bases of hospitality. 2) The host-guest dynamic represents a christological model. At the post-resurrection Emmaus experience, Jesus exemplified a "pilgrim metaphor" of homelessness in his dual guest-host roles. First, in his disguise he accepted the hospitable invitation from the two disciples and became their guest. Second, at table he became the host by blessing the bread and offering it to the disciples, and they ate. Only then did they recognize him (Luke 24:13–35).

These two accounts point to a new hospitality approach, in which home can be systematically decentered. As pilgrims, interpersonal relations would assume a renewed understanding, through which the other, especially the most vulnerable other, becomes anyone's responsibility. The pilgrim metaphor aligns with the theology of migration, which recently seeks "helping those on the move discover an inner identity that fosters their own agency rather than an imposed external identity that increases their vulnerability and subjugation."[15] In practical terms, the metaphor of home, whether real or imaginary, plays out within the host-guest dynamism. In this regard, when Christians assume responsibility for Muslims, Muslims as well would accept Christians as their

14. McNulty, *Hostess,* x

15. Groody, "Crossing the Divide, 644.

own responsibility, especially within the divide in Nigeria between the Northern Muslims and the Southern Christians.

The dynamic tension between host and guest fits into the larger scope of hostility and hospitality. Understood as a functional template, the host-guest metaphor highlights the importance of mutuality and freedom in any interpersonal encounter. Nouwen suggests that a holistic engagement of otherness can be approached through a host-guest dynamic interactivity.[16] His host-guest paradigm clearly indicates hospitality in its holistic sense, whereby the interest of the other enjoys a significant priority over that of the self, or at least demands equal basis. This kind of hospitality, which transcends the basic nicety of eating or sheltering toward strangers, but prioritizes the other's particular interests, sounds more speculative than practical, though not impossible. Nevertheless, the host-guest flexibility engages both parties equally.

To a large extent, the goal of the hospitality paradigm being advanced resonates with Cornille's understanding of the term. For Cornille, "hospitality creates an atmosphere of friendship and trust in which differences are not only tolerated but engaged in an open and constructive way."[17] Cornille's template of hospitality encourages a relationship of responsibility suitable between Muslims and Christians.

In essence, one can argue that the host-guest tension constitutes what defines hospitality, such that any attempt to separate the dual nature would lead to total erasure of hospitality demands.[18] Demands of hospitality both endanger and conquer. They actually "create danger (in the form of jealousy and trespass) and overcome danger (through gestures of welcome and concern)."[19]

McNulty traces the dangerous connotation of *hostis* to the influence of ancient empires. Before the codification of the Roman law called *Corpus Iuris Civilis* (body of civil law), issued from 529 to 534 by Emperor Justinian I, foreign residents in Rome shared equal rights and privileges with Roman citizens.[20] Through this law, *hostis* began emphasizing negative implications, exclusively to a possible enemy, rather than the initial (friendly) guest with divine protection. McNulty also affirmed

16. Nouwen, *Reaching Out*, 55–57.

17. Cornille, "Interreligious Hospitality," 35.

18. Anidjar, "Hospitality," 356.

19. Anidjar, "Once More," 33.

20. Benveniste, "L'Hospitalite," 93.

that simultaneously the Greek *xenos* gradually dropped its common significance of a guest and assumed an exclusive notion of a stranger.[21] These negative connotations of *hostis* have impacted the sociopolitical understanding in the modern world. With this evolutionary trend, *hostis*, according to McNulty, became the linguistic root of hostility, which is antithetical to the institution of hospitality.[22] Nonetheless, hostility not only enriches the relevance of hospitality; it also completes it.

Practices of Hospitality

The paradoxical constituents of hospitality can be broadly categorized into material and immaterial gift-sharing. Whereas the material aspect of gifts accounts for all the tangible privileges the host extends to her guest, the immaterial articulates the spaces shared in the process in order to accommodate the variable otherness that defines the identity of the guest. Even though material hospitality might be essential in the general practice of hospitality, in the interreligious sphere the immaterial dimension, such as an appreciation of otherness, mutual respect, and growth, is most emphasized. Within the context of this research, however, both dimensions are necessary for optimal results in diminishing distorted perceptions about each other, especially between Muslims and Christians in Nigeria. Most often, the material aspect tends to dominate the holistic understanding of hospitality. Pohl's description of hospitality as "welcoming strangers . . . and offering them food, shelter, and protection"[23] affirms the thrust for its multiple dimensional meanings.

In essence, hospitality can be practiced through three main aspects, as argued by Reaves: 1) table fellowship, 2) intellectual hospitality, and 3) protective hospitality.[24] In accord with the dialogue of life, hospitality as that conscious responsibility for the other incorporates the three categories and sustains their connectivity. It is, according to Mona Siddiqui, "a multi-layered concept."[25]

Table fellowship represents the most common and basic depiction of hospitality. Sitting at the same table implies communion or sharing

---

21 McNulty, *Hostess*, xii.

22. McNulty, *Hostess*, xii.

23. Pohl, *Making Room*, 4.

24. Reaves, *Safeguarding the Stranger*, 49.

25. Siddiqui, *Hospitality and Islam*, 29.

(personal intimacy, one dish and under the same roof). Westerners might probably not be familiar with the practice of guest and host eating from the same dish, often with their bare hands, as in India and Africa. However, table fellowship represents a great sense of intimacy, equality, and communion in feeding another person, especially the hungry. Siddiqui affirms that table fellowship "is always the most significant and the simplest act of hospitality."[26]

Sharing provokes a genuine sense of participation in God's abundance and an extension of that to God's people.[27] Ancient hospitality practices, as depicted in the Abrahamic narratives, were aimed at sustaining peace and neighborliness through reconciling and remembering activities.[28] This Abrahamic influence resonates in different religious practices like the Judaistic *Shabbat*, the Christian Eucharist, and the Islamic *Eid*, all of which point to hospitality with emphasis on shared eating and drinking. Such aspect of hospitality, which involves "Eating or drinking together, inviting others into personal space, is an intimate act with sacred connotations."[29] The scope of hospitality this research advances appreciates the cultural, philosophical, and ethical dimensions, but above all emphasizes the theological aspect. From this perspective, genuine hospitality "involves a sacred duty to think beyond our immediate selves in a wide variety of contexts and relationship." Table fellowship, therefore, can only represent one aspect of hospitality.

Intellectual welcome is considered the most vague form of hospitality. How does this even qualify as hospitality? Primarily, intellectual welcome demands the creation of space for the exchange of ideas and the accommodation of a variety of opinions. Sharing one's understanding of God, rather than simply evoking pride in the wisdom of one's tradition, depicts a sense of humility in appreciating the fact that no one person has an exhaustive knowledge of God. Only in sharing can one be further enriched in the fuller understanding of God. Reaves terms such intellectual exercise "a holy rite of disagreement."[30] The disagreement is qualified as holy probably because otherness entails sacredness. Simply put, it is an appreciation of difference for the sake of respect and openness for

---

26. Siddiqui, *Hospitality and Islam*, 29.

27. Reaves, *Safeguarding the Stranger*, 50.

28. Reaves, *Safeguarding the Stranger*, 50.

29. Reaves, *Safeguarding the Stranger*, 51.

30. Reaves, *Safeguarding the Stranger*, 51.

growth. For example: "When we look at teaching in terms of hospitality, we can say that the teacher is called upon to create for his [or her] students a free and fearless space where mental and emotional development can take place."[31] A good teacher communicates knowledge best not only by learning from her students, but also by engaging their different opinions, thereby enriching her pedagogical experiences.

Knowledge gains exponential growth when mutually shared, particularly among pluralistic religionists. The more Muslims and Christians learn to reach out through openness to the other, the more they increase in appreciation of how the other defines herself. As convinced monotheists, charting a bridge of mutual passages would not be an impossibility.

Through the centuries, Abrahamic traditional religions have sometimes engaged in a cooperative theological quest. It was reported that the court of Haruna al-Rashid, ruler of Abbasid, caliphate from Baghdad, provided space for interreligious discourses:

> On countless evenings, the court was transformed into an arena for theological debate. Muslim men of learning, schooled in sharia, the law derived from the Qur'an, offered their wisdom and drew on the philosophical tradition of the ancient Greeks. The works of Aristotle and Plato were translated into Arabic and used not only to enrich Islam, but [also] to create new science and new philosophy. And the caliph was not content simply to take the world of his learned men. He wanted to see how their ideas met opposing theologies, and he invited scholars and preachers of other faiths to his court. Jews, Christians, Buddhists, and Muslims engaged in spiritual and spirited jousts, and each tradition was enriched by knowledge of the others.[32]

A related account took place in the city of Fatepur Sikri in late medieval India under the auspices of the Mogul emperor Akbar. The interreligious discussion room was formed in the shape of a wheel. Each religion's representative sat at the periphery of the wheel, at equal distance to the hub or center of the wheel, believed to represent the mystery of the divine. Akbar has been criticized by some Muslims as not orthodox enough and as too syncretistic in his openness, especially to Hinduism.

Another narrative testifies to what qualifies for an intellectual hospitality in Medieval Iberia. In this particular context, "the Jewish polymath Maimonides, the Sufi mystic Ibn 'Arabi, and a phalanx of Christian monks

31. Nouwen, *Reaching Out*, 60.

32. Karabell, *Peace Be Upon You*, 4.

helped one another unravel the meaning of God and the universe."[33] Reaves regret that such practice of welcome in which differing opinions are amicably engaged has suffered gross neglect[34] and has assumed a radical shift, through which sameness (supersessionism) triumphs.

However, the recent turn toward otherness in the academy constitutes a great retrieval toward the ancient practice of hospitality for the purpose of interreligious understanding and harmony. As Reaves notes, "Welcoming the ideas of traditions other than one's own in order to enhance one's understanding is an act of hospitality."[35] The necessity of "an act of hospitality" among the Abrahamic traditions presupposes the aim "to form pragmatic hypotheses for guiding shared action toward the 'repair' of the failed logic of modernity."[36]

The last aspect, protective hospitality, although clearer than its intellectual form, has not received appropriate independent study. It basically deals with creating safe spaces for the vulnerable other (a homeless person) or one whose life is threatened, which can be riskier for the host than simply offering shelter for a guest for a few days. Scholars sometimes assert that the act of providing space, especially safe space for the other, underscores hospitality. Both Nouwen and Pohl recognize the identical nature of hospitality and the provision of safe space for the other. Pohl, improving on Nouwen's space argument, reiterates its hospitality trait, thereby inferring its aspect of protection. "Hospitality" she insists, "involves sharing food, shelter, protection, recognition, and conversation."[37]

Generally, all forms of hospitality are scarcely separable. From a protective perspective, vulnerability accurately represents the true identity of the poor, widow, orphan, and stranger, because their survival depends solely on others' hospitality. Their commonality identifies them as people in dire need of the greatest amount of protection and support.[38]

True hospitality is identified through its main character of being other-oriented. Leonardo Boff, the Brazilian liberation theologian, confirms that hospitality has the other at its crux.[39] For the other to be that other,

33. Reaves, *Safeguarding the Stranger*, 6.

34. Reaves, *Safeguarding the Stranger*, 53.

35. Reaves, *Safeguarding the Stranger*, 53.

36. Mudge, *Gift of Responsibility*, 123.

37. Pohl, "Building a Place," 27.

38. Katz, *Levinas*, 58.

39. Reaves, *Safeguarding the Stranger*, 38.

as explained by Boff, elements of unfamiliarity (identity), foreignness (language, culture, and habits), class differentiation, marginalization (vulnerability), and/or the absolute Other (God, who disguises in the other) must be present.[40] Hospitality, according to Boff's understanding, embraces all forms of the other, both human and divine.[41] Levinas entirely agrees with the absolute transcendence of the other present in Boff, except that he (Levinas) so much accentuates the human other that only through her face can the divine trace be elicited.

As Levinas argues, it is the presence of the divine in the face of the other that regulates the absorption of the other by the self. In effect, he maintains that monotheism can only be genuinely understood through the self-other relational paradigm.[42] It can be accurately deduced that "In the Levinasian community, individuals will demonstrate their fidelity to God through hospitality by welcoming the non-communal Other."[43] Since Muslims and Christians are professed monotheists, their faith in God could be ascertained by the extent of hospitality each religious group extends to the other. This is the main thesis of this research.

Another important aspect of genuine hospitality entails the courage to deal with certain inherent fear and risk. John D. Caputo advocates for a radical hospitality that must include taking the daring step of welcoming the enemy into one's comfort zone.[44] Otherwise, suspicion and mistrust toward the other fundamentally distorts the practice of hospitality.[45]

Hospitality: A Philosophical Dimension

The main thesis of this section aims at proffering a substantive response to the global question: "If . . . we live in a new open and fluid global village, one with no boundaries, how is the Other actually held at a safe distance?"[46] Scholars like Miroslav Volf remind us of the subtle persistent practices of exclusion, despite the globalization call. Volf identifies three modes of exclusion in the contemporary world: as elimination through

---

40. Boff, *Virtues*, 48–49.
41. Boff, *Virtues*, 48–49.
42. Levinas, *Totality and Infinity*, 214.
43. Eubanks and Gauthier, "Politics," 135.
44. Caputo, *What Would Jesus Deconstruct?*, 76.
45. Reaves, *Safeguarding the Stranger*, 49.
46. Shepherd, *Gift of the Other*, 9.

assimilation, as domination, and as abandonment.[47] While exclusion by elimination is considered the most vicious form of exclusion, Volf adeptly notes that exclusion by subjugation and by abandonment are also forms of violence. He affirms: "If others neither have the goods we want nor can perform the services we need, we make sure that they are at a safe distance and close ourselves off from them so that their emancipated and tortured bodies can make no inordinate claim on us."[48] Examples of exclusive abandonment include Palestinian refugees and African people living in rich natural resource bases like Nigeria and the Democratic Republic of Congo.[49] In all of its three forms, the inviolable rights and identity of the other are grossly infringed upon.

Such terrible social injustices have engendered the philosophers of difference, especially Levinas and Derrida, in charting a persuasive course in defense of the denigrated other. Sameness ideology, according to these scholars, suffocates otherness, and subsequently destroys the beauty of diversity. In essence, sameness enthrones the one-centered self and empowers it as the only judge of reality, including what defines the other. Above all, sameness ideology ruptures the prevalent diversities of reality. In this regard, the other is suppressed into a faceless identity, except as painted by the imperialistic self.

For the liberation of the oppressed other from the imperial hands of sameness, the hospitality key, as an ethical act across religious borders, is being argued against the unjust status quo. Andrew Shepherd contends that "the practice of hospitality as a corrective to exclusions present in the global vision can only be effective if one first eliminates the distortions brought about by the ideologies of the contemporary world."[50] He further argues that hospitality must be redeemed from mere cultural taints through a reestablishment upon theological foundations.[51] In line with this call, our hospitality thesis will undergo an evolutionary development, from philosophical perspectives through ethical considerations to the use of the theological imagination.

The problem of otherness as already identified by Levinas subsists in the Westernized ideology of self-sameness, as seen in the main thoughts

47. Volf, *Exclusion and Embrace*, 60.

48. Volf, *Exclusion and Embrace*, 75.

49. Shepherd, *Gift of the Other*, 8

50. Shepherd, *Gift of the Other*, 13.

51. Shepherd, *Gift of the Other*, 13.

of some of its great minds, including Hegel (*Weltgeschichte*, world history), Heidegger (*Dasein*, Being), Descartes (psychological *cogito*) and Husserl (transcendental *cogito*). On this radical basis of the problem, Richard Kearney wholly agrees with Levinas but also disagrees with him over the identity of the other. In agreement, Kearney firmly states: "Ever since early Western thought equated the Good with notions of self-identity and sameness, the experience of evil has often been linked with notions of exteriority. Almost invariably, otherness was considered in terms of an estrangement, which contaminates the pure unity of the soul . . . Evil was alienation and the evil one was the alien."[52]

Along with determining the historical cause of strangeness, Kearney insists on its contemporary presence. In his analysis, ideological sameness has given rise to a terrifying list of modern historical mayhem. The list includes: "Kristallnacht and Auschwitz, the Soviet show trials and gulags, Mao's cultural revolution and Tienanmen Square, McCarthy's blacklists and Reagan's Starwars, the embargo of Cuba and bombing of Cambodia, Sarajevo and Kosovo, Jerusalem and the West bank, the Twin Towers and Afghanistan."[53] And as a recurring phenomenon among nations, antagonistic relations exist between the known "we" and the unfamiliar "them." In disagreement, Levinas insists that the other remains always as the "unfamiliar," who continues to transcend all attempts to reduce her to the realm of the familiar by the self. Whereas the self is infinitely responsible for the other, the identity of the other must remain mysterious.

As earlier noted, contemporary philosophers of difference like Levinas and Derrida trace the root of the sameness-otherness divide to rigid categorized universals: Logos, Being, Substance, Reason or Ego, which have blurred human perceptions of the other at various levels. Either as 'ontology of sameness' (Levinas) or 'logocentricism' (Derrida), both advocate for a correction of the injustice institutionalized against otherness. The other, using the terminology of Kearney, has in variant ways been "scapegoated."[54] Such pejorative identity of the other demands an urgent dethronement of a sameness construction for the liberation of the victimized other. This advocacy or turn towards the other, as the other, not as an alter ego, assures ethical justice.[55]

---

52. Kearney, *Strangers*, 65.

53. Kearney, *Strangers*, 65.

54. Kearney, *Strangers*, 67.

55. Kearney, *Strangers*, 67.

Such renewed appreciation of otherness aligns with the Levinasian infinite responsibility towards the other, and the Derridan call for absolute hospitality. At this philosophical level, the arguments of these thinkers favor an uncategorized identity of the other, which, *ipso facto*, assures surprise as an inherent quality of the other. The same unknown identity of the other raises, in Kearney's thought, the need for discernment. That the other cannot be fully known or objectivized creates by itself another problem in intersubjective relations—"the problem of discernment."[56]

Should the infinitude of the other exonerate questioning the identity of the other? Is the other benign or is the other malignant? Such critical questions could not escape the philosophical imaginative curiosity of contemporary thinkers. The unpredictability of the other complicates the clues to her true identity. So, contemporary thinkers query the paradoxical possibilities that shroud not only her uncategorized identity but also that of her host. Kearney clearly and rightly perceives the identity impasse thus: "how do we account for the fact that not every other is innocent and not every self is an egoistic emperor?"[57]

Advancing the medium of discernment, Kearney attempts a distinction between the terms "other" and "alien." In his contention, the "other" represents a person (of difference) while "alien" expresses some sort of unfamiliar features of the other. The "other," he asserts, refers to "an alterity worthy of reverence and hospitality" and "alien by contrast, refers to that experience of strangers associated with discrimination; suspicion; and scapegoating."[58] While charting his course on discernment, Kearney recognizes varieties in otherness that show the need to "discern the other in the alien and the alien in the other."[59] Nevertheless, despite their distinctions, the terms "other" and "alien" are essentially inseparable phenomena in a just hospitality. The other invariably includes all her otherness or strangeness.

Contemporary deconstructionist philosophers like Derrida, John Caputo, and Lacoue-Labarthe, even though from different angles, situate justice at the hub of hospitality practices. Prior to these deconstructionists, the nineteenth-century German rationalist Emmanuel Kant had a similar thesis. For Kant, justice should be a determinant for hospitality,

---

56. Kearney, *Strangers*, 67.
57. Kearney, *Strangers*, 67–68.
58. Kearney, Strangers, 67.
59. Kearney, Strangers, 67.

especially in international relations. Justice as a factor, however, comes with its own problems, such as the question of whose laws decides.

Regrettably, the cultural specificity of particular laws weakens their support of genuine hospitality. Altruistic practices seen among different cultures and people, as observed by Pohl, fall into the category of selective hospitality, because of the greater interest in the preservation of citizenry rights and security. With the recognition of law as significant but quite insufficient (for coming to a more universally applicable understanding of justice), deconstructionists argue for a justice that transcends the law. It is only within the ambience of justice, they argue, that the demand for "unconditional hospitality to the alien"[60] can be possible.

In contrast to law, which often relativizes hospitality, true justice demands that genuine hospitality holistically perceive the other, with all the risks of her surprises. Whether benign or malignant, the other is the other in need of hospitality. Further attempts at discriminatory or selective hospitality truncate all that this ethical practice stands for. In this regard, these deconstructionists affirm the default paradoxical nature of hospitality deduced from the (contrasting) dual connotations of *hostis* (as both guest and enemy). In essence, a host, and likewise a guest, can at once designate welcome or invasion; the other is a friend or a foe. Each could also be both. This is so because of the reversible relationship between the host and the guest. A benign host can transform into a malignant host when the presence of the other posits a dangerous threat. In other words, a threatened host could as well discriminate by discerning the identities of his prospective guests.

However, Derrida argues that because the law of hospitality (*hospitalite en droit*) guarantees such a transformative process of identification, it might lead to violence when practiced. In his words: "A certain injustice . . . is present from the outset, at the very threshold of the right to hospitality. This collusion between the violence of power or the force of law (*Gewalt*) on the one hand, and hospitality on the other, seems to be radically integral to the very inscription of hospitality as a right."[61] This Derridean deconstructionism contends that the obvious paradox marking the thin line between hostility and hospitality can be traced to the limits of the conventional ethos concerning laws of hospitality.

60. Kearney, *Strangers*, 68.
61. Derrida, *De L'Hospitalite*, 53.

Consequently, Derrida, in agreement with Levinas, insists that the other must be the nameless (unknown) absolute other, whose identity should transcend the hospitality of law, but is yet deserving of unconditional hospitality. Absolute hospitality "requires that I open my home and that I give not only to the stranger (furnished with a family name and the social status of a stranger etc.), but to the absolute other, unknown and anonymous; and that I give place (*donne lieu*), let come, arrive, let him take his place in the place that I offer him, without demanding that he give his name or enter into some reciprocal pact."[62]

Moreover, that absolute hospitality (as earlier noted) goes beyond its cultural models does not indict the latter. Rather, it strongly speaks to the dynamic flexibility embedded in the various practices of hospitality, thoroughly governed by the ethos of justice. And for there to be a just hospitality, the absolute other, rather than being perceived as vicious alien, should be offered a space to belong, or be allowed some way to share one's home. In so doing, the law or right of hospitality complements the justice of hospitality: "The relation to the alien/stranger (*l'etranger*) is regulated by the law of right (*le droit*), by becoming—right of justice."[63]

Basing hospitality on the right of justice assures an absolute other that comes with absolute surprises (including gifts). Like Derrida, Caputo qualifies this kind of disclosure as an "impossible, unimaginable, un-foreseeable, un-believable, ab-solute surprise."[64] Emphasizing the essence of surprise in hospitality, Derrida concludes, "The newcomer may be good or evil, but if you exclude the possibility that the newcomer is coming to destroy your house, if you want to control this and exclude this terrible possibility in advance, there is no hospitality."[65]

The absolute other that Derrida and Levinas (even though from different perspectives) advocate can be problematic according to Kearney. Dealing with an absolute other implies a disconnection from the self, which sounds a bit contradictory. Kearney describes this brand of absolute hospitality as "hyperbolic hospitality where the self seeks to transcend all laws of hospitality (naming, identifying, certifying, legislating for the other-as-guest) in the search of an unconditional and ultimately

62. Derrida, *De L'Hospitalite*, 29.

63. Derrida, *De L'Hospitalite*, 69.

64. Caputo, *Prayers and Tears*, 73.

65. Derrida, "Hospitality, Justice and Responsibility," 63–83.

impossible hospitality."[66] It worries him that unconditional or absolute hospitality can be paradoxical to the laws of hospitality, because of the priority of individualism against universalism.

Universalism, like totality (as a weapon of the oppressive self), suffocates the infiniteness that Levinas ascribes to the other. For Kearney, analyses of terms like *il y a* (there is) and *illeite* (absolute Other) in defense of asymmetric relations by Levinas are criticized for their implicating hatred or persecution of the self. In his second opus magnum, *Otherwise than Being*, Levinas clearly states that the infinite services of the self toward the other include being "responsible for the persecuting by the persecutor."[67] In essence, "the one is exposed to the other as a skin is exposed to what wounds it."[68]

Furthermore, the perceived extremity of self-abnegation in Levinas engendered Kearney's approval of Simon Critchley's critique:

> Is it not in the excessive experience of evil and horror . . . that the ethical subject first assumes its shape? Does this not begin to explain why the royal road to ethical metaphysics must begin by making Levinas a master of the literature of horror? But if this is the case, why is radical otherness goodness? Why is alterity ethical? Why is it not, we may wonder, "rather evil or an-ethical or neutral"?[69]

Levinas would dismiss Critchley's critique as a predictable reaction expected from the proponents of sameness ideology, whose comfort zone is threatened. Demonization of alterity approves the negative imbalance that sameness implies.

In contrast to the possible exteriority that marks the absolutism of the other, Kearney insists on the intersubjective relationality that grounds hospitality, by demonstrating a legitimate concern about getting trapped if one acts blindly in hospitality.[70] Taking into consideration the nameless identity of the other, Kearney proposes the discernment of identities as the condition for welcome.[71] Such a proposal also borders on justice as the right of the host. Kearney vehemently opposes

---

66. Kearney, *Strangers*, 243.

67. Levinas, *Otherwise than Being* (1991), 75.

68. Levinas, *Otherwise than Being* (1991), 49, 92.

69. Critchley, *Very Little*, 80.

70. Kearney, *Strangers*, 70.

71. Kearney, *Strangers*, 71.

unconditional hospitality. For him, unconditional hospitality as taught by Levinas and Derrida might be "a fine lesson in tolerance, but not necessarily in moral judgment."[72] Kearney thinks that the high risk involved in hosting a stranger questions the moral right of the host to self-protection. However, his attempt to eliminate such paradoxical tension from the nature of hospitality would distort the genuineness of the practice rather than sustain it. Any attempt, as strongly argued by Levinas, to have a premonition of the other infringes on the sacredness of the other's infinite identity.

Who Should Receive Hospitality— the Invited or the Uninvited?

Creating space might be easier than sharing space because the practicality of the latter includes actual threats on comfort zones. Sharing space might question the sacredness of one's sanctuary and violate interpersonal boundaries. The threat and violence that accompany hospitality when space is shared could be real or imaginary, public or private, permanent or temporary.[73] Still, only in common space can welcome and freedom abide.[74] Hospitality cannot be stripped of its constitutive elements of uncertainties and risks.

Derrida agrees that only risk-bearing hospitality is genuine, in these words: "If I welcome only what I welcome, what I am ready to welcome, and that I recognize in advance because I expect the coming of the *hote* (guest) as invited, there is no hospitality."[75] Such endemic risk in hospitality also undergirds a Levinasian infinite responsibility of the host toward the guest.

In his book *Of Hospitality*, Derrida draws two key principles from a *Balga* Bedouin hospitality story of Fawzi al-Khatalin:[76] 1) the dynamic relationship between expected and unexpected hospitality, and 2) the substitutive sacrifice of the host beyond the law of hospitality. About

72. Kearney, *Strangers*, 72.

73. Reaves, *Safeguarding the Stranger*, 39.

74. Sutherland, *I Was a Stranger*, x.

75. Derrida, "Hospitality," 362.

76. Fawzi is a descendant of Ibn Khatlan, the first paramount shaykh of the 'Abbad tribe. He is an electric engineer by training and a famous member of the Jordanian Bedouin bourgeoisie. Known for his proud ancestry legacy, his story on the radical hospitality of his tribe has attracted the interests of scholars.

the seventh century, the nomadic Bedouin tribe, famed for its pride of hospitality, controlled a substantial portion of the commercial and agricultural activities in the Arabian Desert.[77] Today, some *Balga* Bedouins like Fawzi settled in Jordan and other areas outside Arabia. In the story, al-Khatalin recounts how his ancestor, Ibn Khatlan, was proven as the most generous person of his age by the sacrificial gift of his two children in hospitality to honor his guests.[78]

The goal of the story is "to inspire a reverential attitude toward *karam* (hospitality), a respect for its miraculous potential, to which the Khatalin are heirs."[79] Derrida therefore interprets these paradoxes as "intermediate schemas" (to resolve the irresolvable) "between unconditional hospitality and the rights and duties that are the conditions of hospitality."[80] *Of Hospitality* concludes with two biblical passages (Lot's guest in Sodom in Genesis 19:1–8, and the rape and mutilation of the Levite's concubine in Judges 19:22–29) that project portraitures of limitless and enthralling hospitality.

Space creation and sharing presuppose unconditional intentionality and responsibility. Unconditional intentionality and responsibility undergird "one's ultimate calling and obligation . . . [which] is to provide the space and hope, for that Other to unfold and reveal his or her naked identities—while still remaining an Other—a distinct, autonomous being."[81] The strict unconditionality involved assures space that doesn't change people, but rather that which offers the opportunity for transformation to happen.[82] From this perspective, genuine hospitality requires "space and the possibility of transformation, as well as the other and welcome."[83] It also requires that boundaries must be crossed.[84] But for these required elements to transcend manipulations they should be crafted on the universal human standard of justice and equity, which acknowledges another as one's neighbor or as a potential member of one's family.[85]

77. Orji, *Introduction*, 221.

78. Shyyock, "Thinking about Hospitality," 408.

79. Shyyock, "Thinking about Hospitality," 409.

80. Derrida, *Of Hospitality*, 147.

81. Admirand, "Healing the Distorted Face," 303.

82. Nouwen, *Reaching Out*, 51.

83. Nouwen, *Reaching Out*, 40.

84. Shryock, "Thinking about Hospitality," 410.

85. Reynolds, "Improvising Together," 55.

Fear is a major factor in space-sharing. Sharing space can make one tremendously vulnerable, as already discussed, because of its primary target on the person, not merely on what that person believes. According to Ricoeur, there is a protective withdrawal prompted by fear of otherness, which is actually a fear of losing one's own identity. Subsequently, the presence or encounter with the other evokes significant fear and perceived threats to the safety of one's identity. This uncertainty results in the inability to deal with complexity, nuance, and strangeness. In the face of this identity-otherness tension, only the virtue of hospitality can cause the integration.[86] Hospitality in this refined sense takes an anthropotheological meaning of showing concern (with openness for reciprocity) for a concrete other because he/she is human.[87]

One of the endearing qualities of hospitality lies in its ability to achieve fulfillment in bringing together paradoxes. In this regard, hospitality appreciates antinomy as juxtaposition rather than contradiction.[88] A holistic understanding of hospitality cannot ignore the tensions between hostility and hospitality, the invited and the uninvited, welcome and unwelcome, inclusion and exclusion, coercion and embrace, violence and protection, self-identity and human unity.[89] The foreseen paradoxical character of hospitality, on the one hand, accounts for its definitional difficulty, and on the other, orchestrates the inevitability of the contrasting tension.

Understanding hospitality does not stop at knowing the relevance of openness in welcoming the other into one's own space. It is not only about the what, but also about the how of hospitality. In reality, welcoming the stranger into one's own sacred space requires basic uncertainties: the manner of welcoming (material and immaterial means), who should be welcomed (invited and uninvited), and the extent of welcome (shared space and boundary). The ability to harmonize these inherent tensions differentiates genuine hospitality from hypocritical hospitality. Indeed, Scriptures and ancient societies recommended unconditional hospitality to the nameless stranger as a sacred duty.[90]

86. Moyaert, "Biblical, Ethical," 103.

87. Moyaert, "Biblical, Ethical," 103.

88. Reaves, *Safeguarding the Stranger*, 43.

89. Reaves, *Safeguarding the Stranger*, 43.

90. Siddiqui, *Hospitality and Islam*, 30.

In general, hospitality seems to embrace every act that assures the well-being of the other. But the other often comes with an indeterminate identity and otherness that transcend the understanding of the subject or host. In this regard, Caputo thinks that hospitality belongs to a group of complex words that fail to achieve all they promise.[91] In essence, Caputo draws attention to the unavoidable temptation of hospitality, especially the thin line that separates genuine hospitality from artificial hospitality. In Caputo's assessment, when invitations are selective and reserved for the known only, what commonly hides under the shadow of hospitality is basically inhospitality. Caputo regrets such display of hypocrisy, and argues that its practice hybridizes hospitality and inhospitality, thereby perpetuating a circle of sameness that occludes otherness.[92] Therefore, not every welcome qualifies as genuine hospitality.

The tension also extends to the dynamic nature of components of hospitality. Home, for example, constitutes a central metaphor among the defining principles of hospitality. Hospitality implies the significance of home. A home first and foremost plays host to the owner, in terms of granting him protection, comfort, shelter, and other prioritized advantages. By proportional projection, the hospitality gained from a home demands from the owner an appropriate extension of homeness to the homeless stranger. Denial of homeness is tantamount to oppression, because "to be oppressed is to be virtually without a home, in which the oppressor's will is the only rule that counts."[93] By contrast, to be hospitable is to make provision for enough space in which the other feels not only at home, but also defines herself.[94] Such a shared space reflects where both the host and the guest can coexist.[95]

Over time, the centrality of home has generated contrasting perceptions for different people. In other words, home can equally be converted into a locus that perpetuates and/or diminishes conflicts.[96] In essence, what approves activities in a home largely does not depend on what constitutes the owner's priority. Rather, in the home, "it is how the foreign is considered and welcomed or unwelcomed that highlights some

---

91. Caputo, *What Would Jesus Deconstruct?*, 75.

92. Caputo, *What Would Jesus Deconstruct?*, 76.

93. Ogletree, *Hospitality to the Stranger*, 4–5.

94. Reaves, *Safeguarding the Stranger*, 57.

95. Arterbury, *Entertaining Angels*, 20.

96. Reaves, *Safeguarding the Stranger*, 44.

of the tensions within hospitality."[97] In other words, home symbolizes a paradoxical reality that intersects both inclusive and exclusive tendencies. The centrality of home strongly undergirds the hospitality thesis as key toward Nigerian Muslim-Christian relations, wherein the ethnic factor still defines home in a contemporary society. Home as it impacts Muslim-Christian relations in Nigeria will be explored in chapter 8.

A hospitable home, moreover, assures mutual growth between the host and her guest. Even though hosting implies giving, it does not contradict receiving. A good host creates spaces not only for the stranger to belong, but also for the latter to share her (surprising) gift of newness. Invariably, the host "becomes honored and enhanced by sharing [his] space, [while] the vulnerable stranger who allegedly has nothing to offer becomes a source of enrichment to the household, reconfiguring and transforming it, especially when the boundary between them assumes permeability."[98] The greatest gift of the stranger is her otherness, which manifests as newness and enriches the world of the host. This unexpected enrichment by which a hospitable host is blessed agrees with the basis of theological hospitality: "God blesses through the stranger."[99]

By contrast, the serious link between home and identity defines in clear terms the precariousness of welcoming an enemy (*hostis*) into one's home. Theh homelessness of the stranger can be so threatening that the host might even think his own identity will be lost through the dispossession or sharing of his home.[100] No matter how genuine the risk of identity loss could be, it only affirms the continuous tension between hostility and hospitality.[101]

Despite the obvious high risk aimed at home and identity, hospitality ethics demands that doors must not be shut against the homeless other.[102] In addition to the assertion that home is fundamental to the formation of ethics,[103] Levinas affirms that home, as a core element of hospitality, is

97. Reaves, *Safeguarding the Stranger*, 44.

98. Reynolds, "Improving Together," 59.

99. Reynolds, "Improving Together," 59.

100. Derrida, *Acts of Religion*, 360.

101. McNulty, *Hostess,* xiv.

102. McNulty, *Hostess,* xiv.

103. Heidegger, "Letter on Humanism," 234.

"what makes the ethical possible."[104] In support, Derrida sees hospitality not merely as part of ethics, but as "the ethics par excellence."[105]

In summary, tension has shown to be constitutive of hospitality practices.[106] Derrida cautiously identifies a series of paradoxes involved in hospitality. Hospitality, as he describes, should always:

> Wait and not wait, extend and stretch itself [se tender] and still stand and hold itself [se tenir] . . . Intentionality and non-intentionality, attention and inattention . . . [All] at once working, worrying, disrupting the concept and experience of hospitality while also making them possible . . ."[107]

Similarly, spontaneity and intentionality at the core of hospitality do not completely eliminate anticipation and unintentional acts as possible variables of hospitality.[108] Such inherent paradox that characterizes hospitality explains the reasons for its non-exhaustive definition.

Tensions embedded in hospitality also extend toward its understanding among cultures. While Derrida thinks hospitality is central to many cultures, Pohl considers it countercultural.[109] This envisaged dichotomy can be resolved when the expressive terms like "culture" and "counterculture" are replaced with "conventional and unconditional perspectives of hospitality."[110] For hospitality to be reduced to being either cultural or countercultural amounts to a denial of otherness. On the one hand, each culture should be viewed in her own terms and meanings, and on the other hand, the intentionality of a people's culture determines the extent of hospitality implied in its practices. For example, the degree of hospitality among desert nomads, who by default cannot survive without hospitality, would be unjustly comparable to that of agrarian settlers, whose home is the only safe place they call their own. Naturally, the attachment to home often necessitates the threat of its dispossession.

The radical hospitality advocated by Levinas lies in the practice of substitutive altruism. Although the practicality of Levinas's radical

---

104. Katz, Levinas, 59.

105. See Jacques Derrida, "Hospitality and Hostility," a seminar given at UC Irvine, cited in McNulty, Hostess, xvii.

106. Reaves, Safeguarding the Stranger, 46.

107. Derrida, Acts of Religion, 360.

108. Reaves, Safeguarding the Stranger, 46.

109. Pohl, "Building a Place," 35.

110. Kearney, Strangers, 69.

dimension has been severely questioned by scholars, his model of hospitality transcends most existing cultural hospitalities. Transcultural hospitality, rather than condemning, can challenge various cultures and traditions toward evolutionary transformations. In this context, this research aims at engendering substantive provocations among Muslims and Christians by proposing a transcultural model of hospitality that could be key to interreligious healthy competition on altruism. As already demonstrated, the inadequacies perceived in cultural or religious practices of hospitality should be read as inherent, not necessarily as weakness, because "the fluidity and tension within hospitality is its genius."[111] Reaves summarizes, "In hospitality's mystery and tension lies its power to transform."[112]

This section on hospitality in general has sustained a philosophical reflection on mutual hospitality through a host-guest dynamic. The views of some philosophers of difference were articulated in showing that the dual contrasting nature or tensions embedded in hospitality, rather than constituting obstacles to its practice, define genuine hospitality. More so, mutuality was also defended as another constitutive element of genuine hospitality, because the host and the guest engage in an active relationship that culminates in communal growth or enrichment. However, it must be stated that mutual growth happens as a surprise, and not as an intentional expectation for payback. The next section will explore a distinct one-directional view of hospitality, exposing its parallel responsibility, and the reasons for such asymmetric relation.

Hospitality: Ethical Dimension

Welcoming the other derives from ancient tradition with strong divine dimension.[113] Ancient Greek and Roman mythologies contain legendary stories of gods that paid visit in the guise of human beings in order to test the hospitality of their chosen human hosts.[114] Even to date, the undisclosed identity of the guest inspires the sacredness of the guest.[115]

---

111. Reaves, *Safeguarding the Stranger*, 48.

112. Reaves, *Safeguarding the Stranger*, 48.

113. Bolchazy, *Hospitality*, 1.

114. Oden, *And You Welcomed Me*, 18. See Denaux, "Theme," 263–68. Also Stock, "Hospitality."

115. McNulty, *Hostess*, 8–9.

Ancient Greece understood hospitality as a religious practice because it
was the "defining social ethics of *Zeus Xenios*, Zeus god of strangers."[116]
Despite the deep spiritual root of hospitality, some Western contexts
barely emphasize it today due to the demand that sociopolitical aspects
of life exert on boundary respect and sensitivity.[117]

Nonetheless, scholars of hospitality are unwavering about the
centrality of hospitality in the everydayness of intersubjective relations.
For Derrida and especially for Thomas Ogletree, "to be moral is to be
hospitable to the stranger."[118] Reciprocity as argued by Ricoeur, McNulty,
and Reaves constitutes a defining aspect of expressing hospitality. Still,
asymmetric service to the other, in Levinasian terms, articulates a radical level of hosting the vulnerable other. Asymmetric hospitality hones
in on the morality that "makes us human, which is the capacity of unconditional welcome of the other, of being charitable, cooperative, and
communal."[119] In other words, hospitality practices, whether in their
reciprocal or asymmetric dimension, are receiving significant attention
in both the intellectual and the practical worlds. Levinas's teaching on
hospitality is representative of an ethical dimension, and therefore needs
some more highlighting.

Levinasian Hospitality:
The Problem, the Response, and the Evaluation

Levinas's understanding of hospitality inevitably gives rise to four critical questions: 1) What is not right with Western "egology"?[120] 2) What
constitutes Levinas's redefinition of the other? 3) Of what importance is
asymmetric relation to the Christian-Muslim dialogue of life? 4) Is Levinas's ethical hospitality sustainable?

Without any intent of repeating Levinas's background or reviewing
his general thought pattern (included in the introduction), this section
will concentrate on his understanding of ethical hospitality. Here the
focus is on two principles of Levinas's hospitality, namely, (substitutive)

116. McNulty, *Hostess*, vii.

117. Pew Forum on Religion and Public Life in the United States on "The Religious
Dimensions of Torture Debate," cited in Reaves, *Safeguarding the Stranger*, n. 91.

118. Ogletree, *Hospitality to the Stranger*, 1.

119. Boff, *Virtues*, 50.

120. Levinas, *Totality and Infinity*, 44.

responsibility and asymmetry. However, whereas his altruistic responsibility strengthens the thesis of this research, his teaching on asymmetry will be challenged to accommodate the mutuality of responsibility among Christians and Muslims.

Levinas is a specialist in contextualizing the meaning of terms. The greatest difficulty in reading him lays in understanding multiple uncommon terms in his writings within their context-specific connotations. Understanding Levinasian thought on hospitality will therefore entail a fair grasp of the following key terms: totality, infinity, transcendence, face, imperative, responsibility, altruism, hospitality, and asymmetry. Under his hospitality topic, these terms are in no way atomized. Rather, their individual applications confirm their interrelatedness. An attempt at articulating the connectivity of these terms would read: The other as infinity rejects being totalized because of her transcendence, but through the metaphor of the face the other partially manifests herself, while unceasingly commanding an asymmetric responsibility from the self. This succinct expression, I suppose, fairly summarizes Levinas's altruism.

This interconnectivity expresses the beauty of Levinas's altruism, which is solely distinguished by asymmetric hospitality. In other words, Levinas's hospitality engages the distinct identity of the other and how she ought to be cared for. However, the strength of Levinas's argument in defense of the other also provides grounds for its implied limitations. Reading Levinas outside these ascribed terminologies might lead to gross misinterpretations of his thought. A distilling of his thought on these terms constitutes a summary of his entire ethic on hospitality.

A key to Levinas's wider project is to reflect on the ethical significance of what he calls "the Face."[121] Levinas confirms, "The way in which the other presents himself, exceeding the idea of the other in me, we here name face."[122] The face commands self-critique,[123] and demands infinite ethical responsibility. He contends that the noun "I" entails my availability in service for everyone and everything.[124] Levinasian hospitality language can be definitive, which reflects the impact of his philosophical scholarship and his terrible experiences of anti-Semitism, especially

121. Levinas, *Totality and Infinity*, 51.

122. Levinas, *Totality and Infinity*, 50.

123. Levinas, *Totality and Infinity*, 81.

124. Levinas, *Otherwise than Being* (1981), 114.

during the Holocaust. In his exact words, "The face is present in its re-fusal to be contained."[125] The face invites, yet it resists.[126]

Derrida affirms that Levinas's first opus magnum, *Totality and Infin-ity* (1961), is a complete project on his ethical hospitality.[127] Hospitality is such a vital concern in the scholarship of Levinas that it appears over twenty times in the first 150 pages of *Totality and Infinity*,[128] and cuts across his few other works, like *Otherwise than Being* (1974). Theologi-cally, Derrida and Levinas moved beyond Heidegger's critique of meta-physics, but religiously they make this move in radically different ways.

Central to Levinas's philosophy is the reversal of the Western philo-sophical tradition, from that of ontology to a philosophy of relationship among ethical beings. From Plato through modern philosophers, Levinas argues that ontology has been glorified to the detriment of interpersonal ethical responsibilities. Attention was liberally focused on what defines being, rather than on a committed relation toward the other. At the very beginning of *Totality and Infinity*, Levinas systematically assumes the role of an advocate of subjectivity.[129] In his argument, there is need, first, to salvage subjectivity in order to create awareness of its responsibility towards the other. In his words, "I am defined as a subjectivity, as a single person, as an 'I' precisely because I am exposed to the Other."[130]

In reaction to the popular Western thought pattern (*philosophy*, love of wisdom), Levinas strives through his works to establish an ethi-cally based "wisdom of love."[131] He seeks a radical shift from the philoso-phies of totality (ontology) to a philosophy of infinity (ethics), through an articulation of the transcendence of the other. His project builds on Descartes' idea of infinity in his Third Meditation.[132] While Descartes' infinity was applicable to God, Levinas adopts this Cartesian concept and pertains it to the relationship of the human subject to the human other. The twist he achieves by attributing infinity to the other emphasizes in-equality and asymmetry. For Levinas, the absolute exteriority of the other

125. Levinas, *Totality and Infinity*, 194.

126. Levinas, *Totality and Infinity*, 197–98.

127. Derrida, *Adieu to Emmanuel Levinas*, 21.

128. Ferreira, "Total Altruism," 455.

129. Levinas, *Totality and Infinity*, 26.

130. Levinas and Kearney, "Dialogue," 26–27.

131. Shepherd, *Gift of the Other*, 18.

132. Levinas, *Totality and Infinity*, 54.

person assures the infinitude of the other that can never be assimilated or incorporated into a totality.[133]

It is obvious that Levinas is pushing an indefinite identity for the other, which cannot be totalized because the other by nature is quite incomprehensible,[134] in contrast to an object for scientific study. But can the other be known? In his argument, the other is not first and foremost one to be understood, but rather one whose ethical plight we are called to respond to. The other is the absolute other, whose difference exceeds similarities. From his perspective, otherness is nothing less than epiphany, and so must remain strange. Building on Descartes' infinity,[135] Levinas applies its characteristics of inequality, non-reciprocity, and asymmetry to the relationship of the human subject to the human other in such a manner that any reversal of this characterization strangulates the other. In Levinas exact words, "Totalizing the other happens when one conceives that one comprehends or understands the other, as if the relationship with the other is based on correlation, reciprocity and equality."[136]

The absolute portraiture of the other crafted by Levinas recalls a similarity with Buddhist thought. Like early Buddhists, Levinas rejects being based on his claim that Western ontology prevented people from ethical practices; however, he solely emphasizes relations. In early Buddhism, primacy was given to the ethical over the ontological, but there are now (and have been throughout Buddhist history) multitudes of competing Buddhist ontologies. Even the talk of "emptiness" is the expression of an ontology.

Interestingly, Levinas, while elevating the other as transcendence,[137] occluded God, and simultaneously created a form of metaphysical atheism using the metaphor of the face, through which traces of the divine can only manifest. Levinas prioritizes ethics because of its sensitivity to interpersonal human acts. Ethics questions sameness and prioritizes the other to a quasi-transcendental level.[138]

Nevertheless, going by Heidegger's interpretation of the Greek word *physis* (as not nature, but being), Adriaan Peperzak insists that Levinas

---

133. Levinas, *Totality and Infinity*, 79–81.

134. Shepherd, *Gift of the Other*, 51.

135. Descartes, *Meditations on First Philosophy*, Third Meditation, 7:40; 2:28.

136. Shepherd, *Gift of the Other*, 22.

137. Levinas, *Totality and Infinity*, 49.

138. Levinas, *Totality and Infinity*, 79–81.

only initiated a different kind of metaphysics that transcends ontology. Peperzak reiterates, "Better than 'ontology,' the word 'metaphysics' expresses the transcending movement of a thinking that goes beyond the realm of Being."[139]

Maintaining his standpoint that Levinas's scholarship, especially in *Totality and Infinity*, does not constitute a total departure from Western philosophy as popularly claimed, Peperzak concludes, "Just as Heidegger's thought of Being cannot be understood if it is cut off from the classical texts and traditions present in its retrievals, Levinas's philosophy cannot be separated from its polemical connections with Western ontology and its greatest contemporary representative in particular."[140] In contrast, Levinas accuses Heideggerian being of neglecting the transcendence of the other, thereby initiating imperialism[141] or the other that imposes itself. He therefore aims at establishing a radical ethical turn that not only proposes that "Ethics is the spiritual optics," but also asserts that "metaphysics is enacted in ethical relations."[142] In conclusion, he insists, "Morality is not a branch of Philosophy, but first philosophy."[143]

Levinasian ethical hospitality connotes the sacrificial welcoming of the other into the home. As an ultimate fact, home hospitality undergirds Levinas's assertion in *Totality and Infinity* such that the "subject is a host."[144] However, to welcome the other is to put in question the host's freedom.[145] Responsibility towards the other is both imperative and substitutive. There is an infinite debt to the other, meaning that the host is "infinitely responsible"[146] and can never quit[147] from serving the other.

Levinas's "self-recollection" at home,[148] parallel to Panikkar's intrareligious dialogue, prods the host into absolute service to the other, to an extent of being a hostage. The home first offers hospitality of a dwelling to the owner (host). But this hospitable act must be reciprocated for the self to free itself of the sense of indebtedness, and for subjectivity to warrant

139. Peperzak, *To the Other*, 13.

140. Peperzak, *To the Other*, 14.

141. Levinas, *Totality and Infinity*, 46–47.

142. Levinas, *Totality and Infinity*, 79.

143. Levinas, *Totality and Infinity*, 304.

144. Levinas, *Totality and Infinity*, 299.

145. Levinas, *Totality and Infinity*, 85.

146. Levinas, *Emmanuel Levinas*, 18.

147. Levinas, *Éthique et Infini*, 105–6.

148. Levinas, *Totality and Infinity*, 38.

the protection it gets from the home. In other words, the self enjoys a healthy relationship with her home only when she welcomes the other into it.[149] It is interesting how Levinas indirectly approves of reciprocity for the maintenance of the balance between the home and her host, but objects to the same relationship between guest and host.

Significant attention has been given through philosophical and ethical arguments concerning the challenges of otherness. In particular, scholars of difference, from various perspectives, have relentlessly argued for the need for respect and appreciation of the otherness of the other. Despite their different points of emphasis, there is a consensual shift from egocentrism to altruism. However, the consensus seems to stop at identifying the problem with sameness, but far from the methodological approaches for resolving it.

Limitations of the Philosophical and Ethical Views of Hospitality

Hospitality, even though a welcome key to affirming otherness and mutual growth among philosophical and ethical scholars, with its complexity and endemic risks, still engenders diverse conclusions. Hospitality was severally presented as an honorable but risky venture with an inseparable paradoxical dynamism. It was argued that only in paradox can genuine hospitality happen. The complexity of hospitality was seen not only in its ancient Mediterranean practices, through its transformative forms in both Islamic and Christian history, but was also present in its etymological rhetoric. An example runs through the host-guest metaphor and its linguistic implications. In general, the greatest challenge is not only trying to deal with the unknown identity of the other, but also to establish a balance between the self-other dialogic relations. While many advocate for reciprocal hospitality, Levinas uniquely argues for an asymmetric approach as the only way to reassure the inviolable identity of the objectivized other.

Levinas's altruistic hospitality provides a radical responsibility for the other, even to the point of substitution. As previously noted, the radical nature of Levinas's understanding of responsibility constitutes

149. Levinas identifies the other as the individual person and explains the term Third as humanity in general. He centers most of his hospitality arguments on the face of the individual other. However, his dealing on the Third forms his political hospitality.

the ethical dynamism that both Muslims and Christians need in order to turn responsibly toward each other. Without such an essential responsible turn, it would be impossible to perceive the other in her own terms. But when each religious tradition is allowed to communicate itself through its practice of good works, the religious other can unlearn her previous biases and equally transmit her own goodness through hospitality. From this perspective, Levinas's asymmetry poses an obstacle to the thesis of this research due to the restriction on mutuality.

However, the immense contributions of Levinas with some other philosophers of difference expose the underlying principles of hospitality that can be relevant in Muslim-Christian dialogue of life. For ordinary Muslims and Christians who engage in the dialogue of life, the characteristic expositions of hospitality as key to mutual responsibility were shown to work in collaboration with principles such as internal disposition, humility, listening, spontaneity, unconditionality, inclusivity, and sharing of space. Moreover, it was said that for genuine hospitality to happen, these principles might be incomplete if separated from the risks of losing one's comfort zone (home).

Levinas's ethical hospitality could be good enough to awaken one to the injustice toward the other, but it is still inadequate in solving the problem it identified. In order to combat the egoistic monster, Levinas created another monster, other-centrism. Rather than decentralization, Levinas shifted the center of intersubjective relations from one extreme to another. He initiated a radical shift from human subjectivity based on autonomy (self-rule) to human subjectivity based on heteronomy (rule by others).[150]

Summarily, Levinas states: "My ethical relation of love for the other stems from the fact that the self cannot survive by itself alone, cannot find meaning within its own being-in-the world, within the ontology of sameness."[151] His position, even though it has contributed immensely toward the rescue of the manipulated other, still cannot attain the goal of a harmonized relation. If Western self-centrism were the dialectical thesis of intersubjective hospitality conversation, Levinas only provides the antithesis that yearns for a synthesis.

M. Jamie Ferreira summarizes the main problem of total altruism on two counts: 1) theoretical, since it fails to offer a moral agency adequate to ground its imperative, and 2) practical, because it encourages

---

150. Shepherd, *Gift of the Other*, 19–21.

151. Levinas, *Ethics of the Infinite*, 60.

self-hatred.[152] However, she thinks that some of Levinas's critics misinterpret him, and therefore requests that Levinas should be read through an ethic of welcome, in which the host and the guest are already known. Levinas's major critics totally disagree with Ferreira.

In general, critics suggest that by emphasizing the "substitution" of self, total altruism, and the self as hostage, Levinas fails to maintain a sense of self-sufficiency for responsible agency or the dialectics of relation.[153] Ricoeur, a French contemporary of Levinas and a major voice among his critics, stresses the erasure of the agency of the other in asymmetric relations. For him, the other is prohibited from practicing hospitality. Ricoeur, while admitting a deep indebtedness to Levinas, suggests that Levinas's ethics implies the substitution of self-hatred for self-esteem, or at the very least ignores or precludes "solicitude, as the mutual exchange of self-esteems."[154] Oliver Davies, another critic of Levinas, maintains that the hostage self suffers the violence of alterity in oppression, persecution, martyrdom, and obsession, and precludes the self-presence and self-possession necessary to ethical responsibility.[155]

Levinas's strict dichotomy between ethics and ontology constitutes a huge problem. Scholars wonder why the identity of the other (being) can be ignored but a proposal of ethical command is emphasized for her.[156] In this regard, who the other is or who the self is (in Levinas) constitutes a foundational question for this research's thesis on a Muslim-Christian dialogue of life. In essence, the other could be anyone (Muslim or Christian) depending on the circumstances of relative perceptions.

Again, Levinas's radical proposal for a renewed self-other relation fails to take the issue of context seriously. The difficulty encountered in deciphering his anonymous self betrays a sense of indifference in regard to context (home). Eubanks and Gauthier think that Levinas displays greater affiliation to his cultural nomadic life than homeness. Levinas's assertion affirms their guess: "From this point on, an opportunity appears to us: to perceive men outside the situation in which they are placed, and let the human face shine in all its nudity."[157] Levinas's nomadic vi-

---

152. Ferreira, "Total Altruism," 443–44.

153. Ferreira, "Total Altruism," 444.

154. Ricoeur, *Oneself as Another*, 168, 221.

155. Davies, *Theology of Compassion*, 134.

156. Eubanks and Gauthier, "Politics of the Homeless Spirit," 138.

157. Levinas, "Heidegger," 233.

sion, though used here as a critique, supports the Abrahamic pilgrim metaphor, to be explored in chapter 11.

However, caution must be taken against establishing indebtedness via reciprocity as determinant. A check on indebtedness leads to non-reciprocal rule from the same recipient of a hospitable act. Expectations of immediate payback as an inducement, as previously argued by Derrida, destroy the justice of hospitality. In contrast, the beauty of hospitality includes the assurance of its gift of surprise. Any kind of altruism devoid of surprise cannot truly qualify as just hospitality. The pilgrim model in Genesis 18 regarding Abraham and his divine guests has surprises at its center. Nigerian Muslims and Christians are invited to compete with each other by lavishing surprising hospitality across their religious borders.

When this relationship is corrected, hospitality, rather than stemming from impersonal duty, freely flows from within and becomes an outward expression of love for God and God's people. Often enough, it seems to be a thankless responsibility to others, and in this way Shepherd thinks that Catholic theology has a capacity to honor Levinas's insights, but also to understand them critically in light of the incarnation.[158] Christ's incarnation will no doubt be problematic for typical Muslims, but will not necessarily constitute an impasse. Christ, as a true prophet who models a substitutive altruism, in his profound hospitality, similar to the Islamic Bedouin hospitality (who could offer anything to guests, including their wives or children), offered himself for the love of others. Love of neighbor, as an extension for the love of God, should be the goal of both Islamic and Christian teaching and practice. In this regard, Levinas's ethical altruism would be foundational to mutual appreciation and responsibility between Muslims and Christians as they engage in their own dialogue of life. Understanding Levinas's ethics of hospitality through the face can be arduous, but the fruits can be theologically enriching.

---

158. Shepherd, *Gift of the Other*, 160.

8

Hospitality and the African Communality

THE CONTEXTUAL USAGE OF Africa cannot exhaustively be a representative of all peoples living in the Sub-Saharan region. Rather, the term speaks to the major commonalities that every African can generally identify with as a distinct people. Convincingly, most Africans know and believe in an interdependent (triadic) relationship that is too strong for death to destroy. In essence, African relationality is tailored towards communion (of ethnic kin, with deity and cosmos) as its *telos*, while highlighting hospitality as its reliable tool. The problem of otherness has also challenged the African mind, giving rise to certain philosophical views and approaches.

In a traditional African context, the vital force (*ntu*) undergirds her relational or community worldview.[1] Life can be explained in terms of increasing or diminishing the vital force. The extent of cohesion with other entities determines one's spiritual growth in life. At a ripe age of a good life, death is considered a departure journey, with a high expectancy of return (reunion with kin, deity, and cosmos). Although the Fang of Gabon and the Bussa show hospitality to strangers (believed to be disguised ancestors),[2] ancestral reunion, according to Charles Nyamiti, must not be reduced to a physical return.[3]

---

1. Bujo, *Foundations of African Ethic*, 3.
2. Olikenyi, African Hospitality, 105.
3. Nyamiti, *Jesus Christ*, 1:66.

Ancestor veneration has no uniform beliefs and practices in Africa.[4] Only those (male and female) who lived exemplary lives, especially hospitable lives, can be ancestors.[5] However, there are five elements that characterize the merited status of an ancestor: 1) kinship belongingness, 2) superhuman status, 3) mediation role between divinity and kin, 4) exemplarity of behavior, 5) and rights of communication.[6] The most important point in ancestor narrative is a spiritual bond, a connectedness that transcends the bondage of death.

Compared to the Christian universal relational goal of eternal union with God after death, this ethnic exclusivity (kinship) in the African notion of communion exposes its major weakness. Christianity can also be seen as having an ethnic kin expression by the fact that *Lumen Gentium* teaches that the "messianic people, although it does not, in fact include everybody, and at times may seem to be a little flock, is, however, a most certain seed of unity, hope and salvation for the whole human race."[7] Nevertheless, the kinship in Christianity is universally theocentric, whereas the African notion is logically tied to land of origin.

Christians' one-time eternal union might seem unreasonable to Africans, because, whether alive or dead, they never cease desiring an unbroken interconnection with the divine, the kin, and their environment. Moreover, beyond the passage of death, the ancestor (good spirit) acquires a "superhuman status," which strengthens the bond of connectivity and makes the expression of kinship appear real through "the special magico-religious powers."[8]

This African relationality, with a defined communal *telos*, sheds light on the ecclesial community, even though John Zizioulas, an Eastern Orthodox archbishop, insists that only through Christ can communion with God be possible.[9] Zizioulas claims that outside of Christ only a non-personalist relationship with God can actually happen.[10] His christocentric emphasis is a clear shift from the traditional Orthodox theistic

---

4. Hardacre, "Ancestors: Ancestor Worship," 265–68.

5. Dickson, *Theology in Africa*, 198.

6. Nyamiti, *Jesus Christ*, 1:68–69.

7. *Lumen Gentium*, #9, in Flannery, ed., *Vatican Council II*.

8. Nyamiti, *Jesus Christ*, 1:66.

9. Zizioulas, *Communion and Otherness*, 307.

10. Zizioulas, *Communion and Otherness*, 243.

bent. Nonetheless, African communality can be more visible through her hospitality ethics.

African Hospitality

African hospitality is holistic, which is not unusual. Africans seek wholeness of life, which has shaped her pluralistic perception of reality. Reality is one but is composed of the interconnectivity of the divine (including the spirits), the human, and the cosmic spheres.[11] This means that life is generally relational.[12]

African hospitality is a way of life[13] and is in fact a minimum expectation for and from every person, according to Eugene Uzukwu.[14] Uzukwu's thesis highlights an important reason why hospitality transcends charitable acts, as detailed in chapter 7. Uzukwu also strengthens the thesis of this research, since hospitality, in addition to being mandated in both Islam and Christianity, has a strong cultural basis for Africans. Most importantly, looking at African hospitality through a Western lens would be the wrong way.

For Africans, the principle of mutuality, which undergirds interrelatedness, requires that anyone can practice hospitality, anywhere, and at any time. Julius M. Gathogo affirms that "the African carries his hospitality to fields, in politics, economics etc.,"[15] based on the conviction that the stronger the connecting bond among persons, the richer life can be appreciated. The practice of African hospitality primarily aims at establishing and maintaining personal relationships—between individuals, between individuals and communities, and between communities and communities. Broadly speaking, the onus lies on human beings to keep the three spheres of interaction in harmony through sacrificial striving that assures mutual hospitality or interdependence. In agreement with Levinas, it has been argued that Africans talk more of human beings than about God because they believe that anthropological love guarantees divine love.[16]

11. Bujo, *Foundations*, 2.
12. Bujo, *Foundations*, 3.
13. Gathogo, *Truth about African Hospitality*, 4.
14. Uzukwu, "Missiology Today," 158.
15. Gathogo, *Truth about African Hospitality*, 4.
16. Bujo, *African Christian*, 77.

Hospitality, even though a theme that has attracted less scholarly interests, paradoxically pervades the entire fabric of African life and its *Weltanschauung*. John Mbiti attests that hospitality permeates all sectors of African life "so fully that it is not easy or possible always to isolate it."[17] Like the inevitable prevalence of African religiosity, which resists the secular-religious divide, Mbiti categorizes African hospitality on the same level.[18] Traditional African hospitality is so real that its daily practices, in both private and public domains, such as at homes, along the way, in the markets, inside buses, at worship grounds, during ceremonies and festivities, can be taken for granted. Its commonness at socioreligious events and the opposing foreign influences might have contributed adversely to its insufficient presence in some modern African societies. Nonetheless, Gathogo reassures that "even though this ancient hospitality cannot remain intact, it is by no means extinct."[19]

African hospitality eludes a particular definition. Rather, its polysemy can be partially expressed by designating hospitality from several perspectives. In essence, hospitality in ancient African imagination, as earlier remarked, occupies the centerpiece of genuine relational life. The significance of hospitality agrees with the meaning of African life as personalized relationship, in which a person attains fulfillment, not in isolation, but within the whole. As a result, African hospitality offers a positive response toward human existence, which is artfully crafted on interpersonal and interdependent relations. In this light, hospitality defines good life, but life is meaningless without genuine expression of humanness, also known as *ubuntu*.

Ubuntu and Hospitality

Hospitality is deeply tied to the *ubuntu* spirit of the Zulu and Xhosa people. *Ubuntu* originally depicts a profound sense of humanness. It as well offers an understanding of human beings simply as "being-with-others,"[20] which expresses the reality of interpersonal responsibility. *Ubuntu* is a polysemic term that has several synonyms, not only among the South African Zulu, but also among East and Central Africans: *umundu* (in

17. Mbiti, *African Religions*, 1.
18. Mbiti, *African Religions*, 2.
19. Gathogo, "Some Expressions," 275.
20. Gathogo, "Some Expressions," 285.

Kukuyu, Kenya), *umuntu* (in Kimeru, Kenya), *bumuntu* (in kiSukuma and kiHaya, Tanzania), *vumuntu* (in shiTsonga and shiTswa, Mozambique), *bomoto* (in Bomangi, DRC), and *gimuntu* (in kiKongo, DRC, and in giKwese, Angola).[21] From an ontological perspective, "Ubuntu includes all the qualities and traits which go into making a person fully human and includes the willingness and ability to respond positively to the Creator."[22] This assertion does not deny the humanness at creation; rather, it emphasizes the responsibility of actualizing the potencies that define the purpose of humanity. In accord with the teachings of Ireneaus of Lyons (AD 130–202) and Augustine of Hippo (AD 354–430) on the necessity of growth for humanity (growing from God's image into God's likeness), *ubuntu* accentuates the altruistic responsibility that characterizes humanness.

Ubuntu connotes an ideal moral quality of personhood, on the one hand, and an ethos of African communality, on the other. In support of its moral meaning, Archbishop Desmond Tutu writes, "when we want to give high praise to someone we say, 'Yu, u nobuntu'—this implies that he or she has *Ubuntu*."[23] In a related sense, Kenneth Kaunda[24] of Zambia considers African humanism as the nearest translation of *ubuntu*.[25] The two meanings actually relate because a genuine African person actualizes himself or herself only in mutual interdependent relationship with others. Whereas Western humanism excludes religion, African humanism involves the religious because, in the latter perspective, no dualism is perceived between the material, the psychological, and the spiritual.

Similarly, *ubuntu* from a political perspective differs from democracy. Unlike democracy that rules with the majority, thereby disregarding the minority stance, *ubuntu* moves further in seeking a consensus.[26] Even though consensus drags and delays,[27] the *ubuntu* spirit of inclusiv-

21. Kamwangamalu, "Ubuntu in South Africa," 25.

22. Baartman, "Religious Needs," 77.

23. Tutu, *No Future without Forgiveness*, 34.

24. As Zambia's first indigenous president, Kenneth Kaunda chose "Zambian humanism" as the Zambian national ideology and philosophy. It was a form of African socialism, which combined traditional African values with Western socialist and Christian values. At the center of this humanism were God and the human person, for God was known through the human person and also served through human beings.

25. Interview from Kenneth Kaunda, December, 16, 2009; cited in Gade, "What Is Ubuntu?, 448.

26. Teffo, *Concept of Ubuntu*, 4.

27. Mugambi, *From Liberation*, 132.

ity[28] prefers it to the divisive line, which the democratic winner-loser paradigm introduces into the existing communality. The consensual dream of *ubuntu* can become a long-term task for Africans to develop and harness into an alternate political vision, which can benefit the black continent and the rest of the world. J. Teffo confirms in these words: "The ethos of Ubuntu . . . is one single gift that African philosophy can bequeath on other philosophies of the world."[29]

Recently, *ubuntu* usage has been commonly linked with the *Nguni* (Zulu) expression "*muntu ngumuntu ngabantu*" (a person is a person through other persons). In other words, "the meaning of an individual's life is found in and through his relationship with the Other or Others."[30] The *Nguni* proverb, according to Christian B. N. Gade, was not identified with *ubuntu* until the 1990s.[31] Gade traces the reason for such refined meaning among black South Africans to the transitional consciousness against the apartheid segregation experiences.[32] Nonetheless, *ubuntu* could be, originally, a polysemic notion whose various meanings stem from different applications, majorly determined by who used it, why it was used, and in what context, but mostly because the meanings are virtually preserved in poetic languages. These poetic meanings render *ubuntu* difficult to translate into foreign languages. Archbishop Tutu corroborates in these words:

> Africans believe in something that is difficult to render in English. We call it "ubuntu, botho". It means the essence of being human. You know when it is there and when it is absent. It speaks about humaneness, gentleness, and hospitality, putting yourself on behalf of others, being vulnerable. It embraces compassion and toughness. It recognizes that my humanity is bound up in yours, for we can only be human together.[33]

Accepting responsibility for the other provokes a reversal of the biblical Cain's interrogation to God, "Am I my brother's keeper?" Such a fundamental disconnect from the responsibility due to others turned Cain into "[a] desiring self, restless, always on the move, never at rest,

28. Mugambi, *From Liberation*, 132.0

29. Teffo, *Concept of Ubuntu*, 5.

30. Nkemnkia, *African Vitalogy*, 111.

31. Gade, "What Is Ubuntu?, 448.

32. Gade, "Historical Development," 321.

33. Tutu, *Words*, 69.

acquiring and appropriating possessions and yet driven by fear away from others."[34] In contrast to Cain, Abraham understands the theological meaning of human responsibility, which the Letter to the Hebrew attests: "Do not neglect to show hospitality to strangers, for some have entertained angels without knowing it" (13:1–2). This epistle further instructs, "Do not neglect to do good and to share what you have, for such sacrifices are pleasing to God" (13:16). In essence, it is the deceptive option for irresponsibility towards the other that stimulates hostility.

Moreover, the African sense of responsibility for the other questions the immensity of hostility raging in the black continent. If apartheid sprouted from the racial divide between white and black South Africans, what explains the ongoing xenophobic attitudes (of the same black South Africans, who were apartheid victims) against African immigrants? Have the Biafran pogrom (1967–1970), Rwandan tribal genocide (1994), Muslim-Christian conflicts in Nigeria, Liberian fourteen years of civil war, militants wars in the Congo, North-versus-South divide in Sudan and Cameroon, etc. not ridiculed the tenacity of *ubuntu* spirit enough, among Africans?

Nonetheless, *ubuntu* is not a ready-made good. Instead, *ubuntu* remains an ever-evolving process of human personhood,[35] which can hopefully act against the contextual malaise of African morality and politics. For this reason, *ubuntu* continuously requires a proactive imagination in addressing the signs of the time. Such a results-oriented approach can be possible through an improved African hospitality.

In precolonial times, African hospitality was an unrivaled concrete expression of the African communality. It is important to note that African communality, when viewed through a non-African lens, not only distorts the primary purpose, but also renders it absurd. Therefore, this section of the research calls for a preliminary caution against such anachronistic extrapolations. That said, it is pertinent to refresh minds on the basic African worldview in regards to otherness and communion.

34. Shepherd, *Gift of the Other*, 198.
35. Bujo, *Foundations*, 89.

African Hospitality:
A Via Media between Otherness and Communion

The African worldview is structured in a relational paradigm. To understand relation in Africa is to understand the notion of person. A person is not just an individual entity. Rather, personhood implies being in relationship. In African thought, a person cannot achieve fulfillment except in relation with kin, folks, neighbors, and strangers. Individuated life therefore ruptures genuine personality. Speculations are that African society assimilates personal consciousness and suppresses individual freedom. The veracity of such opinion largely depends on the verifying lens. In actuality, interconnectivity constitutes a major problem only when viewed with a foreign lens and measured by a narrow concept of freedom.

For Africans, freedom is broader and guaranteed. In essence, Africans complement "freedom-from" (boundary consciousness) with another aspect John Paul II called "freedom-in"[36] (the liberty to stay in communion). When freedom-from collaborates freedom-in, the African freedom-with becomes a clearer relational gauge. Joseph Ratzinger rejects the atomized individual by teaching in his "Spirit in the Body" that "in simple terms, the single and entire human beings—is marked most profoundly by the fact that one belongs to the totality of humanity, of the one 'Adam.'"[37] By this assertion, Ratzinger distances himself from the solitary I implied in the Cartesian *cogito*, and shows some leaning toward the African relational notion of person. Above all, the African dimension of freedom-in-communion provides level ground for dialogue of life between Muslims and Christians, through which religious otherness can be judiciously engaged. In this light, the African sense of communality can moderate how each religion feels toward the other.

The African sense of communality, engendered by freedom-with, demonstrates a notion of personhood structured on the relational principle: "I am because we are; and since we are, therefore I am."[38] The true and authentic person in this context would be a relational individual— one who understands his own life in relation to those of others. This relational expression necessitates a definition of personhood in discord with the Western epistemological bent initiated by the French Philosopher Rene Descartes.

36. John Paul II, *Veritatis Splendor*, #64.
37. Ratzinger, *Einführung in das Christentum*, 176.
38. Mbiti, *African Religions*, 106.

Distinguished from the Western Cartesian epistemology, "*Cogito ergo sum*" (I think, therefore I am), Africans are said to explain personhood existentially as "*Cognatus ergo sum*"[39] (I am related, therefore I am). The Akan of Ghana[40] says the same thing with a different expression: "I belong by blood relationship, therefore I am."[41] Simply put, African communality emphasizes interdependence or mutual reliance. In other words, mutual hospitality as preached by the African traditional fathers and mothers concretely demonstrates a culture of interdependence. Since this research advocates for the respect of otherness, rather than compare the Western and the African definitions of personhood, it intends showing how the African perspective meaningfully explains life in its context. Both definitions, however, are not without limitations.

The practice of African hospitality underscores communal life, expressed through communications, by which personhood attains fulfillment (being in a responsible relationship with others). In this regard, relationship is not just social, but basically ontological. Chinua Achebe, a renowned Nigerian novelist, stated: "A man who calls his kinsmen to a feast does not do so to save them from starving. They all have food in their own homes. When we gather together in the moonlit village ground it is not because of the moon. Every man can see it in his own compound. We come together because it is good for kinsmen to do."[42] Achebe emphasizes a coming together for sharing and renewing interconnectivity between persons and their kin, in such a manner as to complement otherness with communion.

In order to harmonize respect for otherness and communion, Africans promote hospitality through symbolic elements such as: acceptance, friendship, solidarity, closeness, respect, peace, neighborliness, trust, sharing, mutual love, gratitude, accompaniment, and community.[43] The list could be endless, so long as each leads to communion, in which every individual is given the choice to actualize his personhood.

---

39. Bujo, *Foundations*, 4.

40. Akan people estimate about twenty million in Africa. They are predominantly found (twelve million) in the southern region of Ghana. Some also live in Cote d' Ivoire (eight million), and in Liberia (forty-one thousand). Most Akans speak the Twi Fante language.

41. Healey and Sybertz, *Towards*, 62.

42. Achebe, *Things Fall Apart.* 118.

43. Olikenyi, *African Hospitality*, 112.

African Hospitality: A Socioreligious Dimension

It is no longer surprising that hospitality, as a prominent African practice, embraces the religious dimension as much as the sociocultural, ever
since Mbiti popularized Africans' renowned religiosity,[44] which entails
that "all things would have fallen to pieces if God did not exist."[45] The
inseparable interplay of the divine, the human, and the cosmos, which
depicts a "cosmotheandric"[46] relationship in African thought and belief, manifests vividly in the practices of hospitality. As in some ancient
cultures (already seen), where hospitality has a strong divine dimension,
African hospitality (understood as a constituent part of life itself) is incomplete without the divine sphere.

Some Africans find it fitting to demonstrate the divine dimension of
hospitality within the scope of ancestor belief. "Ancestorship," according
to Charles Nyamiti,[47] "is a sacred kin-relationship, which establishes a
right or title to regular sacred communication with one's kin through
prayer and ritual offering (oblation)."[48] Within such context, extending
hospitality to ancestors connotes a concretized manifestation of interconnectivity between humans and supernatural entities. This does not
exclude a few cultures in which women are not recognized as ancestors.

Ancestors are the living dead in African cosmology. They were humans whose exemplary lives in upholding justice, honesty, truth, and love
(especially sacrificial love) toward others and the Supreme Being transcended the bondage of death and merited them the ultimate reward of
living on among kith and kin.[49] In contrast to the assumption that Africa
is purely patriarchal in structure, many ancestors are women. Though
hotly debated, ancestor belief sheds light on the spirituality of traditional
Africans. For example, the Christian concept of heaven and hell (a linear
movement after death) totally contrasts with the cyclic notion of living
on after death, so long as one lived worthily. Living on does not necessarily mean reincarnation. Rather, it signifies unbroken connectivity with

44. Mbiti, *African Religions*, 1.

45. Idowu, *African Traditional*, 104.

46. "Cosmotheandric" is a coinage of Raimon Panikkar, which accounts for a
triadic bonding that connects the cosmos, humanity, and divinity together.

47. Nyamiti is a foremost African specialist on ancestor study. He has written
extensively on this theme.

48. Nyamiti, *Jesus Christ*, 2:4.

49. Dickson, *Theology in Africa*, 198.

kin beyond the grave. For traditional Africans, the worst damnation is perpetual exclusion from ancestral bonds and interactions, which is the price for dead wicked egoists, and for the forgotten living dead.[50]

In ancient Africa, and probably among some modern ones, the sharing of edibles with the ancestors is common. Usually it happens in the form of pouring a libation and dishing bits of food for these living dead, whose invisible presence is very real for the traditionalists.[51] In Kenya, in the Kikuyu, the Giriama, the Digo, the Chonyi, the Kamba, and the Taita, but most especially in the Pedi community, women commonly dish out food for the ancestors[52] while serving meals for members of their families. Many Africans, East and West, still reverently serve the ancestors first by dropping some portions of the edible on the ground (accompanied by words of thanksgiving) before partaking of any food and drink. In return, the ancestors bless and protect such benevolent givers.[53] It is believed that this amicable bond between the living and the living dead further strengthens their interdependence. As such, the practice resonates with the sense of mutual reliance. Gathogo compares this hospitality or show of gratitude to the ancestors with the African Christian understanding of prayers before and after meals.[54] In essence, he explains it as act of thanksgiving that begets more blessings.

To be truly human in the African context, a person aspires to remain in communion not only with her community, but also with the deity and the cosmos that provides the home. Similar to the Levinasian metaphor of home as that proto-provider of hospitality (protection) to the host, and which thereafter through recollection challenges the owner into being a dispenser of hospitality,[55] in Africa a genuine person is conscious of and strives to maintain a harmonious relationship across the human sphere, the world of divinities and the cosmos, through hospitality acts. He or she understands life in terms of interconnectivity, which must not be breached. Basically, in pre-Christian Africa a customary self-introduction would include one's name (first name), paternity (last name), and ancestral home. Said differently, an African person is

---

50. Mbiti, *African Religions*, 34.

51. Mbiti, *African Religions*, 32–33.

52. Moila, *Challenging Issues*, 3.

53. Nyamiti, *Jesus Christ*, 1:66.

54. Gathogo, "Some Expressions," 278.

55. Levinas, *Totality and Infinity*, 154–56.

a relational individual. Among the very few matrilineal communities, such as the Ashanti (Ghana), a slight shift is noticed, since the last name derives from the mother's ancestry. Above all, while paternity (or maternity) demonstrates the individual's connectivity with his ancestors (kin), the particularity of his root identifies the home (cosmos), and at once acknowledges the deity of the land (divinity). Like Zionists, land and local deity are inseparably personalized. The relational ideology common among Africans informs their perception of the other.

Act of Welcome

Based on the identified factors that constitute African hospitality, the act of welcoming guests (known and unknown) follows a derivative process that acknowledges the person as a relational individual. Africans are not unaware that openness in relationship involves great risks. Consequently, it is believed that "African traditions of hospitality are deep and sincere."[56] It is deep in the sense that the importance of hospitality largely determines good life. Its sincerity is also manifested in the readiness to practice it despite some inherent risks. First, the identity of the unknown guest does not delay or inhibit hospitality. Second, the goal of welcome is achieved in shared communion, aimed at growing, rather than threatening, the existing bond. In this regard, hosting is considered a blessing. Actually, it is the second that fuels the first.

African openness to welcome is severally expressed in words and in deeds. The Baganda people (Uganda) in their daily expression say, "When there is feast, everyone is welcome."[57] Similarly, the Owerri-Igbo (Nigeria) would friendly dispose a guest with, "*Batama, Uyo wu uyo ma'a gi*" (Come in, the home belongs to you and me). These two great expressions from the East and the West regions of Africa attest to the inclusiveness and the willingness to commune with strangers.

In addition to these two underlying motivations, hosting or welcoming a guest well attracts blessings. A Swahili proverb literally translated as "To get a guest is a blessing" resonates with the Kipsigis saying, "Visitors are like the rain, which is a blessing."[58] From this perspective, "the necessity of hospitality provides no excuses for even dubious guests

56. Gathogo, *Truth about African Hospitality*, 26.
57. Gathogo, *Truth about African Hospitality*, 23.
58. Gathogo, *Truth about African Hospitality*, 23.

or uninvited guests."[59] The Igbo people's motif of hospitality fits into similar paradigm as couched in its popular idiom, "When my guest departs peacefully and satisfied, let my creditors come."[60] Igbo people and likewise most other Africans can go an extra mile in satisfying their guests. Overall, a hospitable person is considered an instrument of God's benevolence, a channel through which the prayers of the needy are answered.[61]

Africans know that guests come with surprises (newness). Every genuine act of hosting, rather than impoverishing, enriches both host and guest. Usually, guests complement the hospitality lavished on them, either materially or immaterially. In ancient times, when communication through technological media had not reached Africa, guests were channels for news, both good and bad. Their presence heralded newness, and they often broke up the monotonous life of the community. Mbiti explains the benefits of a guest figuratively preserved in this African proverb: "The visitor heals the sick." This proverb, according to Mbiti, "means that when a visitor comes to someone's home, family quarrels stop, the sick cheer up, peace is restored and the home is restored to new strength."[62] As a result: "Visitors are, therefore, social healers—they are family doctors in a sense."[63] The mere thought of causing unwanted embarrassment on guests would inspire ethical comportment. Practically, the other sets the agenda, as recommended by Levinas.

By extension, the openness to the newness that accompanies strangers and guests explains the overall hospitality shown Christian and Islamic missionaries. Even though mission accounts gravely omitted names of prominent pioneer hosts and their roles, still the success story of missionaries would not be complete without the collaboration of their hospitable hosts. In truth, it was the openness to the surprise of the guest that enabled the hospitable receptions given to European missionaries[64] as well as Islamic *ulamas* and merchants. In other words, the gifts of hospitals and schools established by missions would have been impossible if they had been preceded by an initial hostility.

59. Nkwocha, "Eucharistic Hospitality," 6.

60. Uchendu, *Igbo*, 72.

61. Obengo, "Role of Ancestors," 53.

62. Mbiti, "Forest Has Ears," 23.

63. Mbiti, "Forest Has Ears," 23.

64. Gathogo, *Truth about African Hospitality*, 27.

The process of welcome begins with a cheerful greeting. Greeting in Africa occupies an important aspect of hospitality. Different cultures greet with several gestures accompanied by kind wishes. It is generally an expression of respect for the young to greet their seniors first, while the latter blesses the former in return. Some cultures have profound verbal exchange of greetings.

From a lived experience in Egbemaland (a riverine culture in Imo State, in the southeastern region of Nigeria), when a young person crosses paths with an elder, a detailed dialogic greeting ensues. The young person addresses the elder, *Maa dee* (My elder, may it be well with you). In response, the elder showers the respectful young person with appropriate praises and blessings: *ezenwanyi/ezenwoke* (prospective queen/king), *onyeoma* (a cultured child), *odeuri* (a literate), *okwanka* (an artisan), *nwa Jisos* (a Christian), etc. The young responds with *iyee* (yes) to each praise-title. The high point of this respectful culture is: while each walks away in the opposite direction, the exchange of greetings continues until none can hear the other. Rather than stupidity, this implies a mutual desire of endless blessings for the other. In other cultures, like the Yoruba, greetings are elaborately expressed with various gestures, ranging from simple to more profound: bowing, kneeling, genuflecting, or prostrating, depending on the social status of the elder being addressed by the younger person. In both cultures, respect for the other is greatly cherished and associated with sincere greeting.

Similar to the Levinasian face, which commands discourse, but rejects mere phenomenological disclosure, the African greeting aims at establishing a trustful relationship with a stranger, rather than interrogating her personality for information. It is unusual for the host to express eagerness in asking the stranger-guest for her identity or the purpose of her visit. While initiating a relationship, the host patiently waits for the stranger to reveal her identity and the reason for her visitation.

This approach might sound weird and unwise due to the possibility of danger. Considering that a (homeless) stranger bears enormous risk pertaining to safety of life, a genuine host endangers his comfort home in order to offer protection by sharing in the risk of the undisclosed identity. Nonetheless, the apparently naïve openness reveals an inner impulse and willingness to make sacrifices for the other. As a matter of belief, some African cultures hold that strange guests could be disguised ancestors, thereby mitigating the risk involved.[65] In such substitutive responsibility, the goal to attend to the need of the stranger surpasses the unavoidable consequences. Hospitality will therefore become suicidal only if the goal is either unethical or at par with the negative consequences.

Communion as Goal

The sharing of food and drink complements the verbal dimension of welcome. Siddiqui argues: "Life may be more than food and eating, but there is no life without eating and food. Thus, the theological and philosophical significance of what we eat and who we eat with connect the ordinary life with the higher life."[66] Sharing edibles with guests seals the communion that motivates African hosts. Gathogo confirms: "In most African customs, people eating together is a sacred undertaking."[67] It is sacred because African life constructed on triadic interdependence is central. In general, Africans conceive of life as the most precious and therefore sacred. So, to undertake the risk of eating together with strangers suggests that the purpose of attaining communion with the divine, the living, and cosmos supersedes the threat of physical death. In other words, enemies cannot eat together, since the primary intent of food is communion, which aims at achieving increased bonding, beyond geographic limits.

The logic of exclusive communion can be reasonable. Enmity jeopardizes the relational bond that unites people to their faith, their environment, and with each other. Usually, being guilty of heinous abominations automatically cuts off the culprit from the relational bond, until unity is reestablished through reconciliation. And because abominations are considered serious offenses against the triadic harmony, both offenders and known enemies cannot share meals with community members. In fact, eating together demonstrates friendship and even assures intercommunal peace. When peaceful coexistence is accidentally ruptured through crisis and war, trust and friendship are reinstated through shared meals. Moeahabo Phillip Moila develops this idea further when he argues that any disruption of the well-being of a community calls for the members of a societal group to sit down together and share a common meal.[68] In

65. Moila, *Challenging Issues*, 3.

66. Siddiqui, *Hospitality and Islam*, 13.

67. Gathogo, *The Truth*, 28.

68. Moila, *Challenging Issues*, 4.

this regard, the sacredness of eating together is primarily a covenant that binds all participants. Hospitality therefore strengthens the African sense of community.[69]

Eating together transcends the mere satisfaction of hunger. A Swahili proverb confirms that "Eating together promotes relationship." In the same vein, the Akamba say, "Food eaten together is sweeter." Even though table hospitality constitutes an aspect of hospitality, as Siddiqui rightly observed, "eating together and conviviality are the most obvious ways most of us understand this practice."[70] It is common, therefore, to see traditional Africans sharing meals daily, and especially at ceremonies.

Open invitations at ceremonies, rather than displaying affluence, stem from an existential interconnectivity, which forms the hub of African socialization. Allowing the invited as well as the uninvited into one's celebration proves that joys and sorrows are better managed when shared with sundry others. In most contemporary African communities, the celebration of rites of passages like birth, circumcision, marriages, funerals, etc. among Christians also culminates in the sharing of meals. The survival of such ancient practices of hospitality demonstrates its resilience among African Christians and Muslims, as the Yoruba context would demonstrate. For most Christians, the sacredness of shared meals offers grounds for appreciating the eucharistic Communion, which helps bring about the unity of the partakers. Among Muslims as well, it is not contradictory that, "the theological and philosophical significance of what we eat and who we eat with connect the ordinary life with the higher life."[71]

Being in communion entails sharing. Hospitality basically requires space. Creation of space is a prelude to sharing it. In essence, spaces are created for the other to belong, and not be contained or controlled. Both creation and sharing of space must be characterized by freedom and willingness. Augustine Echema defines African hospitality as "an unconditional readiness to share (give and take)."[72] According to Echema, "give and take," but not necessarily direct reciprocity, completes hospitality. The expectation of instant reward is not the driving force behind African hospitality. Rather, the quest for an integral wholeness of the community fuels its members to reach out to the most vulnerable. In this regard, life

69. Olikenyi, *African Hospitality*, 114.

70. Siddiqui, *Hospitality and Islam*, 80.

71. Siddiqui, *Hospitality and Islam*, 14.

72. Echema, *Corporate Personality*, 35.

at its peak entails the responsibility of each person assuring the connectivity of the whole.

Sharing promotes friendship and dissuades unnecessary enmity. A hospitable person is a global entity whose relational strength is elastic. The Setswana proverb endorses global friendship in these words: *"Lonao ga lo na nko"* (A foot has no nose, meaning you cannot detect what trouble may lie ahead for you).[73] This didactic warning is a reminder of the necessity of hospitality, because no one can accurately predict where and to whom the wind of destiny might land him or her.

Sharing is a way of life in Africa. Sharing includes material and immaterial offers. *"Kwaria ni kwaendana"* is a common proverb that teaches that "Talking makes friendship." Similarly, verbal socializing and material sharing can also go together. In sharing food, for example, topical issues are discussed, thereby enriching all partakers.[74]

A Preserved Legacy

Precolonial Africa lacked literacy but not wisdom. In the wisdom of African forbearers, vital values were preserved in oral proverbs, stories, poems, and songs. Through daily practices and repetitions, these socioreligious standards are handed on to generations unborn. A very important Kikuyu proverb portrays the value of interdependence in African hospitality with these words: *"Iri murungu igiritagia iri kahia"* (The hornless animal leans on the one that has them).[75] One needs to be reminded that meanings of proverbs are typically lost in literal interpretations. So, learning from its owners suggests a right disposition. This Kikuyu proverb from an African perspective simply means that one's momentary need is virtually satisfied through the hospitality of others, because the strength of the whole is revealed in the weakest part.

In addition to preserving hospitality through oral traditions, ethical and socioreligious standards are practically inculcated to the young. Raising kids requires the responsible collaboration of the society and the immediate family, because a cultured child keeps alive the hope of the community. Like the village rooster, which is owned by one man but whose early morning crows alert the neighbors, the responsibility over

73. Kuzwayo, *African Wisdom*, 14–15.

74. Gathogo, *Truth about African Hospitality*, 8.

75. Gathogo, "Some Expressions," 277.

the child is collectively shared. Among the early trainings for the African child, selfishness and greed are rebuked, while hospitality is extolled. However, behavioral results do not often reflect the efforts put in.

As a people, Africans often pay attention to nature's manifestations and learn from them. In Kenya, the pastoral locals of Mwea have through close observation at the symbiotic relationship between their cows and the spotted birds upheld the richness of interdependence or hospitality. This particular species of birds attracted a lot of interest among the Mwea people because of the interdependence it shares with the cow. This is evidenced in several names given it. Among its local names, *Ndeithi* (the one who shepherds) stands out. One notices that the bird untiringly follows the cow about, even more than the human shepherds would; hence its recognition as the true shepherd.

The cow and the bird amazingly share together the space provided by the field. As the cow moves and grazes, grasshoppers and nutritious insects are exposed, and the shepherd-birds feast on them. In reciprocation, the birds hop on the cows and pick parasitic ticks off their skins. Their sense of interdependence for each other has kept them together as friends and collaborators. The symbiotic relationship between the cow and the bird instills deep lessons into the consciousness of these Kenyan pastorists and challenges them into committed hospitality. As argued by Gathogo, such an analogy for African Christians resonates with the biblical Pauline's teaching (1Corinthians 12:12–26) on the corelational importance of every part of the one body.[76]

Articulating such a didactic analogy of interdependence into scholarship, Tutu asserts:

> In our African language we say, "a person is a person through other persons". I would not know how to be a human being at all except (that) I learned this from other human beings. We are made for a delicate network of relationships, of interdependence. We are meant to complement each other. All kinds of things go horribly wrong when we break that fundamental Law of our being. Not even the most powerful nation can be completely self-sufficient.[77]

As an elder, Tutu reiterates for Africans the inevitability of embracing the fuller meaning of a person as one in relationship. Even in the

76. Gathogo, "Some Expressions," 278.

77. Tutu, *Words*, 71.

current socioeconomic hardships that hold Africa down, Tutu's advice still resonates, especially when hospitality has been presented as the hard way, but the only way towards self-emancipation.

That Africans conceive themselves as relational persons entails a consciousness of responsibility towards the other. Compared to much of Western culture, the difference is very clear. In Europe and America people living together in the same block hardly get to know or talk with each other. In this civilized culture, the sense of neighborliness has waned extensively. At best, some immediate families gather with a few friends and celebrate occasionally on holidays, but not as frequently, elaborately, or inclusively as Africans do.

Some Africans even think that African hospitality is unique. G. G. Karuu believes that the uniqueness manifests in the naturalness of hospitality practice and its less pretentious approach.[78] Karuu's opinion agrees with Gathogo's description that African hospitality is "deep and sincere."[79] However, describing African hospitality as unique would not be free of sentimentalism. Its major characteristics are not entirely absent in the ancient Roman, Greek, and other ancient societies in the Mediterranean. The Bedouins share similar practices, if not more. Distinctiveness would better describe African hospitality rather than uniqueness.

Paradoxically, the menaces of poverty, caused by wars, crises, and dictatorial and corrupt leaderships in Africa, strongly question her ancient standard of altruistic responsibility. Indeed, such obvious sufferings might signal doubt, but cannot suggest a total erasure of hospitality. The reason is traceable to the distance between the cognizance of cultural principles and the fidelity to practicing them. It is also a confirmation of the depth of corrosion African hospitality has suffered over time. To a greater extent, the state of misery in Africa, despite her enviable sense of hospitality, reaffirms the cliché: "*Corruptio optimi sit pessimus*" (The corruption of the best is the worst). Truly, the manipulative sociopolitical antics across the continent have so much impacted and impoverished the masses to a breaking point, unleashing perforce a survival instinct that adopts egoism over and above altruism. In other words, enormous obstacles, especially xenophobia, seriously hinder the practice and development of this ancient heritage of hospitality.

78. Karuu, is a senior citizen of Kirinyaga, resident in Nairobi. Cited as interviewee in Gathogo, "Some Expressions," 26.

79. Gathogo, *Truth about African Hospitality*, 26.

Challenges of African Hospitality

Inhospitality is the destroyer of African relationality. As such, it attracts curses from elders. A cursed person becomes a disaster to the society, because through him the relational bond is weakened. Gathogo blames the impact of capitalism on Africa as the source of individual meanness and selfishness.[80] However, capitalism cannot be the only source of inhospitality. The sources of inhospitality should include both internal and external factors.

Inhospitality, or rather the decayed form of hospitality, must be blamed on collective irresponsibility. In addition to capitalism, which is an external factor, another external reason points to the postcolonial system. Most African nations received their independence in the second half of the twentieth century. More than five decades later, these nations are still grappling with identity crises. Many lack the knowledge of that which characterizes their nationality, let alone pursuing a course to preserve it. Others are caught between the hard choices of two extremes, Westernization and Africanization, without making progress at eithher. Besides the likes of Kenneth Kaunda of Zambia, with his humanism, and Julius Nyerere of Tanzania, whose *Ujamaa* philosophies aimed at refocusing their people towards a defined direction, the majority of African's first-generation leaders settled for Europeanization set in place by their colonial predecessors. Europeanization impacted a serious neglect of African values and practices, especially language, culture, and dress. For example, despite the high temperature and unsteady electricity, dressing up in dark suits in Africa has remained a common mark of cultural class. Other influences of foreign cultures are so much widespread that today Africa is home to about two generations of anti-indigenous practices.

Among this group of younger Africans, indigenous languages and customs are misunderstood, disparaged, and consequently hated. Some have even dropped their native names and adopted foreign ones. In this regard, Christianity in general, and Pentecostalism in particular, share the blame of a preached and consolidated anti-African approach. For instance, it is difficult to accept local names for baptism, and to exonerate indigenous customs from fetish acts.

Consequently, Africa is facing the worst form of neocolonization, that of the mind. To date, Africa is currently passing through a formidable identity crisis, decades after the Europeans left. Colonial masters

---

80. Gathogo, *Truth about African Hospitality*, 26–27.

created and cemented ethnic boundaries and barriers in the minds of their African subjects. Since the Middle Ages, Europeans have studied Africans through the lens of the biblical basis (Genesis 9:21–22) of the Hamitic hypothesis, trying to find divine design in nature and human society.[81] A racial claim is stated in the Babylonia Talmud (a collection of oral traditions of the Jews), which appeared in the sixth century AD, that "the descendants of Ham are cursed by being black, and depicts Ham as a sinful man and his progeny as degenerates."[82] In furtherance of this idea, the thesis of C. G. Seligman in his book *The Races of Africa* (1930), which marked the peak of endorsement of the Hamitic hypothesis, engendered an affective impact in the present. It can be summarily said that the chains of slavery were metaphorically loosened from the arms and feet, and fastened in the minds of Africans. Nevertheless, Africa still has both human and natural resources that can reimagine and effectively change her distorted face, by broadening the unity factor.

From an internal perspective, ethnic bigotry has been draining life from the wounded Africa. In successive years, following independence, Africa has not been able to manage ethnic crises ravaging its relational fabric. Little wonder that at the very outset of the Rwandan genocide in 1994, and right at the middle of the first African Synod, a prominent archbishop from Nigeria, Albert K. Obiefuna,[83] prophetically called out, "it seems the blood of family and tribe is thicker than the water of baptism."[84] His observation will indeed remain prophetic until proven otherwise. In addition, Jordan Nyenyembe concludes, "An extreme inclination to tribalism is a sin that is shadowing the construction of fraternity in Africa. Strong misguided tribal feelings have rendered internal unity an almost impossible proposition. Many troubles in Africa, which negates any efforts at finding peace, have roots in tribalism."[85]

The second internal factor constitutes the mother of all other factors. While the other three factors can be categorized as inherited effects, this mother factor sustains them through its passivity. Concerning the Christian-Muslim divide, Bishop Matthew Hassan Kukah has blamed the governance in Nigeria for her inability to manage her pluralistic reality.

81. Stearns, *Dancing*, 23.

82. Gossett, *Race*, 5.

83. Archbishop Albert Kanene Obiefuna (1930–2011) was the metropolitan see of Onitsha province and also the bishop of Onitsha archdiocese in southeast Nigeria.

84. Archbishop Obiefuna, cited in Chukwu, *Church*, 196.

85. Nyenyembe, 90–91.

The accuracy in Kukah's statement aligns well with this mother factor of passivity. However, while Kukah's call draws attention to respective differences that characterize the Nigerian populace, the passivity factor has overlooked the very enviable African values. There is an obvious lack of vision and mission for developing African traits and values, which subsequently will lead to rebranding them for non-African consumption. Hospitality would have been one of those, at least, as an appropriate check on the inhuman effect of capitalism.

Recently, some scholars have pointed to the need for an improved appreciation of indigenous values. Mercy Oduyoye agrees with Rose-Zoe Obianga in her opinion that Africans welcomed Europeans and adopted Europeans' values but have curiously discovered the lack of interpersonal mutuality.[86] The question is: when and how can Africans positively retrieve their treasurable values and enhance them? Timeless values like hospitality call for serious studies and systematization aimed at addressing the ravaging individualism of modernity and its resultant dividing walls. It is the hope of this research to aid in interrupting this prolonged dormancy and passivity, since Africa is not substantially rid of substitutive witnessing for the other.

African Living for the Other

Besides the religious dimension, mutual hospitality understood as substitutive responsibility in Africa also plays a major role in the societal economy and well-being. Unlike Levinasian asymmetric substitution, in which the burden of responsibility falls on the self in service to the other, African hospitality is structured on a paradigm of substitutive disparate mutuality, where the need of each person is responded to proportionately. The interdependent bond that characterizes African society gets translated into daily activities, which encourages healthy competition on the one side and compassion for the less privileged on the other. A true African person struggles in balancing competition with hospitality. Like the mother duck, the pace for crossing a busy road is determined by her ducklings, especially the weakest one.

Most traditional African societies were built and maintained with collaborative industriousness. This idea can be explained with two reasons: through industry, first, laziness is spurned, and second, the sense of

86. Oduyoye, *Introducing*, 94–95.

communality is sustained for community well-being and achievements. The popular saying "*Ekitta obusenza bubu bunaanya*" (A lazy person kills the whole community)[87] among the Baganda reiterates the interdependence structure wherein everyone is responsible for the whole. Benezet Bujo confirms: "Even a handicapped individual has a unique position in the community and becomes a person thanks to other beings, just as these becomes persons thanks to the one who is handicapped."[88] Bujo provides a typical disparate (or asymmetric) mutuality that forms African interdependent existence, and enables fair ground to all in the process of actualizing genuine personhood. In other words, substitutive responsibility entails some sacrifices that also enrich.

Gathogo, reading Jomo Kenyatta, notices how hospitality among the Kikuyu depends largely on industriousness.[89] The undercurrent logic proves that one cannot offer what one does not have. In other words, from the fruits of one's industriousness, the needs of the other and of the self are virtually satisfied. Not only through material exchanges, a hardworking person also represents a hospitable person, who willingly renders services to those in need. Through unparalleled reciprocation, the personal responsibility of a hospitable person attracts communal support. Everyone, including those with disability, is proportionately involved in societal well-being.

One wonders why African hospitality doesn't lead to penury. Hospitality is distinguished from profligacy. In Africa, hospitable people act in prudence, because society also needs them alive and effective. The society regulates ways of checking abuse of hospitality by guests. Guests are not exempt from the industriousness that sustains hospitality. Enshrined in proverbs, the hospitable host is encouraged to engage a guest in the host's means of livelihood after a few days of welcoming entertainment. In support, the Swahili proverb admonishes, "*Mgeni siku mbili, siku ya tatu mpe jembe akalime* (A visitor is a guest for two days, on the third day, put him or her to work (by giving him or her a hoe)."[90] Within this societal structure, the well-being of others attracts the concern of each genuine African person. From this perspective, African hospitality as a daily practice replicates substitutive responsibility.

87. Katongole, "Ethos Transmission," 248.
88. Bujo, *Foundations*, 91.
89. Kenyatta, *Facing Mount Kenya*, 42–44.
90. Healey, and Sybertz, *Towards*, 172–73.

The substitutive dimension in African hospitality was more visible in precolonial times. Lamin Sanneh, in a particularly valued study, unveils the resilient dominance of African hospitality at the first encounters between Islam and Christianity.[91] Popular accounts of such religious contacts usually present Africa as the passive, primitive, unstructured, and timid host, whose natural religiosity dissolved at the confrontation of superior literacy religions.[92] This common but distorted perception, according to Lamin Sanneh, "has been perpetuated that Christianity is locked in a bitter rivalry with it (Islam), with Africa serving as the arena and the prize."[93] The passivity ascribed to Africa by Western colonialism only galvanized the misconstrued supremacy struggle between Islam and Christianity. In accord with Sanneh, the next section will focus on some amicable images of Muslim-Christian relations in an African context.

91. Sanneh, *West African Christianity*, 213.
92. Meyer, "Christianity in Africa," 458.
93. Sanneh, *West African Christianity*, 210.

9

Hospitable Coexistence

The Yoruba Example

THIS SECTION INVESTIGATES A Yoruba (Nigerian) evidence of African cultural, political, and socioreligious impacts on Islam and Christianity, in accord with the already seen argument of Sanneh. A major area of concentration will be on why Muslim-Christian relationship in Yorubaland (southwestern Nigeria) represents a stark opposite of its Northern version, in terms of interreligious intolerance.

With an eye on some fundamental factors responsible for neighborly coexistence, the interest of this research explores the evidence of substitutive responsibility, and how the fruits of such mutual interdependence could be a lesson for a larger society. Therefore, understanding the peculiar Yoruba impact on these two foreign religions will illumine the mediating and moderating role played by African hospitality-driven relationality. Such contextual experience intends also to challenge Muslims and Christians to a renewal of the ancestry bond, which Abraham provides.

In addition, this exploration will attempt to proffer answers to why Christian-Muslim relations in the North are relatively inhospitable compared to the more harmonious coexistence of the two religionists in Yorubaland. In fact, what makes Yoruba Yoruba is solely integral; that is, it cuts across the cultural, the sociopolitical, and the religious dimensions of life in that region.

Common Ancestry

The Yoruba identity[1] gradually evolved and assumed stronger bonding with time. Through mutual exchanges, "non-Oyo areas"[2] gradually adopted the term Yoruba, while Islamic traits and Christian cultures were assimilated without any precondition for conversion.[3] J. D. Y. Peel identifies two high moments of the Yoruba "ethnogenesis" (the making of the Yoruba) as the cultural nationalism in the 1890s[4] and the pan-Yoruba political initiative by Obafami Awolowo's Action Group in 1950s.[5] Christianity (Church Mission Society), according to Peel, was instrumental in both arms of developing the Yoruba identity, through the adoption and propagation of the Yoruba language in schools.

Samuel Johnson, a renowned Yoruba historian, also called "the Herodotus of the Yoruba,"[6] recorded an Oyo version of the Yoruba myth of origin. In the myth as attested by Jacob K. Olupona, Johnson drew from an oral tradition made available by "the Arokin storytellers and Yoruba *intelligentia*," which suggest an Arabian descent of Oduduwa (the progenitor of the Yoruba). As a proof for this Eastern ancestry, a copy of the Qur'an (*Idi*) believed to have been seized from Muslims by followers of Oduduwa (a Meccan polytheist prince) is preserved in the *Ifa* temple as a revered sacred relic.[7] Johnson, however, critiques such an Arabian link and rather explains it away as an adulteration of the story of Mohammad and his idolatrous people of Qurash.

Peel holds to a rather Malian origin of Yoruba Islam, which as well supports the initial usage of the name Yoruba by Ahmad Baba of Timbuktu (d. 1627), prior to its usage by the Hausa (Nigeria).[8] Nonetheless, that the traditional *Odu Ifa* (the corpus of oral texts) used for divination

1. The Yoruba is one of the largest ethnic groups in Nigeria, constituting about 21 percent of the national population with an approximate 20.3 million people. In Nigeria, Yorubaland is divided into seven states: Ekiti, Kwara, Lagos, Ogun, Ondo, Osun, Oyo. The Yoruba are also natives in Ghana, Togo, Benin, Brazil, and the Caribbean.

2. Non-Oyo areas represent the rest of the Yoruba cities besides Oyo. These include: Abeokuta, Esie Ife, Ijebu, Ilorin, Lagos, Oshogbo, Owo, Tosede. The ancient Oyo empire was the military strength and capital city of Yorubaland.

3. Peel, *Christianity, Islam*, 150–51.

4. Ayandele, *Missionary Impact*, chs. 6–8.

5. Peel, *Christianity, Islam*, 150.

6. Olupona, *City of 201 Gods*, 57.

7. Olupona, *City of 201 Gods*, 58–59.

8. Peel, *Christianity, Islam*, 150.

contains some chapters called "Muslim divination texts"—a corrupt form of Arabic idioms and verses (*odu imale*)—evidences a domesticated Islam in Yorubaland.[9]

It is a common belief among the Yoruba that Oduduwa (the god-king) fathered them. Above all, while the Oduduwa common ancestry of the Yoruba belongs to a metahistorical realm, the uniting force it generates has shaped the pan-Yoruba ideology into an unrivaled bonding for the southwesterners in Nigeria.

Yoruba history can be misleading when argued that it lacks conflicts between Christians and Muslims. Indeed, the Yoruba people of the southwest of Nigeria experienced a period of intra-Yoruba wars in struggle for supremacy, conquest, and expansion. It is evident that by 1835 the entire Yorubaland engaged in intra-civil wars.[10] This lasted up to 1893, when the British intervention dismantled the war camps of Ibadan and Ilorin near river Otin.[11] However, in terms of cultural and religious hierarchical structuring, Ile-Ife town stands today as the epicenter of Yoruba civilization and ceremonial city.[12]

The kingship hierarchy also contributed to the Yoruba identity. To date, the *Ooni* of Ife (Oduduwa's vicar) still lives out his responsibility as father figure for all religions and peoples of Yorubaland. The *Ooni*, as the Yoruba hierarchy, strongly symbolizes the hub of family bonds. In that regard, quarrels are controlled or reconciled based on the emphasis of the family concept that unites everyone.

In general, people are discouraged from having religion as the basis of identity. Conscious of their single origin and identity as sons and daughters of Oduduwa, the Yoruba generally consider the other (kin) first as a Yoruba before seeing them in the context of religious affiliations. Referring to the friendly accommodation and spread of Islam in Yorubaland, Peel notices: "For a long time its (Islam) spread was so slow and gentle, unforced by violence and uncomplicated dogma, that an easy cultural intimacy, involving influences running both ways, grew up between Islam and the Oyo Yoruba, sometimes so unobtrusive as almost to escape notice."[13]

9. Olupona, *City of 201 Gods*, 59.

10. http://countrystudies.us/oruba/10.htm.

11. Johnson, *History of the Yoruba*, 628.

12. Olupona, *City of 201 Gods*, 224.

13. Peel, *Christianity, Islam*, 151.

In the North, the reverse is the case. Religion is supreme. Allegiance to the Sokoto caliphate (the religiopolitical seat of the Fulani-Hausa Muslims) is unrivaled and linked to the religious-political authority established by the Sunni (puritanist) jihadist reformer Uthman dan Fodio. Not even Nigerian nationality can compete with it. No Muslim president of Nigeria has publicly disagreed with the opinion of the sultan of Sokoto. The allegiance is so strong that the national constitution can easily be disregarded rather than disagreeing with the stand of the sultan. Even the emirate at Ilorin (Yorubaland) operates as a puppet authority under the Sokoto caliphate.

More so, heterogeneous peoples populate the North, unlike a homogenous ancestry identity that the Yoruba clan represents under the fatherhood of Oduduwa.

Much of the Yoruba sense of inclusivity, as couched in the "live and let live" philosophy, depends on how (by birth or by welcome) and when (time) one came into the Yoruba family. In Yoruba cosmology, every person came into the community with the head or the legs. A person came with the head when born into a family lineage (*ebi*) or with legs when walked into the family—as a guest. Despite these two entrance gateways, cultural taboos are respected by all and sundry in Yorubaland. Symbolically, there is a Yoruba cultural pot. Foreign traits must pass through this pot (a channel of cultural encounter) before being adapted. Such cultural portrayal accounts for the noticed impacts of Yorubaland on Islam and Christianity.

Administratively, calling people to order is the responsibility of the eldest. The eldest, not necessarily by age, but through the oldest unbroken ancestry stalk, is determined by the first who entered with the head. The position of the eldest automatically goes to the first son of the deceased eldest person, and never to his brothers (the son's uncles). A patrilineal system moderated by quasi-gerontocracy for the most part determines who bears the responsibility of leadership. In essence, the eldest son, even if much younger than his uncles, inherits the leadership authority of the late father. Whether a Christian, a Muslim, or a traditionalist, the custodian of the family or the community enjoys respect and obedience from all.

In that regard, religious pluralism is embedded in Yorubaland. The Yoruba philosophy provides a viable context for religious pluralism. A particular family accommodates worshippers of different gods. In families, the disparity of cults in marriages is seriously encouraged, by which peace is maintained, and through which people share sacred spaces. However, there are other factors that shape the overarching hospitality spirit noticed in Yorubaland.

Sociocultural Tolerance

Lai Olurode and P. O. Olusanya identify respect for elders, good conduct, mutual solidarity visits, greetings, and housewarming as major pillars of support for the Yoruba hospitality.[14]

1. Respect for elders: The concept of respect embedded in Yoruba culture guarantees mutual appreciation for each other's religious faith. This is derived from the concept of *omo iyawo ni* (children from the same mother). The culture follows a motherhood bonding in a polygamous family.

   Age difference imposes significant consequences in terms of respect among the Yoruba. The younger person accords respect to the older in age, even with a few months, in Yoruba culture. Yoruba sociologist N. A. Fadipe supports: "The principle of seniority applies in all works of life and practically all activities in which men and women are brought together. The custom cuts through distinctions of wealth, or rank and sex."[15] Under such a sociocultural system, the young are expected to accord respect and prudently yield to the opinions of their seniors, regardless of the relational distance between them.

   Respect is also key toward strangers. Besides the *omoluwabi* (cultured person) concept, often claimed as an inherent trait, the primary motivation for xenophilia among the Yoruba centers on the belief that the gods visit as guests. Moreover, as depicted by the mythic origin, Oduduwa (the Yoruba progenitor) was once a stranger. He came from somewhere, which the *Ifa* oracle prophesied that a great person was coming and should be welcomed.

2. Good conduct: The plural form of address is used for strangers (elders), especially the second-person pronoun. Like the French, "it is and in fact, unthinkable for a person to say *iwo/tu* ['you' in the singular] rather than *enyin/vous* ['you' in the plural] while addressing

14. Olurode and Olusanya, *Nigerian Heritage*, 121–31.

15. Fadipe, *Sociology of the Yoruba*, 29.

an older person unless it is meant as a premeditated form of insult or unwarranted harassment of the junior concerned."[16]

3. Mutual solidarity visits: Interfaith visit exchange is common among the Yoruba. The peak of mutual sharing of sacred places between Muslims and Christians in Yorubaland happened on September 1, 2017, when an incumbent governor of Ekiti state, Ayodele Fayose, attended the *Eid-el-Kabir* celebration. The spectacle was not only about his presence, as a Christian, in the mosque, but also his dressing in Islamic attire reserved for the officiating imam. An online Nigerian newspaper, *Daily Post*, quotes Fayose's reason: "As a leader, appearing in a Muslim regalia with a turban is to say that I must be part of everything the Muslims do and make then realise that we are all one family."[17] It is interesting to note that, beyond political ambitions, Governor Fayose (being a Yoruba) finds support for his action in his official role as the chief custodian of all religions within his jurisdiction.

4. Greetings: In accord with the general sense that Africans value greeting as an important form of hospitality, the Yoruba esteem greetings. "*E ku*" precedes the appropriate instances that prompt a particular greeting, accompanied with postures of prostrating (males) or kneeling (females). Generally, seniors respond with "*Pele*" (bless you) to the greetings of the younger people. Young people who keep these practices alive in the society are regarded as *omoluwabi* (cultured persons).[18]

5. Housewarming replicates a transformed or urbanized form of traditional *saara*. *Saara* is a derivative word from the Arabic *sadaqa* (alms), which the Yoruba have adapted to represent a form of sacrificial giving that begets greater blessings.[19] As an extended religious practice, *saara* connotes two meanings: 1) distribution of alms to beggars (the poor);[20] and 2) in a more general sense, distribution of food to neighbors, relations, and friends (who are not necessarily poor or beggars).

---

16. Olurode and Olusanya, *Nigerian Heritage*, 122.

17. Nwachukwu, *Daily Post Online*, "Why I dressed in Islamic Regalia,"

18. Olurode and Olusanya, *Nigerian Heritage*, 124.

19. Peel, *Christianity, Islam*, 151.

20. Fadipe, *Sociology of the Yoruba*, 94.

Saara usually has adults or minors as primary hosts. In the case of the latter, *saara* entails "an occasion for a child to bring friends together. He or she is gaily dressed and is the center of attention. The invited children eat satisfactorily. They sing and pray for the celebrant" (host).[21] It as well provides the initial occasion for interaction and friendship with the newest member in the neighborhood, irrespective of religious affiliations. *Saara* is different from a birthday party. Often nothing special is celebrated, yet *saara* happens for the sole aim of feasting with others and bringing them together. In this regard, *saara* is an end in itself. A call out (*"Enyin omo kekeke, e wa je saaaaraal,"* Little children, hurry here for *saara*) by the host or her siblings announces the readiness of food, which is followed by a quick response from the children in the neighborhood.

Adult *saara* is usually preceded by the *Ifa* oracle, which links it to a functional means of overcoming current challenges and difficulties. Here, *saara* is a means to an intended end. However, it is differentiated from *ebo* (propitiatory sacrifice to the gods). *Saara* aims at extending goodness purely to humans, usually without anticipation for reward, but with strong conviction that blessings can come from the gods. Besides *Ifa* promptings, adults can freely organize *saara* as a form of substitutive responsibility towards good neighborliness. Such voluntary motivation is rare, especially in the most recent economic recession. The Yoruba popularize the summary of their hospitality ideology in the song: *"Imale/Igbagbo o pe k' awa ma s̀oro; awa o s' oro ile wa o*—tradition is not antithetical to Islam or Christianity and so those who combine both have no apology for doing so."[22]

Rather than being dismissed as religious syncretism, Peel, in *Christianity, Islam, and Orisa-Religion: Three Traditions in Comparison and Interaction*, published shortly before his death in 2015, argued about the peaceful coexistence (which is a process) of the Yoruba religious pluralism as indigenous. He as well appreciated the missionaries, who adapted the existing indigenized Muslim paradigm in planting Christianity in Yorubaland. Such mission strategy resulted in an even Muslim-Christian religious divide. Its gradual permeability of the traditional mutual substitutive responsibility for the other differentiates it from the colonists'

---

21. Olurode and Olusanya, *Nigerian Heritage*, 130.
22. Olurode and Olusanya, *Nigerian Heritage*, 131.

imposed antagonistic stratagem seen in the larger picture of the Nigerian even split between Northern Islam and Southern Christianity.

Yoruba Islam

The Yoruba even divide across Muslim-Christian coexistence in Yoruba-land has witnessed more than a century of interdependent relationality. Although the Portuguese missionaries of the fifteenth century attempted establishing a (failed) Christian presence in Yorubaland, as they did in the Benin and Warri kingdoms, Islam took root first in this Western region of Nigeria. Both religions, however, have displayed better understanding toward accommodating each other than experienced in the Northern region of Nigeria. As a result, immense growth on both sides has generated admirable collaboration, but not without tensions that led to minor religious rivalry.

Islam in Yorubaland can best be appreciated within the wider spectrum of Islam in Nigeria. Despite its envisioned uniqueness that concerns this research, Nigerian Islam in the North provides the basis for the Yoruba context. As vividly accounted for in chapter 3, Islam first arrived in today's Nigeria through commerce. The trans-Saharan trade route connected the eastern horn of Nigeria (Borno empire) to North Africa in the seventh century.[23] Muslim traders and (later) *ulamas* utilized the trade route opportunity for both economic and religious purposes.

Conversion to Islam, leading to today's Nigeria, started slowly but gradually, from two major gates: first in the eleventh century, through the Borno empire, and second in the fourteenth century, through the migration of the Muslim traders and missionaries who came from the Mali and Songhai kingdoms and settled in the Hausa states of present-day Nigeria. In 1370, according to J. Spenser Trimingham, Ali Yaji Dan Tsamiya of Kano became the first of the Hausa kings to convert to Islam.[24]

A reformed Hausa Islam through Uthman dan Fodio's jihad (1804–1810) established a Fulani acquired territory known as the famous Sokoto caliphate, which by the 1830s had extended its conquest southwards, incorporating the Nupe kingdom and part of the Oyo empire (of Yorubaland). The British colonists halted the conquest expansion in 1900, without

23. Adedigba, *Role of Jesus*, 112.
24. Trimingham, *History of Islam*, 107–8.

tampering with the existing Islamic structure, which favored the indirect taxation rule, but also formed the postcolonial political power base.

The Oyo empire, even though the most powerful of the Yoruba states, provided the gateway for Islam into Yorubaland. Toyin Falola notes the sixteenth century as the time of the earliest Islamic encounter in the Oyo empire.[25] Toyin's dating is supported by al-Aluri's claim that the first mosque was built at Oyo Ile (the capital of the empire) in the middle of the sixteenth century.[26] Some other scholars have favored a later Islamic presence in Oyo empire. Samuel Johnson[27] and J. A Atanda strongly argued for an eighteenth century Islamic presence in cities like Old Oyo, Ikoyi, Ogbomosho, Iseyin, Igboho, Ijanna, Ketu, and Lagos.[28] Furthermore, it was also believed that "Islam reached Yorubaland first through Mali and Songhai and later through Borno and Hausaland."[29] Still, scholars like J. F. A. Ajayi and Salau Sule Omotoso agree on the uncertainty of the date of the Islamic arrival on the soil of Oyo due to the unavailability of recorded history.[30]

Notwithstanding the uncertainty that surrounds the actual date of an Islamic presence in the Oyo empire, that the initial encounter happened through military and economic interactions is very certain. T. G. O. Gbadamosi, a Yoruba historian, articulates the initial encounter of Northern Muslims with Yoruba people:

> Yorubaland has some contact with these Islamised areas (the Nupe, the Hausa kingdoms, and immigrants from Mali) both in war and in peacetime through the activities of soldiers, settlers and above all traders. This varied contact meant some intermingling of people and ideas, and intermingling, which facilitated the infiltration of Islam in Yorubaland. From the Islamised areas, especially those to the north-west of Yorubaland, had come the first Muslims in Yorubaland.[31]

Gbadamosi's historic exposition sheds light on the gradual mix (wars and commerce) but also steady penetration of Islam in Yorubaland.

25. Falola and Heaton, *History of Nigeria*, 75.

26. http://yourpedia.com/subjects/oruba-from-19th-to-date/after-the-fall.

27. Johnson, *History of the Yorubas*, 38.

28. Atanda, *Introduction*, 37.

29. Atanda, *Introduction, 37.*

30. Ajayi, "Aftermath," 142. See Omotoso, "Islam in Nigeria."

31. Gbadamosi, *Growth of Islam*, 4.

The Hausas during their earliest encounter first referred the label Yoruba to the Oyo empire, even though Peel attributes the earliest usage to Ahmad Baba of Timbuktu, as mentioned above.

Yorubaland consists of the Igbas, the Ijebus, Ijesha, Oyo (Ilorin was the outpost of the Oyo empire), etc. before the nineteenth century. Are Afonja, the chief of defense, lived in Ilorin (a boundary outpost), and because of his selfish ambition, he sought autonomy and wanted to be *Alaafin* (king), which eluded him eventually.[32]

In 1817, Afonja invited Sheikh al-Salih (popularly known as Alimi), a Fulani jihadist and a Muslim scholar, against the Bashorun, the chief of defense (of the Oyo empire) that lived in the city. The Fulani army led by Alimi arrived, conquered, but also became unruly and later murdered Afonja, leading to the jihad in the Oyo empire and the emergence of the Ilorin emirate.[33] H. A. S. Johnson argues that the defense of the *Alaafin* was weakened by his Muslim faith and friendship with Alimi.[34] Nonetheless, the amicable interactions of Yoruba cultural elements with some foreign religious traits enabled an overall peaceful coexistence in the land.

The Interreligious Impacts: Islam and Christianity

In agreement with the thesis of Anastasios Yannoulatus that African religion "reflects a much higher position on a cultural staircase of different architecture,"[35] Sanneh substantiates the strong impact of Africanness in molding Islamic and Christian religions.[36] He notices how some basic African traits such as hospitality shaped the missionary efforts of the pioneer evangelizers. Moreover, he observed how the Islamic approach produced better results largely because they participated more in African hospitality than the Christian missionaries. Comparing the early Christian missionary approach and that of Muslims evangelizers, Sanneh noticed,

> The Mohammedan teacher is everywhere. He needs no society behind him, no funds to sustain him. He goes forth as the first Christians went with his staff and wallet, and wherever he goes

32. Falola and Heaon, *History of Nigeria*, 74.

33. Atanda, *Introduction*, 37–38.

34. Johnston, *Fulani Empire*, ch. 3.

35. Yannoulatos, "Christian Awareness," 250.

36. Sanneh, *West African Christianity*, 211.

he is at home! He is everywhere welcomed—though perhaps not more freely than the Christian teacher would be. Both have prestige of being Bookmen and God men. The Christian teacher goes as a stranger among foreigners and must be supported from without. The Mohammedan teacher gets paid in kind for blessing crops, sells charms etc. and he doesn't do anything for nothing. The Christian teacher is debarred from these methods of livelihood, consequently must be kept or starve.[37]

The observation of Sanneh validates a thesis this research is defending—that hospitality paves the way for fruitful religious dialogue and fosters evangelization. First, the host Yoruba context was equally hospitable to both religious preachers as they would be to any foreigner. Second, their religions and status were respected as "Bookmen and God men." Nevertheless, their dissimilar approaches impacted their hosts differently.

While the European Christian missionaries kept a distance from their hosts, and solely depended on homeland support, their Muslim counterparts lived out the mutuality that characterizes the African interdependent worldview. Moreover, that Sanneh likened the Islamic teachers' give-and-take practices to those of the Christian apostles shows a radical shift in modern Christian evangelization, in which mutual hospitality has been ignored. In essence, the scenario as captured by Sanneh undergirds the relevance of hospitality, and more so, anticipates the Abrahamic pilgrim model of hospitality, addressed below, where being at home anywhere is central.

Peel, even though writing from a supportive index of Robin Horton's religious evolution theory—ascendency from a microcosmic to a macrocosmic consciousness (in his 2009 research on Yorubaland)[38]—confirms the thesis of Sanneh. Peel observed, "In the early colonial period, Islam still had the negative advantage over Christianity that it demanded less from potential converts by way of cultural renunciation (e.g in the matter of polygamy), though as the number of Christians converts grew, the churches perforce soon became more tolerant of Yoruba custom."[39] But whereas Sanneh roots the preference for Islamic practices on the ability to adapt to the Yoruba relational culture, Peel locates the reason on the attraction for a superior functional monotheistic religions, toward which

---

37. Sanneh, *West African Christianity*, 222.

38. Peel, *Christianity, Islam.*

39. Peel, *Christianity, Islam*, 132.

the natives imagined the "particular monotheism would be its principal beneficiary in any area."[40]

Furthermore, it was also noticed that the African Independent Church (hereafter AIC) in Yorubaland shared a more amicable relationship with Islam than with the mainline churches. Two prominent AIC groups, the Aladura and the Cherubim and Seraphim, identified cordially with Islam. It is a fact that Moses Orimolade Tunolashe[41] was sharing an apartment with a Muslim before his charisma as a prayer leader in the Cherubim and Seraphim church came to light.[42] Close parallels in both religious groups include naming, prayer, dietary habits, religious garb, and structural style.

Concerning common names, Sanneh wrote, "The Yoruba word *aladura* itself, meaning prayer, is not native to the language but is derived from the Arabic *al-du 'a*, meaning supererogatory prayer. Arabic words like *allahumma*, 'O my God'; *al-rabb*, 'Lord' and *majubah*, 'answer, response', find more than echoes in the Holy names of the Church of the Lord (Aladura)."[43] The similarities between the Aladura church and Muslims in the Yoruba context include: five times of prayer daily, raising of arms and heads for blessings from heaven, putting off shoes before entering praying grounds, echoing "Adore his holy name" after every mention of Jesus (equivalent to "Mohammad, peace be upon him"), approval of polygamy, and semblance in dietary rules.[44] The long white religious robes of the Aladura also suggest the Muslim white ceremonial attire.

These Aladura-Islamic parallels attest to the evident interreligious connectivity shared in Yorubaland. In addition to mutual exchanges of religious visits, which are not unusual, liturgical architectural borrowings were tolerated. In Ondo (a modern state in Yorubaland), an Aladura church was constructed in a hexagonal structure, portraying a close pattern with a central mosque in the locality.[45] This Christian-Islamic connectivity has roots in the April 1926 vision of Josiah Oshitelu, of the Church of the Lord (Aladura), in which an opened book was presented

40. Peel, *Christianity, Islam*, 128.

41. Moses Orimolade Tunolase is the founder of the first African Independent Church, the Eternal Sacred Order of the Cherubim and Seraphim, which was established in 1925.

42. Sanneh, *West African Christianity*, 223.

43. Sanneh, *West African Christianity*, 224.

44. Sanneh, *West African Christianity*, 225.

45. Sanneh, *West African Christianity*, 224.

to him with Arabic writings.[46] The dream was believed to be a warning against hostility toward Islam. This warning was taken seriously because divination and dreams are two prominent common features in Islam and the AIC.

Beyond the identified amicability between the AIC and Islam in Yorubaland, cordial exchanges among individuals and corporate bodies were also experienced at the time Christianity met an established Islam. The penetrative impact of Africanness on Yoruba Islam offered Christianity the opportunity of encountering "an acclimatized Islam."[47] Unfortunately, the popularized opinion that rivalry and antagonism mark the Islamic-Christian relationship from its inception is a narrative without the inclusion of the host Africa as the bridge-maker.[48]

Africa, as host, played the important role of bridge-maker. Primarily, the African traditional rulers conceived of themselves as father figures and custodians of all religions. For example, a story has it that the king of Sierra Leone in 1769 "sent one son to learn Islam in Futa Jallon and another to study Christianity in England."[49] Peel recounts a story in which the Yoruba culture of religious tolerance held Islam, Christianity, and African Traditional Religion in a balance. In this particular narrative, the religious tension was between Benjamin Akintunde, a Christian, and his great-uncle, Bello Aromoye, a Muslim, but also the *baale* (family head). That the compound inhabits the *egungu* (ancestral masked spirit) and some other *Orisa* shrines adds to the existing religious pressure. In essence, religious plurality best expresses this little household.

Conscious of the religious mix and driven by the sense of substitutive responsibility prevalent in Yoruba society, both Akintunde and Aromoye knew that only through making room for the otherness of the other would conflict be avoided. As Peel's research demonstrates, Akintunde struggled not to compromise his faith by distancing his nuclear family from participating in the *egungu* festival; but there were limits to what he could control because of the integral responsibility he owed the extended family.[50] He dared not breech the interdependent bond of the

46. Turner, "Typology," 30–31.

47. Sanneh, *West African Christianity*, 213.

48. Sanneh, *West African Christianity*, 212.

49. Sanneh, *West African Christianity*, 216.

50. Peel, *Christianity, Islam*, 133.

larger household and so would tolerate his children participating in the entertaining part of the festival.

Similarly, Akintunde could not avoid obeying the headship instructions from the *baale* (family head). One of such was that the eldest son of every family would witness the slaughtering of the cow at the Muslim *Id el-Kabir* celebration. Akintunde, as the eldest son in his own family, sacrificially complied. In essence, Peel further notices that Akintunde's Christian family "always contributed to and attended the naming ceremonies, marriages and funerals of their Muslim and traditionalist relatives, [and] Muslims in the family always attended the festivities . . . of their Christian relatives."[51] The most interesting point in the reaction of Akintunde is the honest attempts aimed at harmonizing otherness and communion, whose overall motivation derives from a conscious imagination of putting oneself in the situation of the other or allowing the need of the other to engender a positive reaction from the self. Akintunde's household is representative of several daily instances of dialogue of life via hospitality (between Muslims and Christians) present in Yorubaland, from which this research is developing a systematic theological approach based on substitutive responsibility for the other.

The apparent substitutive responsibility that motivates the Yoruba culture of tolerance is often expressed in the "live and let live" philosophy,[52] in which individual lives are judged good to the extent they sustain the well-being of the whole. The ordinariness of an altruistic spirit in Yorubaland is enshrined in the Oshogbo pluralistic song, "*E jonifa o bo Ifa, e jolosun o bo Osun, E jelegun o bo Egun re, k'aye le gun*" (Let the *Ifa* devotee worship his *Ifa*, let the *Osun* devotee worship her *Osun*, let the *Egun* worship his *Egun*, that the world may be straight).[53]

Parallel cordiality is grossly lacking between Northern Muslims and Christians in Nigeria. Two reasons are possibly evident. First, the jihad of Uthman dan Fodio (1804–1808), in a bid to reform the previous Hausa Islam that was culture friendly, distanced itself from the traditional practices of the host community by condemning and overturning the status quo, thereby establishing the Fulani version with a puritanical Sunni face.

---

51. Sanneh, *West African Christianity*, 133–34.

52. Sanneh, *West African Christianity*, 133.

53. A popular song in Osogbo and Odo Otin area made available by Dr. Sola Ajibade of Osun State University, as cited in Peel, *Christianity, Islam*, 261.

However, Sanneh insists that this Islamic radicalness could not entirely terminate the African legacy of tolerance and flexibility.[54]

Second, while the Yoruba Muslims, already tamed by the host hospitality culture, cooperated with Christian missionaries, the colonist British, for purely economic reasons (provided by the Islamic hierarchical structure, which supported indirect taxation), prevented Christian missionary activities in the North as compensation. This earliest divide and distance developed into mega suspicion, antagonism, and hatred when in the mid twentieth century Christians began encountering Muslims in the North. The evil seed of discord and distance that was planted was so powerful that its impact is still strong more than a century afterwards. Fortunately, while distance ferments untold suspicion and mistrust, hospitality generates openness, respect, substitutive responsibility, and unity. The relevance of this research to such a rivalry-ridden context is to awaken the disparate mutual hospitality responsibility, especially in Northern Nigeria, in order that Muslims and Christians will at least reestablish trust and learn to appreciate religious others as they are. The Yoruba sociopolitical activities can be learned from.

The Sociopolitical Impact of Yoruba Identity

In general, Yoruba people claim to be naturally tolerant and also pride themselves on their common ancestral bond (metaphorically stated as "*omo iyawo ni*," children of the same mother) from Oduduwa above religious and political interests. Anthropological records of twenty-first-century research among the Yoruba, reported by Peel, contain vital evidence in support of their claim.[55]

The sociopolitical impulse in Yorubaland constitutes an important marker of the prominence of Yoruba identity over religious affiliations. Here, a broader look at the Yoruba political genre on the national level will be complemented with a similar motivation in Lagos,[56] the largest metropolitan city in Yorubaland. In general, leadership at the local and national levels favors (the more educated) Christians, since their Muslim

54. Sanneh, *West African Christianity*, 213.

55. Peel, *Christianity, Islam*, 125.

56. Lagos was Nigeria's capital city until December 12, 1991, but is still the only functional metropolitan harbor in Nigeria.

counterparts (with little or no Western education) would easily consider them as better representatives of the community's interests.[57]

Western education was a major aspect of the newness that Christianity brought with its presence. The initial passive response[58] to education by Yoruba Muslims gradually turned into welcoming it as a gift when Christians added inclusive Islamic structures such as Arabic studies. As a way of mutuality, Christians concentrated on religious borrowings, such as personalizing prayers for material needs, and internalizing Arabic in order to understand and counter Islam.[59] As a result, the affinity shared between Yoruba Christians and Muslims was pervasive.

It was further noticed that distinctively Yoruba-styled mosques reflected a hybridized Islamic and Christian liturgical architectural form, such as pillared naves, Gothic windows, twin pillars, etc.[60] William Allen, a Christian missionary, made an insightful statement in 1887: Abeokuta and Lagos Muslims "appear to be friendly disposed and devoid of the fanatical spirit which characterize them in the Turkish dominions."[61] The prevalence of tolerance between both religious groups in the two Yoruba cities reveals the strength of the Yoruba identity and community sustenance.

Chief Obafemi Awolowo, a Christian and a London-trained lawyer from Ijebu,[62] was a father figure in the course of achieving Yoruba educational empowerment and a charted Yorubaness as a political goal. This double-winged ambition pushed religious affiliations to the background. Prior to Nigerian independence in 1960, Awolowo formed a pan-Yoruba regional party called the Action Group as a vehicle for the achievement of his sociopolitical dream. An attempt in 1957 to run a parallel Muslim political party in Yorubaland was rapidly suppressed with religious divisive arguments, while the Action Group increased Islamic attractions, such as support for the *hajj* in the party's policies.

Nonetheless, the Mobalaje Grand Alliance party later emerged among the Yoruba with a nationalistic inclusive vision that aligned with the Action Group's arch-rival party, the National Council of Nigeria and

57. Peel, *Christianity, Islam,* 144.

58. Gbadamosi, *Growth of Islam,* 134.

59. Peel, *Christianity, Islam,* 175.

60. Oladimeji, *Islamic Architecture,* 319–20

61. Gbadamosi, *Growth of Islam,* 146.

62. Ijebu is a Yoruba subclan resented by majority of the other Yorubas due to their intimidating warring escapades.

the Cameroons (hereafter NCNC). The well-educated and charismatic Muslim founder of the Mobalaje Grand Alliance, Adegoke Adelabu, effectively combined "radical socialism at the national level and cultural conservatism at the local level."[63] His inclusivity endeared him to most Muslims through the use of Islamic outreach posts, such that the one-time presence of Awolowo in the central mosque in 1957 provoked massive reactions against his imam friend, Muili Abdullah, who brought him.[64] The protesters, according to Peel, interpreted Awolowo's presence as bringing a dog into the mosque.[65]

It was no big surprise that the nationalist party, the NCNC, controlled Lagos,[66] with its outstanding non-indigenous population. With the intimidating population of non-Lagosians, who support the NCNC, the indigenes were threatened and so showed greater allegiance to a pan-Yoruba, Action Group. The strategy includes a formidable network of market women, then under the leadership of a Muslim lady, Abibatu Mogaji. As a result, from the 1960 independence up to 2015, Lagos has sustained a succession of Muslim governors from a pan-Yoruba party rather than from a nationalistic party. Unlike in Ibadan (the ancient city hub of Yorubaland), where Christian politicians dominate, being Muslim and pro-Yoruba are common factors among these past Lagos governors: Lateef K. Jakande, Bola Tinubu, and Raji Fashola, drawn respectively from these ethnic-based political parties: United Party of Nigeria (UPN), Alliance for Democracy (AD), and Action Congress of Nigeria (ACN).[67]

The political seed of pan-Yoruba that Awolowo sowed never grew to fruition in his lifetime, due to the Northern Hausa-Fulani opposition at the national level, which scholars see not so much as a religious divide (between Muslims and Christians) but rather as an ethnic geographic tension (North versus South or Hausa-Fulani versus Yoruba). D. Laitin observed that a little before independence and through the first two decades, it was evident that the Muslim-Christian divide was virtually extraneous to the Yoruba political ambition, except for some internal rift,[68] uncommon in societal blocks.

63. Peel, *Christianity, Islam*, 144.

64. Peel, *Christianity, Islam*, 145.

65. Peel, *Christianity, Islam*, 265, and see endnote 61.

66. Lagos, though a Yoruba city, was then Nigeria's capital, with the highest governmental and business jobs opportunities for non-indigenes.

67. Peel, *Christianity, Islam*, 145.

68. Laitin, *Hegemony and Culture*, 14.

However, in the second and third republics, separated by thirteen years of military control in Nigeria, it was Baba Adinni M. K. O. Abiola, a Muslim, rather than Awolowo, a Christian, who came close to being a national president. Abiola won the 1993 election under the Social Democratic Party (SDP), which was annulled by the incumbent Northern military leader, General Ibrahim Badamosi Babangida (a Muslim). The annulment acerbated the North-versus-South divide, especially following the drastic action of another Northern military dictator, General Sani Abacha (a Muslim), who toppled Babangida's administration and imprisoned Abiola.

This was not a good sign for Yoruba Muslims, because the raging feud was between two Muslims (a Northern Muslim versus a Southern Muslim). But the coincidental deaths of Abiola and Abacha in 1998 seem to have restored the pan-Yoruba interest between Muslims and Christians. In 1999 the result of such a coalition, including overwhelming support from the rest of the Southerners, who were weary of the Northern political domination, produced the first democratic Yoruba president of Nigeria, Chief Olusegun Obasanjo (a Christian)—the very position that Awolowo tenaciously worked for but never saw.[69] The sociopolitical impact on Yorubaness explored thus far would be incomplete without the acidity of the ethnic factor.

The Ethnic Factor

The overall identity tension between indigenes and temporal residents can be viewed as the offshoot of unguided ethnic affiliation. Broadly, the tension is a human problem, the problem of otherness. Undue attachment to territorial settlements has not stopped generating crises, especially among Africans. In Nigeria, for example, the problem of the "identity clause" in the 1979 constitution has bred "violence on account of crisis of identity generated by the indigene/settler dichotomy."[70] This constitution encourages disproportionate privileges to citizens of Nigeria on the basis of the ancestral home of the person. Not even children born and raised in metropolitan cities can receive equal benefits with their counterparts considered as indigenes of that state. In other words, the ancestral root constitutes the basis for identity in Nigeria, by which

69. Laitin, *Hegemony and Culture*, 148.

70. Ogbogho, *Dynamics*, 72.

a child's state of origin determines the limits of opportunities for him. In general, such anomaly has been argued as an ongoing colonizing strategy adopted by Britain in its African territories, to focus more on tribal identity and less on the new nation-state citizenship that emerged from imperialized and colonized Africa. Such preserved colonial structure has been impacting strong negative experiences, which are unconstitutional.

C. B. N. Ogbogho and some other thinkers have observed:

> The dynamics of geographies of citizenship are partly captured in situations such as denial of scholarship awards to non-indigenes, differential policy of tuition fees for indigenes and non-indigenes, non-employment of non-indigenes in the public sector or at best contract employment for non-indigenes. All these not only challenge the spirit of inclusive citizenship envisaged by the constitution, they make the attainment of nation-state an elusive project.[71]

Ogbogho's observation can also be a lens toward the religious colored crises already discussed. In support, scholars like Abdullahi Adamu, in his study on the Tiv and Jukun contexts, which are predominantly Christian regions, identified "inter-group" crises with ethnicity allegiance rather than emanating from religious persuasions. According to Adamu,

> The Jukun and the Tiv are mostly Christians. If religious differences were the sources of inter-ethnic problems, these two tribes would live in total harmony with one another as Christian brothers and sisters. Crises in other communities where people are of the same religious persuasions show that the bond of religious affinity is often not strong enough to hold people together in the unending contest for social, economic and political advantages.[72]

An inverse relationship exists between national citizenship and the locus of home. It is further noticed that the ethnic identity clause legitimately recognized in the constitution has forced millions of Nigerian citizens into a daily encounter with an identity dilemma. Ogbogho identifies the conflicting relationship: "As one moves out of a space he/she can claim indigenity (as native), the quality of his/her citizenship (defined in terms of rights and privileges open to him or her) diminishes."[73]

71. Ogbogho, *Dynamics*, 72–74.
72. Adamu, "Ethnic Conflicts," 23–26.
73. Ogbogho, *Dynamics*, 74.

Consequently, Muslims and Christians in Nigeria hold fast to the perceived advantages of ethnic homeness, which exacerbates differences in political and religious identities. Against ethnic obsession, Levinas warns: "One's implantation in a landscape, one's attachment to Place, without which the universe would become insignificant and would hardly exist, is the very splitting of humanity into natives and strangers."[74]

So, in order to proffer lasting solutions to Muslim-Christian relations, the Abrahamic pilgrim metaphor offers a harmonizing imagination between home and homelessness. An Abrahamic pilgrim imaginative approach idealizes openness to diversity with an aim of creating unity and at once upholding pluralistic inclinations. In accord with the Abrahamic model, and as a contextual step, Ogbogho insists that the 1999 constitution, with its emphatic elements of ethnicity, needs immediate expunging, while the demand for place-of-birth or ethnic identity for the purposes of job opportunities, admission into academic institutions, and travel documentations should be replaced with place of residence.[75] In view of Ogbogho's proposal, the Nigerian context is invited to learn from a theology of substitutive responsibility as exemplified in the Abrahamic pilgrim model of hospitality, in order to be able to reimagine a home that doesn't exclude.

74. Levinas, "Heidegger, Gagarin, and Us," 232–33.
75. Ogbogho, *Dynamics*, 87.

10

Hospitality

A Theological Dimension

IN THE PREVIOUS CHAPTERS, this research engaged two major issues that are foundational to a third concern. The first was the establishment of the problem, whose resolution is intended. The problem as identified is the mutual antagonistic mistrust that has characterized Muslim-Christian socioreligious and political relations at the global level, but particularly in the Nigerian context. Second, this research also demonstrated a noticed monumental turn among concerned Muslims and Christians towards embracing dialogue as a way of building trust and peaceful coexistence. In light of this amicable turn, the dialogue of life, because of its emphasis on daily mutual praxis for all, is being advanced as that medium that offers the needed opportunity for Muslims and Christians to live out their scripture-based altruism, through the familiar tradition of hospitality. Subsequently, the ethics of hospitality was explored from its various perspectives, which include the philosophical, the ethical, and the cultural dimensions. In the chapters that follow, hospitality values found in these three dimensions will be crafted into a theological discourse.

This chapter witnesses to the theological development of a relational antinomy between asymmetry and mutuality that defines the gift exchange, argued here as an illuminative theology of "asymmetric-mutual substitutive hospitality." While developing its primary thesis that proposes asymmetric-mutual hospitality as basic bridge-builder between Muslims and Christians, this research first appreciates the poststructural interventions of Levinas (and his fellow philosophers of difference, such as Jacques Derrida and Paul Ricoeur), but with greater emphasis on his substitutive responsibility for the other. In contrast to the Levinasian radical asymmetric model, this research cautiously borrows Milbank's "asymmetrical reciprocity"[1] phraseology, but remodels it into asymmetric mutuality in order to accommodate the gifts exchange in their disparate nature. In so doing, it aims at reconstructing Levinasian substitutive responsibility into a theological discourse.

Substitutive asymmetric mutuality expresses the exchange of disparate gifts, not borne from indebtedness, but in proportionate responses toward the need of the other. The general idea is the complete avoidance of an oppressive burden on either party. As mentioned in the introduction, asymmetric-mutual hospitality can be imagined in the symbiotic relationship between human beings and trees, through which oxygen from the tree is exchanged with carbon dioxide from man.

The asymmetric-mutual theology being developed is illuminative because it seeks to awaken the latent hospitality spirit among Muslims and Christians in their daily dialogue of life for the establishment of trust and healthy neighborliness, by learning from Abraham (or "Ibrahim"[2]) and his God.

Whether materially or immaterially, both participants of such healthy asymmetric-mutual hospitality attain surprising growth, because of the spontaneity (of the giver) and the unexpectedness (of the receiver) involved. It is the thesis of this tenth chapter that through a theology of substitutive asymmetric-mutual hospitality, Muslim-Christian relations can fix or at least be preparatory for the restoration of trust needed to achieve peaceful coexistence and interreligious neighborliness. In that regard, this theology under construction is located midway between Levinasian asymmetric responsibility and Buber's reciprocal hospitality. Such midway offers fair grounds for the harmonization of otherness and communion.

Order can be possible only when otherness harmonizes communion. Against Thomas Hobbes's (1588–1679) brutish state of nature in *Leviathan*, Andrew Shepherd rightly argued that it was order in creation that preceded chaos, not the converse. Creation, according to Shepherd, was a gift from God in which communion and otherness harmonized each other. It was a concomitant effect of inordinate desire in seeking

1. Milbank's phrase has been explained in the general introduction of this research.

2. In the Qur'an Abraham is called Ibrahim.

distance and separateness from godliness that distorted the order in creation.[3] As a result of that primal self-centeredness, "The Other is no longer perceived as one who comes offering joy, enrichment and mutual beneficence, but rather as a threat to our existence, one to be struggled against and overcome. Fear erupts into violence, hospitality gives way to hostility."[4] Thus Shepherd concludes, "it is communion and hospitality, not conflict and hostility, which are primordial."[5]

Shepherd's observation on the impact of fear largely mirrors the existing relationship between Muslims and Christians. In essence, being fearful of the religious other has been realistically mutual between the two religious traditions. So, how then can Muslims and Christians overcome this fear of the other? What are the steps towards a reestablishment of the lost connectivity between otherness and communion? In other words, what marks the transition or transformation from a hostile to a hospitable perception of the other? And what exactly defines the renewed perception about the other?

In response to the aforesaid questions, but in contrast to a Levinasian anti-self center, Miroslav Volf argues that "personal centeredness must be preserved for the sake of difference."[6] Said differently, personal centeredness should harmonize otherness for the purposes of genuine dialogue and sustenance of order.

This research's attempt in harmonizing otherness and communion agrees more with Volf than Levinas. Virtually, all Levinasian discourses against Western philosophy reflect a mere shift of center, from sameness to otherness. Such, regrettably, sustains rivalry instead.

Paul Ricoeur, in his book *Oneself as Another*, clearly demonstrates the harmony between the self and the other.[7] Like Volf, Ricoeur critiques Levinasian asymmetric relation because of its rejection of mutuality.[8] In the same vein, Volf contests the Derridean center, which he believes acts as "merely a container of the difference."[9] Both Levinas and Derrida in their arguments ascribed absolute infiniteness to the

---

3. Shepherd, *Gift of the Other*, 14.

4. Shepherd, *Gift of the Other*, 176.

5. Shepherd, *Gift of the Other*, 14.

6. Volf and Gundry-Volf, *Spacious Heart*, 38.

7. Ricoeur, *Oneself as Another*, 3; 180–81.

8. Ricoeur, *Oneself as Another*, 183.

9. Volf and Gundry-Volf, *Spacious Heart*, 38.

other, which obstructs mutuality, thereby constituting an additional problem for interreligious relations.

For humanity, absolute infiniteness, while protecting otherness or separation, frustrates mutuality, which is an important ingredient for unity (communion). In accord, the Levinasian self, according to Ricoeur, is denied of self-esteem in the asymmetric infinite responsibility for the other.[10] Oliver Davies also argues that Levinas's portraiture of how "the hostage self" suffers servitude for the other violates the self-presence and self-possession necessary to ethical responsibility.[11] Even though Levinas claims that the gift of self-knowledge comes from the encounter with the other, he insists that such self-knowledge can only be possible through unreciprocated services of the self to the other.

Alternatively, Volf attributes some elements of esteem to the self by redefining it as "a de-centered center."[12] "De-centered center," according to Volf, aims at describing "the kind of unity in which plurality is preserved rather than erased."[13] Therefore, the otherness in plurality must maintain porous and shifting boundaries in order to create space for unity.[14]

Volf knew the work of Paul Hiebert, the missiologist, and actually drew from it.[15] With greater clarity, Hiebert outlines four qualities of a dialogic center: centered, relational, variational, and dynamic.[16] Shepherd asserts that these four elements are present in the biblical metaphor of the gate to the sheepfold,[17] which Jesus identified himself with (John 10:7–10). He backs up his interpretation of the gate with these words from Rodney Whitacre: the gate of the sheepfold "is not that of a door as a barrier for protection, but of a door as a passageway."[18] This gate identifies what stays inside, and still permits free inward and outward movements.

In this light, Muslims and Christians are proportionately challenged to reimagine their respective identities as paradigmatic of a "de-centered center," or "the gate of the sheepfold." This implies envisioning a non-exclusive but permissible community of God's people, which at once assures

10. Ricoeur, *Oneself as Another*, 168, 221.

11. Davies, *Theology of Compassion*, 188, 31.

12. Volf, *Exclusion and Embrace*, 71.

13. Volf, "Trinity," 110.

14. Volf, "Trinity," 111–12.

15. Shepherd, *Gift of the Other*, 188.

16. Hiebert, "Category 'Christian.'"

17. Shepherd, *Gift of the Other*, 188.

18. Whitacre, *John*, 258.

its uniqueness and, as well, creates spaces for a bidirectional relation with the other. Henri Nouwen confirms this openness in these words: "An intimate relationship between people not only asks for mutual openness but also asks for mutual respectful protection of each other's uniqueness."[19]

Since harmony between otherness and communion underscores this chapter's thesis, subsequent subsections will seek to establish theological and cultural grounds for substitutive responsibility, which promotes an asymmetric-mutual hospitality. The sacred books of Islam and Christianity are the most reliable sources for the proposed crafting of a practical interfaith theology. However, an African perspective, through the common ideology of interdependence/interconnectivity, exemplified in *ubuntu* (humanness) personhood, will be presented as a practical support for the sacred textual injunctions, aimed toward a wholesome theological discourse.

Even though Levinas proposes substitutive responsibility from an ethicophilosophical view, it is the claim of this research that a healthy theology can be constructed from its principles by stimulating asymmetric-mutual substitutive responsibility among Muslims and Christians. Such transition reassures one of the scholastic maxims that *philosophia ancillia theologia*—philosophy is the handmaid of theology.

From Philosophical Principle to Theological Praxis

Jean-Luc Marion appreciatively thinks that Levinasian ethical phenomenology can provide a basis for theological reflections because both, as two "recalcitrant cousins,"[20] share a common origin in the givenness of lived experience.[21] In agreement, Michael Purcell interprets the Levinasian notion of theology as that in "which the question about God cannot be asked, without a prior question about who asks the question."[22] Abigail Doukhan also believes that Levinasian hospitality offers the via media for interfaith dialogue, especially among the Abrahamic religions, which respectively considers him a reliable model of hospitality.[23]

---

19. Nouwen, *Reaching Out*, 32.
20. Purcell, *Levinas and Theology*, 28.
21. Marion, *In Excess*, 29.
22. Purcell, *Levinas and Theology*, 2.
23. Doukhan, "Hospitality of Abraham," 81.

Nevertheless, given a philosophical framework by Levinas, how can there be a transition into an interfaith theology? Did Levinas intend doing theology? A fair response combines a yes and a no answer. No, because Levinas never associated himself with any brand of theology that categorized and reflected on God only as a transcendent being. Levinas vehemently attacked the predominant ontological engagement of theologians of his time, which he argued sacrificed ethical responsibility.[24] In reaction, he insists that ethics must be fundamental to both philosophy and theology.[25]

Yes, because even though a philosopher, his brand of phenomenology is so ethically based such that it also grounds theology. According to Purcell, Levinas "offers to theology a new voice, a new grammar of response and responsibility, a new lexicon for articulating the human in its tendency towards the divine which, for Levinas cannot avoid an ethical commitment to the other person here and now."[26]

Corroboratively, the Levinasian metaphorical face of the other reveals the traces of God.[27] Drawing a theological connection with the metaphor of the face, Levinas explains: "The wonderful thing about the face is that it speaks, it says need, vulnerability, it asks, begs me for help, it makes me responsible . . . God, the god, it's a long way there, a road that goes via the Other. Loving God is Loving the Other."[28] Fundamentally, Levinas teaches that the infinite responsibility for the other manifests the infinite God: "The glory of the Infinite is glorified in this responsibility."[29] In essence, Levinasian philosophy undergirds a theological anthropology[30] in which "[t]he dimension of the divine opens forth from the human face."[31]

The discursive ability of the face enables it to manifest God—"a god who loves the stranger, who puts me in question by his demand, and to which my 'here I am' bears witness."[32] Ultimately, substitutive responsibility, as advocated by Levinas, begets a direct favor because through the

24. Zimmermann, *Levinas and Theology*, 21.

25. Purcell, *Levinas and Theology*, 2.

26. Purcell, *Levinas and Theology*, 3.

27. Leirvik, "Towards," 233.

28. Levinas, *Outside the Subject*, 214.

29. Levinas, *Otherwise than Being* (1981), 144.

30. Purcell, *Levinas and Theology*, 2.

31. Levinas, *Totality and Infinity*, 78.

32. Levinas, *Of God*, 166–68.

face of the other the self enjoys a transcendental opportunity.[33] That the human encounter paves the way for the divine encounter[34] proves that Levinasian ethics can be foundational for theology.

Levinasian altruism can also be defended on the basis of its biblical and Qur'anic resonance, in agreement with Oddborn Leirvik's presentation.[35] There are three notable biblical instances presenting the other as an epiphany of God. First, Genesis 33:10 states: "If I have found favor in your eyes, accept this gift from me. For to see your face is like seeing the face of God, now that you have received me favorably." Similarly, the Qur'an highlights seeking the face of God (*wajh Allah*) as the ultimate righteousness (2:272 and 6:52). Second, 1 John 4:20 proclaims, "Anyone who does not love his brother, whom he has seen, cannot love God, whom he has not seen." In consonance with the biblical stance, the Qur'an elaborates: "And they feed, for the love of God, the indigent, the orphan, and the captive,—(saying), 'we feed you for the sake of God alone: no reward do we desire from you, nor thanks'" (76:8–9). Finally, Matthew 25 states, "Truly I tell you, whatever you did [not do] for one of the least of least of these brother and sisters of mine, you did [not do] for me."

Based on these theological insights, this chapter is tailored toward engaging a theological basis of hospitality (from Islamic and Christian sources). Through these scriptural foundations this research intends to tease out support for the development of a theology of asymmetric-mutual hospitality that is practicable among Muslims and Christians in Nigeria, but which can also serve as a lesson at the global context. The goal of this stage of study is to awaken a theology of substitutive responsibility across the Muslim-Christian divide, through which otherness can harmonize communion.

In the course of crafting a practical theology of hospitality toward an Abrahamic pilgrim model, this research seeks to establish a foundational anchor in both Islamic and Christian theologies, before transcending to a convergence on Abraham. In this particular section, attempt will be made to introduce the face of God in the interpersonal dialogue of life, via illuminative substitutive theology of hospitality.

---

33. Doukhan, "Hospitality of Abraham," 89.

34. Levinas, *Totality and Infinity*, 78.

35. Leirvik, "Towards," 234.

Theological Basis for
Asymmetric-Mutual Substitutive Hospitality

As previously explained, asymmetric-mutual hospitality finds its theological basis in the shared belief that God or Allah rewards every good act. Being asymmetric but also mutual encourages disparate gifts exchange, not borne from payback. In that light, the theology of asymmetric-cmutual substitutive hospitality is both illuminative and a form of witnessing. It is illuminative because hospitality has always been at the core of Christian and Muslim teachings, as will be demonstrated. However, its ordinariness and spontaneity, but also societal rules of individualism, have technically forced it into latency. But when illumined, hospitality can be efficaciously invigorated and harnessed. More so, asymmetric-mutual substitution toward the need of the other bears witness to the hospitable God, who demands (my) willingness and surrender.[36] It is therefore the goal of this theological discourse to awaken mutual hospitality from its slumber in order that through a dialogue of life it can pave the way (by establishing trust) for coexistence between Christians and Muslims.

A good theology should be anchored in the sacred texts. To construct a theology of asymmetric-mutual hospitality that is characterized by substitutive responsibility for the other, this research will peruse through the Qur'an, the Bible, and some theological thoughts, but will also review its African understanding, in search of compelling supports. The aim is to establish the presence of mutual hospitality in Islamic, Christian, and African traditions, with a watchful eye on how supportive they reflect substitutive altruism. Substitutive responsibility simply means the willingness to respond positively to the demands of the other by putting oneself in the situation of the other, especially the vulnerable other.

The Qur'an and Islamic Notions of Hospitality

Siddiqui makes a provocative claim: "Hospitality is fundamental to spiritual life."[37] This means that hospitality incorporates more than what could be usually presumed in a particular religion or culture. Hospitality in the Islamic tradition does not differ from its exploration in this research. Rather, Islam in northern Africa inherited a rich Bedouin

---

36. Levinas, *Of God*, 167.

37. Siddiqui, *Hospitality and Islam*, 1.

hospitality culture that goes beyond ethical acts, like doing and giving, and includes most importantly one's "state of mind."[38] As noted, despite the fact that the richness of hospitality has attracted different viewpoints in the academy, the Islamic perspective, especially in modern times, has not been the focus.

Mona Siddiqui acknowledges significant treatment of hospitality in its modern inclusive perspective in the Christian tradition, but notes its multiple nuances in "Islamic thought and piety," such as charity, generosity, and neighborliness.[39] It is interesting to note that modern Muslim intellectual tradition presents hospitality as both "a concept and an act."[40] To be hospitable, therefore, in the Islamic tradition includes "the other-oriented" virtues like forgiveness and compassion. Siddiqui therefore situates compassion at the center of hospitality because of its principal role of initiating surprising solidarity and friendship.[41]

Hospitality in its table fellowship dimension is a pre-Islamic Bedouin practice that was Islamized. It is the closest to the Arabic origin of the term "*diyafa* (equivalent of table fellowship and protective hospitality)."[42] So, having been a commonplace practice, hosting of all strangers as guests, even to the extent of substitution, is prized as a noble act alongside chivalry and honor. In essence, hospitality "was first and foremost an act of chivalry. A man who could make a royal display of his generosity was a true dandy of the desert."[43] Pre-Islamic hospitality, according to Snjezana Akpinar, "was considered as an act of unconditional surrender to the needs of others."[44] Akpinar anticipates the mutual (sacrificial) substitutive hospitality that this research is evolving.

Pre-Islamic legend exemplifies the Arab poet Hatim ibn 'Abd Allah ibn Sa'd al-Ta'I as one of the greatest humans that attained the peak of hospitality. According to Siddiqui, Ibn 'Abd Rabbih's famed *adab*[45]

38. Siddiqui, *Hospitality and Islam*, 1.

39. Siddiqui, *Hospitality and Islam*, 2.

40. Siddiqui, *Hospitality and Islam*, 18.

41. Siddiqui, *Hospitality and Islam*, 19.

42. Siddiqui, *Hospitality and Islam*, 29.

43. Izutsu, *Ethico-Religious Concepts*, 76.

44. Akpinar, "Hospitality in Islam," 23.

45. *Adab* means Islamic etiquette. *The Unique Necklace* (*Al-'Iqd al-Farid*) consists of twenty-five chapters. According to Siddiqui Ibn 'Abd Rabbih, it represents a necklace made of twenty-five jewels. This book embodies some topics like literature, poem, moral, history, politics, humor, etc. It can be compared to a general knowledge

compilation, *The Unique Necklace*, contains several stories about Hatim's substitutive hospitality.[46] However, 'Abd Rabbih, the chronicler, confirms that (as the life of Hatim typified) the nobility of a person was determined with the immensity of his hospitality toward his kinfolk as well as to strangers with all the risks involved.[47]

It is a common claim that *karam/qira* (generosity, alternate of hospitality) was one of the important virtues for pre-Islamic Arabs, especially among the Bedouins. Andrew Shryock affirms: "Arabs, through the ages have hosted a stranger for three days and a third before asking his name."[48] As a virtue, the practice of *karam* connotes nobility of character because of its understanding as both an ethicoreligious obligation and an ancestry heritage.

Karam is described as "a burning in the skin" inherited *harara bi-l-ijlud/min al-abb wa-l-ijdud* ("from the father and the grandfathers").[49] Its extreme form, often expressed as *hiblat al-'arab* ("the Arab madness"),[50] was not discouraged in Islamic Arabia. Rather, its adoption by the Bedouin Muslims merits a host who forgets his prayers while hosting his guest such appealing compliment: *al-karam din-u* ("hospitality is his religion").[51] In this regard, the sacredness of *karam* among the Bedouins perhaps weighs more than religion itself, which explains why they considered it a reliable solution to problems like "the threat of violence, the redistribution of wealth, the rights of strangers, and the placing and crossing of social boundaries."[52] Such a problem-solving notion of *karam* among the Bedouin sets in motion this research's proposal of hospitality as a possible resolution to the antagonistic Muslim-Christian relation. The impact of such a great heritage might be the reason hospitality is tied to Islamic piety, and not to mere ethical demand.

Islam reformed and raised the practice of hospitality into a religious virtue that is obligatory. The polysemic concept of hospitality in Islamic thought might have influenced its engagement with several terms in view

---

encyclopedia or anthology.

46. Siddiqui, *Hospitality and Islam*, 34.

47. Ibn 'Abd Rabbih, *Unique Necklace*, 197–78.

48. Shryock, "Thinking About Hospitality," 407.

49. Shryock, "Thinking About Hospitality," 406.

50. Shryock, "Thinking About Hospitality," 406

51. Shryock, "Thinking About Hospitality," 406

52. Shryock, "Thinking About Hospitality," 406

of capturing the various dimensions to its holistic understanding. Besides the practice of *zakat*, (tied to hospitality) and *al-fatihah* (understood as an expression of divine hospitality leading to true conversion of heart), the Qur'an did not develop any specific theme on hospitality. Rather, in dealing with such principles and notions like guests, wayfarers (*ibn al-sabil*), neighborliness (*jar*), and strangers, the Qur'an expresses its interest in teaching hospitable practices.

Beginning with the concept of guests (*dayf/duyuf*), Siddiqui analyzes its syntactic usages in the Qur'an and notices five appearances of the noun form *dayf*:

> They refused to offer them hospitality (Q. 18:77); So, fear God and do not disgrace me concerning my guests (Q. 11:87); Has there reached you the story of the honored guests of Abraham? (Q. 15:24); And tell them about the guests of Abraham (Q. 15:51); Lot said, Indeed these are my guests, so do not shame me (Q. 15:68); They demanded from him his guests, but we blinded their eyes saying, 'Take my punishment and my warning' (Q. 54:37).[53]

The Islamic teaching on love of God and neighbor includes great concern for wayfarers and strangers, distinguished as distant neighbors:

> Worship God and associate nothing with Him, and to parents do good, and to relatives, orphans, the needy, the near neighbor, the neighbor farther away, the companion at your side, the traveller, and those whom your right hands posses. Indeed, God does not like those who are self-deluding and boastful. [54]

Yusuf Ali explains the distinction between two kinds of neighbors in the Qur'an. The "neighbors who are near," according to him, includes not only local kin, but all those with whom one shares intimate relationship. Similarly, "neighbors who are strangers" includes both distant and unknown persons.[55]

From the modern Islamic perspective, it is difficult to imagine an equivalent of the modernized notion of a stranger in its original socio-cultural context. Franz Rosenthal confirms that neither the terms *gharib* ("strange") nor *ajnabi* ("stranger") are typically present in the Qur'an, despite the former's multiple usages in the hadith. Practically, no one was

53. Siddiqui, *Hospitality and Islam*, 36.

54. Qur'an 4:36. Translation was taken from qur'an.com and from Ali, *Holy Qur'an*. Allah has been replaced with God.

55. Ali, *Holy Qur'an*, 231.

considered a stranger in the then-Muslim world.[56] The reason, according to Rosenthal, borders on the universality of Islamic brotherhood. Moreover, not even a non-Islamic foreigner was considered a problem[57] to an extent that would have attracted xenophobic attitudes.[58] Clarifying further, Rosenthal states:

> No distinction was made between leaving home for good, or staying abroad for some time and gradually losing any intention to return, or just travelling with no thought of permanently changing one's residence such as was done by pilgrims, merchants and fortune seekers; here we may include groups like beggars, crooks and wandering low-class entertainers who often had no place they could call home.[59]

The analysis of Rosenthal provides concrete grounds for the imaginative pilgrim metaphor that this research will later recommend for the possible dissolution of the screen wall established by strict ethnic identification, otherwise called "geogamy."[60]

Besides *gharib* ("strange"), *ajnabi* ("stranger") also suggests outsiders as neighbors, in spite of the latter's obvious distance and differences. From this perspective, *ajnabi* can literally translate as a "distant neighbor," with significant basic rights. Ibn Abbas reiterates the distinctive right of the distant neighbor when he says:

> And unto the neighbor who is kin (unto you) the neighbor who also happens to be your relative has three rights over you: the right of kinship, the right of Islam, and the right of being a neighbor (and the neighbor who is not of kin); the neighbor who is not a relative has two rights: the right of Islam and the right of being a neighbor (and the fellow traveller); a fellow traveller has two rights: the right of Islam and the right of companionship.[61]

---

56. Rosenthal, "Stranger," 36.

57. Rosenthal, "Stranger," 40.

58. Siddiqui, *Hospitality and Islam*, 37.

59. Rosenthal, "Stranger," 41.

60. *Geogamy* is a derogatory neology against the persistent Osu caste system. It articulates the claim of superior bond(age) and entitlement to the native land. Archbishop Anthony J. V. Obinna of Owerri, Nigeria, coined it (in 2011) as a deconstructive argument against the Igbo (Nigeria) ideology of a discriminatory right of purity by a major segment (Diala) against a marginalized minority (Osu), in certain areas of Igboland. *Geogamy* is commonly expressed as "son of the soil."

61. Abbas, *Mokrane Guezzou*, cited in Siddiqui, *Hospitality and Islam*, 38.

That the Qur'an is silent on how the three spheres of neighbors should be treated, offers grounds for a positive attitude to all. The only difference, however, might be that, drawn from Abbas's categorization of rights, there is significant respect for the non-Islamic stranger.

Specificity about hospitality toward the other is lacking in Islamic teaching, as it is in Christianity. The reason is not entirely disassociated from the spontaneity demanded by every particular instance of hospitality. Spontaneous response in reaction to particular needs assures otherness. To an eschatological question from a man, "O Messenger of God, guide me to something which if I do it, will take me to the Garden?," the Prophet Mohammad replied, "Be good to others." And to the question, "How will I know if I am being good to others?," the Prophet insisted, "Ask your neighbors. If they say you are good to others, you are good, and if they say you are bad to others, you are bad."[62]

Without prescribing particular acts, Mohammad gives a form for hospitality, embedded in neighborliness, similar to what Jesus teaches with the story of the Good Samaritan, especially when he said, "go and do likewise" (Luke 10:29–37). Islam and Christianity have robust teachings on the love of neighbor, but the identity and activities of good neighborliness are sketchily portrayed. That only a framework is available from both religious masters allows rooms for spontaneity in implementing the praxis, perhaps as demanded by the immediate need of the other. Certainly, Pohl attests that hospitality converges the form (universality) and the act (personalization) of neighborliness.[63] Viewed from a Levinasian perspective, it is the need of the other that determines the substitutive responsibility.

However, in the Islamic Malik code *Muwatta*,[64] the duration of hospitality is stipulated. Malik's code recommends that a guest "is to be welcomed for a day and a night and his hospitality is for three days. Anything after that is *sadaqa* (extravagance). It is not permitted for a guest to stay with him [his host] until he becomes a burden to him."[65] If strangers value the responsibility of not impoverishing their hosts, the newness of their presence, as gift, invariably benefits their hosts.

---

62. Uthman al-Dhahabi, *Major Sins*, 453–55.

63. Pohl, *Making Room*, 75.

64. Al-Muwatta is the first formulation of Islamic laws compiled and edited by Imam Malik.

65. Anas, *Al-Muwatta*, 708.

Concentrating her research on the Sunni tradition, Siddiqui identifies "surprise and humility" as two important principles of hospitality.[66] The spontaneity of hospitality from the giver comes to the recipient as a surprise. Drawing on a particular life experience, she links surprise with the hospitable act, while humility is said to emerge as a product of the surprising (hospitality) act. Consequently, these Islamic hospitality principles of surprise and humility imply the possibility of unconditional hospitality. So, how would such claim respond to the Derridean impossibility of unconditional hospitality?

Derrida sees hospitality not just as an aspect of ethics, but rather the ethics (itself) for boundary crossing, at both the interpersonal level as well as in the public sphere.[67] His argument reprimands world leaders who prefer safe borders at the expense of the risk-bearing element that constitutes hospitality. Derrida's concern revisits the question of unconditional or borderless hospitality, for which the identity of the welcomed and the unwelcomed are unnecessary.[68]

Concerning the possibility and impossibility (Derrida)[69] of unconditional hospitality, scholars like Roxanne Doty think that the latter becomes the case when hospitable acts are restricted to the territorial laws and policies of sovereign powers.[70] Affirmatively, Siddiqui believes that unconditional hospitality can happen only when governmental norms are transcended.[71] A distinction between a moral person and a legal person can be insightful in differentiating the possibility of unconditional hospitality at its interpersonal level from its impossibility in the public (governmental) realm. While a moral person enjoys absolute value, the worth of a legal person is conditioned by the exclusive norm of her locality.

The Enlightenment philosopher Emmanuel Kant taught that hospitality is a "natural right" to every person because of the collective ownership of earthly goods. Territorial laws, according to Kant, however, moderate this right, when one is in a foreign land.[72] In other words,

66. Siddiqui, *Hospitality and Islam*, 3.

67. Still, *Derrida and Hospitality*, 6–7.

68. See chapter 7 for details.

69. Derrida conceives unconditional hospitality as an impossibility, a promise, a "to come," based on the current world political and economic policies.

70. Doty, "Practices of Hospitality," 46.

71. Siddiqui, *Hospitality and Islam*, 6.

72. Kant, "Perpetual Peace," 106.

human beings have rights according to their respective nativities, and therefore are relatively citizens of the earth.

In contrast, Alasdair McIntyre situates hospitality at the core of every societal life, in particular, for the benefit of the stranger. He argues that hospitality "is important to the functioning of communities that among the roles that play a part in their shared lives there should be that of the 'stranger,' someone from outside the community who has happened to arrive amongst us and to whom we owe hospitality, just because she or he is stranger."[73] McIntyre invariably deconstructs Kant's localized right to hospitality by establishing a universal right to hospitality for the stranger. McIntyre's universal model of hospitality resonates with the substitutive responsibility toward the other that this research advances.

Unlike Derrida or Kant, Siddiqui sees the possibility of unconditional hospitality in Islamic tradition. According to her, Islamic thought regards the stranger with unknown identity as less problematic. The reason given stems from the fact that Islamic hospitality is explained within the category of a "host/guest" or "host/traveler" relationship, rather than that of "host/stranger."[74] Hospitality is one of the noble virtues in the Islamic ethical and spiritual system, inherited from the Bedouin culture, whose sustenance was supported by the harsh arid environment. Hospitality in this regard is both a responsibility toward others and a great reminder for the appreciation of human diversity.[75] Qur'an 5:48 reiterates human diversity as the original plan of God. Notwithstanding that, God has a way of taking good care of them all.

A "hospitable God" might not be a common expression in Islamic theology, similar to the Christian sense of a "self-giving God." While Christians believe in a God whose self-manifestation in the Son atoned for humanity's sins, Muslims perceive the identity of God-Son and God-man extremely problematic. Whereas Christianity situates in Christ the meeting point between transcendence and immanence, Islam considers such teaching irreconcilable. For Muslims, God wants to be known, for he is near (Qur'an 50:16), but only through prophecy and scripture.[76] The absolute transcendence of God held in Islam need not be confused

---

73. McIntyre, *Dependent Rational Animals*, 123.

74. Siddiqui, *Hospitality and Islam*, 10.

75. Siddiqui, *Hospitality and Islam*, 12.

76. Siddiqui, *Hospitality and Islam*, 127.

with distance. Rather, one needs to contextualize the different media of God's revelation in both religions.

Nonetheless, the Qur'an acknowledges Allah as a benevolent, generous, and merciful God. Allah is severally depicted as the God who provides for all. Addressed as *al-Razzaq* (the Provider), the Qur'an sounds a reminder: "O mankind, remember the favor of God upon you. Is there any creator other than God who provides for you from the heaven and earth?" (35:3). The Qur'an unequivocally rejects any intermediary between God's provision and his creatures (11:6).

An account of a woman in the Qur'an can be illuminating here. Mary, the mother of Jesus, is recorded in the Qur'an as a woman whom God specially cared for from her infancy, when she was living under the tutelage of Zachariah in the temple. 3:37 confirms that Mary never lacked supplies, at the utter surprise of Zachariah. And when he questioned her concerning the source of her supplies, Mary answered: "It is from God. Indeed, God provides for whom He wills without account." This story so much aligns with the Islamic teaching on direct providence of God for all his people. But because humans cannot, in a literal sense, provide for God, they are expected to show gratitude to God by extending God's benevolence and hospitality to other humans (neighbors).

Both Islam and Christianity typically agree on the identical closeness of love of God and love of neighbor. In essence, neighbors offer wonderful opportunity for the practice of obedience and gratitude to God, otherwise known as human relationship in which doing good for one another reenacts God's hospitality.[77] This is a form of witnessing to the gratuity of God. From the gratuitous perspective, the giftedness of the other is illumined and appreciated. Siddiqui thinks that the testing for human beings included in the Qur'anic acknowledgement of plurality (5:48) might be for the encouragement of goodness and hospitality to one another as well as obedience to God.[78]

The Biblical and Christian Bases for Hospitality

Arthur Sutherland, in his book *I Was a Stranger: A Christian Theology of Hospitality*, rightly argues that "hospitality is at the center of what it means

---

77. Siddiqui, *Hospitality and Islam*, 123.

78. Siddiqui, *Hospitality and Islam*, 124.

to be Christian and to think theologically."[79] Sutherland supports the thesis that hospitality has been a well-known and highly valued practice in Islam and Christianity, even in African religion and culture. This research is only calling for an awakening attitude toward this ancient practice already enshrined in the sacred books as an act of God, which God also commands for God's people. The awakening is directed to all adherents of both religions in their everydayness such that when mutually adhered to, the individualism of modern society would be defeated, leading to an envisioned neighborliness where otherness harmonizes communion.

The Hosting God

Creation as pure gift manifests the universal hospitality of God.[80] Typically, humanity is the special guest of God. God is the chief host. As guests administering God's goods, Matthew 10:8 provides a guideline for our stewardship. Its injunction, "give freely as you received freely," instructs the disciples to offer hospitality to others in response to God's gift they received. Besides being a sacred duty[81] and in response to the demands of its nomadic life, the ancient Israelites evolved an elaborate code of hospitality[82] in gratitude to God's hospitality. The psalmist's thanksgiving outburst further captures the Israelites' understanding of God as host:

> You prepare a table for me in the presence of my enemies; you anoint my head with oil; my cup is overflowing. Kindness and faithful love shall follow me all the days of my life. And I shall dwell in the house of the Lord, all the days of my life. (Psalm 23:5–6)

Extravagant hosting characterizes the full meaning of divine hospitality. The necessity of hospitality toward strangers, orphans, widows, and the poor was emphasized by God in strident language: "You shall not molest or oppress an alien for you were once aliens . . . You shall not wrong any widow or orphan. If ever you wrong them . . . I will surely hear their cry. My wrath will flare up, and I will kill you with the sword" (Exodus 2:20–23). That God can punish his people's inhospitality towards aliens with death validates the necessity of the thesis this research is defending.

79. Sutherland, *I Was a Stranger*, xiv.
80. Navone, "Divine and Human Hospitality," 329.
81. Olikenyi, *African Hospitality*, 88.
82. Koenig, *New Testament Hospitality*, 16.

Israel's memorial experience of hospitality in Egypt, and of being God's guests during their exodus journey to the Promised Land, epitomizes her prioritization of hospitality.

A reflection on the basis of biblical metaphors of hospitality reveals a hospitable God whose words and deeds invite humanity into the loveship of hospitality, vividly expressed in the substitutive responsibility for the neighbor. Creation was for the well-being of creatures, especially humanity. Without any expectation of a payback, even though an impossibility, God lavishly created and sustains humanity. The need of the other has always been the central concern of God.

Metaphors of hospitality fill both Old and New Testaments. Such abundance points to the centrality of hospitality in Christian life.[83] A slight distinction can be noticed in the way God played host by feeding the Israelites in the desert with manna and quail and how God the Son exemplified the hosting of the crowd also in the desert. God's pattern of hosting agrees with the ancient Israelites' conception of a transcendent God as their God, who shared an indirect relationship with them through a mediation of human agency, like Moses and the prophets.

The gap between God and God's people was later bridged in Christ through his hypostatic union at the incarnation. In Christ, therefore, humanity harmoniously cooperates with divinity. Such divine collaboration defines the hosting of the crowds by Christ and his apostles, in which a shift in approach is noticed. Unlike in Exodus 16:1–29, where God practically provided manna and quail for the people, Christ requested the apostles to host the crowd: "give them something to eat, yourself" (Luke 9:13). The insignificance of five loaves and two fish in comparison to the satisfaction of the crowd, and the twelve wicker baskets of leftover, demonstrate the fruit of divine-human collaboration in hospitality. The point is, in collaboration with God, the chief host, Christian disciples should participate in hospitality toward the (religious) other.

John Navone articulates God's hospitality in a host-guest dynamic:

> We are all guests of God's hospitality. The world in which we live is a pure gift. Our own existence, our human nature, our essential consciousness, intelligence and creativity are all gift. The companionship of other human beings like ourselves is gift. So is the presence on earth of plant and animal life, of water and air and mineral resources, of light, of the firm earth beneath our feet and the blue-sky overhead. We did not make these things

83. Bethune, "Interreligious Dialogue," 15.

nor cause them to come to being. Moreover, we would not exist
for one moment if all these things were not around us to sustain
our existence. God is the Host Exemplar of all his guests. Creation expresses God's hospitality.[84]

In most instances in the Bible, the reversibility of the guest-host
metaphor is common. God is both host and guest. Two accounts, one
from the Old Testament (protective hospitality in Genesis 19) and the
other from the New Testament (Zacchaeus's conversion in Luke 19:1–10)
indicate that God as host doesn't conflict with God being the guest. These
selected scenes not only replicate the three categories of hospitality—table, intellectual, and protective—they also highlight important principles
of hospitality. Gregory I. Olikenyi recaps these hospitality elements,
which were liberally presented in chapter 7, as:

> Complete awareness of the presence of the stranger, spontane-
> ous openness and freedom in the encounter between the host
> and the guest (stranger), obliging invitation, wholehearted
> welcoming, sharing of meal, giving of protection—which can
> be demanding—accompanying on the way, opening of new and
> promising future.[85]

None of Olikenyi's elements falls outside the three broad categories
that Reaves outlined in chapter 7. With the relevance of these elements in
view, this research cannot but agree that "the concept of hospitality is one
of the richest concepts to deepen our insight in the relationship with our
fellow human beings."[86]

In the words of Lucien Richard, "The central image of vision of life
sustaining the law of hospitality to the stranger for Christianity is that
of the kingdom of God."[87] For most Christians, "hospitality is about
seeing the face of Christ in every stranger and living God's triune grace-
filled kingdom on this earth."[88] The host-guest dynamic is most vividly
manifested in the model of Jesus' hospitality; and as such, Christian discipleship has a lot to learn from it for effective practices of substitutive
responsibility towards Muslim neighbors.

---

84. Navone, "Divine and Human Hospitality," 329.

85. Olikenyi, *African Hospitality*, 87.

86. Nouwen, "Hospitality," 7.

87. Richard, *Living the Hospitality*, 38.

88. Richard, *Living the Hospitality*, 16.

A Christological Dimension

Subsequent to demonstrating the Christian God as a universal host, this research further intends establishing the validation of substitutive responsibility for the other in the christological, through the ecclesial, and toward the eschatological aspects of hospitality. The incarnation revealed God's involvement and approval of substitutive responsibility for others (creation in general, but humanity in particular).

Abrahamic hospitality in the Old Testament has severally been read as paradigmatic,[89] but not entirely unconnected with Christ. And for the author of the Letter to the Hebrews, it is the way in which the believers are to welcome the stranger.[90] Although Abraham, an Old Testament figure, might not have met Jesus, to learn from him, still his encounter with Melchizedek (Genesis 14), the prototype of Christ in the Old Testament, suggests some grounds in a similar direction.[91] The bread and wine that Melchizedek offered to Abraham has been explained as prefiguring the New Testament Eucharist,[92] that kenotic expression of Jesus' hospitality to humanity.

Hospitality occupies a very prominent place in the person of Jesus. It is emblematic of almost the entire encounters of Jesus with strangers. Jesus welcomed hospitality from both rich and poor, from the wealthy Zachaeus and from his poor family friends at Bethany. He not only enjoyed hospitality from people, he also practiced and enjoined it. Pohl notices, "The intermingling of guest and host roles in the person of Jesus is part of what makes the story of hospitality so compelling for Christians. Jesus welcomes and needs welcome; Jesus requires that followers depend on and provide hospitality. The practice of Christian hospitality is always located within the larger picture of Jesus's sacrificial welcome to all who come to him."[93]

In his examples, Jesus broke cultural barriers through inclusive hospitality across the borders of gender, class, religion, and sociopolitical taboos.[94] Essentially, he broadened the scope of *philoxenia* to everyone, including enemies (Matthew 5:44). He dined with tax collectors and

89. Allard, "In the Shades," 416.

90. Sykes, "Making Room," 62.

91. Cohen, "Abraham's Hospitality," 168.

92. Cohen, "Abraham's Hospitality," 169.

93. Pohl, *Making Room*, 17.

94. Bethune, "Interreligious Dialogue," 15.

sinners, asked for a drink from a Samaritan woman, and gave audience to foreigners and non-believers without enforcing conversion.

At some moments, he switched roles between guest and host (the Emmaus experience and encounter with the Syro-Phoenician woman). Hospitality demands from everyone the openness to give and ask for it. Jesus taught and practiced both, and instructed his disciples on their first missionary journey to rely on hospitality (Mark 10; Luke 9–10), so long as they do not misconceive of it as a right (Matthew 10:14). De Bethune clarifies that Jesus' instruction to his disciples to traveling light, rather than encouraging asceticism, was intended for the establishment of hospitality necessary for the proper engagement of otherness.[95]

A great moment of encounter that exemplifies substitutive responsibility for the other will be analyzed as a typical christological model of hospitality. The textual passage of John 4 is chosen not only for its rich significances in otherness, but also to orchestrate Jesus' profound model of hospitality, in which substitution for the other was emphatically communicated. This text contains the double otherness of gender (a woman) and foreignness (a non-Jew).

From Jesus's model of hospitality, one can learn, on the one hand, the flexibility and challenges of hospitality, and on the other, the right responses to them. Such proper approaches include spontaneity, respect for the other, and openness to learning or growth, made possible through predilection for the other.

Jesus' spontaneous approach as evident in this biblical encounter not only recalls its Levinasian emphasis, it also agrees with Fernando Segovia's suggestion on the use of bifocal lenses that enable one to see that which is close (one's own social location) and that which is at a distance (the context of the other).[96] Catherine Cornille, aware of the latter (telescopic) lens, confirms,

> The idea of hospitality implies recognition of the other as other, as a stranger who is welcomed in spite of fundamental differences in background, beliefs and way of life. It creates an atmosphere of friendship and trust in which those differences are not only tolerated but engaged in an open and constructive way.[97]

95. Bethune, "Interreligious Dialogue," 15.

96. Brink, "In the Search," 11.

97. Cornille, "Interreligious Hospitality," 35.

Jesus' encounter with the Samaritan woman conforms to the hospitality model that Cornille defends.

The Woman of Samaria

The encounter of Jesus with the Samaritan woman in John 4:4–30 reads:

> Now he [Jesus] had to go through Samaria. So he came to a town in Samaria called Sychar, near the plot of ground Jacob had given to his son Joseph. Jacob's well was there, and Jesus, tired as he was from the journey, sat down by the well. It was about noon. When a Samaritan woman came to draw water, Jesus said to her, "Give me a drink?" (His disciples had gone into the town to buy food.). The Samaritan woman said to him, "You are a Jew and I am a Samaritan woman. How can you ask me for a drink?" (For Jews do not associate with Samaritans). Jesus answered her, "If you knew the gift of God and who it is that asks you for a drink, you would have asked him and he would have given you living water." "Sir," the woman said, "you have nothing to draw with and the well is deep. Where can you get this living water? Are you greater than our father Jacob, who gave us the well and drank from it himself, as did also his sons and his livestock?" Jesus answered, "Everyone who drinks this water will be thirsty again, but whoever drinks the water I give them will never thirst. Indeed, the water I give them will become in them a spring of water welling up to eternal life. The woman said to him, "Sir, give me this water so that I won't get thirsty and have to keep coming here to draw water. He told her, "Go, call your husband and come back." "I have no husband," she replied. Jesus said to her, "You are right when you say you have no husband. The fact is, you have had five husbands, and the man you now have is not your husband. What you have just said is quite true." "Sir," the woman said, "I can see that you are a prophet. Our ancestors worshiped on this mountain, but you Jews claim that the place where we must worship is in Jerusalem." "Woman," Jesus replied, "believe me, a time is coming when you will worship the Father neither on this mountain nor in Jerusalem. You Samaritans worship what you do not know; we worship what we do know, for salvation is from the Jews. Yet a time is coming and has now come when the true worshipers will worship the Father in the Spirit and in truth, for they are the kind of worshipers the Father seeks. God is spirit, and his worshipers must worship in the Spirit and in truth." The woman said, "I know that

Messiah" (called Christ) "is coming. When he comes, he will explain everything to us." Then Jesus declared, "I, the one speaking to you—I am he." Just then his disciples returned and were surprised to find him talking with a woman. But no one asked, "What do you want?" or "Why are you talking with her?" Then, leaving her water jar, the woman went back to the town and said to the people, "Come, see a man who told me everything I ever did. Could this be the Messiah?" They came out of the town and made their way toward him.

This gospel narrative is a typical passage that demonstrates Jesus's hospitality to the other. The biblical narrative, according to Shepherd, contrasts with Levinasian asymmetric responsibility by proving that through "the exchange of gifts (mutual hospitality) with the other, hostility is transformed."[98] By extension, Shepherd strongly supports the main thesis of this research, which intends to assuage the Muslim-Christian inhospitable relationship.

This particular encounter reflects multiple aspects of otherness. If Nicodemus, a Pharisee and a male Jew, in John 3:1–21 engaged Jesus in a theological conversation that left him perplexed, Brink argues that John might have anticipated his audience to expect that such unusual dialogue with a woman of foreign origin would also confound her.[99] Her reasons no doubt stem from the perceived otherness of Jesus' dialogue partner, first as a Samaritan with inferior theology, but also as a woman, culturally considered inferior to men. Besides being a Samaritan woman, she suffered external and internal stigmatization: she was "scapegoated and distanced from her community,"[100] leading to her isolated presence at the well.

Also relevant is the oddness of the locus of the encounter. "Meeting at the well" has been depicted in the ancient Jewish milieu as type-scene of betrothal.[101] As examples: "Abraham's servant finds a wife for Isaac at the well (Gen. 24:4–61). Jacob meets Rachel at the well (Gen. 29:1–20). Moses meets his wife at the well (Exodus 2:15b –21). And here at the well, the woman of Samaria will meet the man of Galilee."[102]

---

98. Shepherd, *Gift of the Other*, 202.

99. Brink, "In the Search," 18.

100. Shepherd, *Gift of the Other*, 203.

101. Alter, *Art of Biblical Narrative*, 61–74.

102. Brink, "In the Search," 18.

The next element is the oddness of the time. It was hot noon, and while his companions went to buy food Jesus stayed at the well (v. 8). Brink notices an additional oddity, not just with regard to the identity of the woman, but rather in her attitude: "Women come in the morning and evening to draw water. Not at the high noon." Brink concludes that "The otherness of the woman is not just her gender, and her religious identity, but also her unusual behavior."[103] The good news is that Jesus did craft these strands of her oddity into a meaningful result.

Jesus' hospitality approach sets forth newness by breaking the Jewish incommunicado rule with Samaritans, and initiated a conversation through a request: "Give me a drink" (v. 7). The woman read the request as odd, because of the obvious degree of antagonism and hostility that marked the relationship between Jews and Samaritans. In her retort, "How can you, a Jew, ask me, a Samaritan woman, for a drink?" (v. 9), she was shocked that Jesus was violating cultural barriers.

Setting a model for overcoming the existing hostility, Jesus introduced a mutual hospitality (the gift exchange) paradigm as key. Jesus might have been in need of ordinary water to drink, but he had the "living water" (v. 14) that the woman couldn't afford in spite of her bucket and the well. Although the woman, seeing herself at home (as host), wondered how a stranger (as guest) would be the one to offer her gifts, still, her initial doubt vanished when she realized the kind of surprise that marked the gift offer from a stranger (v. 14). In essence, the guest usually comes with a surprising gift but needs a welcoming disposition to unveil it.

For gift exchanges to happen, boundaries must be crossed. Jesus' bold steps beyond cultural barriers (by requesting from and making an offer to the other) invited a corresponding transgressing of normal barriers from the woman (to give and to take from the other). Transformed by Jesus' hospitality approach, the woman left her water jar and ran into the town to share her renewed experience. Leaving her jar in total disregard of her cultural prohibitions suggests, according to Shepherd, her willingness for Jesus to use it.[104] At this stage, differences could no longer divide. Rather, the sharing of experiences through gift exchanges begins paved the way for a deeper actualization of otherness's missing rib, that

---

103. Brink, "In the Search," 18.

104. Shepherd, *Gift of the Other*, 206.

is, communion. Communion, which stems from the sharing of gifts, can be developed into intimate sharing of selves (friendship).

Interestingly, the desire to harmonize otherness and communion is impossible without the witnessing drive of substitutive responsibility. Before taking the option of a shorter but dangerous route (through the enemies' territory), Jesus must have prioritized the concern about the disparaged Samaritans over and above the exposure to possible risk to his disciples, and himself (Jews), with the question, "Suppose we were Samaritans?" Without this substitutive willingness, gifts exchanges would be eliminated. Moreover, it is the gift exchange that opens doors for amicable theological discourses.

Overwhelmed by the surprising gifts (prophetic insights on her personal life) from Jesus (the other), the woman disposed herself for theological enlightenment: "Our ancestors worshiped on this mountain, but you say that the place where people must worship is Jerusalem" (v. 20). Though driven together by individual needs to the well (locus of contact), their openness to each other revealed their true identity, which led to mutual growth. The woman revealed her theological limits, and Jesus filled it up: "You worship what you do not know; we worship what we know, for salvation is from the Jews. But the hour is coming, and is now here, when the true worshippers will worship the Father in spirit and truth, for the Father seeks such as these to worship him" (vv. 22–23).

The disciples, having returned from buying food and now shocked by the unusual privacy shared between their master and the woman (an indication of a harmonized otherness and communion), had their confusion dispelled by Jesus. He replaced their microscopic lens with a telescopic lens (opening their gaze to a wider scope) by saying, "Look around you, and see how the fields are ready for harvesting" (v. 35). Jesus used the harvest metaphor in contrast to the disciples' distorted perception of "Samaria as a barren wasteland,"[105] with a renewed vision of huge abundance, where "sower" and "reaper" "rejoice together" in mutual gift exchanges (v. 36). The disciples realized quickly the mutual hospitality model set before them when Jesus personalized his teaching: "I sent you to reap what you have not worked for. Others have done hard work, and you have reaped the benefits of their labor" (v. 38, NIV).

In contrast to the disciples' first missionary report (entangled in self-centeredness), the woman (who was also sent: "go and call you

105. Shepherd, *Gift of the Other*, 206.

husband"), driven by substitutive responsibility towards her people, despite their ostracizing attitude to her, hurried and shared her illuminative mutual hospitality experiences. Her witnessing power desired that others might share the new gift that Jesus brought.[106] Consequently, her status was transformed into a model for missions, and she was no longer that faceless, despised Samaritan woman.[107] Her mission yielded an abundance of fruits because the formerly unsettling community experienced from the "Messiah" a newness in hospitality (based on mutuality, in which otherness and communion cohere) and consequently threw open their doors and hosted their enemies for some days. In essence, gift exchange, purely motivated by substitutive responsibility, constitutes a key for transformation of hostility into hospitality.

Asymmetric-mutual hospitality represents not only a moral injunction, but also a spiritual virtue. Christ's model of hospitality is unconditional, mutually substitutive, and open for gift exchanges. In this light, cultural standards of hospitality beg for reform. In contrasts to Jesus' model, Cornille writes of the Old Testament standard, "Whereas the injunction of hospitality in the Hebrew Bible may have at times been restricted by rules of ritual purity, it places no qualifications on the importance of welcoming and accommodating the stranger."[108] As the corrector of previous standards, Cornille further confirms, "though not belonging to his own ethnic and religious circle, Jesus interacts with these individuals in the most open and receptive way, eventually lifting them up as examples of faith."[109]

Both Jesus and the Samaritan woman retained their otherness but experienced growth. Cornille confirms this informed agreement of otherness and growth. She asserts that "true hospitality—hospitality in its most robust form—involves the recognition of the other as other and openness to the possibility of being transformed by that difference."[110] Growth through crossing boundaries entails the ability to transcend the familiar in search of newness. Moyaert identifies the tension between

---

106. Shepherd, *Gift of the Other*, 207.

107. Thiessen, "Jesus and Women," 53–64.

108. Cornille, "Interreligious Hospitality," 35.

109. Cornille, "Interreligious Hospitality," 35.

110. Cornille, *Im-possibility*, 178.

identity (concern for what is known and familiar) and openness (concern for the stranger) as part of "narrative hospitality."[111]

Jesus' approach demonstrates a genuine model of dialogue of life via hospitality that is being proposed for healthier Muslim-Christian relation. Through Jesus' hospitality approach, which transforms the other without dissolving her otherness, especially as there was no reference to conversion, a new paradigm was set for Christian hospitality. It is a paradigm characterized by spontaneity (not a categorized template), concern for the other, patience, and openness to learning. In other words, the need of the other sets the agenda for the substitutive response. The hospitality model, however, could inspire and invite the other toward conversion, so long as the will of this other is never coerced.

Ecclesial Dimension

How could Christians learn at the feet of Jesus, and what kind of hospitality did he teach? Can the religious other be approached through the portal of this new hospitality? Could this new model of hospitality empower Christians towards overcoming fears and prejudices against Muslims? In other words, how can trust be established among Muslims and Christians?

As a model for Christian discipleship, Siddiqui observes that "Jesus' gracious and sacrificial hospitality—expressed in his life, ministry and death—undergirds the hospitality of his followers."[112] Here is a long quote from Jean Vanier, in which he not only captures the exact relational problems between Christians and Muslims, but also identifies effective solutions for them.

> As long as there are fears and prejudices in the human heart, there will be war and bitter injustice. It is only when hearts are healed that the great political problems will be solved. Community is a place where people can be human beings, where they can be healed and strengthened in their deepest emotions, and where they can walk towards unity and interior freedom. As fears and prejudices diminish and trust in God and others grows, the community can radiate a witness to a style and quality of life, which will bring a solution to the troubles of our

111. Moyaert, "Biblical, Ethical," 99. "Narrative hospitality" connotes a hermeneutical openness towards the unfamiliar account of the other as argued by Moyaert.

112. Siddiqui, *Hospitality and Islam*, 123.

world. The response to war is to live like brothers and sisters. The response to injustice is to share. The response to despair is a limitless trust and hope. The response to prejudice and hatred is forgiveness. To work for community is to work for humanity. To work for peace is to work for a true political solution; it is to work for the kingdom of God. It is to work to enable everyone to live and taste the secret joys of the human person united to the eternal.[113]

The best way to learn from Jesus, reading Vanier, is to be in relationship as ecclesial persons. Relationality must be oriented toward a meaningful *telos*. Undefined *telos* or lack of *telos* renders relationship worthless. An ecclesial person, because of her sense of teleological mutuality in relationship, significantly differs from another involved in a unilateral type, who lacks both qualities. Whereas an undesignated *telos* of a unilateral relation, as proposed by Levinas, does not go beyond the sacrificing self, the ecclesial model derives its purpose from "the joy of mutuality."[114] Shepherd puts it better: "'Being there for others' is therefore not an end in itself but rather is the means to an end, the summoning of the Other to participate in the new economy of gift-exchange, in which gifts of love are freely given and received."[115]

In disagreement also with Levinas, Jurgen Moltmann unequivocally asserts: "Our social and political tasks, if we take them seriously, loom larger than life. Yet infinite responsibility destroys a human being because he is only man and not god."[116] Indeed, Shepherd and Moltmann deconstruct Levinasian asymmetric and infinite responsibility. Moltmann therefore concludes, "being-there-for-others is not the final answer, nor is it an end and not even freedom itself. It is a way, although the only way, which leads to being-there-with-others . . . If this is not our end, our care for others merely becomes a new kind of domination."[117] Only when substitutive responsibility for the other (otherness) is oriented towards communion can the goal of relationality be achieved. However, the relational purpose, as distinguished by Moltmann, becomes real in the face of death.

113. Vanier, *Community and Growth*, 45.

114. Shepherd, *Gift of the Other*, 212.

115. Shepherd, *Gift of the Other*, 212

116. Moltmann, *Theology and Joy*, 46.

117. Moltmann, *Theology and Joy*, 86–87.

Death has challenged people differently. Being face to face with death could be extremely worrisome due to the enormity of uncertainty. Still, some have approached this seeming end with some sense of serenity. What causes a positive attitude at death might not be entirely dissociated from a conscious relational goal.

Ecclesial Relationality

In reflecting on ecclesial relationality and responsibility to the other, it is worth citing the work of the modern Christian martyr and Lutheran pastor Dietrich Bonhoeffer (1906–1945), who displayed a conviction of being in an interdependent relation with a defined *telos*. Incarcerated in Tegel prison (August 1944) as an anti-Nazi dissident, Bonhoeffer set out developing a book about the *telos* of Christian life.[118] In his notes he asserts: "The church is the church only when it exists for others."[119] Reading Bonhoeffer carefully, he is saying that the ecclesial person requires witnessing through discipleship of substitutive responsibility for the other. So, bored with the insipid Christianity in the German church of his time, Bonhoeffer redefines Christianity:

> The experience that [of] a transformation of all human life is given in the fact that "Jesus is there only for others." His "being there for others" is the experience for transcendence. It is only this "being there for others," maintained till death, that is the ground of his omnipotence, omniscience, and omnipresence. Faith is participation in this being of Jesus (incarnation, cross, and resurrection). Our relation to God is not a "religious" relationship to the highest, most powerful, and best being imaginable—that is not authentic transcendence—but our relation to God is a new life in "existence for others," through participation in the being of Jesus. The Transcendental is not infinite and unattainable tasks, but the neighbor who is within reach in any given situation. God in human form . . ."the man for others," and therefore the Crucified, the man who lives out of the transcendent.[120]

Bonhoeffer somewhat reflects the Levinasian face as the locus for the trace of the divine. Unlike Levinas, Bonhoeffer clearly emphasizes

---

118. Bonhoeffer, *Letters and Papers*, 382.

119. Bonhoeffer, *Letters and Papers*, 382

120. Bonhoeffer, *Letters and Papers*, 381–82.

the possibility of existence for the other, though not through "infinite responsibility," but "through participation in the being of Jesus."[121]

Bonhoeffer draws his reason for a christocentric impelled responsibility from the obvious price of Christian discipleship, which entails death to self and being alive in Christ,[122] made possible by sharing in the resurrection of Jesus. Convinced of his christocentrically derived altruistic model of discipleship, Bonhoeffer distinguishes between two heroic deaths, that of Socrates and Jesus, saying, "Socrates mastered the art of dying; Christ overcame death as "the last enemy" (1 Corinthians 15:26). There is a real difference between the two things; the one is within the scope of human possibilities, the other means resurrection."[123]

However, this research foresees a christocentric obstacle for Muslims, who are equally involved in this dialogic conversation. In this light, the illuminative idea of Christian discipleship or witnessing is being developed under the theme "mutual substitutive responsibility"—practically expressible in the form of "asymmetrical mutual gift exchange." The purpose is to awaken mutual substitutive responsibility between Christians and Muslims, which charges them to a renewed hospitality, where asymmetric-mutual gift exchange can happen. In this regard, asymmetrical mutuality replaces mere reciprocity (which connotes a payback).

People who approach ecclesiology from this standpoint pay particular attention to the participation of every member of the community in the life of the church, the process, and context of believing and acting in the name of the Lord, and social, cultural, and historical forces and reflective practices in the shaping of Christian imagination and Christian witnessing for transforming the world.

Bonhoeffer's christocentric ecclesial relationship also resonates with African interconnectivity, where a person's identity is incomplete without living for the other and where divine connectivity is sustained through a "theo-anthropologic"[124] process. The challenge, however, is about the distinctive theological foundation of every ecclesiology. The Christian community is called together by God as a people and is given an identity as God's people through its Trinitarian origin. The question is whether

---

121. Bonhoeffer, *Letters and Papers*, 382.

122. Bonhoeffer, *Cost of Discipleship*, 73.

123 Bonhoeffer, *Letters and Papers*, 240.

124. This a human-medium approach to divinity. As the writer of 1 John 4:20 states: "whoever does not love a brother whom he has seen cannot love God whom he has not seen."

ecclesial tribalism may hamper the Christian mission of uniting God's scattered people toward the eschaton.

As Eschatological Criteria

Islam in its hadith and Christianity in Matthew 25 teach that universal hospitality towards anyone in need, which transcends ethnic or tribal constraints, is the ultimate eschatological criteria for heaven. The standing of the vulnerable other between God and the self is not a strange ethicoreligious idea in Judeo-Christian practice or in Islam. Sacrificial substitutive responsibility toward the other occupies a central position in the teachings of both religious traditions, as shown while establishing its basis in the Bible and the Qur'an. It is therefore the goal of this section to explore the eschatological dimension of mutual hospitality, considering the germaneness of the Last Day in both religions.

A popular hadith in the collection of Imam Sahih Muslim[125] parallels the Christian eschatological ethical standard in Matthew 25. The Muslim version reads:

> Abu Huraira reported Allah's Messenger (may peace be upon him) as saying: Verily, Allah, the Exalted and Glorious, would say on the Day of Resurrection: O son of Adam, I was sick but you did not visit Me. He would say: o my Lord; how could I visit thee whereas thou art the Lord of the worlds? Thereupon He would say: Didn't you know that such and such servant of mine was sick but you did not visit him and were you not aware of this that if you had visited him, you would have found Me by him (la-wajadtani 'indahu)? O son of Adam, I asked food from you but you did not feed Me. He would say: My Lord, how could I feed Thee whereas Thou art the Lord of the worlds? He said: Didn't you know that such and such servant of Mine asked food from you but you did not feed him, and were you not aware that if you had fed him you would have found him by My side (dhalik 'indi)? (The Lord would again say: O son of Adam, I asked drink from you but you did not provide Me. He would say: My Lord, how could I provide Thee whereas Thou art the Lord of the worlds? Thereupon He would say: such and such of servant

---

125. Imam Muslim was born in 202 AH (AD 817/818) in Naysabur, Iran, and died in 261 AH (AD 874/875). He developed outstanding collections for his hadith by traveling widely. Sunni Muslims consider it the second most authentic hadith collection, after Sahih Bukhari.

of Mine asked you for a drink but you did not provide him, and had you provided him drink you would have found him near Me (dhalik 'indi).[126]

The big concern here should not be whether (or not) the hadith plagiarized Matthew 25. Rather, the emphasis is on how important the contribution of the hadith encourages a healthier Muslim-Christian friendship based on ethical concern of the religious other. The Muslim hadith reveals in precise terms an essential Muslim-Christian theological understanding concerning the invisible face of God in the needy other. Such mutual understanding provides a powerful basis for a Muslim-Christian dialogue of life in which ethical responsibility for the religious other does not, by any standard, constitute a serious threat to certain perceived theological differences. Instead, mutual hospitality concretizes and makes present to the religious other the unfamiliar doctrinal principles of both religions. Oddbjørn Leirvik expresses this mutual understanding as an act of "humanizing theological ethics" through which "Christians and Muslims are not merely in dialogue with each other but with secular society as well."[127]

From the Christian account:

> "Then the King will say to those on his right, 'Come, you who are blessed by my Father; take your inheritance, the kingdom prepared for you since the creation of the world. For I was hungry and you gave me something to eat, I was thirsty and you gave me something to drink, I was a stranger and you invited me in, I needed clothes and you clothed me, I was sick and you looked after me, I was in prison and you came to visit me.' "Then the righteous will answer him, 'Lord, when did we see you hungry and feed you, or thirsty and give you something to drink? When did we see you a stranger and invite you in, or needing clothes and clothe you? When did we see you sick or in prison and go to visit you?' "The King will reply, 'Truly I tell you, whatever you did for one of the least of these brothers and sisters of mine, you did for me.'" (Matthew 25:34–40)

In this gospel narrative, Jesus explicitly defines himself as the *xenos* (stranger, alien) whom all believers are required to feed, clothe, welcome, nurse, refresh, and visit (v. 35). In other words, he emphasizes the attitude toward the *xenos* as the eschatological criterion that will separate the

126. Muslim, *Sahih Muslim*, 176.
127. Leirvik, "Towards," 237.

virtuous (to be welcomed into the kingdom, v. 34) from the wicked (to be banished into darkness, v. 41). The reason, Stephen W. Sykes argues, "is because Jesus considers the stranger to be his family member (*adelphos*, v. 41) and someone indelibly connected to him: "just as you did for the least of these who are my brothers, you did for me" (v. 40).

Jesus lived out this eschatological model of hospitality as illustrated in the gospel through his exemplary deeds. His inclusive choice of his close companions from commoners, fishermen, tax collectors, and women, and his many associations with the marginalized and ostracized—sinners, lepers, tax collectors, despised women, and even those possessed—are evidentially the most powerful symbols of hospitality with eschatological vision.[128]

The eschatological standard in the Bible and the hadith of Muslims project the essential dimension of praxis as that inevitable aspect of religious teachings. Being the gauge for the Last Day proves that altruistic praxes maintain an unrivaled prominence among these religious people. The Last Day criterion also seems fitting in both religious and secular contexts.

Cory Booker, an American politician, made this famous statement: "Before you speak to me about your religion, first show it to me in how you treat other people; before you tell me how much you love your God, show me in how much you love all His children; before you preach to me of your passion for your faith, teach me about it through your compassion for your neighbors. In the end, I'm not as interested in what you have to tell or sell as in how you choose to live and give."[129] Equally, Homer rightly noted, "Religious faith, hospitality and civilization are always found together."[130] Similarly, Cardinal Jean Danielou concluded,

> One can say that a civilization takes a decisive step, and perhaps the most decisive step, on the day that the foreigner, the enemy, becomes a guest. Yes, it is on that day that human community has been created. Previously, these humans were battling each other like animals in the primal forest, but on that day when the stranger is seen as a guest and, instead of being held in execration, is invested with conspicuous dignity of a

---

128. Sykes, "Making Room," 64.

129. https://www.goodreads.com/quotes/4504146-before-you-speak-to-me-about-your-religion-first-show.

130. Homer, *Odyssey* 6.19.

brother in humanity—on such day, one can say that something has changed in the world.[131]

Since it is by no means doubtful that Islam and Christianity have substitutive responsibility for the other at the center of their doctrines and practices, a follow-up question is: can hospitality be legitimately extended to the religious other as much as to one's own? Recalling the thoughts of Levinas already explored, the other is the other and should be treated as the other. His asymmetric responsibility towards the other is summarized: "it is my inescapable and incontrovertible answerability to the other that makes me an individual 'I.' I become a responsible or ethical 'I' only to the extent that I agree to depose or dethrone myself—to abdicate my position of centrality—in favor of the vulnerable other."[132] For Levinas, the substitutive obligation to the other can only be compared to "the responsibility of a 'hostage.'"[133] Finally, Levinasian asymmetric hospitality is vividly captured in this one sentence: With an "unmediated summon,"[134] whose first dialogic word begins and ends in obligation,[135] "I am responsible for the other without waiting for reciprocity."[136] Certainly, scholars have traced the source of Levinas's radical asymmetric hospitality to a quote from Dostoyevsky's *The Brothers Karamazov*: "We are responsible for everyone else, but I more than others."[137]

Many scholars disagree with Levinas's objection to mutual hospitality, on the grounds that asymmetric process idolizes the other, thereby creating a similar problem to what he set out to solve (egotism). Among these scholars, Anselm Min reacts, "there is an internal contradiction between Levinas's intention, the defense of the other in her ethical transcendence, and his philosophical procedure, the denial of all historical mediation, which ironically reduces the human other to ahistorical, angelic existence elevated above all contingencies of history, above all vulnerabilities."[138] In defense, the other in Levinas is ethically infinite

131. Danielou, "Pour une theologie," 340.

132. Cohen, *Face to Face*, 27.

133. Hand, *Levinas Reader*, 84.

134. Levinas, *Totality and Infinity*, 200.

135. Levinas, *Totality and Infinity*, 201.

136. Levinas, *Totality and Infinity*, 297.

137. Cohen, *Face to Face*, 31.

138. Min, *The Solidarity of Others*, 13.

because he bears the trace of the divine infinite.[139] It therefore takes a developed ethical sensibility to see the "trace" of the infinite in the "face" of the other and to feel its demand and challenge.[140] Min further argues that such a state of consciousness is possible only "through mediation of culture of care, and respect, a social ethos of compassion and solidarity."[141]

In agreement with Min, Ashoka, a Buddhist emperor of India in the third century BC, once ordered hospitality edicts engraved on columns in the entire province of his nation. One reads: "People are mistaken if they think that they are expressing devotion and glorifying their faith when they praise their own religion while denigrating the tradition of others. In fact, they are harming their own religion." On another column, he asserted: "The king wishes that people of all faiths familiarize themselves with other traditions; in this way they will gain a sound doctrine."[142] Ashoka's observation confirms the centrality of hospitality as an eschatological criterion even among other world religions besides Islam and Christianity.

Basis for Substitutive Theology of Hospitality

As already demonstrated, substitutive sacrifice is a familiar practice in both Islamic and Christian traditions, as much as in the African context. The two religions, as describe in earlier exposition of this research, encourage living for others among their respective adherents as a way of imitating the infinite generosity and universality of the God they worship. By extension, hospitality practices suggest God's approval and our awareness of human diversity.

Although pleasure enhances the practice of hospitality, still, being hospitable also includes some discomforts. Living for the other can happen at the expense of one's pleasure. In "Sufi literature," as noticed by Siddiqui, "giving is also associated with poverty, renunciation, self-denial, because the desired relationship with God leaves no room for any other desire. Worldly possessions or relationships lose meaning as the mystic longs only for a particular intimacy, to be the guest of God."[143] Giving to the point of depriving the self was an ancient Islamic practice. A narration

---

139. Cohen, *Face to Face,* 31.
140. Min, *Solidarity of Others,* 16.
141. Min, *Solidarity of Others,* 16.
142. Nicam and McKeon, *Edicts of Ashoka,* 340.
143. Siddiqui, *Hospitality and Islam,* 13.

has it that one day someone approached the Prophet Mohammad and said, "I love you, O Messenger of God," to which the prophet replied, "Be ready for poverty."[144] The Prophet was not prescribing destitution as a standard; he was rather approving "voluntary poverty" (in Gustavo Gutierrez's term) or substitutive responsibility for the other in need.

One great Christian way of understanding substitutive responsibility is to look at the cross. Looking at the cross implies addressing the question: how should the cross be understood, or more precisely, how might the cross shape Christians' relation to the other?[145] Recently, Moltmann's contributions towards the theological relevance of the cross for interpersonal relations have been remarkable. In general, Moltmann identifies Christ's cross as a willful act of being in solidarity with the most vulnerable ones.[146] Analyzing this definition, one wonders how Moltmann accounts for those (others) who took advantage of the vulnerable. Or are they outside the scope of Christ's redemptive cross?

Indeed, Moltmann's empathy for the weak and poor ones did not obscure the universalistic salvific suffering of Christ. In *The Spirit of Life*, the solidarity theme focuses on victims,[147] but later he includes atonement for the perpetrators.[148] He further adduces that Christ's solidarity on the cross manifests God's substitutive love for creation, especially humanity. Thus he affirms:

> On the cross of Christ this love [i.e, the love of God] is there for the others, for sinners—the recalcitrant—enemies. The reciprocal self-surrender to one another within the Trinity is manifested in Christ's self-surrender in a world which is in contradiction to God; and this self-giving draws all those who believe in him into eternal life of the divine love.[149]

Whereas Moltmann emphasizes solidarity with both victims and perpetrators, Miroslav Volf draws attention to the particularity of Christ's self-donation, through atonement, in reconciling creation with God. Volf argues that since Christ "died for the ungodly" (Romans 5:6), an assertion also defended by theologians like Jon Sobrino as the central

144. Schimmel, *And Muhammad*, 48.

145. Volf, *Exclusion and Embrace*, 22.

146. Moltmann, *Spirit of Life*, 130.

147. Moltmann, *Spirit of Life*, 129–31.

148. Moltmann, *Spirit of Life*, 132–38.

149. Moltmann, *Spirit of Life*, 137.

meaning of the New Testament,[150] then Moltmann's solidarity should be "a sub-theme of the overarching theme of self-giving love."[151] However, Volf clearly does not suggest a severance of solidarity from self-donation. Rather, he reads solidarity for the vulnerable as a partial understanding for the entire episode of love on the cross.

In situating the drama of salvation within the larger perspective of self-donation, Volf seeks to establish a model that humanity can emulate in practicing interpersonal self-donation. Self-donation is equivalent to substitutive responsibility for the other. Self-donation, he argues, is at the center of Trinitarian love, which was made manifest in Christ. In support, Luke Timothy Johnson sees not only the four gospels, but also the entire New Testament, as a retelling of the characteristics of Jesus' life and death, or Jesus as that obedient servant of God who exemplified loving care for his followers.[152] Put in another way, the renowned Orthodox theologian Dumitru Staniloae mentions two basic truths that stand above all else, namely: "the Trinity as model of supreme love and interpersonal communion, and the Son of God who comes, becomes a man, and goes to sacrifice."[153]

Invariably, all these theologians suggest the importance of self-donation as a defining factor for Christian discipleship. Its great importance reverberates further in the conclusive words of Volf: "The will to give ourselves to others and 'welcome' them to readjust our identities to make space for them, is prior to any judgment about others, except that of identifying them in their humanity."[154] Interestingly, Volf's thesis on self-donation parallels Massignon's intuition of the *Badalyia*, discussed in chapter 5. Both fittingly align with the asymmetric-mutual substitutive responsibility that this research is defending.

In Western atonement theology, substitution and sacrifice were not systematized until Anselm's satisfaction theory.[155] Categorizing atonement theories into three typologies, Shepherd notices its motifs throughout the history of the church, but locates *Christus Victor* in the Middle

150. Sobrino, *Jesus the Liberator*, 231.

151. Volf, *Exclusion and Embrace*, 24.

152. Johnson, *Real Jesus*, 165.

153. Staniloae, *7 Dimineti*, 186.

154. Volf, *Exclusion and Embrace*, 29.

155. Shepherd, *The Gift of the Other*, 150.

Ages, whereas the moral influence theory of Abelard and the satisfaction theory of Anselm dominated in the last millennium.[156]

Not all welcomed the Anselmian atonement theology. Some anti-atonement scholars, especially feminists and liberationists, interpret sacrificial discipleship as violent, with the belief that it spiritualizes oppression and suffering. Many in this group draw from Denny J. Weaver's anti-atonement thesis: "Jesus came not to die but to live, to witness to the reign of God in human history. While he may have known that carrying out that mission would provoke inevitable fatal oppositions, his purpose was not to get himself killed."[157]

In reaction, some theologians have questioned the argument that atonement and sacrifice are integrally violent. While Weaver's anti-atonement thesis might appeal to Muslims, his stance, as argued by Christopher Marshall, will amount to a purposeful overturning of biblical and historical theological evidence.[158] In essence, a repudiation of atonement theology questions the foundation of Christian Christology.

Furthermore, similar minded theologians also accuse another group of anti-atonement proponents, who basically draw from Rene Girard's thesis that sacrifice inherently assures violence, of a shallow interpretation of the significance of sacrifice. Perusing ancient cultures, these scholars, like John Dunnill, discovered that, rather than bloodlust, the native people were engaged (during festivity) in gift-giving.[159] Invariably, the motivation draws on offering their deity the highest and the best of gifts, for the noble cause of sustaining communal well-being, through a harmonized relationship among the people, their god, and their land.[160]

Gift-giving in the form of self-donation, as evident in Christ, must imply freedom and joy. In most cases, the willingness is explicitly expressed in self-donation. Far from violence that expresses power control and insensitivity towards the other, self-donating sacrifice derives its meaning from love for others and shared interrelatedness. The heroic victim is usually inspired by the *telos* of his action, that is, harmony and communion.[161] In addition to sacrifice through self-donation, which

---

156. Shepherd, *The Gift of the Other*, 150.

157. Weaver, *Nonviolent Atonement*, 211.

158. Marshall, "Atonement," 81.

159. Dunnill, "Communicative Bodies," 87.

160. Shepherd, *Gift of the Other*, 154.

161. Shepherd, *Gift of the Other*, 154.

could lead to death, living for the other could as well be sufficiently expressed without having to die.

The experiences of growing up in Nigeria offered me the opportunity to witness self-sacrifice without death. In this regard, most traditional African families engaged in mutual substitutive responsibility. It was common among Igbo people of Nigeria, up to the 1980s, for the first child of low-income earners to forfeit his early education for the sake of the younger siblings, in order that the family's petty trading, farming, or crafting be adequately supported. Often such a challenged family might be one that lost its breadwinner so early that the eldest or a younger volunteer steps into the gap created by death. The self-sacrifice engendered by the well-being of the entire family was usually responded to freely.

While some of these heroic volunteers might later acquire education, others sacrificed theirs for their families. At times, and in mutual gift exchanges, some would receive full sustenance, including having their own children well trained in school by their educated siblings. In such African contexts, where the government has failed in providing scholarships for the less privileged and where life insurances are not efficiently established, the family or community through interdependent responsibility constitutes the pillar of support for human development and sustenance. Within this particular structure, the successes of the educated siblings become the joys and fulfillment of the sibling that sacrificed his or her education. Conversely, her would-be regrets were also shared by the entire family. In essence, life becomes more meaningful and survival assured when its component parts are mutually shared through substitutive responsibility.

At the community level, resources were eagerly pooled in providing training overseas for brilliant children. In a certain village, attorney Michael Eze was a beneficiary of the community responsibility that covered his education in London. His graduation with first-class honors has not stopped being referenced in the entire community by his non-biological benefactors. Anyone in this community can boast to other communities about Michael's academic excellence and successes, which in a way challenges those other communities into harnessing human resources for the benefit of all. As a show of gratitude to his people, Michael has kept his promise of defending for free the civil rights of his benefactors in court.

Evidently, in his book *The Sacrifice of Africa*, Emmanuel Katongole tells the story of a sacrificial intervention of Angelina Atyam, a Ugandan nurse and midwife, which demonstrates substitutive relationality. After

Yoweri Museveni took over power in Uganda in 1986, war started raging between the government army, the National Resistance Army, led by Museveni, and a rebel group, the Lord's Resistance Army (hereafter LRA), headed by Joseph Kony. Kony rained havoc in Northern Uganda, torturing, raping, murdering, and abducting over twenty-six thousand children, who were forcefully initiated into the LRA as child soldiers and sex slaves.[162] At fourteen, Charlotte, Angelina's daughter, was among the abducted girls from St. Mary's Catholic boarding high school in 1996. The mothers of the missing girls, who began a routinized Saturday prayer and fasting, seeking divine intervention, later learned forgiveness for the enemies while praying the Lord's Prayer, and also spread such a difficult message, to the utmost chagrin of many.

This group of mothers after a few years organized themselves into the Concerned Parents Association, which sought an unconditional release of all the abducted children and a peaceful resolution of the Northern Ugandan conflict, by creating local and international awareness of the crises through overseas travels and negotiations.[163] Due to the attraction of the United Nations and other international bodies towards Angelina's advocacy, Kony offered to release Charlotte on condition that she ends her crusade. Angelina sacrificially turned down the offer, saying, "getting my child back would be absolutely wonderful, but if I accepted the offer, I would be turning my back on all the other families. I'd destroy the new community spirit we had created—the hope of getting all the boys and girls back."[164]

Most people, as well as her own family, perceived the rejection of Kony's offer as senseless, but Angelina insisted that "all those children had become my children."[165] Angelina love Charlotte and earnestly prayed and worked for her return, but not at the expense of the other children. According to her, "there are hundreds of Charlottes in my country and beyond . . . Every child is my child." After seven years in abduction, on July 22, 2014, Charlotte miraculously escaped and reunited with her mom, Angelina.

Though a rare feat, Angelina's exemplar of substitutive responsibility for the other not only idealizes the entire picture of the African bond of

162. Katongole, *Sacrifice of Africa*, 150.

163. Katongole, *Sacrifice of Africa*, 157.

164. http://biography.jrank.org/pages/2895/Atyam-Angelina.html.

165. Personal interview at Bujumbura, 2009; cited in Katongole, *Sacrifice of Africa*, 158.

communality, it also sheds light on Christ's (hard) discipleship condition of prioritizing love for God and neighbor before the self (Luke 14:26).

Nonetheless, no matter how impressive African communality manifests itself, it barely transcends ethnic blocks. The geographic borderline constitutes the weakest link on the chain of community strength in African society. Like the wall of an environment, it provides refuge and protection to what stays inside but excludes what is outside. This imaginary wall has as well framed minds to an extent that ethnic home determines the center of existence in people's lives. To date, "geogamy" has remained a formidable force militating against the African sense of communality. In other words, the African community, with its developed altruism, is not entirely free from the self-centeredness that Levinas condemned in Western philosophy. The communal spirit is so structured in a web-like connectivity that the center is the land of birth; thus, the farther from this geocentric point, the weaker the bond.

The homeness thrust in African communality therefore needs to be healed with the homeless imaginative conception of Abraham. The God of Abraham is a universal God, whose hospitality not only extends to all peoples, but also mandates his friends to act accordingly. Homelessness, rather than being anti-home, aims at decentering the (original) home by discovering and appreciating being at home in any place and everywhere. When the home is decentered, a transformative process reveals a newness of homeness (neighborliness) among peoples of different religions and disparate ethnicities. This is the core of Abrahamic hospitality that Christians and Muslims are invited to emulate.

1 1

The Abrahamic Model

IN THIS INCLUSIVE PILGRIM metaphor of Abraham, it will be shown how the Abrahamic pilgrimage concept first reminds Muslims and Christians of their individual and collective pilgrim status in God's world. As seen in Abraham, a pilgrim is a metaphorical depiction of a friend of God whose willingness sacrificially prioritizes the concerns of God and his people. It could be further understood as a collaborative journey (of life) with the universal God, whose approval for diversity demands being at home with the otherness of all God's people and places. In essence, the pilgrim metaphor accounts for genuine commitment toward universality and the infinite love for God.

The importance of the Abrahamic figure for these two religions, as attested by Louis Massignon (1883–1962), derives from the God of Abraham they worship. Massignon asserts that anyone who accepts "the equality of the origin of the three Abrahamic religions, Israel, Christianity and Islam, knows that they refer to the same 'God of Truth.'"[1] As stated in chapter 4, theologians like D'Costa have critiqued Massignon's controversial stance on the grounds that it doesn't represent the church's official position. Second, it will challenge Muslims and Christians into embracing hospitality as a concrete means of demonstrating gratitude to God, the owner and the host of humanity. It is central in this argument that revitalizing such an altruistic ancient practice like a conscious pilgrim imagery in both religious traditions can definitely invigorate the numbness that obstructs the dialogue of life.

1. Massignon, "Islam and the Testimony," 52–53.

While highlighting the importance of interfaith hospitality between Muslims and Christians, greater attention is given to Abrahamic commonality. Both Islam and Christianity posit Abraham as a hospitality model that can enhance interreligious dialogue. For example, it is virtually uncontested that "Abraham inspired a theology of hospitality often echoed in Jewish, Christian and Islamic literature and used as framework for interreligious dialogue."[2]

Not only scholars, but also most practitioners of these major religions of the world align their belief toward Abraham as that human model of faith or a special friend of God from various perspectives. Jews, Christians, and Muslims make sincere claims on him in their different religious traditions. In accord, Jon Paulien asserts: "All three faiths share a common appreciation for the role of Abraham as 'founding father' of the faith."[3] Michael Lodhal, in his book *Claiming Abraham*, articulates how Judaism, Christianity, and Islam all share Abrahamic faith, but he also argues that Abraham provides at least as much contested ground as common ground.[4] In line with this cautionary statement of Lodhal, this research intends to first establish a convergence in Abraham, but then emphasize the appreciation of otherness he epitomizes. Ayoub, describing Abrahamic uniqueness among the three monotheistic religions, asserts: "Abraham is said to be the physical father of Arabs and Jews and, by extension, the moral and spiritual father of all Christians and Muslims as well."[5]

Unfortunately, the fatherhood of Abraham (among the three monotheistic faiths) is still contestable, and has provided equal grounds for convergent and divergent views among the three monotheistic religions. In a very broad sense, the term "Abrahamic" does not only denote the religious traditions of Judaism, Christianity, and Islam, but also Ba'hai, Druze, and Rastafarianism.[6] But in a strict and narrower sense, Abrahamic religions articulate those who claim the spiritual ancestry that has God as a friend of Abraham, and as recorded in three respective faith narratives: the Torah, the Bible, and the Qur'an. Even though "Abrahamic" as a term is practically suspect, hospitality is one outstanding

2. Siddiqui, *Hospitality and Islam*, 10.

3. Paulien, "Remnant of Abraham," 51.

4. Lodhal, *Claiming Abraham*, 9.

5. Hinze and Omar, *Heirs of Abraham*, 97.

6. Reaves, *Safeguarding the Stranger*, 31.

characterization of Abraham that has developed with some nuances among these traditions. But for this research, whose purpose centers on Muslim-Christian conversations, Abrahamic hospitality will be explored within the biblical and the Qur'anic texts.

In essence, Abraham's fatherhood constitutes a major controversy between Muslims and Christians, and as a result of that this research presents him from a different but more agreeable perspective. From this viewpoint, Abraham's pilgrim status is being argued as a positive disposition that necessitated his exemplar model of substitutive hospitality. This pilgrim metaphor can be substantiated in the Qur'anic identification of Abraham as the "leader/model for mankind"[7] who followed God's instructions to the end. As a pilgrim with God, Abraham proved himself as the true submitter to God, and therefore a *Khalil Allah* (friend of God).[8]

According to Shepherd, the common role model of mutual substitutive responsibility (toward the other) between Muslims and Christians

> is the Patriarch Abraham, whose travel is not directionless, but rather is a journey, originating in the gift of faith from the Divine Other; who heads towards a final destination, the promised land of rest, and whose arrival in this new land is characterized by the building of relationships of mutuality with the inhabitants.[9]

While journeying, therefore, Abraham had in view a destination he willingly transformed into a home, with the consciousness of being at the service of God and his people. As such, Abraham was more than an alien traveler. A distinction at this point between a pilgrim and a mere traveler or tourist might help in substantiating the pilgrimage metaphor of Abraham.

A Tourist?

A pilgrim and a tourist share similarity and difference. Both leave home embarking on a journey, but for different purposes. Their distinct purposes motivate contrasting attitudinal relationships at the point of arrival. While a tourist seeks pleasurable sites that enlighten the self, a pilgrim such as Abraham is at home with her new environment. The latter

7. Qur'an 2:124.

8. Siddiqui, *Hospitality and Islam*, 22.

9. Shepherd, *Gift of the Other*, 198.

identifies with both people and their context, with an envisioned aim of belonging and growing through the newness of available opportunities.

Most tourists are conscious of the invisible tie to their native places, which compels their return. This return consciousness suggests the self as basis of judgment for the contextual otherness that the tourist encounters. In essence, the foreignness of the land, including citizens, could be related to as phenomena. As if viewed through a high-resolution camera, the other is often perceived as an object of study, whose otherness gets a premonitory interpretation within the scope of a familiar paradigm.

One basic distinction between the two approaches stems from the fact that, whereas a tourist even in foreign land is headed home, an Abrahamic pilgrim, away from his native home, discovers a new home. In his journey, a true pilgrim seeks to harmonize otherness and communion, through mutual substitutive hospitality, as Abraham did: "Understood symbolically, Yahweh's command to Abraham implies that human beings are morally compelled to sever their ties to their fatherland."[10]

Thomas Michael supports this assertion in the following words:

> The experience of being forced to leave one's home because of poverty, threats, or fear of violence is one that most of us have fortunately not experienced, but it occurs so frequently in the lives of the principal characters of the Bible and the Qur'an that it is clear that this experience is fundamental to God's message for humanity. Abraham forced to leave his father's house, Moses and his people fleeing Egypt in the middle of the night, the baby Jesus carried off to Egypt by his parents a step ahead of Herod's soldiers, Muhammad's early disciples taking refuge in Ethiopia, and the prophets Muhammad's own hijra to Medina—these dramatic stories show the centrality of the refugee experience for God's word.[11]

Faith is a journey. Abraham manifested exactly that. He was not perfect—though faithful to God's covenant with him, he trusted, was merciful and hospitable, but also doubted. Abrahamic faith is described as that faith which "sees to the extent that it journeys, to the extent that it chooses to enter into the horizons opened up by God's word."[12] The faith process demonstrated in the journey of Abraham with God was a

---

10. Eubanks and Gauthier, "Politics of the Homeless Spirit," 144.

11. Michael, "Where to Now?" 533–34.

12. Francis, *Lumen Fidei,* #9.

constant description of dependency through an evolving faith. Abraham lived in the here and now as he journeyed into the unknown.

Abraham the pilgrim can be distinguished from other biblical patriarchs, especially Moses. Between the homeless Abraham and the homeward Moses exists respectively a paradox of homeness and strangeness, hospitality and hostility, toward their host contexts. Similar to the resolve of Ruth to Naomi, her mother-in-law, "your people shall be my people, your God shall be my God" (Ruth 1:16), Abraham the pilgrim heartily embraced and felt at home with places and peoples he encountered in his journey towards the unknown home. The tension between the uncertainty of his destination and his unwavering trust in God might have enlarged his openness to being at home with anyone in any place. As a conscious pilgrim, each stopover or resting place was home. In contrast, Moses, comparable to a tourist, kept a distance from his transient environments, engulfed by an envisioned home where ethnicity ruled supreme. Unfortunately, he never reached that kind of isolated home. Indeed, he never tasted his dream home.

The story of Abraham is a story of departure from home (the familiar) to an unknown destination (the alien).[13] Abraham's pilgrim metaphor is ethically sacrificial because he freely embarked on his covenantal journey in order to be available to the services of the divine other as well as human others. The Levinasian "*Me voici*" (Here I am) rightly articulates the disposition of Abraham at the inception and throughout his pilgrimage experiences. Cecil L. EuBanks and D. J. Gauthier affirm: "By responding to God's voice, Abraham distinguishes himself as an 'obedient servant' of the Other."[14]

However, Levinas's admiration of the Abrahamic pilgrim or homelessness questions his initial position on the home (in *Totality and Infinity*) as a recollecting refuge that motivates altruism.[15] Even though Levinas discussed dwelling in *Totality and Infinity*, "in the most part, his focus on the Self-Other relationship renders him largely indifferent to the question of context."[16] Eubanks and Gauthier trace reasons for such underdeveloped attention on context to Levinas's preference of nomadic relationship to home: "From this point on, an opportunity appears to us:

13. Eubanks and Gauthier, "Politics of the Homeless Spirit ," 144.

14. Eubanks and Gauthier, "Politics of the Homeless Spirit ," 144.

15. Levinas, *Totality and Infinity*, 156, 171.

16. Eubanks and Gauthier, "Politics of the Homeless Spirit ," 138.

to perceive men outside the situation in which they are placed, and let the human face shine in all its nudity."[17]Eubanks and Gauthier certainly believe that "the story of Abraham has profound Levinasian import. Like the Levinasian journey toward otherness, Abraham's journey is exterior in its trajectory. Indeed, not only does Abraham depart from his fatherland, he also 'forbids his servants to bring his son to the point of departure.'"[18]

From the Levinasian point of view, the Abrahamic exodus from home mirrors a true self's journey. Levinas confirms: "To the myth of Ulysses returning to Ithaca (self-centeredness), we wish to oppose the story of Abraham who leaves his fatherland forever for a yet unknown land, and forbids his servant to even bring back his son to the point of departure."[19]

Jesus also identified himself as a pilgrim. When asked about his home, his reply depicted homelessness: "Foxes have holes, birds have nests, but the Son of man has nowhere to lay down his head" (Luke 9:58). Inasmuch as his metaphoric answer does not condemn home, it seems to imply that homelessness is not just a barrier, but rather an effective model or imagination for authentic discipleship.

Jesus' earthly life demonstrates the essence of pilgrimage imagination. Like Abraham, Jesus' idea of home transcends a limited location with its cultural and religious ties and biases. Homelessness must not be understood as mere lack of shelter and ancestry; instead, it connotes a conscious imagination of being at peace in any environment. In reality, no one is originally without a home. So, whether in the home context or elsewhere, the imagination of the pilgrim offers a kind of freedom and dependency that can pave the way for interfaith coexistence.

As noted above, Jesus' story from birth to death attests to the importance of the pilgrim metaphor. His childhood started while his parents were pilgrims in Jerusalem, and he experienced firsthand inhospitality from birth—"there was no room for them in the inn" (Luke 2:7). Like his ancestors, though an infant, Jesus with his parents sought refuge in Egypt against the evil plot of Herod. His pilgrim imagination was problematic even to his own family. At some point, the family members, including his mother, concluded that he was out of his mind (Mark 3:21) because his pilgrim self-understanding shaped his practical life over against some local ethics and religious standards.

17. Levinas, "Heidegger, Gagarin," 233.

18. Eubanks and Gauthier, "Politics of the Homeless Spirit," 144.

19. Levinas, "Trace of the Other," 348.

That the church on earth is addressed as the pilgrim church is no mistake, based on her master's pilgrim identity. Spiritual masters like Pierre-Francois de Bethune attest to the discovery of the ecclesial pilgrim identity: "The church is like the great house of my parents; it is essential to my identity. But I no longer identify myself solely with reference to any dwelling place where I feel truly at home. On the contrary, I feel called upon to open wide the doors to all places where I live and to see that they stay open to everyone."[20] From this perspective, one can see a personal testimony to the possibility of a pilgrim imagination at the level of spiritual experience. At such level, de Bethune confirms that, rather than being occupied with geographic boundaries or limited to a physical or geographical place called home, he is preoccupied with asking the question, "Of whom am I the neighbor?"[21]

In Luke 10:29, the scholar of the law asked Christ, "Who is my neighbor"? In this biblical passage, two questions are pertinent. Why did Christ tell a story of the Good Samaritan, rather than define the neighbor? And what lessons does the story teach contemporary Christians? From the story, however, we may understand that it is the willingness to respond to the need of the other that substantially defines a neighbor. In essence, the readiness for a substitutive witnessing towards the need of the other qualifies one as a neighbor. Love of God does not happen in isolation. The danger, as envisioned by the scholar of law who questioned Jesus about the greatest commandment, lies in severing love of God from love of neighbor. Choosing one without the other, if possible, distorts what genuine love stands for.

Dualism constitutes an aberration of love. Christians are called to express God's love practically through love of neighbor. Christ stunned the mischievous scholar of the law and his cohorts when he explained that love of God and love of neighbor provide the basis for all the Law and the Prophets (Matthew 22:40). In other words, the kingdom of God as preached is to be realized in interpersonal sharing, in a life of communion that leads back to the Trinitarian source. The intra-Trinitarian communion invites *ad extra* the participation of several communities back to the Father, in and through Christ, and by the promptings of the Holy Spirit, leading to what has been called the divinization of the disciple:

---

20. Bethune, "Interreligious Dialogue," 21.

21. Luke 10:36–37.

To be divinized means to have the grace of Christ within you, to lay down your life for your neighbor and to wash the feet of the poor. To be divinized is to be like Christ, unafraid to go to the margins and touch the sick, the wounded, the sinners and all those shunned by society. To be divinized is ultimately to live in the spirit of martyrdom, willing to offer up one's life for the sake of the gospel. It is no wonder that we never desire to be divinized because it is easier to follow fleeting earthly images than to risk one's life for a person we really don't know or love someone who cannot repay us in return. Yet divinization is what lies at the base of our deepest desires. We want to be "like God," only we are unsure of what God we want to be like: the God of Jesus Christ, the god of culture, the god of progress or the god our own self-centered egos.[22]

Being divinized entails being true ambassadors of God, whose faith-witnessing lives reflect nothing but God's *intrumentum laboris* (instrument of work). Abraham's divinization journey impacted his living with and for the other.

Evidence of Abrahamic Substitutive Responsibility

Substitutive theology empowers willing disciples into asking or imagining the fundamental question: what does the other most need? It aims at reversing the common desire of expectation from the other. The usual motivational questions—what do I gain from the other in this encounter? and of what use can this other be?—are radically overturned by the question: what does the other need? That the self should imaginatively and instantly substitute the other, even before the other asks for it, constitutes the core of theological substitution.

Certain characteristics of dialogue of life, as explained in chapter 5, such as spontaneity, everydayness, mutuality, interfaith relations, substitution, otherness, and communion, present in this Abrahamic model, confirm its essential place for Muslim-Christian relations. In essence, the Abrahamic pilgrim model of substantive hospitality is presented as not only a practical interfaith spirituality, but more so as leverage for an effective dialogue of life between Christians and Muslims.

In addition to the distinct hospitality scene accounts in Genesis 18 and in sura 11 (also in suras 15 and 51), which will be given broader

22. Delio, *Humility of God*, 149.

analysis, two other events in the life of Abraham will be referenced in order to establish his substitutive responsibility towards both near and distant neighbors.

As Host to Wayfarers

The biblical scene at the Oak of Mamre totally exemplifies substitutive theology. Both Abraham and his angelic guests engaged in substitutive responsibility for each other. The sight of the wayfarers might have prompted a foundational question: what would they need most? And probably an answer came through the inner voice; some refreshing comfort against the harsh desert heat. That Abraham took the initiative of inviting in and hosting unfamiliar passersby indicates the extent of responsibility he owed to the well-being of the other. The profundity of his hospitality towards his ad hoc guests, in both the Qur'anic and biblical accounts, stresses his commitment in substitutive responsibility. Qur'an 51:24–30 reads:

> Has there reached you the story of the honored guests of Abraham? When they entered upon him and said, "[We greet you with] peace." He answered, "[And upon you] peace, [you are] a people unknown." Then went to his family and came with a fat [roasted] calf and placed it near them; he said, "Will you not eat?" And he felt fear of them. They said, "Fear not," and gave him good tidings of a learned boy. And his wife approached with a cry [of alarm] and struck her face and said, "[I am] a barren old woman!" They said, "Thus has said your Lord; indeed, He is the Wise, the knowing."

Genesis 18:1–10 states:

> The Lord appeared to Abraham by the Oak of Mamre, as he sat at the entrance of his tent in the heat of the day. He looked up and saw three men standing near him. When he saw them, he ran from the tent entrance to meet them, and bowed down to the ground. He said, "My Lord, if I find favor with you, do not pass by your servant. Let a little water be brought, and wash your feet, and rest yourselves under the tree. Let me bring a little bread, that you may refresh yourselves, and after that you may pass on—since you have come to your servant." So they said, "Do as you have said," And Abraham hastened into the tent to Sarah, and sad, "Make ready quickly three measures of choice

flour, knead it, and make cakes." Abraham ran to the herd, and took a calf, tender and good, and gave it to the servant, who hastened to prepare it. Then he took curds and milk and the calf that he had prepared, and set it before them; and he stood by them under the tree while they ate. They said to him, "Where is your wife Sarah?" And he said, "There, in the tent." Then one said, "I will surely return to you in due season, and your wife Sarah shall have a son." And Sarah was listening at the tent entrance behind him.

Abraham's hospitality depicts a kenotic practice, which spurred him to go out of his way to welcome his guests and to make them feel at home in his tent.[23] The spontaneous movement of Abraham towards the strangers marks a strong distinction between hospitality to those on our way and its higher form (set forth by Abraham), which motivates one to move out of one's way, attracted by the presence of that strange other, in order to show him/her welcome. Moving out of one's way towards the way of the other, as depicted by the Good Samaritan story, forms the basis of solidarity present in theology, especially that of Gustavo Gutierrez.[24] In line with Gutierrez, the neighbor is not necessarily the one that comes my way in need of my help, but more so the one I move out of my comfort zone to attend to.

Always, it is the need of the other as argued by Levinas that should solicit rapid response from the self. Abraham did not only move out of his way, but humbly served the other himself. Indeed, Abraham "himself *va-yiten lifnehem* [sets it before them], and does not delegate the task to a servant. *Vehu omen ale hem* [He himself stood by], and he himself waits upon them while they eat."[25]

As demonstrated earlier in chapter 7 concerning the inseparability of hospitality and sacrificial risks, it is the willful responsibility that overcomes these hurdles while serving the other that defines genuine hospitality. In this context, Abraham overcame significant ones. First, he kept God (his friend) on hold (Genesis 18:1) in order to entertain strangers. This can be judged an odd option. Second, he endured pain from the fresh cut he received during circumcision a few days prior, for hospitality.[26] And finally, as noted above, he inconvenienced himself,

23. Moyaert, "Biblical, Ethical," 96.

24. Gutierrez and Groody, *Preferential Option*, esp. the Introduction.

25. Gutierrez and Groody, *Preferential Option*, 169.

26. Ginzberg, *Legends of the Jews*, 1:240.

not only by sacrificing his rest and wealth, but also by undertaking the service by himself, instead of designating his servants to do it.

In his forty-first homily on Genesis, John Chrysostom emphasizes Abrahamic substitutive responsibility toward the wayfarers. First, he argues that Abraham had 318 servants, which he didn't involve. Second, Abraham transcended the excuses implied in his very old age. And lastly, his choice of resting outside, rather than inside his tent, was an indication of the Abrahamic disposition in rendering hospitable services to travelers.[27] Summarily, Chrysostom's analysis highlights the internal and external readiness of Abraham for substitutive hospitality. Indeed, Abraham created and shared his spaces. Most probably, God rewarded his hospitable heart with a personal visit, and also permitted what seemed to be his odd priorities. God appeared unbothered by Abraham's decisions of keeping him on hold for hospitality's sake.[28]

In this regard, Abraham performed an ethical act within a theological context. Keeping God on hold never meant the absence of God, but rather a shift in focus on the other. Abraham rediscovered the face of God in the human other. This Abrahamic priority was misplaced in the story of the Good Samaritan by the priest and the Levite, who thought that the concern for ritual purity was more important than a hospitable service to the abused victim (Luke 10:31–32). Moreover, "God comes into view as 'God incognito', to whom we do or do not offer hospitality."[29] The Mamre story also teaches that hospitality takes precedence over the spiritual enjoyment of an encounter with God.[30] The Talmud affirms this horizontal bent (interhuman relationship) as indeed the correct prioritization.[31] Summing this up, Jonathan Sacks confirms:

> There is God as we meet Him in a vision, a mystical encounter in the depths of the soul. But there is also God as we see His trace in another person, even a stranger, a passerby; in Abraham's case, three Arab travelers in the heat of the day. Someone else might have given them no further thought, but Abraham ran to meet them and bring them rest, shelter, food and drink. Greater is the person who sees God in the face of the stranger than one who sees God as God in a vision of transcendence,

27. John Chrysostom, *Homilies on Genesis 18–45*, 405.
28. Moyaert, "Biblical, Ethical," 98.
29. Moyaert, "Biblical, Ethical," 98.
30. Moyaert, "Biblical, Ethical," 98.
31. Moyaert, "Biblical, Ethical," 98.

for the Jewish task since the days of Abraham is not to ascend to heaven but to bring heaven down to earth in simple deeds of kindness and hospitality.[32]

In general, anthropomorphic depiction of the presence of God, even though an inconceivable discourse in Islamic tradition, fits into the Trinitarian-monotheistic theology of God as a relational being, *ad intra* and *ad extra*. Christianity believes that God, as a relational being, can and does manifest Godself in both symbolic and anthropomorphic forms, in order to remain in contact with helpless humanity. This relational perspective on God separates Christian monotheism from the Islamic strict transcendent otherness in which Allah has no partners. These two different understandings greatly inform the textual divergences of the Abrahamic hospitality in the Bible and the Qur'an.

According to the Qur'anic narrative, these strangers are angels, not God in the guise of men, so that when Abraham first encountered them they appeared particularly, "unknown, uncommon, unusual, not customary";[33] yet the duty of hospitality resulted. Later Muslim tradition goes further in naming the angels "Gabriel, Michael, and Israfil."[34] The Qur'an does not mention God at all, partly because of its anti-anthropomorphic depiction of God. To further substantiate the angelic claim, the guest in the Qur'anic account did not eat the food Abraham served them, simply because they have no need for human food.[35] Based on this Islamic teaching, the eighth-century (fourteenth-century in the Islamic calendar) Muslim exegete Ibn Kathir critiqued Christians: "According to the people of the book, the fatted calf was roasted and served with rolls, fat and milk. And according to them, the angels ate, but this is not right."[36] Despite the discordance in the biblical and Qur'anic accounts, none entertains doubt about the willingness and sacrifice with which Abraham hosted his guests.

However, the Christian Old Testament notes two sets of guests visiting Abraham almost at the same time: God and the three anonymous wayfarers. Unfortunately, the distinction between these guests can only be implied because the biblical account displays a back-and-forth switch

32. Sacks, "Abraham and the Three Visitors."

33. Ali, *Holy Qur'an*, 1428.

34. Lodhal, *Claiming Abraham*, 11.

35. Siddiqui, *Islam and Hospitality*, 25.

36. Ibn Kathir, cited in Wheeler, *Prophets*, 96.

from singular to plural expressions in reference to the guests. This (one but three) depiction of divine guests, according to Augustine, can find explanation in the triune-God paradigm of the Trinity.[37] It can as well distinguish the three wayfarers from God. But of major importance here is how Abraham responded to his one and three mysterious guests.

One peculiarity that marks the Abrahamic hospitality model is the verbal persuasiveness of his appeal. The remarkable persuasive force is noticed in his words of invitation towards the mysterious wayfarers. The gradual ascent pattern of Abraham from very simple to more engaging appeals lobbied the interlocutor into a serious commitment: "Now let a little water be fetched, wash your feet, and rest yourselves under the tree . . . I will get a morsel of bread so you can refresh your heart. After that you may go your way . . ." But a little water and a morsel of bread later turned into a sumptuous meal (Genesis 18:4–8). However, he reassured his guests that they were no burden at all.[38] In essence, Abraham initiated a humble hospitality approach, despite the strangeness of the wayfarers—"these seeming unusual people" (Qur'an 51:25).

A similar account is seen during the conversation with God on the justification of his intended punishment of the righteous with sinners in Sodom and Gomorrah. The number of the righteous decreased proportionally until God had to cut Abraham off. In this regard, Abrahamic hospitality manifests itself and shows Abraham's excessive sensitivity to the needs of others: "By downplaying his efforts, he accentuates their dignity."[39] And because of his ability to combine superabundance and simplicity, Abraham has become the prototype of hospitality, not only in Christian tradition but also in the Islamic traditions, where he is called *Abu l-Dhifan* (Father of Hosts).[40]

Because asymmetric mutuality is usually inseparable from substitutive responsibility, the angelic guests gifted Abraham with what he and Sarah needed most. Their reaction as well reflects substitutive responsibility, because they relieved the old couple from their burden of childlessness. According to an early church father, Clement of Rome, Abrahamic reward came not only through faith, but through faith and hospitality.[41]

37. Arterbury, "Abraham's Hospitality," 371.

38. Arterbury, "Abraham's Hospitality," 371.

39. Arterbury, "Abraham's Hospitality," 371.

40. Arterbury, "Abraham's Hospitality," 97.

41. Clement I, *Letter to the Corinthians* 10.

Not every act of hospitality ends in instant (concrete) blessing, the way Abraham's hospitality yielded the birth of Isaac from a barren Sarah and her aged husband. Nevertheless, the blessing and transformation that accompanied Abraham impacted the New Testament understanding of hospitality, on the one hand, as in: "Do not neglect to show hospitality to strangers, for by doing that some have entertained angels without knowing it" (Hebrew 13:2). On the other hand, Islamic tradition teaches, for example, that "strangers embody the presence of God and carry with them the possibility of blessing."[42]

Indeed, both Abraham and his guests participated in gift exchanges because they lived for the other. Both responded aptly to the need of the other. Gifts, as seen in this context, need not be material alone. The praxis of substitution involves materiality, but also extends to the immateriality of presence or promise. The ability to imagine and to satisfy what the other needed most confirms respect and connectivity toward otherness. It also explains the significance of asymmetric mutuality, which guarantees exchange of disparate gifts, solely determined by the need of the other. Indeed, the other always sets the agenda.

However, when the identity of the other varies, what difference could that make? What lessons can be drawn from Abrahamic examples? In other words, did he treat the near neighbor and the distant neighbor equitably or partially? From the many instances of Abrahamic substitutive responsibility toward the other, attention is paid to two more instances commonly reported in the biblical as well as the Qur'anic texts.

As Advocate for Sodom and Gomorrah

The Abrahamic hospitality model of intercession balances particularity and universality. It is no coincidence that the story "of the honored guests of Abraham" (Genesis 18) is located between Abraham's request to God that "Ishmael might live under your blessing!" (family) in Genesis 17:18 and his intercession for the people of Sodom and Gomorrah (foreigners) in Genesis 18:20–21.[43]

A smooth connection exists between Abrahamic hospitality to the wayfarers, which God approved by his patient wait, and the revelation of the purpose of his visit (plans against Sodom), which engendered

42. Omar, "Embracing the 'Other,'" 439.
43. Snodgrass, "Has the Story?," 181.

another dimension of Abraham's hospitality. Hospitality as exemplified in Abraham needs not be limited to eating and drinking. Instead, it embraces all forms of willful responsibility to the other for the sole interest and well-being of this other. In this regard, Abraham transitioned from one form of hospitality to another when he solicited before God on behalf of Sodom. With the interest of a few righteous Sodomites in mind, Abraham boldly confronted God on the issue of justice.

> Abraham drew near and said, "Will you consume the righteous with the wicked? What if there are fifty righteous (people) within the city? Will you consume and not spare the place for fifty righteous, who are in it? Be it far from you to do things like that, to kill the righteous with the wicked, so that the righteous should be like the wicked. May that be far from you. Shouldn't the judge of all the earth do right?" (Genesis 18:23–25)

For a second time, Abraham put God on the spot, not for his own sake but for the sake of others, in hospitality. A hospitable person cannot lack in mercy, kindness, and righteousness, for these characterize the noble act known as hospitality. With this second virtuous act of Abraham, "he sets himself up as advocate of all just people in Sodom and Gomorrah. In doing so, he realizes his true calling: to be a host for strangers, and advocate for those who are threatened to become victims of ruined circumstances."[44]

Justice is another virtue that plays out in the two moments that Abraham showed hospitality to others despite their otherness as total foreigners to him. Hospitality as practiced by Abraham shuns exclusivity but promotes universality in relation to God. Abrahamic hospitality distinguishes itself as one that has God at its center, which suggests that he strived to replicate God's universal hospitality and most probably had to practice it under the watchful eye of God for approval. That he took up the justice of God was not a challenge on the competence of God, but through it the elasticity of God's love for humanity was revealed, in which justice and mercy are brought into harmony.

Rav Alex Israel confirms that there is no difference between near and distant neighbors in the life of Abraham with this assertion: "Abraham is the man on earth who epitomizes kindness to all. Independent of who you are, you are invited into this home, unquestioningly, you are

---

44. Moyaert, "Biblical, Ethical," 99.

escorted back into the desert."[45] In contrast to Noah, who simply endorsed what God asked him to do, Abraham argued with God. He took the fate of the Sodomites to heart even though they did not belong to his covenantal clan.[46]

Moyaert argues that Abraham's life shows how the virtue of hospitality is deeply connected to friendship with God. For her, "where strangers are hospitably welcomed, God is present to uphold worldly commandments, as hospitality is the highest possible form of religion, and vice versa; a prayer life can never result in disregard of neighborly love."[47] Indeed, every believer in the Abrahamic tradition knows that a stranger asking for hospitality is not necessarily an intruder, nor an enemy (despite the obvious possibility).

Nevertheless, in the Qur'an (sura 11) it is inconceivable for mere mortals to challenge God. Conversely, "it is Abraham who is told to be silent, to hold his tongue, to submit to Allah's judgment."[48] Lodahl thinks that the Qur'anic silence on this aspect of debating God is understandable.[49] For example, whose standard of justice was Abraham appealing to in order to probe God's decision? In this portraiture, the Qur'an attempts defending God's image colored in biblical anthropomorphism: "O Abraham, desist from this, the command of your Lord has come and an irreversible punishment shall surely smite them" (11:76). A reader easily observes the consistency of total submissiveness to Allah that Islam propagates and not its converse. On the other hand, the biblical approach permits more flexibility in relation to God, i.e., humanity's free collaboration.

As Mediator between Sarah's Resentment and Hagar's Vulnerability

The inclusion of Abraham's household shows that the challenges of hospitality are not restricted to strangers only, but also extend to one's own people, whose higher expectations can be more demanding. Genesis 21:8–14 narrates:

45. Israel, "Parshat Vayera."

46. Moyaert, "Biblical, Ethical," 101.

47. Moyaert, "Biblical, Ethical," 101.

48. Moyaert, "Biblical, Ethical," 17.

49. Lodhal, *Claiming Abraham*, 16.

> And the child grew and was weaned. And Abraham made a great feast on the day that Isaac was weaned. But Sarah saw the son of Hagar the Egyptian, whom she had borne to Abraham, laughing. So she said to Abraham, "Cast out this slave woman with her son, for the son of this slave woman shall not be heir with my son Isaac." And the thing was very displeasing to Abraham on account of his son. But God said to Abraham, "Be not displeased because of the boy and because of your slave woman. Whatever Sarah says to you, do as she tells you, for through Isaac shall your offspring be named. And I will make a nation of the son of the slave woman also, because he is your offspring." So Abraham rose early in the morning and took bread and a skin of water and gave it to Hagar, putting it on her shoulder, along with the child, and sent her away. And she departed and wandered in the wilderness of Beersheba.

After the Mamre scene, this narrative account depicts Abraham yielding to the desire of his wife, Sarah, by sending Hagar and her child, Ishmael, away against his own intent. Again, for the sake of the peace and happiness of Sarah, Abraham escorted Hagar into the desert but implored God for their protection. Even though it appears odd to interpret this act as hospitable for a kind and compassionate father, who would exile his own son and maidservant just to please the aversion of his wife towards otherness, hospitality can still be implied.

Hospitality, with its characterization of *kenosis*, humility, and compassion are virtually mixed in this context. The Islamic tradition goes beyond the Christian narrative to lend a clearer picture of Abrahamic compassion through his later search after Hagar and the son. One tradition has it that the "abandoned Hagar" in the desert received welcome by a local Bedouin tribe of Southern origin. The Bedouins inculcated in Ishmael (later forefather of all Arabs) their hospitable spirit.[50] This welcome and settlement in an area close to today's Mecca, granted by the Bedouins, is important for Muslims as it validates their center of worship.

The same Islamic tradition holds that Abraham, who had been searching everywhere for Hagar, found her and the child by the well (*zamzam*) and built a house for them. Later, Abraham, with the help of the young Ishmael, built the Ka'ba for the worship of God, which Muslims believe to be the first building on earth dedicated to the worship of

---

50. Michael, "Where to Now?," 535.

the one God.[51] In Bukhari's account, Abraham left Hagar and Ishmael at Mecca with some provisions, but it was the angel that dug the *zamzam* well with his heel or his wing for the supply of water.[52] In essence, the God-centered orientation that shaped Abraham's hospitality had a way of vindicating his (conflicting) hospitable acts, insofar as he unwaveringly relied on God and acted toward his neighbors for the sake of God.

Why an Abrahamic Model, but Not African Communality or Levinas's Ethics?

Substitutive responsibility similar to that exemplified by Abraham is not absent in the discussed Levinasian ethics and in African communitarianism. The major difference, however, is found in the purpose for those altruistic actions. Whereas Levinasian altruism strictly serves the other (other-centric) and the African perpsective is technically tied to kinship bonding (communion), the Abrahamic model is universally theocentric. In essence, the inherent beauty in the Levinasian and African models is suffused by their respective particularities, which fail to harmonize otherness and communion. In context, Levinasian altruism and the African kinship bond would exacerbate rather than attenuate the Muslim-Christian mistrust.

A theocentric model of substitutive responsibility for the other, which Abraham personifies, is exemplary because of its indirect motivation. De Bethune describes the fundamental principles of Abrahamic hospitality thus: "that it is freely given, respectful, attentive, tactful, and that it holds out the possibility that one has welcomed God Himself."[53]

In conformity with Abraham, it is always for the sake of God that sacrificial responsibilities for the other are undertaken, even when the human beneficiaries justly do not deserve the hospitality. God is the primary motivation for good deeds to near and distant neighbors, on two counts. First, as the owner of the universe, God's inclusive love accommodates all persons as children of one Father. In other words, any attempt to separate the love of God from the love of his children necessarily ends in futility. Second, the God of Abraham that Muslims and Christians claim to worship is a hospitable God who graciously commands

51. Michael, "Where to Now?," 535.

52. Wheeler, *Prophets in the Qur'an*, 96.

53. Bethune, "Interreligious Dialogue," 8.

mutual substitutive hospitality among his children. Above all, God chose hospitality as the essential eschatological standard for these two religious traditions. Therefore, a universal reimagination of God for Muslims and Christians challenges both into living for the other (doing good)—not necessarily for what the other stands for (otherness), but for who he is: a child of God and a co-pilgrim with Abraham (communion). In this light, dialogue of life with its spontaneity and everydayness offers the appropriate level ground for mutual substitutive responsibility towards the religious other, as a proof for genuine submissiveness and discipleship of the hospitable God.

Abrahamic hospitality challenges Muslims and Christians from two angles. First, his model assures otherness. The high point of Abrahamic hospitality, according to Abigail Doukhan, is antithetical to appropriation and assimilation such that: "To be hospitable is not to convert, nor to naturalize. To be hospitable is to encounter the Other while acknowledging that they will always remain other, and never be 'wholly in my site.'"[54] Second, his model encourages mutual growth. Both the self and the other are renewed after every encounter because when the former runs the risk of allowing the unknown other to share his sacred space, the gift of newness from the other activates the process of correcting distorted perceptions of each other.

---

54. Doukhan, "Hospitality of Abraham," 91.

Conclusion

THEISTIC SPIRITUALITY CAN BE expressed as a collaborative journey with God wherein God points out the direction as well as the destination. Christian discipleship and Islamic submission fit into the journey metaphor in the sense that both have a defined *telos* and each aspires towards reaching the communion goal through humble and obedient companionship with God. In essence, the journey with God embraces God's people, through whom the love for God can be practiced.

Like Abraham, genuine Muslims and Christians desire transiting from earth into eternity as the Promised Land for the friends of God. Friendship with God entails learning the asymmetric-mutual substitutive hospitality for the other that Abraham represented. Abraham lived for the divine other through human others, irrespective of the religious, cultural, and sociopolitical otherness involved, because he understood the universal hospitality of God. In other words, when the universality of God is the primary focus, otherness, rather than dividing, beautifies unity as different colors form the rainbow.

Doing good or being committed to the responsibility of the religious other for the sake of God, as this research is proposing, reestablishes the lost trust between Muslims and Christians and also paves way for fruitful dialogue. Bukhari's al-Adab al-Mufrad concurs: "Whoever believes in Allah and the Last Day must honor his neighbor. Moreover, whoever believes in Allah and the Last day must honor his guest with required hospitality,"[1] on condition that the guest must not stay too long as to oppress his host. In other words, asymmetric-mutual substitutive hospitality is that altruistic praxis, in the form of dialogue of life, preparing the ground for healthy reflections pertaining to doctrines.

1. See Bukhari's *Al-Adab al-Mufrad*, "The Guest Must Not," in Hasan, *Way of the Prophet*, 153.

This research sets out developing its overall thesis of giving voice to an unpopular but practical faith-based witnessing approach for interfaith dialogue between Muslims and Christians, aimed toward a healthier co-existence. Such doctrinal-adaptive praxis identifies the relevance of dia-logue of life via hospitality as the primary thesis proposed by this research.

In order to substantiate its major thesis, this research critically established the essence of the theological praxis of hospitality, in light of both Islamic and Christian scriptures, as an inevitable eschatologi-cal condition. It as well demonstrated the spirit of African *ubuntu* as a veritable ground for the Abrahamic pilgrim model of hospitality, through the promotion of substitutive hospitality. Prior to the exploration of the thesis proposal on dialogic hospitality, four chapters were developed (the first through the fourth) in which the Muslim-Christian problem of in-ability to manage otherness overtime and their consequential ugly past were reviewed, both globally and contextually. In the course of exploring the Christian-Muslim problematic history, exemplary positive views and actions were identified as possible basis for the progress of dialogic rela-tions. Then the fifth chapter was a build-up chapter that established a turn toward dialogic options, having learned from the mutual lost caused by violent approaches. The gradual dialogic growth shown in this chap-ter culminated in the concentration on the development of dialogue of life via hospitality, using Levinasian substitutive altruism and African cultural practice, as a platform for its Abrahamic asymmetric-mutual remodeling, evidenced in chapters 6–11.

Prompted by the post-Vatican II intervention of the Pontifical Council for Interreligious Dialogue, the (latent) hospitality practice was recommended from a Catholic perspective as key for dialogue of life, whose characteristics of spontaneity, surprise, and everydayness can ju-diciously engage religious otherness in pluralistic societies.

The research drew from several Islamic, Christian, and traditional African sources in demonstrating the possibility and efficiency of its proposal for dialogue of life through asymmetric-mutual substitutive hospitality. The culminating argument in this research lies in its ability to establish an Abrahamic theistic meeting point for both religious tradi-tions. *Inter alia*, Muslims and Christians revere Abrahamic faith practic-es, especially his unwavering love for God, concretized in his hospitable acts to near and distant neighbors. However, the Abrahamic fatherhood contestation was carefully supplanted with his pilgrim metaphor, which puts Muslims and Christians on fairest ground for hospitable collaboration of each other with good works.

Asymmetric-mutual substitutive hospitality as modeled by Abraham challenges Muslims and Christians of all cultures to live out their faith-based beliefs proportionately, as wisely shaped by context. The Abrahamic figure not only provides the common ground for Muslims and Christians, it also assures their distinct otherness. As argued, Abraham demonstrated appropriate openness and respect to both near and distant neighbors (the religious other). His pilgrim model was presented in such a manner that it can impact Muslims and Christians differently in accord with their respective faith commitments. The idea of aligning the Abrahamic theology of asymmetric-mutual responsibility on Qur'an 5:48 and Matthew 25 affirms this claim. The asymmetric-mutual substitutive hospitality model also offers a synthesis of Levinasian and Buberian altruism. As partly Buberian and partly Levinasian, true hospitality is best appreciated when perceived as asymmetric-mutual responsibility, rather than when practiced either as required reciprocity or the exclusive asymmetric form.

Pope Francis's recent clarion call for a turn toward dialogue of life is both apt and challenging. Even though the thesis proposal of this research was applied to a particular African context, the faith-awakening lessons therein extend beyond its borders. The baseline lesson is to unlearn the ignorance-induced biases and shun imperialistic perceptions toward the religious other and his faith activities. And for a way forward, those shells of insulated religiosity need to be broken through discursive and hospitality acts, allowing the (need of the) other to always set the agenda, as mandated in Matthew 25 and Qur'an 5:48. Against the disclosure key of phenomenologists, the religious other must define itself in her own terms through dialogic interactions oriented toward mutual growth in newness and faith commitment. Invariably, asymmetric-mutual substitutive hospitality aims at interfaith enrichment, leaving room for conversion only as fruit of personal conviction in every dialogue.

Incidentally, the seeds of these amicable principles can only be sown and nurtured toward maturity through daily and concrete relationship, aimed at healthy neighborliness. In contrast, insulated isolations from both traditions would constitute an interfaith disaster. Although security risks, as shown, constitute the offshoot of encountering otherness, still, peaceful coexistence, as the ultimate goal of human society, can only be possible when ignorance-induced suspicion and antagonism are surpassed with trust and respect for the otherness of the religious other. Encounter generates trust. Invariably, otherness, as this research has argued, must be harmonized with communion, since the unfamiliar does not necessarily destroy the familiar. Antinomy coexists.

As an interfaith proposal, this research does not claim to have the last word on Muslim-Christian dialogic hospitality relation. The envisaged fruits of this research notwithstanding, its concrete applications might remain challenging, especially due to the informality that governs dialogue of life. However, the encouragement for the pursuance of this research's thesis lies in the strength of its commonness and concreteness, without necessarily involving doctrinal debates and conversion.

Moreover, Pope Francis's recent preference of dialogue of life for ecumenical and interfaith interactions assures the future of this research. In light of Pope Francis's recommendation, the provocative aspect of this research will surely open up further research inquiries, like: 1) How could dialogue of life via hospitality speak to every Muslims and Christians? 2) What defines good works in each religious tradition? 3) How can a functional theology of dialogue of life be developed without imposition of particular faith categories? 4) What guarantees a balance between faith commitment and openness to otherness among ordinary Christians and Muslims? Won't conversion be an unavoidable threat? These outlined scholarly inquiries will further set in motion the thesis of this research toward its fruitful goal.

Bibliography

Abbas, Ibn Tafsir. *Great Commentaries on the Holy Qur'an*. Translated by Mokrane Guezzou. Jordan: Royal Ahl al-Bayt Institute for Islamic Thought, 2007.

Abdul-Hamid, Mustapha. "Christian-Muslim Dialogue in Ghana: A Model for World Dialogue and Peace." *Ilorin Journal of Religious Studies* 1.1 (2011) 21–32.

Achebe, Chinua. *Things Fall Apart*. Reprint, Oxford: Heinemann, 2008.

Adam, Karl. *The Spirit of Catholicism*. Translated by Dom Justin McCann. New York: Macmillan, 1933.

Adamu, Abdullah. "Ethnic Conflicts in Nigeria." Paper presented at the Presidential Retreat on Peace and Conflict Resolution, National Institute for Policy and Strategic Studies, Kuru, January 23–26, 2002.

Adedigba, Francis A. "The Roles of Jesus at the Final Judgment in Christianity and Islam: A Proposal for Inter-Religious Dialogue in Yoruba Culture." PhD diss., Pontificiam Universitatem S. Thomae in Urbe, 2014.

Admirand, Peter. "Healing the Distorted face: Doctrinal Reinterpretation(s) and the Christian Response to the Other." *One in Christ* 42.2 (2008) 302–17.

Adogame, Afe. "Politicization of Religion and Religionization of Politics in Nigeria." In *Religion, History and Politics in Nigeria: Essays in Honor of Ogbu U. Kalu*, edited by Chima J. Korieh and Nwokeji U. Ugo, 125–39. Lanham, MD: University Press of America, 2005.

Akpinar, Snjezana. "Hospitality and Islam." *Religion East and West* 7 (2007) 23–27.

al-Abidin, A. Z. "Introduction to the Sudan Charter." *BICMURA* 6.1 (1988) 1–12.

al-Azimi. "La Chronique Abregee d' al-Azimi." *Jornal Asiatique* 230 (1938) 353–448.

al-Bukhari, Muhammad. *Sahih al-Bukhari: The Translation of the Meanings of Sahih al-Bukhari*. Translated by Muhammad Muhsin Khan. Medina: Dar al-'Arabiyah, 1981.

al-Dahabi, Muhammad Husein. "Israelitic Narratives in Exegesis and Tradition." *Fourth Conference of the Academy of Islamic Research* 13.88 (September 1968, Rajab, Cairo) 579–35.

al-Faruqi, Isma'il Raji. *Islam and Other Faiths*. Leicester, UK: Islamic Foundation and International Institute of Islamic Thought, 1998.

Ali, Maulana Muhammad, trans. *The Holy Qur'an*. Lahore: Ahmadiyyah Anjuman Isha'at Islam, 1973.

———. *A Manual of Hadith*. Lahore: Ahmadiyya, Anjuman, 1951.

Ali, Yusuf, trans. *The Holy Qur'an*. Medina: King Fahd, 1989.

Allard, Silas Webster. "In the Shades of the Oak of Mamre: Hospitality as a Framework for Political Engagement between Christians and Muslims." *Political Theology* 13.4 (2012) 414–24.

Allen, John L., ed. "Francis Eschews His Own Safety to Back the 'Three Saints of Bangui.'" *Crux*, November 22, 2015. https://cruxnow.com/church/2015/11/francis-eschews-his-own-safety-to-back-the-three-saints-of-bangui/.

Alter, Robert. *The Art of Biblical Narrative*. New York: Basic Books, 2011.

Ammah, Rabiatu. "Muslim-Christian-Muslim Relations in Contemporary Sub-Saharan Africa." *Islam and Christian-Muslim Relations* 18.2 (April 2007) 139–53.

Anas, Malik b. *Al-Muwatta*. Vol. 1. Cairo: Dar al-Haddith, 1999.

Anawati, George. "An Assessment of the Christian-Islamic Dialogue." In *The Vatican, Islam, and the Middle East*, edited by Kalil C. Ellis, 52–68. Syracuse, NY: Syracuse University Press, 1987.

———. "Excursus on Islam." In *Commentary on the Documents of Vatican II*, edited by Herbert Vorgrimler, 776–83. New York: Herder, 1976.

Anees, Munawar Ahmad. "The Dialogue of History." In *Contemporary Islam: Christian-Muslim Relations*, edited by Merryl Wyn Davies, 6–35. London: Grey Seal, 1991.

Anidjar, Gil. "Hospitality." In *Acts of Religion*, by Jacques Derrida, edited by Gil Anidjar, 356–420. New York: Routledge, 2002.

———. "Once More, Once More: Derrida, the Arab, the Jew." In *Acts of Religion*, by Jacques Derrida, edited by Gil Anidjar, 1–31. New York: Routledge, 2002.

Arterbury, Andres E. "Abraham's Hospitality among Jewish and Early Christian Writers: A Tradition History of Gen 18:1–16 and Its Relevance for the Study of the New Testament." *Perspectives in Religious Studies* 30.3 (2003) 359–76.

———. *Entertaining Angels: Early Christian Hospitality in Its Mediterranean Setting*. New Testament Monograph 8. Sheffield, UK: Sheffield Phoenix, 2005.

Asbridge, Thomas. *The Crusades: The Authoritative History of the War for the Holy Land*. New York: HarperCollins, 2010.

Ashafa Muhammad N. (Imam), and James M. Wuye, eds. *The Pastor and the Imam: Responding to Conflict*. Lagos, Nigeria: Ibrash, 1999.

Askari, Hasan. "The Dialogical Relationship between Christianity and Islam." *Journal of Ecumenical Studies* 9.3 (1972) 477–88.

Atanda, Joseph Adebowale. *An Introduction to Yoruba History*. Ibadan: Ibadan University Press, 1980.

Augustine of Hippo. *Contra Faustum*. Translated by Richard Stothert. In *The Nicene and Post-Nicene Fathers*, 1st series, edited by Philip Schaff, vol. 4. Buffalo, NY: Christian Literature, 1887.

Ayandele, Emmanuel Ayankanmi. *The Missionary Impact on the Modern Nigeria, 1842–1914*. London: Longman, 1966.

Ajayi, Jacob F. Ade. "The Aftermath of the Fall of Old Oyo." In *History of West Africa*, edited by Jacob F. Ade Ajayi and Michael Crowther, 2:129–66. London: University of London Press, 1974.

Aydin, Mahmut. "Religious Pluralism: A Challenge for Muslims—A Theological Evaluation." *Journal of Ecumenical Studies* 38.2/3 (Spring-Summer 2001) 330–52.

———. "Towards a Theological Dialogue between Christians and Muslims." *Islamochristiana* 26 (2000) 1–31.

Ayegboyin, Deji. "Religious Association and the New Political Dispensation in Nigeria." *Journal for Studies in Interreligious Dialogue* 15.1 (2005) 101–13.

Ayoub, Mahmoud M. "Christian-Muslim Dialogue: Goals and Obstacles." *The Muslim World* 94 (July 2004) 313–19.

———. *Islam: Faith and History*. Minneapolis: Oneworld, 2004.

———. *The Qur'an and Its Interpreters.* 2 vols. Albany: State University of New York Press, 1984, 1994.

———. *Redemptive Suffering in Islam.* Hague, Netherlands: Mouton, 1978.

———. "Roots of Muslim-Christian Conflict." *The Muslim World* 79.1 (January 1989) 25–45.

———. "Towards an Islamic Christology: The Death of Jesus: Reality or Delusion." *The Muslim World* 70.2 (1980) 91–121.

Baartman, E. "The Religious Needs of Children and Young People: A Panel Discussion." *Journal of Theology for Southern Africa* 33 (1980) 49–77.

Baldick Julian. "Massignon: Man of Opposites." *Religious Studies* 23.1 (1987) 29–39.

Baum, Gregory. "Interreligious Dialogue: A Roman Catholic Perspective." *Global Media Journal* 4.1 (2011) 5–20.

Benoit, Standaert. *Sharing Sacred Space: Interreligious Dialogue as Spiritual Encounter.* Translated by William Skudlarek. Minnesota: Liturgical, 2003.

Benveniste, Emil. "L'Hospitalite." In *Le Vocabulaire des Institutions Indo-Europeennes,* 1:87–101. Paris: Minuit, 1969.

Berkley, Jonathan Porter. *The Formation of Islam: Religion and Society in the Near East, 600–800.* Cambridge: Cambridge University Press, 2003.

Bethune, Pierre-Francois de. "Interreligious Dialogue and Sacred Hospitality." *Religion East and West,* October 2007, 1–21.

———. "Monastic Interreligious Dialogue." In *The Wiley-Blackwell Companion to Inter-Religious Dialogue,* edited by Catherine Cornille, 34–50. West Sussex, UK: John Wiley, 2013.

———. "Monks in Dialogue with Believers from other Religions." *Studies in Formation Spirituality* 14.1 (1993) 129–38.

Boer, Jan Harm. *Missionary Messengers of Liberation in a Colonial Context: A Case Study of Sudan United Mission.* Amsterdam: Rodopi, 1979.

Boff, Leonardo. *Virtues for Another Possible World.* Eugene, OR: Cascade, 2011.

Bolchazy, Ladislaus J. *Hospitality in Early Rome: Livy's Concept of Its Humanizing Force.* Chicago: Ares, 1977.

Bongo, Kenneth C. *Christianity in Danger (as Islam Threatens): The Five Whys.* Diquadine: Admiral, 1989.

Bonhoeffer, Dietrich. *The Cost of Discipleship.* Translated by R. H. Fuller. London: SCM, 1948.

———. *Letters and Papers from Prison.* Translated by Reginald Fuller et al., edited by Eberhard Bethge. London: SCM, 1971.

Bonner, Michael. "Poverty and Economics in the Qur'an." *Journal of Interdisciplinary History* 35.3 (2005) 391–406.

Borrmans, Maurice. *Guidelines for Dialogues between Christians and Muslims.* Translated by R. Marston Speight. Interreligious Documents 1. Mahwah, NJ: Paulist, 1990.

Boullata, Issa J. "Fastabiqul-Khairat: A Qur'anic Principle of Interfaith Relations." In *Christian-Muslim Encounters,* edited by Yvonne Haddad and Wadi Zaidan Haddad, 43–53. Gainesville: University Press of Florida, 1995.

Boyarin, Daniel. *Border Lines: The Partition of Judeo-Christianity.* Philadelphia: University of Pennsylvania Press, 2004.

Braswell, George. *Islam.* Nashville: Broadman and Holman, 1996.

Brink, Laurie. "In the Search of the Biblical Foundations of Prophetic Dialogue: Engaging a Hermeneutics of Otherness." *Missiology: An International Review* 41.1 (2013) 9–21.

Browne, Laurence. E. "The Patriarch Timothy and the al-Mahid." *The Muslim World* 21.1 (1931) 38–45. Adapted from Dr. Mingana's English translation of the Arabic version, 1928.

Buber, Martin. *I and Thou*. Translated by Walter Kaufmann. New York: Scribner, 1970.

———. *Pointing the Way: Collected Essays*. Translated and edited by Maurice Friedman. Atlantic Highlands, NJ: Humanities, 1990.

Buck, Dorothy C. "A Model of Hope: Louis Massignon's Badaliya." *SUFI: A Journal of Sufism* 59 (Autumn 2003). http://www.dcbuck.com/Articles/ModelofHope/modelhope.html.

Bujo, Bénézet. *African Christian Morality at the Age of Inculturation*. Reprint, Nairobi: Paulines Africa, 1998.

———. *Foundations of African Ethic: Beyond the Universal Claims of Western Morality*. Translated by Brian McNeil. New York: Herder, 2001.

Bullock, Alan, and Steven Trombley, eds. "Otherness." In *The New Fontana Dictionary of Modern Thought*. 3rd ed. London: HarperCollins, 1999.

Bureau, Rene. "Sorcellerie et Prophetisme en Afrique Noire." *Etudes*, April 1967, 467–81.

Burton, John. *The Collection of the Qur'an*. Cambridge: Cambridge University Press, 1977.

Caner, Ergun M., and Emir F. Caner. *Christian Jihad: Two Former Muslims Look at Crusades and Killings in the Name of Christ*. Grand Rapids: Kregel, 2004.

Caputo, John D. *The Prayers and Tears of Jacques Derrida: Religion without Religion*. Bloomington: Indiana University Press, 1997.

———. *What Would Jesus Deconstruct?: The Good News of Postmodernism for the Church*. Grand Rapids, Michigan: Baker, 2007.

"CAR's Archbishop and Imam in Peace Drive." *BBC News*, April 9, 2014. http://www.bbc.com/news/world/Africa.

Casey, Thomas G. "Levinas' Idea of the Infinite and the Priority of the Other." *Gregorianum* 84.2 (2003) 383–417.

Caspar, Robert. *A Historical Introduction to Islamic Theology: Muhammad and the Classical, Period*. Translated by Penelope Johnstone. Rome: Pontificio Instituto di Studi Arabi e d' Islamistica, 1998.

———. "Islam according to Vatican II, vol.1." *Encounter: Documents for Christian Muslim Understanding* 2.21 (1976) 1–7.

Casarella, Peter. "Wholes and Parts: Ecumenism and Interreligious Encounters in the Pope Francis's Teologia del Pueblo." In *The Whole Is Greater than Its Parts: Christian Unity and Interreligious Encounter Today (Jan. 8–10, 2018)*. Conference report. https://www.academia.edu/35700977/Conference_Report_The_Whole_is_Greater_Than_its_Parts_Christian_Unity_and_Interreligious_Encounter_Today_Jan_8_10_2018_.

Catholic Bishops' Conference of England and Wales. *Meeting God in Friend and Stranger*. London: Catholic Truth Society, 2010.

Cavanaugh, William T. *Being Consumed: Economics and Christian Desire*. Grand Rapids: Eerdmans, 2008.

"The Christian Concept of the State." *CAN News*, Zaria, March 10, 1988, 5.

Chukwu, Donatus Oluwa. *The Church as the Extended Family of God: Toward a New Direction for African Ecclesiology.* Bloomington, IN: Xlibris, 2011.

Clarke, Peter, and Ian Linden. *Islam in Modern Nigeria: A Study of a Muslim Community in Post-Independence State (1960–980).* Mainz, Germany: Gruenewald, 1984.

Clooney, Francis X. *Comparative Theology: Deep Learning Across Religious Borders.* Malden, MA: Wiley-Blackwell, 2010.

Cohen, Jeffrey M. "Abraham's Hospitality." *Jewish Bible Quarterly* 34.3 (2006) 168–72.

Cohen, Richard, ed. *Face to Face with Levinas.* Albany: State University of New York Press, 1986.

A Common Word between Us and You. Jordan: Royal Aal al-Bayt Institute for Islamic Thought, 2009. https://rissc.jo/docs/Common_word.pdf.

Congregation for the Doctrine of the Faith. "Letter to the Bishops of the Catholic Church on Some Aspects of Christian Meditation." Vatican City, October 15, 1989. https://www.vatican.va/roman_curia/congregations/cfaith/documents/rc_con_cfaith_doc_19891015_meditazione-cristiana_en.html.

Constable, Giles, ed. *Letters of Peter the Venerable.* Vol. 2. Cambridge, MA: Harvard University Press, 1967.

Cook, David. *Understanding Jihad.* Berkeley: University of California Press, 2005.

Cornille, Catherine. *The Im-Possibility of Interreligious Dialogue.* New York: Crossroad, 2008.

———. "Interreligious Hospitality and Its Limits." In *Hosting Strangers Between Religions,* edited by Richard Kearney, 35–44. New York: Continuum, 2011.

Cornille, Catherine, and Christopher Conway, eds. *Interreligious Hermeneutics.* Interreligious Dialogue Series 2. Eugene, OR: Cascade, 2010.

Cross, Frank Leslie, and Elizabeth A. Livingstone, eds. *The Oxford Dictionary of the Christian Church.* 3rd ed. Oxford: Oxford University Press, 1997.

Culpepper, R. Alan. "Luke." In *The New Interpreter's Bible,* edited by Leander E. Keck, 9:102–9. Nashville: Abingdon, 1995.

D'Costa, Gavin. *The Meeting of Religions and the Trinity.* Maryknoll, NY: Orbis, 2000.

———, ed. *Vatican II: Catholic Doctrines on Jews and Muslims.* Oxford: Oxford University Press, 2014.

Daniel, Norman. *Islam and the West: The Making of an Image.* Rev. ed. Oxford: Oneworld, 2009.

Danielou, Cardinal, Jean. "Pour une theologie de l' hospitalite." *La Vie Spirituelle* 367 (November 1951) 339–47.

Davies, Oliver. *A Theology of Compassion: Metaphysics of Difference and the Renewal of Tradition.* London: SCM, 2001.

Davis, William Stearns, ed. *Readings in Ancient History: Illustrative Extracts from the Sources.* Boston: Allyn and Bacon, 1913.

Delio, Ilia. *Humility of God: A Franciscan Perspective.* Cincinnati, Ohio: St. Anthony Messenger, 2005.

Denny, Frederick. *An Introduction to Islam.* New York: Macmillan, 1985.

Denaux, Adelbert. "The Theme of Divine Visits and Human Hospitality in Luke-Acts: Its Old Testament and Graeco-Roman Antecedents." In *The Unity of Luke-Acts,* edited by J. Verheyden, 263–68. Leuven: Leuven University Press, 1999.

Derrida, Jacques. *Acts of Religion.* Edited by Gil Anidjar. New York: Routledge, 2002.

———. *Adieu to Emmanuel Levinas.* Translated by Paschale-Anne Brault and Michael Naas. Stanford, CA: Stanford University Press, 1997.

————. *De L'Hospitalite*. Paris: Calmann-Levy, 1997.

————. "Hospitality." Translated by Barry Stoker with Forbes Morlock. *Angelaki: Journal of the Theoretical Humanities* 5.3 (December 2000) 3–18.

————. "Hospitality, Justice and Responsibility." In *Questioning Ethics*, edited by R. Kearney and M. Dooley, 65–83. London: Routlege, 1988.

————. *Of Hospitality: Anne Dufourmantelle Invites Jacques Derrida to Respond*. Stanford, CA: Stanford University Press, 2000.

Dhavamony, Mariasusai. "Evangelization and Dialogue in Vatican II and in the Synod." In *Vatican II, Assessment and Perspectives Twenty-Five Years After (1962–1987)*, edited by Rene Latourelle, 3:264–81. Mahwah, NJ: Paulist, 1989.

Dickson, Kwesi. A. *Theology in Africa*. Maryknoll, NY: Orbis, 1984.

Doty, Roxanne Lynn. "Practices of Hospitality in a Sovereign World." *Theory in Action* 8.2 (2015) 45–68.

Doukhan, Abigail. "The Hospitality of Abraham: Reflections on a Levinasian approach to Interfaith Dialogue." In *The Three Sons of Abraham: Interfaith Encounters between Judaism, Christianity and Islam*, edited by Jacques B. Doukhan, 81–92. London: I. B. Tauris, 2014.

Dowd, Robert A. *Christianity, Islam, and Liberal Democracy: Lessons from Sub-Saharan Africa*. New York: Oxford University Press, 2015.

Drew, Rose. "Christian and Hindu, Jewish and Buddhist: Can You Have a Multiple Religious Identity?" In *Controversies in Contemporary Religion*, edited by Paul Hedges, 1:247–72. Sancta Barbara, CA: Praeger, 2014.

Droge, Arthur J., trans. *The Qur'an: A New Annotated Translation*. Bristol, CT: Equinox, 2013.

Dunnill, John. "Communicative Bodies and Economies of Grace: The Role of Sacrifice in the Christian Understanding of the Body." *Journal of Religion* 83.1 (2003) 79–93.

Dupuis, Jacques. "Inter-Religious Dialogue into the Churches Evangelizing Mission: Twenty Years of Evolution of a Theological Concept." In *Vatican II: Assessment and Perspectives Twenty-Five Years After (1962–1987)*, edited by Rene Latourelle, 3:264–81. Mahwah, NJ: Paulist, 1989.

Eboh, Camillus. "Nigeria (DSS) Arrests Iran-Linked Cell Targeting US, Israel." Reuters, February 21, 2013. http://news/nigeria-says-arrests-iran-linked-cell-targetting-us-093721751.html.

Echema, Augustine. *Corporate Personality in Igbo Society and the Sacrament of Reconciliation*. Frankfurt am Main: Peter Lang, 1995.

Eck, Diana. "What Do We Mean by Dialogue?" *Current Dialogue* 11 (1986) 5–15.

Ela, Jean Marc. *Repenser la théologie africaine: Le Dieu qui libère*. Paris: Karthala, 2003.

Engineer, Asghar Ali. "Da'wah or Dialogue." *Journal of Ecumenical Studies* 39.1/2 (Winter/Spring, 2002) 26–31.

Esack, Farid. *Qur'an, Liberation and Pluralism: An Islamic Perspective of Interreligious Solidarity against Oppression*. Grand Rapids: Oneworld, 1997.

Esposito, John L. *The Islamic Threat: Myth or Reality?* New York: Oxford University Press, 1992.

Eubanks, Cecil L., and David J. Gauthier. "The Politics of the Homeless Spirit: Heidegger and Levinas on Dwelling and Hospitality." *History of Political Thought* 32.1 (2011) 126–80.

Evans, Joseph W., and Leo R .Ward, eds. *The Social and Political Philosophy of Jacques Maritain: Selected Readings*. London: Geofrey Bles, 1956.

Fadipe, N. A. *The Sociology of the Yoruba*. Ibadan: Ibadan University Press, 1970.

Falola, Toyin, and Matthew M. Heaton. *A History of Nigeria*. New York: Cambridge University Press, 1989.

Ferreira, M. Jamie. *Love's Grateful Striving: A Commentary on Kierkegaard's Works of Love*. Oxford: Oxford University Press, 2001.

———. "Total Altruism in Levinas's Ethics of Welcome." *Journal of Religious Ethics* 29.3 (2001) 443–70.

Firestone, Reuven. *Jihad: The Origin of Holy War in Islam*. Oxford: Oxford University Press, 1999.

Fisher, Humphrey. "Conversion Reconsidered: Some Historical Aspects of Religious Conversion in Black Africa." *Africa* 43.1 (1973) 27–40.

Flannery, Austin, ed. *Vatican Council II: The Conciliar and Post Conciliar Documents*. New rev. ed. Dublin: Dominican, 2007.

Foucauld, Charles de. *Letters from the Desert*. Translated by Barbara Lucas. London: Burns and Oates, 1977.

Francis, Pope. *Evangelii Gaudium*. Apostolic exhortation, November 24, 2013. http://www.vatican.va/content/francesco/en/apost_exhortations/documents/papa-francesco_esortazione-ap_20131124_evangelii-gaudium.html.

———. *Lumen Fidei*. Encyclical letter, June 29, 2013. http://www.vatican.va/content/francesco/en/encyclicals/documents/papa-francesco_20130629_enciclica-lumen-fidei.html.

Franz Rosenthal, "The Stranger in Medieval Islam." *Arabica* 44.1 (1997) 35–75.

Fredericks, James. *Faith Among Faiths: Christian Theology and Non-Christian Religions*. New York: Paulist, 1999.

———. Review of Gavin D'Costa, *Vatican II: Catholic Doctrine on Jews and Muslims*. *Studies in Christian-Jewish Relations* 10.1 (2015) 1–5.

Fredericks, James, and Tracy Sayuki Tiemeier, eds. *Interreligious Friendship after Nostra Aetate*. New York: Palgrave Macmillan, 2015.

Gade, Christian B. N. "The Historical Development of the Written Discourses on Ubuntu." *South African Journal of Philosophy* 30.3 (2011) 303–29.

———. "What Is Ubuntu?: Different Interpretations among South Africans of African Descent." *South African Journal of Philosophy* 31.3 (2012) 484–503.

Gailey, Harry A. *Lugard and the Abeokuta Uprising: The Demise of Egba Independence*. Totowa, NJ: Frank Cass, 1982.

Gathogo, Julius M. "Some Expressions of African Hospitality Today." *Scriptura* 99 (2008) 275–87.

———. *The Truth about African Hospitality: Is There Hope for Africa?* Mombasa: Salt Productions, 2001.

Gaudeul, Jean-Marie. "Christianity, Islam, and Nation-Building in Africa." *Encounter* 70 (1980) 3–25.

Gbadamosi, Tajudeen Gbadebo O. *The Growth of Islam among the Yoruba, 1841–1908*. London: Longman, 1978.

Ginzberg, Louis. *The Legends of the Jews*. Vol. 1, *From the Creation to Jacob*. Translated by Henrietta Szold. Baltimore: John Hopkins University Press, 1998.

Gossett, Thomas F. *Race: The History of an Idea in America*. New ed. Oxford: Oxford University Press, 1997.

Griffin, David Ray. "Religious Pluralism: Generic, Identist, and Deep." In *Deep Religious Pluralism*, edited by David Ray Griffin, 3–38. Louisville: Westminster John Knox, 2005.

Griffith, Sidney. *Arabic Christianity in the Monasteries of Ninth Century Palestine.* London: Variorum, 1992.

Groody, Daniel G. "Crossing the Divide: Foundations of a Theology of Migration and Refugees." *Theological Studies* 70.3 (2009) 638–67.

Guillaume, Alfred. *The Life of Muhammad.* London: Oxford University Press, 1955.

Gutierrez, Gustavo. *Las Casas: In Search of the Poor of Jesus Christ.* Translated by Robert R. Barr. Maryknoll, NY: Orbis, 1993.

Gutierrez, Gustavo, and Daniel Groody, eds. *The Preferential Option for the Poor Beyond Theology.* Notre Dame, IN: University of Notre Dame Press, 2014.

Hand, Sean, ed. *The Levinas Reader.* Oxford: Blackwell, 1989.

Hardacre, Helen. "Ancestors: Ancestor Worship." In *The Encyclopedia of Religion*, vol. 1, edited by Mircea Eliade, 263–68. New York: Macmillan, 1987.

Harris, Elizabeth J, et al., eds. *Twenty-First Century Theologies of Religions: Retrospection and Future Prospects.* Leiden: Brill Rodopi, 2016.

Hasan, 'Abd al-Ghaffar. *The Way of the Prophet: A Selection of Hadith.* Translated by Usama Hasan. Leicestershire, UK: Islamic Foundation, 2009.

Haykal, Muhammad H. *The Life of Muhammad.* Translated by Isma'il Ragi and A. al Faruqi. Indianapolis: North American Trust, 1976.

Healey, Joseph, and Donald Sybertz. *Towards an African Narrative Theology.* Nairobi: Paulines, 1996.

Hedges, Paul. *Controversies in Interreligious Dialogue and the Theology of Religions.* London: SCM, 2010.

Hegel, Georg Wilhelm Friedrich. *The Phenomenology of the Spirit.* Translated by A. V. Miller. Oxford: Oxford University Press, 1807.

Heidegger, Martin. "Letter on Humanism." In *Basic Writings: From Being and Time (1927) to The Task of Thinking (1964)*, edited by David Farrell Krell, 191–242. New York: Harper, 1977.

Hemmer, Hippolyte. *Les Peres Apostoliques.* Vol. 2. Paris: Picard, 1909.

Hensman, J. Mark. "Beyond Talk: The Dialogue of Life as the Locus of Nonverbal Interreligious Dialogue." *East Asian Pastoral Review* 36.3 (1999) 323–37.

Herskovits, Melville. *The Myth of the Negro Past.* Boston: Beacon, 1958.

Hick, John. *Disputed Questions in Theology and the Philosophy of Religion.* London: Macmillan, 1993.

———. *God and the Universe of Faiths: Essays in the Philosophy of Religions.* London: Macmillan, 1973.

Hiebert, Paul. "The Category 'Christian' in the Mission Task." *International Review of Mission* 72 (1983) 421–27.

Hinze, Bradford E., and Irfan A. Omar, eds. *Heirs of Abraham: The Future of Muslim, Jewish, and Christian Relations.* Eugene, OR: Wipf & Stock, 2012.

Hiskett, Mervyn. *The Development of Islam in West Africa.* London: Longman, 1984.

Hodgkin, Thomas. *Nigeria Perspectives: An Historical Anthology.* London: Oxford University Press, 1960.

Hofman, Murad Wilfried. *Al-Islam Kabadil.* Translated by Muhamad Gharib Gharib. 1st ed. Kuwait: Majalah al-Nur-al-Kuwaytiyyah, 1993.

Hone, C. A. and D. Hone, eds. *Seventeen Years in the Yoruba Country: Memorials of Anna Hinderer, Wife of the Rev. David Hinderer, C.M.S. Missionary in West Africa.* London: Religious Tract Society, 1872.

Hourani, Albert. *Arab Thought in the Liberal Age, 1798–1939.* Oxford: Oxford University Press, 1962.

————. *Islam in European Thought.* Cambridge: Cambridge University Press, 1991.

Huntington, Samuel P. *The Clash of Civilizations and the Remaking of World Order.* London: Simon & Schuster, 1997.

Ibn 'Abd Rabbih. *The Unique Necklace: Al-'Iqd al-Farid.* Vol. 1. Translated by Issa J. Boullata. Reading: Garnet, 2007.

Ibn al-Mubarak, Abdallah. *Kitab al-jihad.* Beirut: Da al-Nur, 1971.

Idowu, Bolaji. *African Traditional Religions: A Definition.* London: SCM, 1973.

Ifemesia, Chieka C. "Bornu Under the Shehus." In *A Thousand Years of West African History: A Handbook for Teachers and Students,* edited by J. F. Ade Ajayi and Ian Espie, 284–93. Ibadan: Ibadan University Press, 1967.

————. "States of the Central Sudan." In *A Thousand Years of West African History: A Handbook for Teachers and Students,* edited by J. F. Ade Ajayi and Ian Espie, 72–112. Ibadan: Ibadan University Press, 1967.

Ipgrave, Michael. Editor. *Scriptures in Dialogue: Christians and Muslims Studying the Bible and the Qur'an Together.* London: Church House, 2004.

Israel, Alex. "Parshat Vayera: The Importance of Chesed." http://www.alexisrael.org/vayera—-angels-humans-chessed.

Iwuchukwu, Marinus C. *Muslim-Christian Dialogue in Postcolonial Northern Nigeria: The Challenges of Inclusive Cultural and Religious Pluralism.* New York: Palgrave Macmillan, 2013.

Izutsu, Toshihiko. *Ethico-Religious Concepts in the Qur'an.* Montreal: McGill-Queen's University Press, 2002.

Jacobs, Dale. "The Audacity of Hospitality." *Journal of Advanced Composition* 28.3 (2008) 563–81.

Jason, Zachary. "A Deliberate Walk." *Boston College Magazine,* July 10, 2015.

John Paul II, Pope. "Address to Participants in the Annual Meeting between the Secretariat for Non-Christians and the World Council of Churches (WCC) Sub-Unit on Dialogue." April 11, 1986. http://w2.vatican.va/content/john-paul-ii/en/speeches/1986/april/documents/hf_jp-ii_spe_19860411_consiglio-ecumenico.html.

————. Christmas address to the Roman Curia. December 22, 1986. http://www.vatican.va/content/john-paul-ii/it/speeches/1986/december/documents/hf_jp-ii_spe_19861222_curia-romana.html

————. *Redemptoris Missio.* Encyclical letter, December 7, 1990. https://w2.vatican.va/content/john-paul-ii/en/encyclicals/documents/hf_jp-ii_enc_07121990_redemptoris-missio.html.

————. *Veritatis Splendor.* Encyclical letter, August 6, 1993. http://www.vatican.va/content/john-paul-ii/en/encyclicals/documents/hf_jp-ii_enc_06081993_veritatis-splendor.html.

John Chrysostom. *Homilies on Genesis 18–45.* Translated by Robert C. Hill. Fathers of the Church 82. Washington, DC: Catholic University of America Press, 1990.

Johnson, Luke Timothy. *The Real Jesus: The Misguided Quest for the Historic Jesus and the Truth of the Traditional Gospels.* San Francisco: HarperSanFrancisco, 1996.

Johnson, Samuel. *The History of the Yorubas: From the Earliest Times to the Beginning of the British Protectorate.* Edited by Dr. O. Johnson. London: Routledge, 1921.

Johnston, Hugh Anthony Stephens. *The Fulani Empire of Sokoto.* London: Oxford University Press, 1967. http://www.webpulaaku.net/defte/hasJohnston/ch13.html.

Jomier, Jacques. *How to Understand Islam.* Translated by John Bowden. New York: Crossroad, 1999.

Kamwangamalu, Nkonko Mudipanu. "*Ubuntu* in South Africa: A Sociolinguistic Perspective to a Pan-African Concept." *Critical Arts* 13.2 (1999) 24–41.

Kant, Immanuel. "Perpetual Peace: A Philosophical Sketch." Translated by H. B. Nisbet. In *Kant: Political Writings*, edited by Hans Reiss, 93–115. Cambridge: Cambridge University Press, 1991.

Kaplan, Stephen. *Different Paths, Different Summits*. Lanham, MD: Rowman & Littlefield, 2002.

Karabell, Zachary. *Peace Be Upon You: Fourteen Centuries of Muslim, Christian and Jewish Conflict and Cooperation*. New York: Vintage, 2008.

Kärkkäinen, Veli-Matti. *An Introduction to the Theology of Religions: Biblical, Historical, and Contemporary Perspectives*. Downers Grove, IL: InterVarsity, 2003.

Katongole, Emmanuel. *The Sacrifice of Africa: A Political Theology for Africa*. Grand Rapids: Eerdmans, 2011.

Katongole, J. C. "Ethos Transmission through African Bantu-Bantu Proverbs: Proverbs as a Means for Transmitting Values and Beliefs among African with the Example of Bantu-Baganda." PhD diss., Würzburg, 1997.

Katz, Claire Elise. *Levinas, Judaism, and the Feminine: The Silent Footsteps of Rebecca*. Bloomington: Indiana University Press, 2003.

Kaufmann, Walter. "Buber's Religious Significance." In *The Philosophy of Martin Buber*, edited by Paul Arthur Schilpp and Maurice Friedman, 665–85. 2nd ed. LaSalle, IL: Open Court, 1991.

Kearney, Richard. *Strangers, Gods, and Monsters: Interpreting Otherness*. New York: Routledge, 2003.

Kearney, Richard, and James Taylor, eds. *Hosting the Stranger Between Religions*. New York: Continuum, 2011.

Kenny, Joseph. "Islam and Christianity in Nigeria: Islam and a 'Secular' State." *Journal of Religion in Africa* 26.4 (1996) 338–64.

———. "Sharia in Nigeria: A Historical Survey." *Bulletin of Islam and Christian-Muslim Relations in Africa* 4.1 (1984) 1–21.

———. "The Spread of Islam in Nigeria: A Historical Survey." Paper presented at the Conference on Sharia in Nigeria, Spiritan Institute of Theology, Enugu, March 22–24, 2001.

Kierkegaard, Soren. *Works of Love*. Edited by Howard V. Hong and Edna H. Hong. Kierkegaard's Writings 16. Princeton, NJ: Princeton University Press, 1995.

Kimball, Charles. *Striving Together: A Way Forward in Christian-Muslim Relations*. Maryknoll, NY: Orbis, 1991.

Knitter, Paul. "Doing Theology Interreligiously Union and the Legacy of Paul Tillich." *Crosscurrents* 61.1 (March 2011) 117–32.

Knitter, Paul. *Introducing Theologies of Religions*. Maryknoll, NY: Orbis, 2002.

———. *No Other Name?: A Critical Survey of Christian Attitudes toward the World Religions*. London: SCM, 1985.

———. *One Earth, Many Religions: Multifaith Dialogue and Global Responsibility*. Maryknoll, NY: Orbis, 1995.

Koenig, John. *New Testament Hospitality: Partnership with Strangers as Promise and Mission*. Philadelphia: Fortress, 1985.

Korieh, Chima J., and Nwokeji Ugo, eds. *Religion, History and Politics in Nigeria: Essay in Honor of Ogbu U. Kalu*. Lanham, MD: University Press of America, 2005.

Krey, August C. *The First Crusade: The Accounts of Eye-Witnesses and Participants*. Princeton, NJ: Princeton University Press, 1921.

Kukah, Matthew H., and Kathleen McGarvey. "Christian Muslim Dialogue in Nigeria: Social Political, and Theological Dimensions." In *Fractured Spectrum: Perspectives on Christian-Muslim Encounters in Nigeria*, edited by Akintunde E. Akinade, 12–29. New York: Peter Lang, 2013.

Kukah, Matthew Hassan. "Christian-Muslim Relations in Sub-Saharan Africa: Problems and Prospects." *Islam and Christian-Muslim Relation* 18.2 (April 2007) 155–64.

Küng, Hans, et al. *Christianity and the World Religions: Paths to Dialogue with Islam, Hinduism and Buddhism*. London: Collins, 1986.

Kuzwayo, Ellen K. *African Wisdom: A Personal Collection of Setswana Proverbs*. Cape Town: Kwalw, 1998.

Laitin, David D. *Hegemony and Culture: Politics and Religious Change among the Yoruba*. Chicago: University of Chicago Press, 1986.

Lamptey, Jerusha Tanner. *Never Wholly Other: A Muslim Theology of Religious Pluralism*. Oxford: Oxford University Press, 2014.

Lane, Edward. *An Arabic-English Lexicon*. London: Williams and Norgate, 1865.

Las Casas, Bartolomé de. *The Only Way*. Edited by Helen Rand. Mahwah, NJ: Paulist, 1992.

Last, Murray. *The Sokoto Caliphate*. London: Longman, 1967.

———. "Some Economic Aspects of Conversion in Hausaland." In *Conversion to Islam*, edited by Nehemia Levtzion, 236–46. New York: Holmes & Meier, 1979.

Leirvik, Oddborn. "Towards a Relational and Humanizing Theology: A Christian-Muslim Dialogue." In *Twenty-First Century Theologies of Religions: Retrospection and Future Prospects*, edited by Elizabeth J. Harris et al., 223–38. Leiden: Rodopi, 2016.

Levenson Jon D. "Judaism Addresses Christianity." In *Religious Foundations of Western Civilization: Judaism, Christianity, and Islam*. Nashville: Abingdon, 2006.

Levinas, Emmanuel. *Emmanuel Levinas: Basic Philosophical Writings*. Edited by Adriaan T. Peperzak, Simon Critchley, and Robert Bernasconi. Bloomington: Indiana University Press, 1996.

———. *Ethics and Infinity*. Edited by Philippe Nemo, translated by Richard A. Cohen. Pittsburgh: Duquesne University Press, 1985.

———. *Éthique et Infini: Dialogues avec Philippe Nemo*. Paris: France Culture, Livre de Poche, 1982.

———. "Heidegger, Gagarin, and Us." In *Difficult Freedom: Essays in Judaism*, translated by Sean Hand, 231–34. Baltimore: Johns Hopkins University Press, 1990.

———. *Of God Who Comes to Mind*. Translated by Bettina Bergo. Stanford, CA: Stanford University Press, 1998.

———. *Otherwise Than Being, or Beyond Essence*. Translated by Alphonso Lingis. Boston: Nijhoff, 1981.

———. *Otherwise Than Being, or Beyond Essence*. Translated by Alphonso Lingis. Boston: Kluwer Academic, 1991.

———. *Outside the Subject*. Translated by Michael B. Smith. Stanford: Stanford University Press, 1993.

———. "The Trace of the Other." Translated by Alphonso Linguis. In *Deconstruction in Context: Literature and Philosophy*, edited by Mark Taylor, 345–59. Chicago: University of Chicago Press, 1986.

———. *Totality and Infinity: An Essay on Exteriority*. Translated by Alphonso Lingis. Pittsburgh: Duquesne University Press 1969.

Levinas, Emmanuel, and Richard Kearney. "Dialogue with Emmanuel Levinas." In *Face to Face with Levinas*, edited by Richard A. Cohen, 13–35. Albany, NY: SUNY Press, 1986.

Lewis, Bernard. *Culture in Conflict: Christians, Muslims and Jews in the Age of Discovery.* Oxford: Oxford University Press, 1995.

———. *The Muslim Discovery of Europe.* London: Weindenfeld & Nicolson, 1982.

Lodhal, Michael. *Claiming Abraham: Reading the Bible and the Qur'an Side by Side.* Grand Rapids: Brazos, 2010.

Madigan, Daniel. "Muslim-Christian Dialogue." In *The Wiley-Blackwell Companion of Interreligious Dialogue*, edited by Catherine Cornille, 244–60. West Sussex, UK: Wiley, 2013.

Marcel, Gabriel. *Homo Viator: Introduction to Metaphysics of Hope.* Translated by Emma Crauford. New York: Harper, 1962.

Marion, Jean-Luc. *In Excess: Studies of Saturated Phenomena.* Translated by Robyn Horner and Vincent Berraud. New York: Fordham University Press, 2002.

———. *The Visible and the Revealed.* Translated by Christiana M. Gschwandtner. New York: Fordham University Press, 2008.

Marshall, Christopher. "Atonement, Violence and the Will of God: A Sympathetic Response to J. Denny Weaver's *The Nonviolent Atonement.*" *Mennonite Quarterly Review* 77 (2003) 69–92.

Maskulak, Marian. "The Mission and Dialogue of Encounter." *Missiology: An International Review* 41.4 (2013) 427–37.

Massignon, Louis. "Islam and the Testimony of the Faithful." In *Testimonies and Reflections: Essays of Louis Massignon*, edited by Herbert Mason, 43–53. Notre Dame, IN: University of Notre Dame Press, 1989.

———. *Opera Minora.* Paris: Presses Universitaires de France, 1969.

———. *The Passion of al-Hallaj: Mystic and Martyr of Islam.* Translated and edited by Herbert Mason. Abridged ed. Princeton, NJ: Princeton University Press, 1994.

———. "Visitation de l'Etranger." In *Parole Donnee.* Paris: Seuil, 1983.

Massignon, Louis, and Mary Kahil. *L' Hospitalite Sacree.* Edited by Jacques Keryell. Paris: Nouvelle Cité, 1987.

Mbiti, John S. *African Religions and Philosophy.* London: Heinemann, 1969.

———. *African Religions and Philosophy.* 2nd ed. Oxford: Heinemann, 1990.

———. "The Forest Has Ears." *Peace, Happiness and Prosperity* 7.7 (July 1976) 17–26.

McAuliffe, Jane. *Quranic Christians: An Analysis of Classical and Modern Exegesis.* Cambridge: Cambridge University Press, 1991.

McDermott, Gerald R. *World Religions: An Indispensable Introduction.* Nashville: T. Nelson, 2011.

McIntyre, Alasdair. *Dependent Rational Animals: Why Human Beings Need the Virtues.* London: Duckworth, 1999.

McNulty, Tracy. *The Hostess: Hospitality, Femininity, and the Expropriation of Identity.* Minneapolis: University of Minnesota Press, 2007.

Menocal, Maria Rosa. *The Arabic Role in Medieval Literary History: A Forgotten Heritage.* Philadelphia: University of Pennsylvania Press, 1987.

Merton, Thomas. *The Asian Journal of Thomas Merton.* Edited by Naomi Burton. New York: New Directions, 1975.

Meyer, Birgit. "Christianity in Africa: From African Independent Churches to Pentecostal-Charismatic Churches." *Annual Review* 33 (June 17, 2004) 447–74.

Michael, Thomas. "Where to Now? Ways Forward for Interreligious Dialogue: Images of Abraham as Models of Interreligious Encounter." *The Muslim World* 100.4 (2010) 530–38.

Michel, Thomas, and Michael Fitzgerald. *Recognize the Spiritual Bonds Which Unite Us: 16 Years of Christian-Muslim Dialogue*. Vatican City: Pontifical Council for Interreligious Dialogue, 1994.

Micklethwait, John, and Adrian Wooldrige. *God Is Back: How the Global Revival of Faith Is Changing the World*. London: Penguin, 2009.

Milbank, John. "The Soul of Reciprocity, Part Two: Reciprocity Granted." *Modern Theology* 17 (2001) 485–507.

Milbank, John, Catherine Pickstock, and Graham Ward, eds. *Radical Orthodoxy: A New Theology*. New York: Routledge, 1999.

Miles, William F. S. "Religious Pluralism in Northern Nigeria." In *The History of Islam In Africa*, edited by Nehemia Levtzion and Randall L. Pouwels, 209–25. Athens, OH: Ohio University Press, 2000.

Miller, J. Mitchell. "Otherness." In *The Sage Encyclopedia of Qualitative Research Methods*, edited by Lisa M. Given, 587–89. Thousand Oaks, CA: Sage, 2008.

Min, Anselm Kyongsuk. *The Solidarity of Others in a Divided World: A Postmodern Theology after Postmodernism*. New York: T. & T. Clark, 2004.

Mingana, Alphonse, ed. *Woodbrooke Studies: Christian Documents in Syriac, Arabic and Garshuni*. Vol. 2. Cambridge: Herffer, 1927.

Minority Rights Group International. *World Directory of Minorities and Indigenous Peoples—Central African Republic*. June 2018. Available online at https://www.refworld.org/docid/4954ce4723.html.

Moila, Moeahabo Phillip. *Challenging Issues in African Christianity*. Pretoria: C.B. Powell Bible Centre, 2002.

Moltmann, Jurgen. *The Spirit of Life: A Universal Affirmation*. Translated by Margaret Kohl. Minneapolis: Fortress, 1992.

———. *Theology and Joy*. Translated by Richard Ulrich. London: SCM, 1973.

Moorman, John R. H. *Richest of Poor Men: The Spirituality of St. Francis of Assisi*. London: Darton, Longman and Todd, 1977.

Morel, Edmund Dene. *Nigeria: Its People and Its Problems*. London: Cass, 1968.

Moyaert, Marianne. *Absorption or Hospitality?: Two Approaches to the Tension between Identity and Alterity*. Eugene, OR: Cascade, 2010.

———. "Biblical, Ethical and Hermeneutical Reflections on Narrative Hospitality." In *Hosting the Stranger Between Religions*, edited by Richard Kearney and James Taylor, 95–108. New York: Continuum, 2011.

———. *Fragile Identities: Towards a Theology of Interreligious Hospitality*. Amsterdam: Rodopi, 2011.

Moyaert, Marianne, and Joris Geldhof, eds. *Ritual Participation and Interreligious Dialogue: Boundaries, Transgressions, and Innovations*. New York: Bloomsbury, 2015.

Mudge, Lewis S. *The Gift of Responsibility: The Promise of Dialogue among Christians, Jews, and Muslims*. New York: Continuum, 2008.

Mugambi, Jesse N. K. *From Liberation to Reconstruction: Africa after the Cold War*. Nairobi: East African Educational, 1995.

Müller, Karl, Theo Sundermeier, Stephen B. Bevans, and Richard H. Bliese, eds. *Dictionary of Mission, Theology, History, Perspectives*. Eugene, OR: Wipf & Stock, 2006.

Munro, Dana C. *Urban and the Crusaders*. Philadelphia: University of Pennsylvania Press, 1896.

Muslim, Imam. *Sahih Muslim*. Translated by Mahmoud Matraji. Beirut: Dar El Fiker, 1993.

Nasr, Seyyed Hossein. *Islamic-Christian Dialogue: Problems and Obstacles to be Pondered and Overcome*. Washington, DC: Georgetown University Press, 1998.

———. "Religion and Religions." In *Towards a Muslim Theology of Other Religions in a Post-Prophetic Age*, edited by Mohammad Suheyl Umar, 59–81. Lahore, Pakistan: Iqbal, 2008.

———. "Response to Hans Küng's Paper on Christian-Muslim Dialogue." *The Muslim World* 77.2 (April 1987) 96–105.

Navone, John. "Divine and Human Hospitality." *New Blackfriars* 85.997 (2004) 329–40.

Neusner, Jacob, ed. "Judaism." In *Religious Foundations of Western Civilization: Judaism, Christianity and Islam*, edited by Jacob Neusner, 27–69. Nashville: Abingdon, 2000.

———. *A Rabbi Talks with Jesus*. Montreal: McGill-Queen's University Press, 2000.

Nicam, N. A., and Richard McKeon, eds. and trans. *The Edicts of Ashoka*. Chicago: University of Chicago Press, 1959.

Nkemnkia, Martin Nkafu. *African Vitalogy: A Step Forward in African Thinking*. Nairobi: Paulines, 1999.

Nkwocha, Levi. "Eucharistic Hospitality: A Bi-Directional Dynamics." *Vincentian Heritage Journal* 33.1 (2016) art. 10.

Nouwen, Henri J. M. "Hospitality." *MonS* 10 (1974) 1–28.

———. *Reaching Out: The Three Movements of the Spiritual Life*. Glasgow: Collins, 1974.

Nsofor, Chukwunulokwu Fyne. "Muslim-Christian Relations, in a Contemporary Multiethnic, Multireligious Society: Toward Nigerian National Identity." PhD diss., Trinity International University, 2004.

Nwachukwu, John O. "Why I Dressed in Islamic Regalia." *Daily Post*, September 2, 2017. http://dailypost.ng/2017/09/02/sallah-dressed-islamic-regalia-fayose.

Nwaiwu, Francis O. "Inter-Religious Dialogue in African Context." PhD diss., Pontificia Universitas Urbaniana, 1989.

Nyamiti, Charles. *Jesus Christ, the Ancestor of Humankind*. 2 vols. Studies in African Christian Theology 1–2. Nairobi: Catholic University of Eastern Africa, 2005, 2006.

Nyenyembe, Jordan. *Fraternity in Christ: Building the Church as Family*. Nairobi: Pauline, 2005.

Obengo, Tom Joel. "The Role of Ancestors as Guardians of Morality in African Traditional Religion." *Journal of Black Theology in South Africa* 2.2 (November 1997) 44–63.

Oden, Amy G., ed. *And You Welcomed Me: A Source on Hospitality in Early Christianity*. Nashville: Abingdon, 2001.

Oduyoye, Mercy A. *Introducing African Women's Theology*. Sheffield: Sheffield Academic, 2001.

Ogbogho, C. B. N., R. O. Olaniyi, and O. G. Muojama, eds. *The Dynamics of Inter-Group Relations in Nigeria Since 1960*. Ibadan, Nigeria: University of Ibadan Press, 2012.

Ogletree, Thomas W. *Hospitality to the Stranger: Dimensions of Moral Understanding*. Philadelphia: Fortress, 1985.

Ojo, Matthew A. "Pentecostal Movements, Islam and the Contest for Public Space in Northern Nigeria." *Islam and Christian-Muslim Relations* 18.2 (April 2007) 172–88.

Okpanachi, Eyene. "Building Peace in a Divided Society: The Role of Civil Society in Muslim-Christian Society in Nigeria." Paper presented at SHUR International Conference on Human Rights in Conflict: The Role of Civil Society, Rome, June 4–6, 2008. http://www.shur.luiss.it/files/2009/06/.

Oladimeji, T. A. O. "Islamic Architecture in Ijebuland, 1926–1994: A Historical Study of Forms." Ph.D diss., University of Ibadan, 2001.

Olikenyi, Gregory I. *African Hospitality: A Model for the Communication of the Gospel in the African Cultural Context.* Nettetal, Germany: Steyler, 2001.

Olupona, Jacob K. *City of 201 Gods: Ile-Ife in Time, Space, and the Imagination.* Berkeley: University of California Press, 2011.

Olurode, Lai, and P. Olufemi Olusanya. *Nigerian Heritage: The Yoruba Example.* Lagos: Rebonik, 1994.

O'Mahony, Anthony, and Peter Bowe, eds. *Catholics in Interreligious Dialogue: Monasticism, Theology, and Spirituality.* Leominster, Herefordshire: Gracewing, 2006.

Omar, A. Rashied. "Embracing the "Other" as an Extension of the Self: Muslims Reflections on The Epistle to the Hebrews 13:2." *Anglican Theological Review* 91.3 (2009) 433–34.

Omotoso, Salau Sule. "Islam in Nigeria." http://www.nou.edu.ng/noun/NOUN_OCL/pdf/df2/Is1%20056%20IslaminNigeria.

Orji, Cyril. *An Introduction to Religious and Theological Studies.* Eugene, OR: Resource, 2015.

Orman, Irfan A., ed. *A Muslim View of Christianity: Essays on Dialogue by Mahmoud Ayoub.* Maryknoll, NY: Orbis, 2007.

Paden, John N. *Religion and Political Culture in Kano.* Berkeley: University of California Press, 1973.

Palacios, Miguel Asin. *On Muslim Influences on Dante.* Madrid: Editorial Maeste, 1919.

Panikkar, Raimon. *Christophany: The Fullness of Man.* Translated by Alfred DiLascia. Maryknoll, NY: Orbis, 2004.

———. *The Cosmotheandric Experience: Emerging Religious Consciousness.* Edited by Scott Eastham. Maryknoll, NY: Orbis, 1993.

———. *The Intra-Religious Dialogue.* Rev. ed. New York: Paulist, 1999.

———. *Invisible Harmony: Essays on Contemplation and Responsibility.* Minneapolis: Fortress, 1995.

———. "The Jordan, the Tiber, and the Ganges." In *The Myth of Christian Uniqueness: Toward a Pluralistic Theology of Religions,* edited by John Hick and Paul F. Knitter, 89–116. Maryknoll, NY: Orbis, 1987.

———. *Myth, Faith and Hermeneutics: Cross-Cultural Studies.* New York: Paulist, 1979.

Parsons, Mikeal C. *Luke.* Paideia. Grand Rapids: Baker Academic, 2015.

Patey, Ariana. "Sanctity and Mission in the Life of Charles de Foucauld." *Studies in Church History* 47 (2011) 365–75.

Paul VI, Pope. *Dignitatis Humanae.* Apostolic exhortation, December 7, 1965. http://www.vatican.va/archive/hist_councils/ii_vatican_council/documents/vat-ii_decl_19651207_dignitatis-humanae_en.html.

———. *Ecclesiam Suam.* Encyclical letter, August 6, 1964. http://w2.vatican.va/content/paul-vi/en/encyclicals/documents/hf_p-vi_enc_06081964_ecclesiam.html.

————. *Evangelii Nuntiandi*. Apostolic exhortation, December 8, 1975. http://www.vatican.va/content/paul-vi/en/apost_exhortations/documents/hf_p-vi_exh_19751208_evangelii-nuntiandi.html.

Paulien, Jon. "The Remnant of Abraham." In *The Three Sons of Abraham: Interfaith Encounters between Judaism, Christianity and Islam*, edited by Jacques B. Doukhan, 45–63. New York: I. B. Tauris, 2014.

Peel, John David Y. *Christianity, Islam, and Orisa Religion: Three Traditions in Comparison and Interaction*. Oakland: University of California Press, 2016.

Peperzak, Adriaan. *To the Other: An Introduction to the Philosophy of Immanuel Lévinas*. West Lafayette, IN: Purdue University Press, 1993.

Peters, Francis. "Alius or Alter: the Quranic Definition of Christians and Christianity." *Islam and Christian-Muslim Relations* 8.2 (1997) 165–76.

Peters, Rudolph. *Jihad in Classical and Modern Islam: A Reader*. Princeton, NJ: Markus Wiener, 1996.

Pew Research Center. "Mapping the Global Muslim Population." October 7, 2009. https://www.pewforum.org/2009/10/07/mapping-the-global-muslim-population/.

————. "Sunni and Shia Muslims." In *The Future of the Global Muslim Population*. January 27, 2011. https://www.pewforum.org/2011/01/27/future-of-the-global-muslim-population-sunni-and-shia/.

Pignedoli, Sergio. "Lettre a l'Abbe Primat." *AIM Bulletin* 17.62 (1974), Vanves.

Plessner, M. "Mukatil b. Sulaiman." In *The Encyclopaedia of Islam*, edited by M. Th. Houtsma et al., 3:711–12. Leiden: Brill, 1936.

Pohl, Christine D. "Building a Place for Hospitality." In *Hospitality*, edited by Robert B. Kruschwitz, 27–36. Special issue of *Christian Reflection*, 20f07.

————. *Making Room: Recovering Hospitality as a Christian Tradition*. Grand Rapids: Eerdmans, 1999.

Pontifical Council for Interreligious Dialogue. *The Attitude of the Church Toward Followers of Other Religions: Reflections and Orientations on Dialogue and Mission*. Vatican City, Pentecost 1984. https://www.pcinterreligious.org/the-attitudes-of-the-church-towards-the-followers-of-other-religions.

————. *Dialogue and Proclamation: Reflections and Orientations on Interreligious Dialogue and the Proclamation of the Gospel of Jesus Christ*. Vatican City, Pentecost 1991. http://www.vatican.va/roman_curia/pontifical_councils/interelg/documents/rc_pc_interelg_doc_19051991_dialogue-and-proclamatio_en.html.

————. "Discourse of the Pope to Zen and Christian Monks." *Bulletin* 23.1 (1988) 5–6.

Pratt, Douglass. "The Vatican in Dialogue with Islam: Inclusion and Engagement." *Islam and Christian-Muslim Relations* 21.3 (2010) 250–51.

Purcell, Michael. *Levinas and Theology*. Cambridge: Cambridge University Press, 2006.

Raboteau, Albert J. *Slave Religion: The "Invisible Institution" in the Antebellum South*. Oxford: Oxford University Press, 1978.

Race, Alan. *Interfaith Encounter: The Twin Tracks of Theology and Dialogue*. London: SCM, 2001.

Rahman, Fazlur. *Major Themes of the Qur'an*. 2nd ed. Minneapolis: Bibliotheca Islamica, 1994.

Ratcliffe, Krista. "Rhetorical Listening: A Trope for Interpretive Invention and a "Code of Cross-Cultural Conduct." *College Composition and Communication* 51 (1999) 195–224.

Ratzinger, Joseph. *Dominus Iesus*. Congregation for the Doctrine of the Faith. August 6, 2000. http://www.vatican.va/roman_curia/congregations/cfaith/documents/rc_con_cfaith_doc_20000806_dominus-iesus_en.html.

————. *Einführung in das Christentum: Vorlesungen über das Apostolische Glaubensbekenntnis* (Introduction to Christianity: Lectures on the Apostolic Creed). Munich, 1986.

Reaves, Jayme R. *Safeguarding the Stranger: An Abrahamic Theology and Ethic of Protective Hospitality.* Eugene, OR: Pickwick, 2016.

Reynolds, Gabriel Said. *The Emergence of Islam: Classical Traditions in Contemporary Perspective.* Minneapolis: Fortress, 2012.

————. "Gavin D'Costa, Vatican II and Islam." *Nova et Vetera*, English ed., 16.1 (2017) 291–99.

————. *A Muslim Theologian in a Sectarian Milieu: Abd al-Jabbar and the Critique of Christian Origins.* Islamic History and Civilization, Studies and Texts, 56. Leiden: Brill, 2004.

Reynolds, Thomas, E. "Improvising Together: Christian Solidarity and Hospitality as Jazz Performance." *Journal of Ecumenical Studies* 43.1 (December 2008) 45–66.

Richard, Lucien. *Living the Hospitality of God.* New York: Paulist, 2000.

Ricoeur, Paul. *Critique and Conviction: Conversations with François Azouvi and Marc de Launay.* Translated by Kathleen Blamey. New York: Columbia University Press, 1998.

————. *Oneself as Another.* Translated by Kathleen Blamey. Chicago: Chicago University Press, 1992.

————. "Reflection on a New Ethos for Europe." *Sage Journals* 21.5/6 (1995) 3–13.

————. *Reflections on the Just.* Chicago: University of Chicago Press, 2007.

Sacks, Jonathan. "Abraham and the Three Visitors." Vayera 5767. *Covenant and Conversation* 11 (November 11, 2006). https://rabbisacks.org/covenant-conversation-5767-vayera/.

Sahas, Daniel. *John of Damascus on Islam: The Heresy of the Ishmaelites.* Leiden: Brill, 1972.

Salihu, Joseph, ed. *Interreligious Dialogue and the Sharia Question.* Contributions to an interfaith dialogue held June 8–11, 2005, and a paper presented by the editor in August 2005. Kano, Nigeria: Jaleyemi Group, 2005.

San-Martín, Ines. "Now a Cardinal, This African Prelate Was Already a "Saint."" *Crux*, October 19, 2016. https://cruxnow.com/cardinals/2016/10/now-cardinal-african-prelate-already-saint/.

Sanneh, Lamin. *Piety and Power: Muslims and Christians in West Africa.* Maryknoll, NY: Orbis, 1996.

————. *West African Christianity: The Religious Impact.* Maryknoll, NY: Orbis, 1983.

Schimmel, Annemarie. *And Muhammad Is His Messenger: The Veneration of the Prophet in Islamic Piety.* Chapel Hill: University of North Carolina Press, 1985.

Schumann, Olaf. *Der Christus der Muslime: Christologische Aspekte in der arabisch-islamischen Literatur.* Köln: Böhlau, 1988.

Schweig, Graham M., ed. *Bhagavad Gītā: The Beloved Lord's Secret Love Songs.* New York: HarperCollins, 2007.

Shehu, Fatmir M. *Nostra Aetate and the Islamic Perspective of Interreligious Dialogue.* Kuala Lumpur: International Islamic University of Malaysia Press, 2008.

Shepherd, Andrew. *The Gift of the Other: Levinas, Derrida, and a Theology of Hospitality.* Cambridge: Clarke, 2014.

Shryock, Andrew. "Thinking About Hospitality, with Derrida, Kant, and the Balga Bedouin." *Anthropos* 105.2 (2008) 405–21.

Siddiqui, Mona. *Hospitality and Islam: Welcoming in God's Name.* New Haven, CT: Yale University Press, 2015.

Silas Webster Allard. "In the Shade of the Oaks of Mamre: Hospitality as Framework for Political Engagement between Christians and Muslims." *Political Theology* 13.4 (2012) 414–24.

Silberstein, Laurence J. "Buber, Martin." *Encyclopedia.com*. August 8, 2020 (updated). https://www.encyclopedia.com/people/philosophy-and-religion/philosophy-biographies/martin-buber.

Sintang, Suraya, et al. "Dialogue of Life and Its Significance in Inter-Religious Relation in Malaysia." *International Journal of Islamic Thought* 2 (December 2012) 69–79.

Sirry, Mun'im. "Compete with One Another in Good Works: Exegesis of Qur'an Verse 5.48 and Contemporary Muslim Discourses on Religious Pluralism." *Islam and Christian-Muslim Relations* 20.4 (October 2009) 423–38.

Smith, Wilfred C. *Faith and Belief*. Princeton, NJ: Princeton University Press, 1979.

———. *Toward a World Theology*. Philadelphia: Westminster, 1981.

Snodgrass, Bowie. "Has the Story Reached Thee, of the Honored Guests of Abraham?" *Anglican Theological Review* 92.1 (2010) 175–81.

Sobrino, Jon. *Jesus the Liberator: A Historical Theological Reading of Jesus of Nazareth*. Translated by P. Burns and F. McDonagh. Maryknoll, NY: Orbis, 1993.

Standaert, Benoit. *Sharing Sacred Space: Interreligious Dialogue as Spiritual Encounter*. Collegeville, MN: Liturgical, 2003.

Staniloae, Dumitru. *7 Dimineti cu Parintele Staniloae*. Edited by Soriu Dumitrescu. Bucharest: Anastasi, 1992.

Stearns, Jason K. *Dancing in the Glory of Monsters: The Collapse of the Congo and the Great War of Africa*. New York: Public Affairs, 2011.

Stendahl, Krister. *Meanings: The Bible as Document and as Guide*. Minneapolis: Fortress, 1984.

Still, Judith. *Derrida and Hospitality: Theory and Practice*. Edinburgh: Edinburgh University Press, 2010.

Stock, St. George. "Hospitality (Greek and Roman)." In *Encyclopedia of Religion and Ethics*, edited by James Hastings, 808–12. New York: Scribner, 1959.

Sutherland, Arthur. *I Was a Stranger: A Christian Theology of Hospitality*. Nashville: Abingdon, 2006.

Swidler, Leonard. "The Age of Global Dialogue." In *Islam and Christianity: Mutual Perceptions since the Mid-20th Century*, edited by Jacques Waardenburg, 271–92. Leuven: Peeters, 1998.

———. *Dialog in Malaysia and the Global Scenario*. Edited by Azizan Baharuddin. Kuala Lumpur: University of Malaysia, Centre for Civilisational Dialogue, 2003.

———. "The History of Inter-Religious Dialogue." In *The Wiley-Blackwell Companion to Inter-religious Dialogue*, edited by Catherine Cornille, 3–19. West Sussex, UK: Wiley, 2013.

Sykes, Stephen W. "Making Room for Other." In *The Religious Other, Hostility, Hospitality, and the Hope of Human Flourishing*, edited by Alon Goshen-Gottstein, 53–68. Lanham, MD: Lexington, 2014.

Teffo, Joseph. *The Concept of Ubuntu as a Cohesive Moral Value*. Pretoria: Ubuntu School of Philosophy, 1994.

Thatcher, Oliver J., and Edgar H. McNeal, eds. *A Source Book for Medieval History*. New York: Scribner, 1905.

Thiessen, Karen Heidebrecht. "Jesus and Women in the Gospel of John." *Direction* 19 (1990) 53–64.

Theunissen, Michael. *Der Andere: Studien Zur Sozialontologie der Gegenwart*. Berlin: De Gruyter, 1977.

Trimingham, J. Spencer. *A History of Islam in West Africa*. Oxford: Oxford University Press, 1962.

Troll, Christian. "Changing Catholic Views of Islam." In *Islam and Christianity: Mutual Perceptions since the Mid-20th Century*, edited by Jacques Waardenburg, 19–77. Leuven: Peeters, 1998.

———. "Christian-Muslim Relations in India: A Critical Survey." *Islamochristiana* 5 (1979) 119–45.

———. *Dialogue and Difference: Clarity in Christian-Muslim Relation*. Maryknoll, NY: Orbis, 2009.

Turner, Harold W. "The Typology of African Religious Movements." *Journal of Religion in Africa* 1.1 (1967) 1–34.

Tutu, Desmond Mpilo. *No Future without Forgiveness*. New York: Doubleday, 1999.

———. *The Words of Desmond Tutu*. Selected by Naomi Tutu. London: Hodder & Stoughton, 1989.

Ugwoji, Matthew. "Inter Religious Relations and Solidarity: Contextualization the Vision of Francis Cardinal Arinze for Religious Education in Nigeria." PhD diss., Fordham University, 2008.

Ukah, Asonzeh. "Born-Again Muslims: The Ambivalence of Pentecostal Response to Islam in Nigeria." *In Fractured Spectrum: Perspectives in Christian-Muslim Relations in Nigeria*, edited by Akintunde E. Akinade, 43–62. New York: Peter Lang, 2013.

ur-Rehmaan, Shah. *Jihaad: Fardh ayn or fardh kifaayah: A Refutation of the Takfeeree Jihaade Groups*. Maktabat, Cairo: Ashab al-hadeeth, n.d.

Uthman al-Dhahabi, Muhammad b. *The Major Sins*. Translated by Mohammad M. Siddiqui. Beirut: Dar al-Fikr, 2007.

Uzukwu, Eugene E. "Missiology Today: The African Situation." In *Inculturation: A Nigerian Perspective*, edited by E. E. Uzukwu, 146–73. Religion and African Culture 1. Enugu: Spiritan, 1988.

Vanier, Jean. *Community and Growth*. 2nd ed. Sydney: St. Paul, 1980.

Volf, Miroslav. *Exclusion and Embrace: A Theological Exploration of Identity, Otherness, and Reconciliation*. Nashville: Abingdon, 1996.

———. "The Trinity Is Our Social Programme: The Doctrine of the Trinity and the Shapes of Social Engagement." In *The Doctrine of God and Theological Ethics*, edited by Alan J. Torrance and Michael C. Banner, 105–24. London: T. & T. Clark, 2006.

Volf, Miroslav, and Judith M. Gundry-Volf. *A Spacious Heart: Essays on Identity and Belonging*. Harrisburg, PA: Trinity, 1997.

Wainwright, William J. "Wilfred Cantwell Smith on Faith and Belief." *Religious Studies* 20.3 (1984) 353–66.

Wansbrough, John. *Quranic Studies: Sources And Methods Of Scriptural Interpretation*. Oxford: Oxford University Press, 1977.

Watt, William M. "Islamic Conceptions of the Holy Way." In *The Holy War*, edited by Thomas P. Murphy, 141–56 Columbus: Ohio State University Press, 1976.

———. *Muslim-Christian Encounters: Perceptions and Misperceptions*. New York: Routledge, 1991.

Weaver, Denny J. *The Nonviolent Atonement*. Grand Rapids: Eerdmans, 2001.

Wessels, Antonie. "Some Biblical Considerations Relevant to the Encounters between Traditions." In *Christian-Muslim Encounters*, edited by Yvonne Yazbeck Haddad and Wadi Z. Haddad, 54–64. Gainesville: University Press of Florida, 1995.

Wheeler, Brannon M. *Prophets in the Quran: An Introduction to the Quran and Muslim Exegesis*. New York: Continuum, 2002.

Whitacre, Rodney A. *John*. IVP New Testament Commentary. Downers Grove, IL: InterVarsity, 1999.

Wielandt, Rotraud. "Menschenwürde und Freiheit in der Reflexion zeitgenössischer muslimischer Denker." *Schwartländer (Hg.), Freiheit der Religion* 171.1 (1993) 179–209.

Winter, Tim. "The Last Trump Card: Islam and the Suppression of Other Faiths." *Studies in Interreligious Dialogue* 9.2 (1999) 133–55.

Winterbottom, Thomas. *An Account of the Native Africans in the Neighborhood of Sierra Leone*. 2 vols. Reprint, London: Cass, 1969.

World Council of Churches, Office on Interreligious Relations. "Striving Together in Dialogue: A Muslim-Christian Call to Reflection and Action." *Islam and Christian-Muslim Relations* 12.4 (2001) 481–88.

Yannoulatos, Anastasios. "Christian Awareness of Primal World Views." In *Faith Meets Faith* (*Mission Trends* 5), edited by Gerald H. Anderson and Thomas F. Stransky, 249–57. New York: Paulist, 1981.

Zebiri, Kate. *Muslims and Christians: Face to Face*. Oxford: Oneworld, 1997.

Zimmermann, Nigel. *Levinas and Theology*. New York: Bloomsbury, T. & T. Clark, 2013.

Zizioulas, John D. *Communion and Otherness: Further Studies in Personhood and the Church*. Edited by Paul McPartlan. New York: T. & T. Clark, 2006.

Zoe, Hersov. "A Muslim's View of Charles De Foucauld: Some Lessons for the Christian-Muslim Dialogue." *The Muslim World* 4.3 (1995) 295–316.

Index

Index